D0931512

NOBLES IN NINETEENTH-CENTURY FRANCE

THE JOHNS HOPKINS UNIVERSITY STUDIES IN
HISTORICAL AND POLITICAL SCIENCE 105TH SERIES (1987)

Nobles in Nineteenth-Century France

THE PRACTICE OF INEGALITARIANISM

David Higgs

THE JOHNS HOPKINS UNIVERSITY PRESS
Baltimore and London

The Johns Hopkins University Press
701 West 40th Street
Baltimore, Maryland 21211
The Johns Hopkins Press Ltd., London

*The paper used in this publication meets the minimum requirements of
American National Standard for Information Sciences—Permanence
of Paper for Printed Library Materials, ANSI Z39.48-1984.*

LIBRARY OF CONGRESS CATALOGING-IN-PUBLICATION DATA

Higgs, David, 1939–
    Nobles in nineteenth-century France.

    (The Johns Hopkins University studies in historical and political science; 105th ser., 1)
    Bibliography: p.
    Includes index.
    1. France—Nobility—History—19th century I. Title. II. Series.
HT653.F7H54 1987   305.5'223'0944   86-7393
ISBN 0-8018-3061-3 (alk. paper)

Contents

List of Tables and Figures

Acknowledgments

This book examines themes first investigated when I was a student of Professor Alfred Cobban and elaborated over the years since his untimely death. Among those who so benignly made valiant efforts to improve earlier drafts of this book I particularly thank J. F. Bosher, J. H. Galloway, T. J. A. Le Goff, P. Mansel, D. A. McQuillan, F. W. O. Morton, and D. M. G. Sutherland. Jean Meyer suggested the use of Révérend's genealogy as a source, and Herb Klein showed me how the S.P.S.S. computer program might be of use. I am indebted to the published works and kind suggestions, not all of which was I able to follow up, of Maurice Agulhon, Guy Chaussinand-Nogaret, and Jean Tulard. Tom Beck was generous with the statistical information he has amassed, and Peter Simoni kindly gathered information on the Caderousse estate. My brother Michael aided in the detection of grammatical errors. The remaining errors and imperfections in the book are, of course, my responsibility. I am grateful to Bill Callahan for loyal and collegial friendship over the years, to Olwen Hufton for her wise counsel on how to "just bash on," and to Kaoru Kamimura for domestic arrangements that made it possible to do so. The 1975 France-Canada Exchange of Scholars, the Social Sciences and Humanities Research Board of Canada, and the Research Fund of the University of Toronto provided financial help at different stages of the preparation of this study, and I am greatly beholden to them.

I have made use of materials consulted during the summers of 1962 and 1963 in the private archives of the Villèle family at Mourvilles-Basses (Haute-Garonne). I am enormously grateful to the late comte and to Mme de Villèle for the kindnesses shown to the Canadian student who came droning up the drive to their château on a dilapidated Vélo-solex. In more recent years I have restricted my research on noble families in the nineteenth century to documents in the public domain. A great many librarians and archivists in France and elsewhere gave generously of their skills, and I would like to express one historian's admiration for those who make it possible for us, as best we may, to ply our trade.

Introduction

Since Juarès many writers have argued that the French Revolution marked the political triumph of a capitalist bourgeoisie over a landed aristocracy, but led by the late Alfred Cobban, some historians began to put into question the assumptions that followed about social changes in France since 1789.[1] Scholarship uncovered so much in common between nobles and upper bourgeois at the end of the Old Regime that it became doubtful whether the leaders of the third estate felt any intrinsic animosity towards the hierarchy in society represented by the second estate. Members of the third estate wanted instead to widen the access to privilege, which was a far cry from the notion of egalitarianism. As the Revolution unfolded, however, successive waves of new leaders moved to persecute nobles, particularly during the Directory. The individual and property rights of nobles enshrined in the Declaration of the Rights of Man and the Citizen were denied to them in 1793–94 and especially in 1797–98, when they were deprived of French citizenship. Individual responsibility for crimes was replaced by collective noble guilt. Ink may yet be spilled on the motivations of this animosity: was it genuine fear of an internal fifth column or a coldly calculated attempt to provide the masses with a hate figure? By 1800, when nobles were readmitted to the conservative consensus of land-owners anxious to preserve their station in life, they had been deeply shaken.[2] Together with the *notables*, the men of political and economic weight in each department of the nation, they were terrified by any prospect of a revival of sans-culottism. In return for the right to keep the properties that most of them had never vacated, they fell silent over the spoliation of the Church. What is even more important, they nevertheless accepted, albeit sullenly, the irretrievable losses that the Revolution had inflicted on them: the end of seigneurial dues, tax privileges, and special status before the courts, as well as the complete disappearance of the society of orders. Politically, and in some measure economically, they were now on a par with the notables; but that does not mean that they thought in the same way as their new bedfellows. Yet the Revolution was a political lesson in which the wealthiest 5 percent of the national population discovered the merits of cooperation over conflict. In 1800 nobles had perhaps forgotten little of the Old Regime; however, they had certainly learned a great deal about the new one.

Two schools of thought have predominated in describing the effect of the Revolution on the nobility. The first, associated with Marx and Jaurès, saw nobles as social fossils, moribund remnants of the feudalism swept away in 1789 by the triumph of the capitalist bourgeoisie. A quaint anachronism, the nineteenth-century nobility did not merit close study save, perhaps, by antique dealers and other antiquarians. Nobles were no longer crucial to the nation's destiny. A second school of thought derived from questioning the political triumph of the allegedly capitalist bourgeoisie. Changes in the individual rights of Frenchmen before the law were recognized by historians as having ended the discrimination of the society of orders, but historians also saw the political and social conservatism of the elite. After the destruction in 1789 of the legal basis of the society of orders, and before the onset of mass politics in the 1870s, for almost a century France was effectively ruled by a hybrid political form, the notables. Writers like Guy Chaussinand-Nogaret and Louis Bergeron maintain that cautious, landed, well-off notables simply ingested the remnants of the pre-Revolutionary *noblesse*. They affirm that henceforth there were no "real" differences between nobles and notables. For dissimilar reasons, then, both Marxist and revisionist historians are uninterested in the separate study of post-Revolutionary nobles.

In this book, however, I want to sustain a third argument: that nobles were similar to an ethnic group, in the familiar North American sense of "a self-perceived group of people who hold in common a set of traditions not shared by the others with whom they are in contact."[3] My thesis is that the sum of psychological and social variances between nobles and commoners of similar wealth constituted real differences which left an enduring mark on nineteenth-century France. That is not to say that those traditions were fixed for eternity. In a similar vein we may add that French nobles today are quite different from their peers of a century earlier, while they generally maintain a pride in family separateness and a distinct way of life. This book studies the French dimension during the years 1800–70 of a larger historiographical issue put by Arno Mayer:

> Scholars of all ideological persuasions have downgraded the importance of preindustrial economic interests, prebourgeois elites, pre-

democratic authority systems, premodernist artistic idioms, and "archaic" mentalities. They have done so by treating them as expiring remnants, not to say relics, in rapidly modernizing civil and political societies. They have vastly overdrawn the decline of land, noble, and peasant: the contraction of traditional manufacture and trade, provincial burghers and artisinal workers; the derogation of kings, public service nobilities, and upper chambers; the weakening of organized religion; and the atrophy of classical high culture.[4]

The history of the nineteenth-century nobles is thin and patchy, while a great flow of material on the Old Regime nobility continues to respond to the appeals made in the *Annales* articles of 1936 by Marc Bloch, Lucien Febvre, and the comte Neufbourg for serious study of the changing contours of the nobility—their fortune, family structure, choice of profession, regional incidence, and ideological behavior. Similar questions about post-Revolutionary nobles remain largely unanswered despite some recent advances. To some it may appear foolishly premature to attempt to generalize about those noble residues in France when we still lack monographs free of hagiography for such exemplary nineteenth-century families as the Crillons, the Beauvaus, the Dreux-Brézés, and the Aligres. Investigations into the less wealthy nobles of provincial prestige like the Aiguirandes of the Berry and a myriad more are scarce. What follows is advanced with the hope that an overview, whatever its imperfections, may assist in suggesting those areas of the terrain that are most in need of further examination.

French nobles changed with their century, but given their numbers in the national population, they kept a hugely disproportionate presence in politics, in culture, among the wealthiest landowners, and in economic life. Nobles bequeathed to their progeny, new recruits, and imitators their faith in status, formality, inegalitarianism, some racism, ideas of "la distinction" and their authority in the symbolism of power. Having realized that they could no longer aspire to be a ruling caste, nobles sought to permeate the new ruling body with their old ideas. This was reflected in the changing but constant polarities of noble self-description between the *bonne compagnie* (in the Saint-Germain, right-wing, and Catholic correct-thinking sense) and the *haute société* (from aristocrats and wealthy socialites like those who founded the celebrated Jockey Club in November 1833 down to smart Parisian café society). Individuals might be part of both, but not all of the latter could enter the former, and vice versa. The study of nineteenth-century nobles reveals the power of the noble mystique in France, the disproportionate social authority of nobles in relation to their numbers in the population at large, and the deference accorded to Old Regime attitudes by post-Revolutionary commoners. There are certainly more pressing reasons than the antiquarian to examine the social role of nobles in nineteenth-century France.

At least three generations of French nobles might be arbitrarily discerned in this book: those adults who experienced the Revolution and the transformation into the Napoleonic Empire (1800–1814); those nobles who flourished under the constitutional monarchies (1815–48); and those nobles who reached adulthood in a France transformed by railways and the first stirrings of mass politics (1848–70). Speaking of generations in this way is artificial, however, not simply because the limits of each are political events but also because the very invocation of generations overlooks the continuing presence in noble families of individuals of different ages. Indeed, with the longer life expectancy of the rich in any population, nobles were more likely than Frenchmen at large to have family contact with a remoter past. Marie-Paul-Gabriel du Pac, marquis de Badens, former page of Louis XVI and a chevalier de Saint Louis, died on 27 December 1869 at the age of almost one hundred, having lived through all three "generations." He breathed his last in Nice, a more salubrious climate for retirement than that of the family château in the Aude, where he was born in May 1770. He was second deputy of the Carcassonne *sénéchaussée* noble assembly in 1789. The family château was sold as confiscated national property on 27 ventôse II. Doubtless an exceptional example, the marquis's long life span reminds us that nobles with political attitudes first formed under the Old Regime were not extinct until the end of the Second Empire.[5] However, there was change as well as continuity in the opinions passed along the "generations" in the patriarchal château setting which was the idyll of all aspirants to nobility. Even inside the sentimental family chronicle lovingly elaborated by elderly relatives there was a slippage, a steady adjustment to new political systems, to prestigious appointments to the Chamber of Peers or the Senate, to the departmental consultative councils or charity boards, and to novel investment possibilities or opportunities in agriculture or housing.

The place of nobles in France from 1800 to 1870 has received surprisingly little systematic study. During the great wave of investigations into past French social structures the affection and concern of scholars for the lower classes was so evident that it led one historian to reflect that in contemporary French social historiography there was a much faster advance in knowledge of the ruled classes than in that of the ruling class.[6] This assertion may appear paradoxical in light of the many thousands of genealogies, books of heraldry and coats of arms, and memoirs published during the nineteenth century and afterwards. Those books rarely served the analytical aims of history, for they were formulating and elaborating mythology rather than explaining it. They were part of noble discourse, not an examination of it. In the case of professors of history, the classic three-generation climb from artisan to schoolteacher to professor means that academics, as in the case of the present writer, frequently of petty bourgeois origins and in a profession with scant recruitment among the truly wealthy and socially prominent, find it difficult to study dispassionately nobles and their collective mythology of superiority. In general one may observe that historians of modern France, for their part, often have scant interest in "losers" or un-progressive elements in the national past. Modern nobles steadily de-clined in numbers despite their obvious ubiquity and leverage; like others who do not fit conveniently into a meliorist view of the past, they are frequently ignored. The historian is too often assumed to side with the people he is studying. More than one French historian has been frightened off the subject by the commendable desire to escape his colleagues' suspicion of indulging vicariously in snobbery.

When nobles themselves wrote history, they usually set out to under-line their uniqueness. In the nineteenth century family members un-able to afford their ancestors' life style were correspondingly proud of former wealth and distinction. That would seem to be the case of André-Joseph-Jules Mondot de Lagorce et de Beaujour (b. 1791), an engineer for the Ponts et Chaussées who, in addition to his official reports, wrote a genealogy of Christ's family, studies of political history of right-wing views, and a *Code de l'état actuel de la noblesse en France*. In Burgun-dian retirement at Auxerre after a lifetime of improving roadworks, he could feel wistful that the former family seigneury of Mondot, in the wine-producing Saint Emilion district near Bordeaux, had passed into the hands of that high dignitary of the Second Empire, *premier prési-dent* Troplong.[7] So it is that many of the thousands of volumes listed in one superb genealogical bibliography are suffused with the nostalgia, and sometimes the bitterness, of declining families and individuals looking back to the pre-1789 *noblesse*.[8] Their feelings are those of the cartoon dog who declaims: "I'm too good to die. I'm too *me* to die." Ciphers, signet rings, coats of arms, and engraved cutlery were but one part of the laborious compilation of traditions and rituals that attested to "good blood." The nobles' genealogies affirmed their importance through that of their ancestors. Rich treasure-houses await the histo-rian of *mentalités* and the linguistic structuralist in these paeans to family distinction.[9]

In the past, the subject of nobles has been cursed by the insistent study of family origins which is the primary obsession of nobles reflect-ing on their own comparative status. Yet titles were legally bestowed during most of the seventy years considered in this book. Numerous titles were appropriated for general use without any legal basis by the unscrupulous. Some families had a more venerable claim than others to the perquisites of rank, but the first step in investigating titled French people, those who claimed to be noble in the nineteenth century, is to jettison Old Regime taxonomies of robe, sword, cloche, and so forth, which no longer applied to the new society after 1800.[10] It remains useful on occasion to distinguish the descendants of the former second estate, the *noblesse*, from the newly titled *titrés*. In fact these two groups were connected, both by individuals who figured in both and by the fact that in society at large nobles were considered to be alike, despite exclamations of disapproval in Legitimist salons. A third group of people was the aristocracy, those skillful and adroit titled families who persisted in the corridors of power from Versailles to the Tuileries court of Napoleon and thence to every other focus of patronage, position, and fashionability in the century. *Noblesse, titrés,* and aristocrats may be figuratively described as engaged in a gambling game with winnings paid in prestige, and all three accepted as self-evident the merits of a distinctive noble style. Some brought to the gaming table substantial wealth that survived the Revolution, like that of the Aiguirande family of ancient *noblesse* from the Cher, who also bought a great deal of *biens nationaux,* or the Villèles in the Toulousain, who did not but kept their estates intact. Others were in more reduced circumstances, particularly the poor military *noblesse* who emigrated and whose property fell into the hands of the Republic. The nineteenth-century hereditary *titrés,* in the traditions of the former monarchy, were necessarily wealthy and asserted rank to go along with their riches. The aristocracy knew court politics too intimately to be long detained by such quaint notions as loyalty to former masters or by inconvenient ideas of honor. They are well represented by the Choiseul-Praslins, the first of the great to rally to Bonaparte.

If we see nobles in this way, we can trace the different trajectories of families within the "ethnic" universe of those who wished to stand apart from their fellow Frenchmen. Families of *noblesse, titrés,* and aristocrats, defined in turn by origin and wealth, valued otherness.[11] Historians have been too quick to assign noble individuals or families to political categories based on origin or ideology instead of stressing the diversity and flexibility of the linkages between those whose belief in their distinction was the common bond.[12]

This introduction might conclude with some admissions of what I have not attempted. I made no use of the 14,766 items in the o^2 series in the *AN* dealing with the sovereigns' households in the nineteenth century. I did not try to trace the luxuriant development of the nobles' discourse about themselves in a variety of publications from 1800 to 1870. I am also aware that in speaking of the power of families I have constant recourse to individuals. Despite those obvious lacunae and more not mentioned, I hope that this book—which looks especially at how nobles behaved in a society they perceived as a network of families with special traditions rather than as an aggregate of individuals with shared rights—will further understanding of the place of nobles in the development of modern France.

Note to the Reader

NOTE ON SPELLING AND MEASURES

In this book dealing with French nobles I have used French spelling of titles. *Emperor, empress, king, queen, prince,* and *princess* follow English usage. One hectare is 2.4711 acres. In 1802 the franc was a silver coin weighing 5 grams and containing one-tenth alloy. Its value in relation to the pre-Revolutionary livre tournois was in the proportion of 81 to 80; that is, 1 franc was worth 1 livre, 0 sous, 3 deniers.

NOBLES IN NINETEENTH-CENTURY FRANCE

1

The Number of Nobles

Before the French Revolution some nobles boasted, in the manner of Orlando's forebears, that their families came out of the mists wearing coronets.[1] They claimed *noblesse immémoriale,* meaning that they were descendants of the factions who put Hugues Capet on the throne in 987 or simply that their family's distinction was of time out of mind. Their filiation was too antique to have left so mundane a trace as a written grant of title. However, the larger portion of the *noblesse* dated from the previous two or three centuries and recalled that French kings bestowed membership in the second estate, titles, and sometimes financial rewards for valor in battle, ready cash, sexual favors, or governmental and other services.[2] Throughout their history the French nobility accepted new members, since only in that fashion could they compensate for losses sustained from war, pestilence, poverty, an absence of male heirs, or sterility. There was always a discrepancy between aristocratic evocations of ancient antecedents, or at the least three generations of titled relations, and the constant recruitment of fresh nobles. This led to collective hypocrisy over the actual recruitment, contrasted with the resounding statements about the need to uphold endogamy and to sustain family honor against contamination by the vulgar. At any time in the nobility's history, it is important to contrast what was said and what in fact was done. This is particularly true of the nineteenth-century nobles, who, facing new pressures exerted on their self-imagery, needed to explain how they defined themselves in a France where, henceforth, all men were equal before the law. Who was noble after 1800?

Posing this question might suggest that for the time before the Revolutionary decade we have its answer, but this is very far from the truth. No accurate, let alone widely accepted, count was ever completed in France, despite various "registrations" of nobles under Louis XIV and

1

Louis xv, which were essentially devices for making financial levies on the *noblesse*. There is an enduring margin of uncertainty, unlikely ever to be definitively dispelled, as historians juggle disputed and inaccurate genealogies, unreliable statistics, and shifting definitions of rank in an effort to produce a plausible count of nobles. Many years have passed since Marc Bloch's unanswered call for reliable statistics about the ratio of nobles to the populations of the French provinces over time.[3] Almost equally difficult to know is how numerous nineteenth-century nobles were in the nation at large. Unless we investigate those who should be counted as noble, we can say little, save in the most speculative way, about their place in the national elite. Moreover, the latter concept commands no consensus among sociologists and historians. There is a tacit agreement about the existence of an establishment, a ruling class, a top drawer, or of a dominant group under some other name, singular or plural, and there is a distinctly healthy trend towards thinking about the elite(s) as a significantly large category of people, in the top 5 percent of the national population in total wealth, including almost all those who hold public office above the level of mayor and local judge.[4] In nineteenth-century France, as we shall see, the nobles played a fluctuating but leading role in that larger national elite from 1800 to 1870 and, indeed, afterwards.

A summary of estimates of the nobility's numbers before 1789 is instructive. Between Louis xiv's accession to the throne at the age of four in 1643 and the abolition of the second estate on 19 June 1790, the nobility shrank in numbers, just as the national population grew. In the mid-seventeenth century the population of France was perhaps 20 million, of whom half a million made some claim to nobility. By the eighteenth century's end the national population probably exceeded 25 million, and R. Dauvergne estimated the nobles as some 400,000 persons.[5] This estimate exceeds by 50,000 the long-established estimate popularized by Mathiez, who counted the second estate in 1789 as numbering 350,000. More recent scholarship has attacked these figures: Guy Chaussinand-Nogaret has advanced a figure of 110,000 for the end of the Old Regime, while Thomas Beck extrapolated from documentation of the 1830s a similarly emaciated total.[6] Despite the eighteenth-century practice of ennoblement—here again historians are at odds in their estimates, with Jean Meyer counting 10,000 individuals and Chaussinand-Nogaret 6,500, multiplied by a factor of five per family—the infusion of perhaps as many as 50,000 individuals was insufficient to reverse the steady drying up of the demographic pool.[7] These variations in the numbers put forward by historians derive from the necessary use of mathematical probabilities and regional extrapolations in the absence of any satisfactory census of nobility during the Old Regime. Yet if there.

is no agreement on the precise size of the second estate or the number of new recruits to it, there is unanimity in one direction: the steady shrinkage of the number of nobles as a proportion of the French population.

After 17 June 1790 the use of *qualifications nobiliaires*, together with the display of coats of arms and distinctive liveries on servants, was prohibited. No longer were titles like monseigneur, éminence, grandeur, excellence, altesse, prince, duc, comte, vicomte, vidame, chevalier, écuyer, messire, or noble homme to be used. Withdrawal of legal recognition and consequently of record of titles—save in the case of unfortunate nobles arrested on charges of counterrevolutionary activities—made estimations of the numbers of the *noblesse* ever more difficult. Family archives were dispersed as a result of emigration and property confiscations. Under the Reign of Terror, the *noblesse* suffered more cruelly from executions in proportion to their place in the national population than did the middle and lower classes. There was a surge in mortality among the *noblesse* still under arms in the Republican and Napoleonic armies, as well as in those of their opponents. Perhaps as many as 30 percent of the Republic's officers were like Caulaincourt, *noblesse* who remained on active service or, like Noailles, part of the wave of new aristocratic recruits under Napoleon too young to have served before 1789. The cumulative effects of absence, injury, and death among eligible partners affected the matrimonial prospects of an entire cohort of noblewomen. Combined with the suppression of ennoblements in the 1790s, these effects thinned the ranks of the *noblesse* more brutally than during any decade since the sixteenth-century Wars of Religion.

The Reign of Terror once past, there were signs that fondness for ranks and hierarchy had not died in all hearts. In private gatherings the government's fulminations against titles remained more or less a dead letter. After the fall of Robespierre, the fashionable affected the prefix *ci-devant* in the conversation of a smart salon or reactionary circle, which were often one and the same. A British visitor to Paris in 1802 said of the *noblesse*: "In the course of conversation, take special care not to omit the title of the person to whom you address yourself. Such an instance of forgetfulness savours of a man of the new régime."[8] Under the authority of First Consul Bonaparte, the revulsion against the excesses of Jacobin egalitarianism seemed to encourage its opposite. There was a return to the use of titles in conversation and even in correspondence by those engaged in a pinprick war against egalitarian behavior. This was effective when the experience of Jacobinism was fresh in the minds of flustered notables. In 1807, a year before Napoleon introduced a new system of titles, the police reported that more than 150 family seals had been cut by jewellers whose shops were on fashionable streets in Paris. Those who had ordered seals had names like La Rochefoucauld, Choiseul-Stainville, Levis-Mirepoix, Saint Aignan, and others of the Old Regime court aristocracy.[9] Curiously, in that atmosphere it was easier than before the Revolution to affect titles or to slip particles into surnames. Benjamin Constant de Rebecque, as he called himself during the Directory, was only one of innumerable social climbers. In that diffuse invocation of rank and distinction we find the necessary preparation for Napoleon's revival of titles.

Except during the brief Second Republic, titles were to be used to reward partisans by every regime in France from 1808 to 1870. How did those new nominations affect the nobility at large? To answer this it is vital to abandon the exclusivist position that only those with a title legally recognized before June 1790 were "true" nobles. Despite the sympathy of biological descendants of the former second estate to the notion that they were of another noble essence from those with titles created after the end of the Old Regime, the social historian can safely abandon that hypothesis to the student of *mentalités*, or the psychohistorian.[10] Instead, we discern various strata among the post-Revolutionary nobles, the largest of which was the pre-1790 *noblesse*. Without renewals, this collection of individuals slowly shrank over the decades before Sedan. The second stratum adapted to the century by taking or renewing a title from the ruler, and this included, besides *noblesse*, individuals and foreigners whose families had no previous French claim to rank. In what follows, this adaptable and accommodating group will be called *titrés* when it is necessary to distinguish them from the *noblesse*. The third stratum was the smallest and was also characterized by adaptability and wealth: the aristocracy.

The contours of the aristocracy are not easily defined, for even among the courtiers who surrounded the ruler there were those who, at different times, belonged more definitely than did others. Sometimes this was by reason of royal approval, so with Louis xvIII's fondness for Elie Decazes; or by association with aristocratic rituals, as in the case of the Dreux-Brézé family's administering under the Restoration the lessons of protocol learned at Versailles; or simply because of the antiquity and splendor of the lineage, as in the case of the Noailles. The court festival guest lists convey the relative standing of families, as in the case of the 1830 invitations to the Tuileries in honor of the visiting king and queen of the Two Sicilies.[11] The aristocracy was an amalgam of *noblesse* and *titrés* but transcended both, marching to its own drum in the pursuit of power, distinction, and wealth. The great names of the last century at Versailles were common among them—Noailles, Choiseul, Gramont,

Talleyrand-Périgord, Bauffremont—and *as families if not as individuals* they were never far from the focus of power.

Aristocracy, *titrés*, and *noblesse* were themselves the top of a pyramid of those who hungered for visible signs of success, some of whom were ready to "crash" the nobility. Under the Old Regime, if those who wanted to accede to nobility had the means and patience to support a distinctive life style, they almost always reached their goal. Ennoblement by gradual acceptance remained possible in the nineteenth century if the newcomers showed themselves ready to undertake the adjustments necessary for the osmosis to occur.

The social history of the nineteenth-century nobles in France should, at least initially, skirt those endless battles between genealogists over who was the noblest of them all. Disputes of that ilk were intrinsic to *Homo hierarchicus* in France as much as elsewhere in Europe, and since the prestige of the nobility is intimately bound up with age, relative scarcity, and family traditions, it is only natural that these are all systematically exaggerated. Before 1789 there was a known pecking order of more or less proven origins among nobles that could be modified by radical changes in wealth or governmental patronage. After the Revolution the *noblesse* were likely, in line with the historical principles of evaluating eminence, elegance, distinction, grace, and other intangibles, to denigrate more recent titles as gewgaws. The historian with no brief for particular families is concerned with understanding a whole universe of status aspirations. The vital element for the study of nobles in modern France is *the desire to appear noble*. That volition was essential in a society where all Frenchmen were equal before the law. Lazare Carnot never used the title of comte with which he was decorated in the decree naming him minister of the interior on 20 March 1815. *Noblesse* who wished to shed their rank could do so by no longer using a title, seal, or visiting card embossed with the appropriate crown. Impoverished nobles were most likely to do this. Others with the means to live nobly could arrange to be granted a title by the regime or perhaps simply claim a title or affect a resounding family name complete with particle.[12] There is in all this an element of imprecision and overlap inevitable in the pursuit of rank, but the historian of the nineteenth century, and indeed the twentieth, needs to depart from a conception of French nobles frozen in late eighteenth-century terminology and eternally discussed in the light of the French Revolution and its success or failure.

The elections that ratified the Constitution of the Year VIII made it clear that, at least among the wealthier sectors of French opinion, order and hierarchy in the nation were much longed for. In the years before the establishment in 1808 of his own honorific system with noble titles and coats of arms, Napoleon included some *noblesse* in the taxonomies of the departmental lists of notables (1801), the Legion of Honor (1802), the Senate (1803), and the six hundred highest taxed individuals (1805). Despite his own origins in the Corsican gentry, Napoleon seems to have had little regard for the intrinsic merits of the *noblesse*, but he was interested in harnessing any residual prestige they might still command among the peasantry. The initial intention was to absorb all well-disposed nobles into the new enumerations of supporters of the regime. A variety of studies have shown that the *noblesse* figured on the lists of notables and among the greatest landowners in the departments, although with regional variations.[13]

In establishing the Legion of Honor on 19 May 1802, Napoleon hoped to produce something between a Praetorian Guard and Janissaries, loyal and beholden, to which the bravest combatants were to be named and rewarded with a high salary. The two thousand or so recipients of *armes d'honneur* were automatically members of the new order. The pay in fact never materialized in the tight money situation of the war years. In 1805 the orders of the Iron Crown and of La Réunion were set up. In due course the Legion of Honor would be fitted into the system of hereditary honors that came into being in March 1808 when it was laid down that the title of chevalier was hereditary after it had been passed on for three generations to the eldest male with a minimum salary of three thousand francs. However, the thirty thousand or so members of the Legion named by Napoleon were too demotic and too variegated in their relationship to distinction to achieve the prestige or social authority envisaged.

Napoleon's conception of power was monarchical at least from the time when he was first consul and moved his lodgings, significantly, to the former royal palace of the Tuileries in the heart of Paris. Almost immediately a staff and protocol proliferated to ensure the foremost representative of the Republic a stately setting. The young general's entourage came increasingly to resemble a court, and the first enterprising members of the Versailles aristocracy began to make their appearance. The *noblesse* found the military uniforms at the new "court" rather oppressive after the multicolored costumes of Versailles: comte de Saint-Aulaire, whose father had been a page to Louis xv, thought court events were like reviews with ladies taking part. Busy conquering Europe, Napoleon had little time for the niceties of etiquette and tailoring, but he wanted around him those who did. He believed that ritual and show were necessary to the exercise of power. Napoleon frequently said that formality and magnificence were needed to overawe the French into respectful obedience, especially the Parisians.

In 1803 Napoleon tried to link honor, wealth, and politics by singling out senators to be especially requited with incomes to enable them and their families to live in great style. In the jurisdiction of each regional appeal court, an estate and a house enjoying an annual revenue of between twenty thousand and twenty-five thousand francs was to be awarded as a *sénatorerie* for life to the senator chosen by Napoleon from the three nominated by their colleagues (14 nivôse II). The senators were the acme of the opportunist and manipulative political class spawned by the Revolution, as they demonstrated in 1814. Napoleon soon disabused himself of the notion that he was endowing a loyal territorial peerage. He realized that his senatorial endowments were aimed at a small set of people too close to the levers of power to feel lasting hereditary gratitude for particular rewards, while the Legion of Honor was so unevenly and widely spread a distinction that membership in it could not constitute a hereditary Praetorian Guard.

After his coronation Napoleon returned to an old vocabulary for new purposes. In 1806 he created the hereditary dignities of the Empire, carrying the titles of prince and altesse sérénissime, with eldest sons to be styled duc and with "fiefs" in conquered Italian and German territories. Even the president of the Senate was to be called excellence. The intention was to make his ministers and high officials more impressive to the public (imperial edicts dated 30 March 1806 and 28 May 1807). Cambacérès, the plump, shrewd southerner who so enjoyed society life, quickly divined the drift towards monarchical hierarchy in France. He was appropriately rewarded with the title archichancelier and grand dignitaire of the Empire and was encouraged to give glittering dinner parties to those clearly loyal to the regime. Only a few dozen great officials enjoyed such opulence and resounding titles. The remaining republicans had deep suspicions of ever more sinister designs being forged upon the anvil, and these were confirmed when Napoleon set up what is usually called the imperial nobility.

To do this the emperor used a decree of 1 March 1808 rather than a fundamental law, which would have gone to discussion by the Corps législatif. The Legion of Honor was created by a fundamental law that did not pass without legislative criticism of the growth of hierarchical spirit in French society and expression of fears of revived feudalism. Napoleon seemed intent on avoiding even the limited public discussion of his parliamentary assemblies on the subject of restoring titles to use in French life. The 1808 decree never employed the word *noblesse* but spoke only of titles that could become hereditary to the eldest son on certain financial conditions. The newly titled individuals were to be an honorific aggregate, a rather obscure entity intended to "nourish in the hearts of our subjects praiseworthy emulation, by perpetuating illustrious memories and by conserving for future ages the ever-present image of the recompenses which under a just government follow great services rendered to the state." In order to underline that the purpose of these titles was also to strengthen loyalty to the regime, the imperial monopoly of titles was emphasized. Articles 14 and 15 of the decree spelled this out:

14. Those of our subjects upon whom we shall confer titles shall not display other armorial bearings nor have other liveries than those that shall be set out in the letters patent of creation.
15. We forbid all our subjects to arrogate to themselves such titles and qualities as we shall have not conferred upon them, and to officials of the public registry [*état civil*] notaries and others to use them [in public documents]; renewing in so far as necessary against those who contravene those provisions laws presently in force.

The Council of State reiterated in 1809 the prohibition of the display of feudal coats of arms stated in various laws of 1791, 1793, and 1798. The 1810 Criminal Code included an article prohibiting the use of titles or the wearing of uniforms not permitted by the government. The intention of these measures was perfectly plain: only those loyal to the regime would have the trappings of title and rank.

Between 1808 and 1814 Napoleon bestowed 3,263 titles.[14] Over half of the recipients (58 percent) had not held a title previously. They were mainly officeholders, lawyers, and landowners from families who either had risen in social position before 1789 or had made rapid advances thanks to the Revolution. Among the most famous was a former canon of Chartres and author in 1789 of "Qu'est-ce que le Tiers Etat?" Emmanuel-Joseph Sieyès, named comte in May 1808. Another was Joseph Fouché, the infamous pacifier of Lyons in 1793, who became successively a comte (April 1808) and duc d'Otrante (August 1809). The imperial nobility translated into the traditional forms of prestige the achievements of the new men of the Revolutionary decade. Twenty-two percent, however, had been noble before 1789, and they were by no means restricted to recent additions to the second estate but included men of antique lineage.[15] One member of the Somme electoral college noted that the nobility of the Chassepot de Pissy family dated from 1300, that they originated in Buguey of the former Savoye: "[The family] has always been devoted to the service and defense of the State and of its Prince."[16] In June 1810 Napoleon noted of these *anciens nobles* that "above all it was necessary that they should have kept wealth [in order to be useful to him]."[17] In the years immediately following 1808 Napoleon gave most titles to military men, ranging from members of the *noblesse* like Marmont, Davout, Caulaincourt, Le Lièvre de la Grange, and

Flahaut de la Billarderie to commoners like Masséna, Soult, and Ney. This prominence among the *titrés* of military men continued under later regimes, as will be shown below.

A striking illustration is the successful request by Charles-Reynald-Laure-Félix, son of senator Antoine-César Choiseul-Praslin (whose family property is discussed in more detail in chapter 3), a year after the setting up of the imperial titles to be named a comte and to establish a *majorat*. The young man sought to explain why he had resigned from the military service but still considered that he merited a title: "in favor of the services of his ancestors, most of whom spilled their blood for the defense of their country and who had the glory of upholding the honor of French arms." He pointed out that since his father had died before receiving the title of comte, he was asking for it himself. He recalled that he had been a student at the Ecole polytechnique in the year IV (virtually from its first days), in the engineering school in the year VII, and a captain in the year X and that his brother had been killed in action. As a result, he had been obliged to resign in order to render to his relatives the necessary consolations and care.[18] Napoleon also used new titles to secure the affections of influential local worthies who could form opinion. Henri Maloteau de Guerne, member of the Douai municipal council, former *président à mortier* in the Parlement of Flanders and a member of his local electoral college, as well as the possessor of an income of more than twenty thousand francs from *biens nationaux,* went on from the enumeration of his substance to point out a strong devotion to family tradition:

> The petitioner who has not ceased to be in the ranks of the National
> Guard since its establishment joins with his son to ask you, Sire, for
> comtal letters [patent]. Both would find in that grace a compensation
> for the [hereditary judicial] post of *président à mortier* of which the
> Revolution deprived them. This grace would also recompense a
> distinguished act carried out by the forefather of the petitioner, who,
> being chief provost of the Valenciennes magistrates in 1722,
> marched at the head of the workers to stop the fire that was
> beginning to take hold in the powder magazine as the result of a
> violent storm.[19]

This recitation of praiseworthy past acts presented to the sovereign, in the event Napoleon, as evidence of the continuing merit of the Maloteau de Guerne family was accepted, and the title of baron was bestowed in 1814. A *majorat* was set up in 1817.

In a similar vein, the widow of a marquis and *maréchal de camp* of Louis XVI, Charles-Louis d'Hautefeuille, unsuccessfully petitioned Napoleon in 1813 to ennoble one of her sons, an officer in the Second

Dragoons: "Your Majesty would complete all his benevolences for the sons, and would cause the gratitude of the mother, who would never forget for the rest of her life the honor that her ancestors and she had to lodge in their country and town residences Henri iv in 1603, Louis xiii in 1620, and Your Majesty at an epoch that will never be effaced from her memory and from that of her relatives."[20] Such fulsome sentiments may be dismissed as merely sycophantic, but they were in fact utterly within the logic of a service *noblesse*.

The primacy of family ambitions over political loyalties to a particular dynasty was a striking feature of nineteenth-century nobles, although a certain demure prudery prevented this obvious truth from being trumpeted too loudly. Perhaps many nobles did not themselves see any inconsistency in their conduct. Theories about political change in France (the feudal nobility vanquished by a capitalist bourgeoisie), just as much as earlier disputes in royalist and liberal historiography (the ultra and noble Restoration locked in battle with the liberal and commoner Monarchy of July), have distracted attention from the striking continuities in the defense of family interests from the second estate to the post-Revolutionary nobles. Of course individuals might hold passionate loyalties, as did the devoted Avaray (d. 1811), whose dukedom was the only title created in exile by Louis xviii, and Ferdinand de Bertier, whose royalist beliefs shaped an entire life. Some old aristocratic families were less opportunist than others: the Damas, Fitzjames, Duras, and Croys were among those who remained aloof from Republic and Empire. Overall, however, the aristocracy and *noblesse* accommodated themselves to political change, just as they had always done earlier, and accepted new recruits and gradually ingested the *titrés* of successive regimes.

This amalgamation was not automatic. Not all *noblesse* who sought a Napoleonic title were accepted. Jacques Rose de Voisins, a former artillery captain and mayor of the village of Burgairolles in the Aude, hoped for the title of comte not merely to reward his efforts as a former *président de canton* who was now a member of his department's general council. He wished even more to refurbish a lineage approved by Chérin before the Revolution. (Perhaps mention of the celebrated court genealogist was to recall that the last Chérin to be charged with checking the ancestry of those to be presented at court died a general of the Republic.) Voisins petitioned that he was "jealous to perpetuate in my race honorable memories."[21] Similar avid pursuit of new titles among the *noblesse* can be studied in the dossiers of both successful and unsuccessful applicants for titles. The motives of families who went early to the Tuileries have been set down to the relative penury of families like the Rémusats or Ségurs, or to the hope of protecting their fortunes by fabulously wealthy aristocrats like the Luynes and the Choiseul-Praslins. Ambition motivated able striplings like Molé and Broglie. Self-interest and self-esteem are not easily separated in the circumstances of the Revolutionary aftermath, but one can confidently advance the idea that the observed behavior of the *noblesse* was *attentiste* in the sense that family went before royalism. From the inner circle of the fewer than one thousand individuals who comprised the Versailles court nobility there was a keen interest in again getting close to power. On 1 January 1814 the emperor's chamberlains included Mercy d'Argenteau, Montesquiou-Fézensac, Aubusson de la Feuillade, Talleyrand, Galard de Béarn, Mun, Choiseul-Praslin, Contades, Nicolay, Miramon, Louvois, Rambuteau, d'Alsace, Turenne, Brancas, Gontaut-Biron, Saint-Aulaire, Gramont, Montalembert, Lur-Saluces, Haussonville, and Montmorency; écuyers, Chabrillan de Moreton and Lauriston; and pages, Bougainville and Dreux-Brézé. Aristocratic ladies at court included Fontanges, Rochefort, Chabrillan de Moreton, Montmorency, Bouillé, Montalembert, Beauvais, and Noailles.[22] These prominent and wealthy individuals had links with families of similar extraction.

The dispassionate opportunism of the great aristocratic families was less frequently visible among those of the provincial *noblesse* who were less active solicitors. They remained far from determined opposition to the Empire. In Toulouse in 1812 the prefect reported that the *noblesse* thought that speaking warmly of the regime showed bad form, but that did not mean that they opposed it. Although the more conservative local nobles were increasingly appalled by the numbers of new titles being dispensed and accepted, the shrewder among them pointed out that titles from any source were useful in buttressing French nobles' prestige. The latter believed that the *noblesse* would rise to a commanding position because of the simple fact of inherent superiority, despite any irritation caused to less enlightened relatives. These wiser heads prevailed, and their families cooperated with the Empire.[23] The accommodations by nobles, if not all nobles, to each succeeding regime will be considered further below.

In 1814 Louis XVIII returned to his capital. Article 71 of the new constitution of France, the Charter, baldly referred to "la nouvelle noblesse," although Napoleonic legislation about titles never employed the world *noblesse*. The Bourbons recognized the more than three thousand titles bestowed by Napoleon as having the same currency as those of the second estate's remnants: "The former noblesse takes up again its titles; the new keeps its own. The king creates nobles at will, but he only accords to them ranks and honors with no exemption from the burdens and the duties of society." This was an obvious olive branch proferred to recent recruits to the French elite, and it was not only extended to imperialists. Marshal Jourdan, a soldier and a small-ware dealer in Limoges before the Revolution who then became a republican die-hard, was made a hereditary comte on New Year's Day, 1815, a grace Napoleon I had always refused him. In March 1819 Louis XVIII named him a peer.[24] However, in an inexplicably inconsistent gesture, Louis XVIII refused to wear the decoration of the Legion of Honor until the last days of the first Restoration, with Napoleon already on the return from Elba. Louis was perhaps not unconscious of the irony of wearing on his portly person an award for courage in battle, but his sense of the ridiculous slighted the pride of many thousands of brave men. In general, however, there were no ruptures in the honorific system of the Empire, although some slight adjustments were made in the mechanism of granting titles.[25] The officials charged with verifying, registering, and setting fees payable drew attention to the fact that royal letters, not the possession of office, were the way to ennoblement. The ennobling venal offices of the former provinces of the kingdom were now transmuted in the nineteenth century to more bureaucratic, more Parisian forms. As one 1817 pamphlet lamenting the absence of an accurate census of nobles put it, "By contrast with the former nobility, one had the new, wherein all was constant and certain."[26] It was a novel thought that recent titles were less open to question than the old. Candidates for titles discovered that partial claims to ennoblement derived from services rendered before the Revolution were discounted. This *noblesse inachevée*, holders of pre-1789 ennobling office whose tenure necessary to gain title had been brought abruptly to an end by the suppression of offices early in the Revolution, found scant sympathy in the chancellery. Individuals requested a title not merely citing the years spent in the defunct office but invoking other grounds for approval, including, significantly enough, titles bestowed by Napoleon. The Commission du sceau accepted some requests, especially from former *trésoriers de France* such as Pierre-Anne Delpech, born in 1758 (Tarn-et-Garonne), and Jean-Marius Devoisins de Lavernière, born in 1744 (Haute-Garonne), both ennobled in 1816–17. Nevertheless, the refusal of other candidates and the brushing aside of claims based on Old Regime practice underlined that the Napoleonic centralized dispensation of titles would be maintained by the Bourbons.

The epic events of the Hundred Days, when Napoleon escaped from his island prison of Elba (March 1815) to seize power again until his defeat on the field of Waterloo (18 June), did not change the trend but revealed the lively animosities that the *noblesse* had excited. Enthusiastically welcomed into Lyons during the "Flight of the Eagle" from the Mediterranean coast to Paris, Napoleon decreed that all émigrés who had returned to France since 1 January 1814 were again exiled. These measures were aimed at the most loyal retainers of the Bourbons, and their property was to be confiscated under the supervision of the prefects and tax officials. This was understandable enough, since only the most irreducible loyalists of the Old Regime had not made their peace by 1814. However, on the same day, 15 March 1815, "Napoleon, by the Grace of God and the Imperial Constitutions," abolished the *noblesse* that had been resuscitated by the 1814 Charter: "Feudal titles are suppressed." This, of course, did not include *noblesse* who held imperial titles, but in its aggressive rejection of the others it ran contrary to the earlier policy of encouraging their rallying to the Empire. The Chamber of Peers convened in a truncated form and claimed to support the emperor's return. However, in the dramatic and crucial situation of that spring, Napoleon hoped for more short-term gains from the support of vengeful egalitarians than rewards from his long-term aim of co-opting the *noblesse*. During his last days of power prior to the fall on 4 June 1815 the emperor bestowed only a handful of new titles: twelve comtes and five barons.

The returned Bourbons simply took up where they had left off. Their policy was to weld together *titrés* and *noblesse* in a steady dispensation of titles, after a cursory vetting of political suitability and a more thorough one of wealth. Louis XVIII accepted that the peerage should be hereditary in the summer of 1815, although he regretted that this would give them too much independence.[27] The crown tried to weld the Legion of Honor with the older titles of chevalier of the orders of Saint Louis, Saint Michel, or the Saint-Esprit, in line with the traditions of the military nobility. On 8 October 1814 Louis XVIII had issued an ordinance repeating *légionnaires'* right to a personal title of chevalier if they had net income of three thousand francs from real estate located in France and adding that if the forefather, the sons, and the grandsons had been members of the Legion of Honor with the necessary letters patent, the grandson would be noble by right and would transmit his nobility to all of his descendants.[28] Here the words *noble* and *noblesse* in the ordinance text showed the government's intent to encourage the proliferation of a petty nobility: at any given time the number of chevaliers was unlimited, although the higher grades were limited to a total of 2,640. In fact the title never established itself in popular esteem in the nineteenth century.

Almost two-thirds of all the titles granted between 1815 and 1830 were bestowed during the first five years. This revealed the rush of families who wanted to take a rank they had been unable or unwilling to solicit from Napoleon. Efforts were made to clear old debts of gratitude. They included the shower of honors bestowed upon one of Louis XVIII's favorites in the emigration, the *provençal* Blacas, who became a peer

(1815), a chevalier of the Order of the Saint-Esprit, a hereditary comte (1817), and a duc (1824), and the more modest appreciation shown a Parisian barrister, Chauveau-Lagarde, who in April 1817 was given letters patent that "bestowed on him *noblesse* and authorized him to use the title écuyer" in recognition of his courage and devotion to the defense, before the Revolutionary tribunal, of Marie-Antoinette and the sister of Louis XVI, Madame Elisabeth.[29] Business was honored in the person of Ternaux, the textile manufacturer and businessman who also sat as a deputy for the Seine department (1818–24) and Haute-Vienne (1827–31). Given letters of nobility in 1816, he was made a baron in 1819 but caused a scandal when he renounced his title in 1821 to protest against the "lettres de relief" given to a man whose father had derogated from the nobility by engaging in commerce.[30] Titles were also bestowed on officials, such as the judge who asked for a title on the occasion of his nomination to preside over the Poitiers Appeal Court:

> I venture to say to Your Excellency that an honorific title which I could pass on to my son would have for me in this connection much more worth if it were linked to my nomination; it would serve as a recommendation to him and his family in recalling in the future the circumstances in which it would have been granted; and from the present time it would testify that my nomination has been the spontaneous testimony of the confidence of H.M. and you, Monseigneur, and in giving more weight to the acts which the public good and the needs of the service dictate to me in the exercise of my functions, and in giving me more credit with my new colleagues and those under my jurisdiction it would make it easier to serve H.M. more efficaciously, which shall ever be the goal of all my efforts.[31]

He was made a hereditary baron, and his son succeeded to both the title and a judgeship at the Poitiers court.

In their effort to bind nobles to them in loyalty the Bourbons ennobled fewer commoners than had Napoleon; before 1789, 56 percent of all *titrés* were commoners and 42 percent were nobles, with a margin of uncertainty for the remainder. Of those receiving a Bourbon title, 27 percent already possessed an imperial one, an important contingent of individuals showing the continuity of their search for family distinction under regimes of opposing loyalties. The regilding was quite evident in 1816–17: a Toscan du Terrail (a gendarmery captain from the Hautes-Alpes), a Borel de Bretizel (a judge at the Paris Cour de cassation), a Faulcon (a member of the Vienne electoral college), and a Tarrible (a *maître des comptes*) are examples of the hundreds who added a Bourbon title to one given by Napoleon. Continuity was particularly striking among the military *noblesse*. General Tilly, at the seventeenth degree of a family with Norman origins, enlisted before the Revolution, fought under the Republic, became a general on the day of Louis XVI's execution, and received further distinctions under Napoleon, who named him, successively, chevalier, baron, and then comte de Tilly et de l'Empire. His son Charles-Edouard showed a similar appetite for status. A midshipman in 1813, he continued to serve through the Restoration (which made him a *comte héréditaire* in 1823) and remained on active service under the July Monarchy. In fact, officers made up the largest professional group among those granted titles by the Restoration (40 percent), trailed by those in central administration (12.5 percent), local administration (10.6 percent), and others. However, as will be seen, the same proportions did not apply for those who actually entailed land for a hereditary title (*majorat sur demande*). Talents outside the well-beaten tracks of state service were rarely recognized, although Ancelot, the playwright and member of the Académie française, was given letters of nobility in April 1830. More representative of the newly titled was Andlau, at the fifteenth degree of an Alsatian aristocratic family. Armand, son of a lieutenant general of the Old Regime army, was a chamberlain of Napoleon named comte in April 1810 and a hereditary peer in November 1827, who entailed an estate to carry the title of *majorat* the following year.[32]

Heredity for nineteenth-century titles was to be linked to entailed property to ensure the continuance of the holder's family wealth. Napoleon donated land from his German and Italian conquests to some of those he wished to gratify, but this property was lost when the French were driven out. The Bourbons also required peers, or individuals who established *majorats sur demande,* to possess entailed property. Individuals with *majorats sur demande* without the political right of a seat in the Chamber of Peers represented "pure" status for its own sake. Holders of a *majorat sur demande* were not a power elite in the reductionist sense beloved of the C. Wright Mills school, with its vision of societies manipulated by tiny, and usually sinister, minorities. No *majorat sur demande,* for example, figured on the painting of the main court dignitaries at the coronation of Charles x.[33] It would be wearisome to demonstrate at length that the bulk of the *noblesse* who took *majorats sur demande* were of families of decidedly secondary prestige under the Old Regime. The Falentin de Saintenacs were condemned for usurpation of *noblesse* in 1666, although this was reversed by a decision of 1701; the Drouilhet de Sigalas only registered in 1784 letters patent first bestowed in 1654; the elder Boutray had been an *écuyer avocat* and a *trésorier général et payeur* of the Paris municipality, which, while lucrative, were faintly unseemly positions. However, those who set up *majorats sur demande* linking wealth and title knew that henceforth with every passing year their rank would gain luster.

Enough has been said to establish the overlapping and layering of *noblesse,* aristocracy, and *titrés* discernible under the Empire and Restoration and flagrant by the Second Empire. The amalgamation desired by Napoleon and Louis XVIII had in fact taken place. The intermarriage that consolidated the process will be discussed in chapter 7, dealing with the noble family, but the taking of titles and position from successive regimes had the same meaning in civil society. An aristocrat like Auguste-Michel-Félicité Le Tellier de Souvre, marquis de Louvois, the wealthiest voter in the Yonne, whose extensive holdings at Ancy-le-Franc (Yonne) escaped Revolutionary confiscation, showed the style: he became a comte in 1811 thanks to Napoleon and a marquis in 1819 thanks to Louis XVIII, and in 1830 he was the most prominent noble in his region to rally to Louis-Philippe.[34] Another example of this de facto *noblesse* acceptance of the new status was the second son of the Bois-le-Comte family, one of robe origins, who received his first title in 1825 and another in 1847. The cavalry officer Commaille, son of an Old Regime tax collector from the Orléans region, established a *majorat* of baron just before the 1830 Revolution. Like Pandin de Narcillac and other officers, he completed the formalities of his new letters patent under a different regime but in the same year. Later, in 1837, he added to his name a papal marquis bestowed by Gregory XVI. Claude-Etienne Chaillou was an official in Lower Silesia in 1806 and then a prefect (Ardèche and Creuse) from 1810 to 1815; despite his Hundred Days service, he was created a hereditary chevalier in January 1816, with the right to add *des Barres* to his surname, and raised to a hereditary baron in 1825, which in turn was confirmed by new letters patent from Louis-Philippe of 29 March 1842. In 1805 he married Mlle Nompère de Champagny, the daughter of the duc de Cadore. These random examples drawn from Révérend show the behavior of the most adaptable of the *titrés,* which in turn was emulated by their more timid fellows bent also on the pursuit of family status over that of political loyalties.

More than seven thousand titles were granted between 1800 and 1830. Some were based on entailments to support hereditary transmission, while others existed simply for the lifetime of the recipient. In practice, families that did not set up *majorats* continued to use their titles among their descendants. This evolution was sanctioned by the general aspiration for nobility in the adding of particles to names and in a climate of opinion that was sympathetic to the use of titles in daily life. This generalized interest was evoked by one descendant of the robe *noblesse* of Toulouse who said that the descendants of more recent municipal officials under the Old Regime had suddenly and miraculously transformed themselves into "high and mighty seigneurs" and now called their modest rural residences *châteaux, comtés,* or *mar-*

quisats and that never had there been more titled personnages in the city.[35]

The Restoration Bourbons produced for the first time an amalgam of families with legally recognized nobility before 1789, those post-Revolutionary titles given by Napoleon and themselves, and a relative tolerance towards a *noblesse* of pretension more numerous than during the Old Regime. By the mid-1820s ennoblement was less cluttered with political references to the recent past. Gradations of rank and title were understood as markers on a *cursus honorum* of success at court, in the administration, especially in the army, and more rarely in law, business, or other professions. The title marquis, not used in the 1808 decrees, retained the strongest royalist connotation. Among the *noblesse* who received Napoleonic titles it was usual after 1815 to prefer the Old Regime title. However, de Caulaincourt bequeathed one of his titles to each of two sons: the eldest was duc de Vicence (an imperial title), and the younger, marquis de Caulaincourt (Old Regime).[36] By the closing years of the Restoration there was a substantial fusion of the nobles, with a focus on the court of Charles x to provide a glittering focus for "the palace dignitaries, the three hundred gentlemen of the king's bedchamber, the masters of horse, the officers of the venery, of the household, the pages, the bodyguards, the officers of the royal guard, everybody covered with gold and embroideries."[37]

After the July 1830 Revolution, in order to underline the contrast with the practice of the Restoration and to assuage the jealousy of the middle classes, the Orleanist regime in its early years seemed opposed to noble pretensions. Ninety-three recent peers were unseated on 7 August 1830, and the Chamber of Peers was warned that it was to be reorganized. The aging liberal aristocrat La Fayette was noisily opposed to the maintenance of the Chamber of Peers. During the 1831 debate over the complete abolition of Article 259 of the Penal Code, which punished illegal use of noble titles, he observed that after the Revolution it would be quite grotesque to defend noble titles with an article of the code.[38]

Among the military honorific orders only the Legion of Honor was maintained. In the new governing class there seemed to be a widespread hostility to rank and hierarchy. Eusèbe de Salverte, a Parisian deputy notorious for his ferocious atheism, denounced in the Chamber of Peers the probable results of failing to abolish the heredity of the peerage, whose three hundred leaders would "soon despise the rights of the nation and who would believe they were only in contact with it in order to absorb property, favors, and dignities."[39] The deputies went further in the opposition to the use of titles: between 1831 and 1835 a cluster of decrees were issued that, particularly as they related to hereditary titles, sharply slowed the induction of nobles. The apparatus for administering new titles was dismantled when the prestigious Commission du sceau de France was demoted to an ignominious subbureau in the Ministry of Justice. Although Article 23 of the revised Charter gave the king after 1830 the same unlimited right to create peerages, either for life or as hereditary titles, this was docked by the law of 6 October 1831, which restricted the possession of newly created peerages to one generation. On 17 January 1834 the setting up of *majorats* on titles bestowed before 1831 was forbidden, in order to prevent some Legitimist families from becoming titled dynasties, as many of those who held Restoration titles now belatedly went through the legal process of entailment in order to make them hereditary under law. In May 1835 the deputies' attack on hereditary titles went a step forward with a prohibition of the *majorats* for new titles: Article 2 of the ordinance prohibited existing *majorats* based on personal property from remaining in force for more than three generations. In 1837 another law declared a *majorat* to be unnecessary for the transmission of any title originally based on an entailment. This cluster of legislation throughout the 1830s attempted to halt the strengthening of a wealthy hereditary nobility. It also attests to the deputies' continuing preoccupation with rank.

From this brief survey of Orleanist legislation against hereditary titles and entailments, one might wrongly conclude that the July Monarchy drastically accelerated the decline of the French nobility. In society at large there was no such reticence about noble pretensions, and increasing numbers of individuals began to use the particle in their family name. Among famous writers, Balzac first added *de* to his name in 1831, and both Gobineau and the Maupassant family did the same around 1846. Gérard Labrunie became Gérard de Nerval, and Barbey exhumed the long abandoned suffix *d'Aurévilly*.[40] As so often happens, practice was quite different from bureaucratic regulation. Innumerable textbooks have propagated a misconception by describing Louis-Philippe as a citizen-king, but although affable, unprepossessing, and considerate to the bourgeois, the monarch was of the blood royal and did not forget it. He created his own titles, maintained an urbane court, and although less exacting than under Charles x, the ceremonial surrounding the royal family emphasized their rank. Moreover, in the last years, the entourage of the duc and duchesse de Nemours provided a socially exclusive venue for the Orleanist aristocracy. Legitimist nobles who supported the elder line affected to question the regime's moral authority, and at a splendid ball at the Austrian Embassy in 1847 literally turned their backs on the Orleanist aristocrats.[41] However, lines of cleavage beteeen families and individuals were rarely complete ruptures. Earlier and in a similar way there had been a cool, face-to-face formal civility between Napoleonic *titrés* and the more ultraroyalist members of the *noblesse* but one that left enough room for subsequent accommodation. The nobility never saw a complete breakdown of communication between its pre-Revolutionary members and the modern titles. Similarly, there was no definitive rupture of contacts between Legitimists and Orleanists after 1830.

Throughout the whole period a new usage created titles independently of the crown: the so-called decrescendo of titles, initially envisaged by Louis XVIII as a right limited to the eldest son of a hereditary peer (*sur majorat*) to carry a title before he inherited that of his father. This was based on a hierarchy of rank: the son of a duc called himself marquis; the son of a marquis, comte; the son of a comte, victomte; and the son of a vicomte, baron. Under the July Monarchy's new conditions, and even more under the Second Empire, this device multiplied the use of titles considerably. In 1868 one genealogist denounced the carelessness with which the nobility used the decrescendo, which he mistakenly believed inflated its total numbers.[42] In the hope of restricting a proliferation of titles, another writer suggested that all males of a lineage should carry the same rank, as was done in high aristocratic French families, and cited the La Rochefoucauld, Choiseul, Croy, Montesquiou, and Broglie families.[43] Louis-Philippe also gave titles to his partisans, but there were fewer title registrations than under either Napoleon or the Bourbons. The Orleanist monarchy's political program was at least to avoid confrontations with the country *noblesse*, if not to win their support. Leading commoner Orleanists like Guizot did not appear to covet titles as avidly as their predecessors in other assemblies.

An increasingly elaborate de facto certification of modern nobility was that of genealogies and guides to nobility. These were nothing new in France: nobles had long used checklists to know their fellows should instinctual recognition fail. They employed professional genealogists to provide satisfactory accounts of their forebears.[44] The crown had entrusted the checking of proofs of nobility, on the best hereditary principles, to the Hozier family. The last of them, Ambroise, was using the family archives to produce a revised *Armorial général* in 1823.[45]

Compilations of family genealogy fascinated nobles of scholarly disposition. Early in the Restoration there was a desire to catalog the *noblesse* survivors of the Revolution, those who died for the counter-Revolution, and to distinguish between old and recent titles. An 1817 prospectus for a "Martyrologie de la Révolution française, ou recueil monumental consacré à la mémoire des victimes par leurs familles" is an example. Contributing noble families were promised a discount for providing memoirs and portraits of individuals for the publication. A single copy, printed on black paper with tasteful silver lettering, was promised to the individual who sold the most subscriptions. Subscribers were assured that their name, title, and residence would be printed. This project may have appeared a trifle ostentatious, for it seems not to have been published.[46] Courcelles (1759–1834), who had written a genealogical dictionary of the peers of France, proposed to produce a "Conservateur de la noblesse territoriale et légale de la France" dealing with families whose members, although only titled with such as bannerets, chevaliers, or écuyers, were no less illustrious than families who possessed lands that transmitted titles. In an open letter of 25 October 1827 the comte de Croy-Chanel published a denunciation of Courcelles as venal, without any official authorization, without any claim to the title chevalier, and being in fact named Jullien, a former notary at Orléans.[47]

Other works, such as the *Manuel héraldique* and the *Etrennes de la noblesse,* were republished, as though to continue the format used in the 1780s, but the volumes were doubled in size by the inclusion of interleaved blank pages on which the owner could update, in alphabetical order, his—or her—genealogical researches. From the 1840s, there was a remarkable proliferation of vanity publications dealing with noble families. The inauguration of the Salle des Croisades at Versailles in 1839–40 has often been derided as an example of romantic fascination with medievalism in a completely inappropriate setting, but it also reminds us how congenial the mental climate was to the compilers of dictionaries of provincial nobilities, of engravings of châteaux, of guides to aristocratic usage, and of journals for nobles and their mimics, the whole decked out with heraldic devices and bad poetry in fake old French. Yet gradually this accumulation of publications began to confer its own legitimation.

The publication of the *Mémorial historique de la noblesse,* edited by A. J. Duvergier, in 1839 serves as a convenient marker for a sharp increase in the network of publishers and experts on heraldry, genealogy, and the like. These congeries of publishers, archivists, and editors of the reviews of learned societies and local newspapers became a variant of the *Armorial de France.* With the revival of genealogical literature, the compilers' expertise was questioned. Certification of noble standards progressively passed into the hands of specialists. In the past the court of appeal on such matters was the Commission du sceau de France, and earlier still the crown's genealogists. By the time of the July Monarchy the downgrading of the registration procedures, as well as the noncooperation of the Legitimists, left the judgment of contentious matters of lineage in the hands of self-appointed experts. The *Revue historique de la noblesse* (1841) evoked its authority to judge these matters:

In the absence of heralds of arms and of royal genealogists whose
functions have been abolished by the French Revolution, the *Revue
historique de la noblesse* gathers together archivists, paleographers,
and students of the Ecole des chartes, the only official genealogists
of our age, only inheritors of the de Marle, the de Chérin, the
d'Hozier, and the learned Benedictines . . . for in the insertion of
genealogical notices and articles the one requirement is a severe and
conscientious examination made by the editorial committee which,
located near the big archival depots of the capital, can itself
undertake researches and investigations necessary for the families
involved.[48]

Not only technical skill and archival research were pressed into service to justify the new works. It was thought desirable that France
should enjoy publications of the type found in other countries. A prospectus produced by de Milleville for an *Armorial de France* cited England, where "on every household table one or several of these volumes
are always to be found, and if you wish to know more precisely the
family connections, the dates of the life of a man of *bonne compagnie*
whom you saw a moment before, you have only to open the volume." A
catalog of every profession's members was a necessity: "However obscure or modest, there is no artisan who cannot find in a special book the
names of his confreres."[49] Nobles expected no less. Comte François de
Croy-Chanel, who had savaged "M. de Courselles [*sic*]" nine years earlier, published in 1836 a vehement attack against Lainé—"great author, faker, and seller of genealogies supposedly truthful but really
false, abusive, grotesque, and mendacious."[50] The same P. Louis Lainé
denounced André Borel d'Hauterive in 1850 as an intriguer and the son
of a Lyonnais ironmonger and perfumer who tried to palm himself off as
descending from a Dauphinois noble family extinguished by the Revolution. In his efforts to attract clients, Borel claimed to be the only official
genealogist of the time thanks to his training at the Ecole des chartes.
This was contested by Lainé and others, who pointed out that France
lacked an official genealogist. Lainé claimed roundly that most of the
genealogies published under the Restoration by Saint Allais (whose
Nobiliaire universel de France appeared in twenty-one volumes from
1814 to 1843) and de Courcelles were his work, and he gave references
that he felt constituted acknowledgments. On 20 October 1845 Lainé
had struck Borel on the rue Vivienne and was judged on 10 December
1845 at the 7th chamber of the court of petty sessions.[51] Lainé's aversion was fueled by jealousy of Borel d'Hauterive's archival training
which gave him an advantage over Duchesne, Anselme, and La Roque,
who lacked it. For his part, Borel d'Hauterive sued Aubert for publishing

an almanac of the nobility, but although initially successful at the commercial tribunal, his case was dismissed by the first chamber of the Paris Appeal Court on 26 June 1847.[52]

These disputes illustrate the animosities among this heterogeneous group, including nobles and commoners, who made a living from the nobility's concerns. Men like Gabriel Eysembach or Clairefond, of the *Mémorial*, claimed a special expertise as historians. Others had legal training, such as Louis de la Roque, an *avocat* at the Paris Appeal Court, or Edouard de Barthélemy, who had been an *auditeur* at the Council of State. These men were nobles, but A. J. Duvergier had only the particles in his family name. The commoner publisher Bachelin-Deflorenne was the most successful in this line of publishing: he had a Paris printing house which produced *nobiliaires* for other authors, as well as his own directories. He found the business sufficiently profitable to persist in it from the 1860s to the 1880s, listing titles, coats of arms, addresses, and the heads of families.

The authors mentioned above worked on a national scale and with an eye on the aristocracy and its mimics, but in each part of France there were provincial experts. They probably found less reward for their efforts. Some journalists specialized in genealogical matters, such as the chief editor of the Bordelais *Revue d'Aquitaine*, Joseph Noulens, who often dealt with family histories in his newspaper pages. From 1861 he wrote a series of books and pamphlets on the subject, including regional publications (*Maisons historiques de Gascogne ou galerie nobiliaire* [1863]), family histories, and documented attacks on those whose claims he wished to crush, such as that of the comtes de Bréda against "la rédaction anonyme" of *Le Chartier français* or that of comte P. J. T. J. de Pardaillan against members of the Treil family, "the first calling himself comte de Pardaillan, the second baron de Pardaillan, the third de Pardaillan." In Toulouse, always a hotbed of noble pretension, Alphonse Brémond produced listings of nobles and lost heavily on the publication of his *Nobiliaire toulousain*. When they realized that costs would not be covered, the printers sold the remaining copies, as Brémond bitterly complained, "dirt cheap and at auction," leaving him with no profit after years of labor.[53] Quite striking to the twentieth-century mind is the lack of "market research." Among people as touchy as nobles the credibility of a *nobiliaire* was crucial. To be listed in the right one was heaven; to appear in the pages of one thought to be the work of an unscrupulous compiler was ridiculous. Brémond tried to amass local credibility by producing a series of lesser publications, but his major commercial venture was a flop.

The Parisian and provincial developments of genealogical silk-purse factories emphasized the widening gap between *noblesse* certified by royal letters patent, *titrés* with similar enactments from the nineteenth century, and the transformation of status by commercialism and ambition. Library shelves groaned under the weight of large volumes with tooled leather and gilt inlay, the apparatus of a self-sustaining genealogical scholarship. This resurgence of noble pretensions in the years following the regime's change in 1830 explains the virulent reaction against them under the Second Republic in 1848.[54] All titles were abolished in France (29 February 1848), and it was forbidden to mention them in public documents such as marriage contracts. The next month saw the prohibition of the public display of coats of arms or the use of outriders with carriages: in general "are abolished forever all noble titles, all distinctions of birth, class, or caste." General Alphonse d'Hautpoul commented indignantly on the loss of titles of nobility and of official positions that overtook him in the spring of 1848: "At that time I remained, however, without a shred of prestige. As a result of the Revolution I lost at one blow my qualities of peer of France, of general councillor of the Aude, and of lieutenant general: I could not *even* [my emphasis] use my title of hereditary *noblesse*. I was just citizen d'Hautpoul but surrounded, it is true, with the esteem and consideration of the public."[55] On 22 December 1849 the son of the Napoleonic duc d'Istrie called himself in a procuration "Mr Napoléon Bessières d'Istrie, ancien pair de France," which constituted at least an echo of former distinctions.[56] Others forced to sacrifice to modesty were doubtless vexed by enforced egalitarianism.

The hurt of those who had lost their titles was assuaged four years later on 24 January 1852 when the *prince-président* revoked the suppression of former French titles. Throughout the 1850s and 1860s the campaign to solicit support from nobles and notables was evident. One newspaper editor was outraged in 1857 that two-thirds of the Senate and 48 percent of the Corps législatif had either titles or particles in their surname, and his book denouncing this trend went through three editions.[57] Nobles who complained that the state had ceased to give them any aid or comfort in maintaining a proper sense of distinctions in social place were soon to be answered.[58] On 7 May 1858 a proposed law was introduced to the Corps législatif by Duvergier and two other state councillors that provided a rotund defense of the concept of hereditary honor. Reinstatement of Article 259 of the Penal Code suppressed in 1832 was called for:

It is neither timely nor moral to abandon to the encroachments of vanity or to fraudulent maneuvers an institution to which are attached the great memories of the former monarchy, which the glories of the Empire surrounded with a new brilliance and which

are upheld at the same time by the respect due to the antiquity of
traditions and by the obedience that is due to the most solemn acts
of contemporary legislation.[59]

The speaker emphasized that the force of law was required to prevent
the proliferation of illicit use of titles and particles. He took up the
fundamental objection to the existence of ranks of in society, that of
egalitarianism, by saying that such a principle did not demand a sacrifice of purely honorific titles and decorations which were rewards for
talent, courage, and faithful service to the state. This point was elaborated by de Beauverger, du Mirail, General Parchappe, and de Rigaud,
the leading speakers supporting the committee report. This the assembly endorsed, but not without signs of reticence about appearing to
nurse retrograde enthusiasms. The proposed article included the word
noblesse: "Anybody who shall wear in public a costume, a uniform, or a
decoration that does not belong to him or who shall have taken without
right a title of *noblesse* shall be punished with imprisonment of from six
months to two years and a fine of from 500 to 5,000F." A highly significant change was made before the law was accepted (211 for, 23
against): the word *noblesse* was replaced by *distinction honorifique,*
which seemed more appropriate to the legislators.[60]

With the pragmatism of the Bonapartist tradition, Napoleon III used
for the benefit of his regime those tendencies among nobles already
discussed. He preferred to "confirm" earlier claims to a title or to renew
them rather than to create new titles *ex abrupto.* Of course, the Second
Empire was particularly congenial to the beneficiaries of the First, that
is, to those of them who retained sufficient wealth, connections, and
skills to be politically or socially useful. By imperial decree of May 1859
the *avocat* Sieyès was declared comte by the transmission of his bachelor great-uncle's title. While the titles of the First Empire were naturally well-thought-of, Napoleon III did not view titles of other prove-
nances as anything more than a decoration of that part of the national
elite prepared to throw its lot in with his. Adélaïde-Joséphine Bachasson
de Montalivet was the granddaughter of a comte and donatory of the
First Empire who had passed a hereditary peerage to her father during
the Restoration. Her father, a liberal and a minister of state under the
July Monarchy, had been blessed with five daughters and no sons, so
Adélaïde, married to Antoine-Achille Masson, was authorized to add the
name Montalivet to that of her sons. By a decree of the Third Republic (5
January 1892) the three sons were permitted to raise (*relever*) the Bachasson de Montalivet name—and presumably to drop the less sonorous
patronym Masson. Although titles had never been more lavishly used in
society, it is interesting that the Second Empire gave out fewer titles

than either the First Empire or the Restoration: about five hundred. This included the valued permissions to add the particle *de* to a surname, conferred in letters patent rather than by the less elegant procedure of obtaining a court order. In short, by the Second Empire there was a synthesis in matters of nobility. Titles were considered the decorations of success across a broad band of elite opinion.[61]

One example of how a family might rise and fall over time shows the difficulty of deciding who is in the top drawer of society at any given moment. In the eighteenth century the Baudon de Mony might have been looked down upon from the more commanding heights of the *bonne compagnie*. They sprang from a seventeenth-century fines collector and, one hundred years later, a *secrétaire du roi* and tax farmer whose son married another tax farmer's daughter. Evidently they had an atavistic skill with money, for they were wealthy enough in the nineteenth century to have the adoptive grandson of Senator Colchen made a baron in 1843 and to marry their daughters into such aristocratic houses as the Maillé de la Tour Landry, the Rohan Chabot, and the Rosanbo. The men of the family were less grand—for example, the Cour des comptes official who added the name Colchen in 1843—but they were extremely well-connected under the Second Empire. Napoleon III hoped to encourage just this type of supporter in his effort to found the regime on the affection of the prosperous, conservative nobles and notables.

A circular of 19 June 1858 from the Ministry of Justice to the *procureurs généraux* condemned pretensions that an "excess of permissiveness has permitted to emerge" but underscored the need to apply the new May 1858 law with as much prudence as firmness.[62] In 1859 the Commission du sceau des titres was reestablished, another sign of the keen interest the regime bestowed on regulation of the honorific system. The Second Empire did not apply Article 259 with much rigor, which is understandable, since those likely to transgress it were precisely those who supported the regime. Enquiries to *procureurs généraux* of the appeal courts were almost invariably returned marked "néant"—at least if the Marseilles file copies are representative. The *procureurs* were instructed not to initiate prosecutions on their own initiative but to do so only after preliminary consultation with the *garde des sceaux*. However, the introduction of legislation on the subject and the definition of administrative procedures illustrate the political importance attached to the question of hierarchy in society by the Second Empire.

Legislators were equally vexed by the ursurpations of what they called nobiliary names: "as much as the title, more even than the title, the particle is added to the name, makes a part of it which communicates and is transmitted. In our customs it decorates the name almost to the same extent and sometimes heightens the prestige of a name's origin . . . its usurpation is damaging to the respectable rights of those who possess it legally."[63] The idea that the particle in itself was an honorary distinction was vigorously criticized by various authors, such as the lawyer P. Biston in several diatribes published around 1860. What Biston had in mind was exemplified by another, more prominent lawyer, Paul Bresson, for a time *avocat général* at the Cour de cassation and a member of the Conseil du sceau de titres, who in 1863 added the particle *de* to his name, in 1865 was granted the reversion of his dead brother's title of hereditary comte awarded by Louis-Philippe in 1838, and in 1866 had his own son's right to the hereditary title confirmed. Although before 1789 members of the second estate did not all have a particle in their family name, nineteenth-century practice increasingly linked titles, particles, and nobles together.

Despite the Second Empire's reputation as a paradise for social climbers, the rate of legalized "cosmetic" alterations to family names was no greater than during the Restoration and the July Monarchy. A decision of 10 April 1818 laid down that notification of name changes should appear in the official government newspaper, *Le Moniteur*. Some alterations scarcely demand comment: MM. Chieux, Cochon, Cocu, and Couillaud understandably found their patronyms a trial.[64] Various Jews Gallicicized their names—from Abraham to Abrand, for example. Between 1803 and 1868, however, nearly eighteen hundred alterations were made that were distinctively ornamental—such as Bobé de Moyneuze (1826) or Bobière de Valière (1861)—but the changes were made at a fairly regular rhythm over the years between the First Empire and the Second. This pursuit of a resounding name, of the use of the particle, and of titles was vexing to contemporaries of egalitarian disposition but also witnessed the hunger among the elite, or the elite among the socially hungry, for a distinctive appellation. The journalist Edmond About, whose *hobereau* wife had been disowned by her family after their wedding, railed bitterly against the whole trend as degrading.[65]

One curious feature in the new world where status was signified by title was the decline of some older forms. Most striking was the fading of the prestige in being called chevalier. Napoleon had established chevaliers at the bottom of his hierarchy of titles: the revenue in francs required to established a hereditary *majorat* (3,000F) was only a fifth of that required for baron, the next title in the ascending series (15,000F). There were also numerous chevaliers of the Legion of Honor. Both its ubiquity and its low price level, together with its association with elderly and often penurious chevaliers de Saint Louis named under the Old

Regime, lowered its prestige. The Bourbons were fairly prodigal in bestowing it on businessmen and others whose financial abilities commanded respect, but not to excess. Antoine-Joseph Le Marchant de Gomicourt, son of the farmer-general of a *marquisat* in Picardy, had been active at the Amiens finance bureau before 1789 and subsequently a deputy to the Conseil des Cinq-Cents and the Corps législatif. He was named chevalier both by the Empire (February 1814) and by the Restoration (February 1815), but he had no children to carry his hereditary title. In general it can be said that by the 1830s, use of the title chevalier had gone out of style save for among the elderly.

Another venerable appellation that withered away was that of écuyer. Before the Revolution this had been the basic building block of the honorific system: the March 1600 edict of Henri IV linked it to exemption from the taille and hence to the fundamental privilege of the second estate. Napoleon did not revive the title in 1808, perhaps because it was already used at court by equerries (*écuyer de l'empereur*). Under the Restoration it was occasionally bestowed simply to indicate ennoblement, as in the case of the barrister Chauveau-Lagarde mentioned above, and was found, although infrequently, on formal documents, such as the 1829 marriage contract of a judge from the Chartres *tribunal de première instance,* who had the word entered alongside his profession.[66] Thirty years later, however, even in the backwaters of provincial society, even to another noble the use of écuyer had become grotesque: "I shall never forget the effect produced on the numerous company gathered, twenty-five years ago, in the main room of the Poitiers town hall, at the reading aloud of a marriage certificate that included along with the name of the bridegroom's father this quality of écuyer. The most worthy man, who had exercised his right in this solemn occasion, seemed to return from the other world, and the most indulgent listener at that time thought him ridiculous."[67] The incident took place at a legal ceremony, where under the Old Regime participants would have been absolutely punctilious in enumerating their "qualities."

It falls outside this book's framework to explore the situation after the fall of the Second Empire in 1870. However there is a strong impression that the autorecruitment of the nobility by vanity publications, name changes, and use of the particle actually accelerated sharply. The *Belle Epoque* may have seen a brief reverse in the declining numbers of those who lived as nobles and who wished to advertise the fact. The Third Republic permitted the use of titles to those who felt so inclined. Showers of grandiloquent additions to surnames were registered for little more trouble than the legal fees. M. Barbier, a barrister from Alençon, must have felt like an emergent butterfly that first morning in 1891 that he awoke as Faulcon de la Parisière, if in fact he existed.[68] Those who still clung to Old Regime genealogical concerns and who were unhappy that nineteenth-century nobility mirrored wealth, success, and style rather than bloodlines were outraged. Representative of disdainful recrimination by the *noblesse* (an enduring literary genre) was an 1898 article later expanded into a book replete with contempt for the "the coats of arms that *les misses américaines* bought with their cash" and for aristocrats who intermarried with Jewish families: "Let them frankly admit that their half-commonness, half-Jewishness, and half-cosmopolitanism ['leur mi-roture, leur mi-juiverie et leur mi-cosmopolitisme'] henceforth prevents their claiming to be part of *la noblesse française:* that of Agincourt and of Denain."[69] In the twentieth century other specimens of this xenophobic, exclusionist, and hierarchic literature would be published in France, but that cannot concern us at present. At

TABLE I. French Nobles over Time by Components from Pre-1789 *Noblesse*, Nineteenth-Century *Titrés*, Name Changes, and Aristocrats, 1790–1870

	Noblesse		*Titrésa*			
Year	Individuals	Families	Born Common	Born Noble	Name Changesb	Aristocrats
1790	400,000c	70,000d				2,000
	350,000e	25,000–30,000f				
	140,000f					
	110,000g					
1800						
1810			2,790	1,220		1,000
1820	25,000h	45,000h	2,226	1,374	638	
1830		17,000i				
1840		15,246j			541	800
1850						
1860					594	
1870	[90,000]b	20,000b				2,000

Sources:

aRévérend.

bAntoine Bachelin-Deflorenne, *Etat présent de la noblesse française, contenant le dictionnaire de la noblesse contemporaine . . . 1866* (Paris, 1866).The edition of 1868 gave 30,000. Other editions swelled the numbers in 1869, 1884, and 1887. The 1884 edition gave "Les noms, qualités et domiciles de plus de soixante mille nobles . . . 5e édition, revue, corrigée, expurgée et considérablement augmentée." The introduction noted that "aujourd'hui le nombre des nobles, ou ayant la prétention de l'être, peut être évalué à environ 60,000. Mais combien en est-il réellement? 8 à 9,000 peut-être" (p.xix).

this point a table usefully summarizes the probable evolution of the French noble population between 1800 and 1870 by showing the range of estimates put forward by historians and others (see table 1).

The most inexorable distraint upon remaining noble was poverty. This grieved the fellows of the impecunious, who liked to think of the nobility as innate and imperishable. After the Revolution, when a privileged access to public position was no longer assured to them, nobles were obliged to be highly attentive to private financial concerns. De Tocqueville remarked in *L'Ancien Régime* that a lasting divorce between nobility and wealth was a chimera that led either to the destruction of the first or its amalgamation with the second. The need for careful management of one's funds was equally evident to a twentieth-century noble who observed: "Simply to last it is necessary to be sober, thrifty master of one's passions, prudent. To remount the slope it is necessary to join to these virtues work, courage, and luck. Families that last are the result of a selection."[70]

All editions of the *Etat présent* count adult males primarily, and for the total noble estimated population the numbers should be multiplied by 4.5. Names changes were calculated from the appendix to Bachelin-Deflorenne: "Les changements de noms ou liste alphabétique d'après le *Bulletin des lois* de toutes les personnes qui ont obtenu du gouvernement l'autorisation de changer ou de modifier leurs noms par l'addition de la particule ou autrement depuis 1803 jusqu'à 1868, contenant les noms, prénoms, professions et lieux de naissance de chaque individu cité dans ladite liste."

[c]R. Dauvergne, "Le Problème du nombre des nobles en France au XVIIIe siècle," *Sur la population française au XVIIIe et au XIXe siècles* (Paris, 1973), 181–92.

[d]Guy Guérin, *Législation et jurisprudence nobiliaires* (Lille, 1961), 15.

[e]Jean Meyer, *Noblesses et pouvoirs* (Paris, 1973), 30.

[f]H. Taine, *Les Origines de la France contemporaine*, 27th ed. (Paris, 1909), 20.

[g]Guy Chaussinand-Nogaret, *The French Nobility in the Eighteenth Century: From Feudalism to Enlightenment*, trans. William Doyle (Cambridge, 1985), 30.

[h]Charles Ganilh, *De la contre-révolution en France* (Paris, 1823), XXIX: "L'ancienne classe privilégiée est réduite à quarante-cinq mille familles ou à deux cent vingt cinq mille individus, ce n'est pas le vingtième des classes qui vivent du revenu, et la centième partie de la population."

[i]Charles Nodier, "De la loi des élections et de l'aristocratie," *Le Défenseur* 1 (1820): 460, which says that this is the number of noble families "qu'on dit exister en France."

[j]Thomas D. Beck, "The French Revolution and the Nobility: A Reconsideration," *Journal of Social History* 15, no. 2 (1981): 223: "My lists on the electorate of the July Monarchy, which contained 13,721 nobles, covered 90 percent of the population [of male adults paying a *cens electoral* of 200F]. The missing lists, therefore, should have contained approximately 1,525 nobles, which would raise the total for all of France to 15,246. In round numbers, then, there were 3,000 titled nobles and 12,000 nontitled nobles fifty years after the revolution."

Note: There is an element of overlap and extrapolation in each category, and the table is meant to show the variety of estimates and rough proportions.

The strangling noose of poverty was tightest on the fringes of France, in poorer regions, Brittany's north coast, or the recesses of Gascony. Marriage into the aristocracy was quite impossible for families who could never raise the necessary dowries. Even in the remoter valleys of the Pyrenees or Burgundian backwaters, everywhere lurked the threat of wealth insufficient to maintain a noble station as understood by one's fellows. Exclusion was not a brutal breaking of minimal civilities or respect to individuals diminished by financial distress and who still had the self-esteem necessary to meet with other nobles; rather, the eye of the needle through which such individuals could no longer pass was the contract of suitable weddings for themselves or their children. That was how the Revolution definitively expelled many of the *noblesse*, such as the impoverished bachelor chevaliers de Saint Louis, who although admitted to the salons of good society in the provinces could never make a suitable match. For many the 1825 legislation that gave compensation for those émigrés whose property had been confiscated, in the main from western and northwestern departments, came too late.[71] Noble marriage patterns are investigated in more detail below, in chapter 7; here it suffices to bear in mind that the value of dowries governed the social reproduction of the nobles.

A number of authors have tried to calculate the rate of decline in the numbers of nineteenth-century nobles, although they have not always measured the same thing. In 1923 the Belgian baron Woelmont thought that of 50,000 French families with claims to nobility at that time, some 5,200 were of authentic chevaleric descent, although he subsequently revised that figure downwards.[72] In the second edition of a book on the modern French nobility, published in 1946, vicomte Marsay was less generous in listing the chevalresque families of his day. In the century and a half since 1800, 20–46 percent of those families had disappeared, leaving a mere 1,314 families surviving.[73] Both Woelmont and Marsay were obsessed above all with identifying descendants of the sword *noblesse*. In a 1959 discussion Guérin calculated that 3,100 families descended from the pre-1789 second estate survived, ennobled by any means, and he expressed them as a percentage of the number of nobles in 1790 (half of the figures advanced by Woelmont) and claimed that only 12.4 percent of them still had direct male descendants carrying the family name. He considered separately those with a claim to nobility from offices held just before the Revolution (he counted 3,900 offices), and then multiplying them by the same rate of decline as that of the older families, he suggested that $3,900 \times 0.0124$ equals 480— although his own nominal count convinced him that 350 was more likely.[74] A demographic study of the high dignitaries of the First Empire, a third of whom had belonged to the *noblesse* previously, revealed a striking decline over the nineteenth century. Of fifty-nine dignitaries born before 1785 only thirteen had male descendants born after 1900 and still alive around 1960; stated another way, only 22 percent of a wealthy and powerful group of *titrés* survived in direct line after 160 years.[75] There is thus plenty of evidence of rapid declines in generational replacement for old and new noble families.

As a further cause for decline one can consider the effects of emigration by marriage or residence abroad, although there was always a countervailing immigration, particularly of Slavic nobles. Foreign nobles who were naturalized French needed authorization to carry their titles. This requirement was spelled out again by the royal ordinance of 31 January 1819 and yet again by a decree of 5 March 1859. Croy-Chanel was refused the right to use the title of prince during the 1860s.[76] Foreigners appeared briefly among *titrés*, for example, Georges Stacpoole, born in Cork, Ireland, was named *comte héreditaire* with a *majorat* based on *rentes sur l'état*. His son was first a comte after his father's death in 1825 but then became a papal marquis (Leo XII in 1828) and later a papal hereditary duc (Gregory XVI). The son was born and died in England and had a large family: in 1859 his seventh daughter married Auguste Fornier de Boisaiyrault, known as the comte d'Oyron. As a result of the emigration some nobles were "exported," such as the children of M. de Bombelles, who had lived abroad as an ambassador before the Revolution, entered orders in 1803, became a canon of Breslaw, and was named almoner of the duchesse de Berry in 1816 and then bishop of Amiens. His children never returned to France but remained in the Austrian service with court positions. The first born to the third marriage of the marquis de Raigecourt was an émigré who served in the Austrian army and lived out his life in Vienna. Similarly complicated international families did not, however, reverse the overall shrinkage of the French noble population.

Neither the making of new *titrés* nor the more amorphous recruitment of *noms à particule* reversed the steady decline in the number of French families who could claim to be nobles between 1800 and 1870. The *titrés* added perhaps 35,000–45,000 individuals. In the late 1890s the writer who used the name vicomte Royer de Saint-Micaud and whose outburst was quoted above waxed indignant that 45,000 families claimed to be nobles.[77] Bachelin-Deflorenne, one of the most successful publishers of a directory of the nobility, included ever greater numbers of individuals in each edition: in 1866 he listed 20,000, and by 1884, 60,000.[78] This may reflect a search for subscribers as much as anything else, but it also suggests that in Marcel Proust's world there was a rally against the steady shrinkage in the numbers of nobles. That may explain the 1875 prohibition of collateral lines taking over existing *majorats* or the proposal in 1882 for a complete abolition of titles and "particules nobiliaires." That fascinating period brought to an end by the Great War is not here our concern.[79] However, it is highly unlikely that even in the sunshine heyday of the *Belle Epoque* the numbers of those who claimed to be nobles seriously reversed their continuing decline as a percentage of the French population which had been afoot since the middle of the seventeenth century.

2

Noble Landholders

THE GEOGRAPHY OF NOBLES IN FRANCE

Just as the distribution of nobles as a percentage of the European population varied widely from country to country during the Old Regime, so it did within France.[1] A brilliantly innovative study of eighteenth-century Brittany contrasted a penurious but pullulating petty nobility on the north coast of the peninsula with the wealthier, titled families around Nantes.[2] The eastern marches of France, Alsace and Lorraine, counted a smaller noble component of their populations than in the south; for example, Provence, Languedoc, or Gascony with its proverbial swarms of erstwhile d'Artagnans. Evidence of this uneven geographical presence of nobles in Old Regime France is varied but persuasive, and during the nineteenth century this regional contrast remained. Of course, within smaller provinces, or *pays*, there were also variations in the number of nobles compared with the local populations.[3] In Provence, where individuals from the Bouches-du-Rhône and Var departments took more than half of the titles awarded between 1800 and 1870, the Hautes-Alpes and Basses-Alpes represented no more than 10 percent each.[4] Thus the former departments were overrepresented among new nobles proportionate to their population, and the latter, underrepresented. To complicate matters still further, one might point out that some regimes preferred *provençaux* nobles more than others (see table 2). This makes plain the uneven pace of creation of nineteenth-century nobles and thus warns us against geographical determinism over time.

The implications of this distribution of nobles in France, especially their tendency to cluster on the richest lands, those with the highest value yield per hectare as given in the agricultural statistics collected in 1836, are examined in more detail below. A detailed departmental map based on the declared "political domicile" of male voters of the requisite age and tax payments during the late 1830s has been drawn by Thomas

TABLE 2. *Provençaux* Given Titles by Successive Regimes, 1800–1870

Regime	Number of Individuals	Percentage
First Empire	89	35.4
First Empire and Restoration	43	17.0
Restoration	95	37.8
Restoration and July Monarchy	1	0.3
July Monarchy	5	1.9
Second Empire "Confirmations"	18	7.2
Total	251	99.6

Source: S. Icard, "Les Provençaux titrés et anoblis au XIXe siècle," *Mémoires de l'institut de l'histoire de Provence* 4 (1927), 181–202.

Beck,[5] but we are less well served for the periods twenty years before and twenty years after his compilations. From samples of birthplaces recorded in vicomte Révérend's genealogies, the almost three hundred individuals who established *majorats sur demande* between 1814 and 1830, and over two thousand entries from a directory of nobles published in 1866 a strikingly consistent picture of regional distribution emerges (see table 3). Based on major geographical contrasts superimposed on departments, those regions do not, of course, chart the geographical variety of French *pays*. There are no universally accepted criteria for contrasting the different parts of France, although individual writers on agriculture have advanced their own schemes. In 1844 Lullin de Chateauvieux proposed a map of eight agricultural regions: (1) North, (2) Northeast, (3) Southeast or the Alps, (4) South or the olive trees, (5) Center or the mountains, (6) Southwest or the Pyrenees, (7) West, and (8) Northwest or heaths and gorse. This was a rather unequal mixture of points on the compass, natural features, and vegetation.[6] A century later a French geographer enumerated more than 425 agricultural regions.[7] Despite this diversity, any geographical study of nobles in France after the Revolution shows that they were not to be found everywhere in the same proportions in the population.

Besides showing the persistence of regional proportions, table 3 indicates a slight decline in the number of nobles in eastern France, the most economically innovative area of the nation in embracing the new industrialism of the nineteenth century. Brittany changed hardly at all, but the southwest seemed to provide a home for increasing numbers of nobles. However, these changes on the peripheries of France merely underscore that the noble heartland of the nineteenth century was the Paris region with the rich farmlands to the northwest. At a time when the absolute number of nobles in France was in decline (as pointed out in chapter 1), their concentration waxed in Paris and the northern lowlands. Much evidence from almanacs and directories points to the growing preference of nineteenth-century nobles for the northwest of the country. If the birthplaces of individuals who set up *majorats sur demande* under the Bourbon Restoration are compared with those of the Second Empire titled, a rise in the proportion of those born in the capital is apparent. Paris and its immediate region—Seine, Seine-et-Marne, and Seine-et-Oise—predominate. Despite the advance in *titrés* from the southwest and the Massif Central during the Second Empire, the south of France overall, with its plethora of relatively impoverished *noblesse*, shrank in its representation among the new titles awarded. Under the Bourbons 26.8 percent of *titrés* were born in the southern region at a time when 37.9 percent of the French population lived there, but under the Second Empire this dropped to 23 percent of the *titrés* when the south still contained more than a third of the French population. If Paris supplanted Versailles as the central stage of noble life, this was (in geographical terms) merely a small adjustment, since the two

TABLE 3. The Distribution of Nobles in Nineteenth-Century France, by Major Natural Regions

Region	1814–1830[a] (Birthplace)		1814–1830[b] (Birthplace)		1866[c] (Residence)	
	Number	%	Number	%	Number	%
Paris region	221	18.0	58	24.0	523	22.9
Northern lowlands	264	21.5	67	27.7	617	27.0
Vosges-Meuse	59	4.8	6	2.5	64	2.8
Armorica	104	8.5	12	5.0	195	8.5
Rhône-Saône	95	7.7	18	7.4	144	6.3
Alpine	62	5.1	10	4.1	62	2.7
Massif Central	135	11.0	16	6.6	192	8.4
Southwest	114	9.3	16	6.6	218	9.6
Mediterranean	111	9.1	23	9.5	133	5.8
(Foreign)	61	5.0	16	6.6	137	6.0
Total	1,226	100.0	242	100.0	2,285	100.0

Sources:
[a]Révérend.
[b]AN BB²⁹783–84.
[c]Antoine Bachelin-Deflorenne, *Etat présent de la noblesse française contenant le dictionnaire de la noblesse contemporaine . . . 1866* (Paris, 1866).

FIGURE 1. The Location of Entailed Estates, 1816–1830

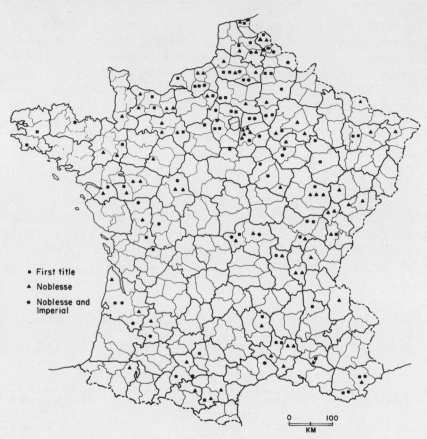

Source: Data from *AN* BB²⁹783, 784.

centers were separated by less than thirty kilometers. Figure 1 shows the location of the entailed estates of candidates for hereditary titles under the Bourbons—a map that is arguably an indicator of where the most successful nineteenth-century nobles lived.

NOBLE URBAN LIFE

Another, less sweeping way of looking at the distribution of nobles in nineteenth-century France is to consider those towns and cities that under the Old Regime were fountains of nobility, that is, places where courts or the municipality offered to those who staffed them access, under specific conditions of tenure, to the second estate. In 1800 many

FIGURE 2. The Average Yield per Hectare per Arrondissement, 1836

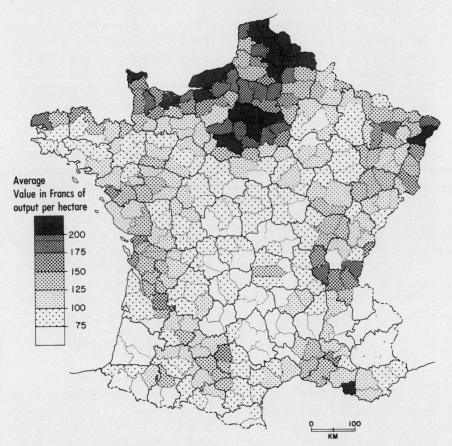

Average
Value in Francs of
output per hectare

200
175
150
125
100
75

0   100
KM

Source: Adapted from H. D. Clout, *French Agriculture on the Eve of the Railway Age* (London, 1980).

nobles still had property and an attachment to the towns where, over two or three generations, their families underwent the transformation from *roturiers* into accepted nobles. A quarter-century after the *parlement*'s abolition and that of venality of office in Aix-en-Provence, Rennes, Grenoble, Dijon, Besançon, Douai, and other administrative centers, numerous nobles lived close to the site of the source of their family's distinction. When Napoleon ordered a particular effort to recruit members of *parlementaire* families back into the judiciary at the 1811 reorganization of the regional appeal court, those robe families who remained loyal to their localities felt, justifiably, that their hour had returned. This was particularly true in a backwater like Pau, where the family names of the eighteenth-century *parlement* constituted a fifth of the mid-nineteenth-century regional appeal court.[8]

Small towns or big cities sometimes boasted a distinct noble district, although its location changed at the behest of taste and fashion. Restoration Toulouse had a "rue des nobles." One scholar noted that in nineteenth-century Bordeaux the townhouses of the great landed nobility, families such as the Lur-Saluces, the Carayon-Latours, and the Myre-Morys, were concentrated around the former archepiscopal palace, but they were gradually given up during the course of the century.[9] In the nineteenth century there was also a blurring of the often remarked preferences under the Empire and the Restoration of the Parisian aristocracy to live in the Saint-Germain district (especially the rues de Lille, de l'Université, de Grenelle, Saint Dominique, and so on), while the *titrés* and more recent nobles of the Empire settled for the right bank. In fact, large estates and smart addresses in Paris united the aristocracy and the *titrés* while deepening the gulf between them and the provincial *noblesse*. Some towns attracted nobles because nobles had always been drawn to them. Of nowhere was that more true than the *quartier* Saint Louis of Versailles, where lived "the old Legitimists of that last stronghold of French aristocracy deeming an error in pedigree a sin which no amount of penitential contrition can obliterate." The same journalist noted that it was to Versailles that the families of the noble faubourg of Paris made their escape during the panic over the cholera outbreak in October 1865.[10]

With its echoes of the Old Regime, Versailles held an understandable attraction for nobles, but the draw of other places was less evident. For instance, in 1819 the Norman town of Bayeux boasted eleven nobles on the urban electoral list, while nearby Honfleur, with approximately the same population of ten thousand, possessed only one noble family.[11] Chartres, Arles, Sens, and Pamiers had a similar allure for nobles, while nearby centers did not. This was either because they provided cheaper living than commercial towns or because nobles within their walls were not jostled, figuratively speaking, by an aggressive commercial group. In nineteenth-century Rouen, for example, the old *parlementaires* and their descendants increasingly lost their eminence in local society to business and manufacturing families. In Rennes, on the other hand, the nobility remained at the peak of local society; baron Régis de Trobriand wrote ironically of the "brilliant and select society" of nobles who set the tone of social life and were in a position of prestige.[12]

Some towns gained a seasonal popularity in the nineteenth century that had no connections with the life of the Old Regime. From the 1820s Dieppe became fashionable as a temporary residence in summer thanks to repeated visits by the young duchesse de Berry. Deauville and

Dinard became the beau monde's refuge from the Parisian summer during the 1840s. Biarritz owed its prosperity in the 1860s to the empress Eugénie's fondness for a resort on the road to Spain.

As mentioned above, the noble district of nineteenth-century Bordeaux shrank in size, not only because of the demographic decline pointed to in chapter 1. Investigations into the movements of noble families suggest that impoverished former residents of large townhouses in Amiens, Rouen, and similar regional capitals sometimes relocated to Paris, or else they moved to cheaper lodgings in the smaller cities.[13]

Save through family letters and account books, it is difficult to find reliable information on the changing location of the principal residence of nobles. Did nobles become more urban or more rural, or were rich nobles more likely to live in the country than poor nobles? In the first thirty years of the eighteenth century the Toulouse nobility lived mainly in the country, although after 1740 improved incomes permitted more purchases of townhouses.[14] In the Sarthe the same flow to regional centers and even Paris was evident in the later Old Regime, at least prior to the difficulties before 1789.[15] Something can be gleaned from the declarations of residence on the printed electoral lists of the constitutional monarchies or from the registers of the *enregistrement*.[16] One investigation in the Sarthe found that the nobility moved away from Le Mans in the 1830s and 1840s to smaller places in the department.[17]

A family's principal residence is germane here. Long before the eighteenth century an alteration existed between the urban "season" and a rural retreat for the hot and harvest times. Of course, a winter in Paris was not at all the same as one in Bordeaux or, even less, Sens or Bourges. An aristocrat interviewing his bailiffs or indulging in a little hunting on his estates during a brief rural escape from Paris had a very different sense of country life than did a Breton gentleman conscious that economies in running the family estate would permit the annual extravagance of spending the winter in a rented house in Rennes. The relation of rural *noblesse* with their tenants was different from that of a duc d'Uzès, whose wife, Anne de Mortemart, described a series of visits in 1867 to the various family properties at Boursault, Bonnelles, Uzès, Entrains, Sancerre, and Villers-en-Prayères. At Uzès they were welcomed by twenty-five shots from a cannon with the family crest upon it. She claimed that the château had been protected during the Revolution by local people, who, to conceal their aim, turned the building into a school, an act approved by the authorities.[18] (The same thing happened to the La Rochefoucauld château at Liancourt.) After the Revolution Uzès was too delicate to take over his old home before a new school had been found—to the costs of which he made a generous contribution, we are assured—and only then, around 1830, did the family return under the ancestral roof. Anne de Mortemart added that the estate manager (*régisseur*) had received permission to take home some furniture and barrels of wine at the time of the Revolutionary confiscations and that in those barrels were all the Uzès family papers: "And that is how our precious archives remained intact."[19]

Such visits from aristocrats living in Paris were not the same thing as inspections by penny-pinching country squires. Faced with crucial decisions about investing limited funds in either urban or rural property, increasingly the poorest of the *noblesse* chose provincial towns. Yet sometimes the choice was dictated by the unpredictable demands of age and health, as when one recently widowed grandfather gave over to his son, around 1808, the running of his estate and château of Aguts and took up residence with a sickly daughter-in-law living in Toulouse.[20] A common lament was that urban pleasures had seduced the rich away from their rural responsibilities. Emmanuel d'Harcourt wrote in 1822: "Today the charm of the countryside is not the same; the towns are depleted of rich people, who, no longer enjoying in them their former respect, willingly leave their province and their manor in order to go and look in Paris for the liberty that is born in the middle of the crowd and the diversity of pleasures."[21]

Noble attitudes in the Oise were deplored by the prefect Boudet de Puymaigre, who served there from 1824 to 1828: "As for the others, avid for the rewards of the court, they come to their lands in order to economize, to check the accounts with their managers [*intendants*], and the common people, who do not receive any sign of interest from them, feel no obligation in their regard."[22] Forty years later another noble voiced the same perennial complaint with a slightly different emphasis: "Everyone comes back to town when the autumn leaves are falling, and then, having paraded during long months all the magnificence of ruinous extravagance, they decide to go back to their uncared-for châteaux to live in solitude in order to repair by strict economy the mad prodigality of the winter season."[23]

Ferocious economies could be undertaken in the country. At the other end of the noble social hierarchy, the aristocracy lived *primarily* in Parisian townhouses although spending the summers on a large estate not far from the capital. Generalizations about the "emigration to the interior," that shunning of the Orleans regime by disgruntled supporters of the Bourbons, have greatly exaggerated and obscured this increasing metropolitanism. Leading nobles were well aware that suitably genteel hostility to the regime could be expressed in their townhouses, especially by the family women. One noble newspaper's gossip columnist claimed in the 1840s that "the Hôtel Castellane [71, rue de Grenelle] has become, without doubt, the rendezvous of the *noblesse* and of the best Paris society . . . the Polignacs, the Bauffremonts, the Sainte-Aldégondes, the Bondys, the Crillons, the Villoutreys, the Brissacs, etc., are all to be found there."[24] Great aristocrats, as well as those who hoped to be considered such, needed a season in the capital and its contacts to maintain their claim to rank.

To sum up we can turn to the labors of Thomas Beck, who counted 13,721 adult male noble voters, that is, those with titles and those whose surnames included particles, in the 1830s. One fifth of these can be considered rural—resident in cantons with less than 5,000 in the chief town. This is broader than the French definition of *rural* in the 1846 census, when the number was fixed at 2,000. Conversely, more than half of the nobles lived in cities with over 10,000 people. The remainder lived in small towns, where there was also the sharpest contrast in the average amount of tax paid between the northern half of France and the southern half. Overall, despite points of detail that might constitute matters of contention between historians, Beck's computer analysis revealed that most nobles were predominantly urban dwellers.[25] Despite the doleful clamor of traditionalist commentators, nobles were well in the forefront of urbanization in France.

THE VARIETY OF ESTATES

Landownership remained the touchstone of the noble social hierarchy even more than in the last century of the Old Regime. I shall return below to the vexed question of precisely what losses the nobles sustained as a result of property confiscations during the Revolutionary period. Moreover, those given awards under the compensation known to French history as the Emigrés' Billion, individuals frequently of an advanced age, often transferred payments into state bonds, the interest of which paid for apartment rentals. Yet the newest recruits to the nobility, the *titrés,* wanted to add to the landholdings that underpinned their new dignity. For example, of thirty-eight adjustments to the terms of *majorats sur demande* between 1814 and 1830, thirty registered changes in the locations of entailed estates or increased their value. Only two reduced the total value entailed, and one transferred the entailment from land to *rentes.*[26] These very wealthy aspirants to respectability hungered for broad hectares. As a result, the aristocratic families found more and more *titré* neighbors in traditional preserves of large properties close to Paris: Seine-et-Oise, Seine-et-Marne, Oise, Aisne, Eure, Eure-et-Loire, Loiret, and Orne. Choiseul-Praslin (at Vaux-Praslin), Lafayette (Rozay-en-Brie), Montmorency-Laval (Beaumesnil), Davout (Savigny-sur-Orge), and many other great names had estates relatively close to the capital.

The descriptions of general fortunes contained in the same registers of the *majorats sur demande* gave thumbnail sketches of noble estates in different parts of France. Clerel de Tocqueville, prefect of the Moselle when he was named a hereditary comte in 1820, owned in the Manche department the Tocqueville château, five farms, and three mills, all of which he said were in his family "from time immemorial"; domaines in the Cherbourg arrondissement worth over half a million francs; and forty-nine fractions of annual incomes (*parties de rentes*) on various individuals. When subtracting the dowry reserves of Mme de Tocqueville, he estimated his net worth at 861,484F, or an annual revenue of 45,611—and this did not include his prefectoral salary. Moussaye, also of old *noblesse*, described his Breton château, the buildings and lands around it, the *métairies* (rather than the *fermes* of the Norman Tocqueville estate), mills and meadows situated in the Saint Brieuc arrondissement, Côtes-du-Nord, containing some two hundred hectares in arable land and thirty hectares of heath—in all an estate producing a revenue of 8,860F. This was a very low per-hectare yield compared with that of regions producing more than 200F per hectare. The very first Restoration request for a *majorat sur demande* was by comte Jean de Gouey de la Besnardière, a *conseiller d'état* in charge of the political section at the Foreign Ministry who put forward a property in the Indre-et-Loire purchased in July 1808 from a Fouasse de Noirville comprising the principal *manoir* and ten *métairies,* totaling about four hundred hectares, for which he had paid the modest price of 148,125F. In the Midi, Duplessis de Pouzilhac, living at Avignon, described property he possessed in the arrondissements of Uzès, Nîmes, and Arles which produced a net revenue of 30,191F; a hotel in Avignon and a country house nearby, producing a net revenue of 3,989F, and two 5 percent bonds—giving him a net revenue of 35,343F annually. Pouzilhac château had been bought in 1781 by his uncle, at that time the local curé, from comte de Lannion for 166,000 livres. This uncle had made him the sole owner by bequest some thirty-three years before. A grander estate in Provence of 651 hectares inherited from his mother carried the ducal *majorat* of Emmanuel-Marie-Pierre-Félix-Isidore de Caderousse-Gramont:

> Institution par M. le duc de Gramont, père du futur époux, dud. S. de Gramont son fils, comme donataire du Tiers des Biens immobiliers qui composeront sa succession, et ce à titre de préciput; Donation entre vifs, à imputer sur ce Tiers, mais sous réserve d'usufruit, (Le Donateur est décédé depuis) entr'autres Biens des Isles et Islots dits Vernet, de Codolet, Glanon, Pipi, Gazargues des Islons, Prés, Pelory etc. consistants, en grande partie, en Bois et Terres labourables, et situés en la Commune de Codolet; ce qui a été . accepté par le Donataire, impétrant: Pension, Douaire ou plutôt rente viagère de 11 000F; et Donations de 2400F en d^ers compt^ts; le

tout sous l'hypothèque des Biens donnés aud. futur époux. . . .

Etat, signé par lui, des Biens composant sa fortune, lesquels sont: 1º Le Château de Caderousse et ses dépend^{ces}, de 190 ares 2º une maison à Orange; 3º Le Domaine de la Durbanne et ses dépend^{cs}, de 10 hect. 58 ares 50 c/a 4º La Terre de la Perron, d'env. 24 hectares; 5º Les grand et petit Pelory, d'environ 457 ares; 6º Le Moulin dit de la Ville; 7º des Prés, de 4 hectares 19 ares 47 c/a 8º d'autres Terres et prés de 3 hectares 63 ares 87 c/a; 9º Les Islons de Gazargue de 17 hectares 7 ares 60 c/a; 10º la Traverse de Gazargue, de 13 hectares 42 ares 60 c/a 11º L'Islot de la Traverse, de 32 hectares 48 ares 44 c/a; 12º le Domaine de Panier, de 31 hectares 10 ares; 13º Le Mautemps etc. de 6 hect. 14a 22c/a, 14º L'Isle du Colombier de 192 hectares, 15º Les haut et bas Bassins et Bassin du milieu, de 21 hect. 34 ares; 16º L'Isle de Vernet de 68 hect. 14 ares 60c/a; 17º L'Isle de Taillan, de 28 hectares 18a; 18º Les Islots, de la Beaumatte de 95 hect. 19º une Oseraie et des graviers, de 13 hectares 54 ares; 20º les Terres du Prince 21º et celles des Fonesse-Loubers, ensemble de 101 hectares; et 22º L'Ilon de Codolet, Pipi et Glandon, de 71 hectares 69 ares, arrondt. de Bagnols, Dépt. du Gard. Arrond^t d'Orange (Canton Ouest) et Communes de Caderousse et Piolenc, Dépt. du Gard. Tous ces biens d'environ 651 hectares produisant net 94 261F [144.7F/ha.] Et Déclaration y insérée que ces immeubles proviennent à M. le Duc de Caderousse comme les ayant acquis de la D^e sa mère; du Gouvernement par suite d'une transaction entre ses auteurs et la Ville de Caderousse; ou recueillis dans la S^{on} du Duc son père sus dénommé. Déclaration par M. de Caderousse qu'il destine au Majorat ceux de ces Biens compris sous les articles 1er, 5, 7, 9, 10, 16, 22 ensemble de 191 hectares et produisant net 30 066F. Ventes à M. de Caderousse, Impétrant, par Dlle Sinety, Veuve de Mr de Caderousse de Gramont, sa mère, 1º du château de Caderousse et de ses dépend^{ces} 2º de la Terre du Pelory, 3º des Prés etc. par deux contrats passés devant Pons, notaire à Avignon, des 13 7bre 1824 et 20 avril 1826 contenant relation de la propriété antérieure. etc.

These random examples from Normandy to Provence show something of the wide range of noble estate sizes and configurations.

THE NOBLES AND THEIR CHÂTEAUX

All nobles wanted a château in their family. Of course, not all châteaux belonged to nobles, and not all nobles possessed châteaux. However, the prestige of spacious (if often uncomfortable) living which derived theoretically from the feudal past lasted into the nineteenth century. When Napoleon inhabited the Tuileries, it was called a palace, but when the more genteel Bourbons were in residence, the court spoke of the château.[27] Indeed, nobles in general did have more spacious housing than commoners. There were châteaux throughout France.

The comparison of the living space of nobles and commoners as revealed by the doors-and-windows tax on the electoral lists of the constitutional monarchies revealed that titled individuals paid more than two and a half times as much house tax as commoners, and twice as much as those with a particle in their name.[28] Commoners and nobles who paid a similar total tax did not pay a similar doors-and-windows tax: nobles lived in larger establishments.[29] Moreover, since nobles were overrepresented in the wealthiest part of the electorate, spacious dwellings were more likely to be associated with them. In the Manche, payment of a doors-and-windows tax of more than ten francs was more frequent among those with a title or a particle in their name than among those without.[30]

Although the splendor or mere suitability of housing should match the owner's pocket, there is no doubt that maintaining the château, the adjacent lands, and the country life style was one of a noble family's highest imperatives. Descriptions of château life are found in many nineteenth-century memoirs. Mme d'Armaillé recalled the annual stay of the Ségur family at their elegant château near Fontainebleau, with its famous groves of chasselas white wine grapes and impressively large grounds, which her father had bought in 1829. The annual visit followed an immutable timetable. At the beginning of June they went to the château of La Rivière, overlooking the Seine at Thoméry (Seine-et-Marne), taking with them piano, safe, her father's manuscripts—he, like his own father, belonged to the Académie française—and cartloads of other furniture and linens. In the countryside, she emphasized, the social life was different from that in town. Their visitors varied in background more than they did in the capital, and at lunch there was almost always a peasant farmer or former soldier and sometimes the priests from the environs. After lunch there were more visitors and informal conversation.[31]

There was not a specific nineteenth-century definition of a château, but it was generally understood to be a large and imposing country house, preferably with a chapel. Joseph de Villèle had a chapel constructed next to his château at Mourvilles-Basses (Haute-Garonne). The 1832 Seine-et-Oise almanac listed a "maison bourgeoise, jardin et terres" belonging to comtesse Lepie, the adjoining château of general Lepie, a "château peu important" belonging to comtesse de Lastour, a "petit château" (de Singensse), a "château assez considérable" (Lerat de Magnitot), another which was not only considerable but had an "ancienne tour" (duc de la Rochefoucauld-Liancourt), and a "Grand et beau Château" (Tourteau de Septeuil). Of the almost one hundred châteaux listed, 61 percent belonged to noblemen, 6 percent to noblewomen, 32 percent to commoner men, and 1 percent to commoner women.[32] There were infinite variations on this 1831 description of a property near Toulouse: "The lands designated under the name of Lafitte château in the commune of Castelnau d'Estrefonds [were] composed of the château buildings of all kinds, park, garden, orange trees, arable lands, vines, permanent and temporary [*artificielles*] meadows."[33] In the event that the residence could not pass muster to be called a château without drawing the neighbors' smiles, it might pass under the label of *maison de maître*, manor, *gentilhommière*, or among the peasantry of the southwest, a *castel*. The château and its surroundings were, in theory if not always in fact, the tangible backdrop of the family existence, impregnated with traditions, memories, and prompts to appropriate conduct. This was very true of the château of the comte de Selve, a former cavalry officer, located near La Ferté-Alais (Seine-et-Oise). His family had started their climb into the nobility from a series of sixteenth-century robe positions, and by the eighteenth they were military men. We can see the château layout from the 1836 inventory of its contents.[34]

In the case of a family lacking such historical baggage or of a cadet starting a fresh branch, a new château was required. There was also the desire for more comfortable lodging for the family, as when the father of Corélie de Gaix decided in the early years of the nineteenth century, thanks to good agricultural profits, to pull down the old citadel (*château fort*), with its towers and ruined ramparts which dominated part of the countryside near Castres, and build a more commodious structure in its place. His daughter had a romantic nostalgia for the antique discomforts of the old building.[35] That was not the case of baron Deschamps de la Vareinne, who produced an attestation from the subprefect and seven other witnesses that the embellishments and additions he had made to his château, together with the buildings, canals, and plantings added since 1811, had made it "one of the most agreeable places in the Montluçon arrondissement."[36] Some families found such efforts impoverishing. One young noble wife of Mayenne, upon marrying Alfred Doublard du Vigneau, replaced his modest house on the Vaucençay estate with a château complete with balustrade, *donjon*, two pointed towers, a library, and large reception rooms, thereby plunging the family into severe financial difficulties.[37] Even the fortune of the duc de Choiseul-Praslin was strained by the expenses of repairs and improvements to the family seat at Vaux-Praslin (today Vaux le Vicomte), near Melun, when he acceded to the title in 1841.[38]

Indeed new constructions in the "noble" style were almost as numerous between the 1820s and 1880s as during the seventeenth century. In Mayenne, for example, there were on the average, two château per commune by 1900.[39] There was a similar proliferation of noble buildings in the Hautes-Pyrénées in the same period.[40] Périgord also saw a rash of new châteaux, including the château of Rastignac, which appears to be a replica of the White House.[41] Others were repaired, enlarged, remodeled. Madame de Dino lavished money on the Rochecotte château (Indre-et-Loire), which she bought in 1825 and which the aging Talleyrand so much enjoyed. The newer châteaux were necessarily simplified from the remains of earlier centuries to serve the needs of modern life. Moats, fortifications, and drawbridges were no longer needed save as decorative accents. By contrast, prestige rooms for dining, dancing, and receptions were emphasized to the limits of expense, as were the park, serving no purpose at all save for good-weather sauntering, and the *grande allée*, lined with stately trees or at the least potted flowers, which served as a repeated motif marking the progression from the gate to the main entrance. Historical whimsy was sometimes indulged, as when baron James de Rothschild had a château built at Ferrières (Seine-et-Marne) in English Elizabethan style, which attracted the visit of Napoleon III in 1862 to enjoy the opulent appointments: six carriages decorated with the baron's livery and drawn by thoroughbreds followed the imperial coach from the railway station at Ozoir la Ferrière.[42]

Perhaps the supreme town planner of the nineteenth-century, baron Georges Haussmann, showed a mixture of vanity and shrewdness when he took over a large property at the death of his parents-in-law and purchased an adjoining château (remodeled by the architect of the Paris Halles, Victor Baltard), to which he added a large *H* on the pediment. He needed "a residence where I might honorably fix my domicile and lead a sufficiently comfortable life, although less expensively than at Paris."[43]

To enable one to live with honor—that was the purpose of the château. Even if they were not all exclusively in the hands of nobles, the châteaux affirmed an earlier form of dignity. It was for that that they were prized. Even if the nobles had no monopoly of the cash required to buy status, the association with nobles made the purchase of a château alluring. That was clear as far away from the Paris region as the Pyrenean foothills, where an 1854 pamphlet lauded a property near Pau not merely for its fertility but also for the neighbors: "One is there quite in the country but without being at an inconvenient distance from town. That is, once again, an advantage which many families look for, rather than that of excessive propinquity." Besides invoking the rising land values as a result of the railway's arrival, the pamphlet pointed out the fashionability of the property:

> One can add that it [the property] is in a classy district [*des mieux habités*]. In fact one finds there the vacation homes [*les maisons de*

plaisance] and the properties of M. le comte de M. (one of the finest
names of the Empire); of M. le baron P.L., former peer of France; of
M. le marquis d'A. (one of the oldest and richest families of Béarn); of
Mme La maréchale marquise de G.; of M. de C., on the Taillefer
estate; of MM. de P. et F., honorary judges at the imperial law court at
Pau; and finally of several other good families both foreign and of the
pays.[44]

Ideally, each château was part of a network of relatives' properties
between which individuals moved. The de Maupas family, for example,
was listed in one 1868 directory as follows:

(1) Le marquis de M. au château de Poissons (Haute-Marne);
(2) Le vicomte de M. au château de la Gérinière, par Château-
Renault (Indre-et-Loire);
(3) de M., grand officier de la légion d'honneur, sénateur, préfet
chargé de l'administration du départment des Bouches-du-Rhône,
conseiller général à Bar-sur-Aube, et 44 rue St. Dominique, St.
Germain (Paris);
(4) de M., au château de Maupas par Aix-d'Anguillon (Cher);
(5) Paul de M., maître des requêtes, 72 rue de Varenne (Paris);
(6) Edouard de M., à Soissons (Aisne).[45]

The antiquity and respectability of family property—which should
not be made up of land confiscated and sold during the Revolution—
was desirable for the setting up of *majorats* during the Restoration.
When Henri de Cadevac, marquis d'Havrincourt, upgraded an 1810
comtal title to one of marquis in 1825, he proposed that the newest rank
be established on the Havrincourt *terre* bestowed on his ancestors by
letters patent dated at Chantilly in 1693.[46] Comte de Rancher put up
the Matetour château in the Seine-et-Oise, a property he held as the
only inheritor from his brother, the marquis de Rancher, who had died
before the Revolution.[47] Other châteaux were innocent of any family
cachet. Baron Gaullier, son of the Tours *procureur du roi,* received
farms from his father's 1810 will; his father before him had received
them from his father, a *secrétaire du roi,* who had bought them from
comtesse d'Adhémar in 1784.[48] Comte Lejéas paid 226,800F in 1811 to
buy a fine château, farmyard, and nearby land at Aiserey (Côte-d'Or),
sold by the creditors of a bankrupt.[49]

Yet, possession of a château however come by, ancient or modern, was
a large part of effective claim to rank. The *bonne compagnie* immediate-
ly recognized a noble family without a country seat as distinctly odd.
There was a sense of the appropriateness of property to pretension.
Armand de Melun described the Montalembert château at Roche-en-
Brénil (Côte-d'Or) in 1856 as "a château that, if neither princely nor too

gothic, has, however, enough moats and towers without, enough es-
cutcheons, old tapestries, and emblems within, to suit the son of a
crusader and the historian of Saint Elisabeth."[50] This importance shone
through family attitudes to buildings often extremely uncomfortable
and expensive to maintain. A roseate recollection of the Rességuier
château at Drudas (Haute-Garonne) during the Restoration gives a
rather positive account of the family's country seat:

> A considerable property surrounded the château. Two steps away lay
> the church and village. In a word, from the size and number of the
> farms that were attached to it and the extent of the inhabited
> buildings and rooms, this agglomeration richly deserved the name
> *château* which it was given in the district. The land was fertile, the
> hunt abundant; the only fault was of being of a difficult, almost
> forgotten, access . . . it took a good seven hours to cover the forty
> kilometers that separated Drudas from Toulouse.[51]

The Rességuiers occasionally called the château Druidas to evoke drui-
ds and cultivated mistletoe on the oaks to underline the Ossianic touch.
   Mary Boddington had a less lyrical response to the country houses of
the same district: "The châteaux within view are sad castles of discom-
fort, the campagnes worse; I remarked two, each with the embellish-
ment of a huge straw stack planted exactly in the middle of the avenue
which led to the entrance door, so as to interdict all approach. . . . Yet
some have a look—half farm, half manor house—that is not amiss."[52]
"Half farm, half manor house" was how many châteaux appeared to
visitors used to the great country establishments of English aristocrats,
generally wealthier than their French counterparts.[53]

THE PLACE OF NOBLES IN THE RURAL ECONOMY

Curiously, it is harder to examine the place of the nobility in the agricultural economy of the nineteenth century than a hundred years earlier. After the Revolution, however, nobles were not separated from non-
nobles on the tax roles, so details of their estate size or tax assessments
became swallowed up in the general taxonomies of the enquiries of
1840, 1852, 1862, and 1882. Historians are still hard at work trying to
arrive at a better understanding of the changes that took place in French
agriculture during the nineteenth century, and until they reach some
conclusions, the participation of nobles can be gauged only from observations made by informed contemporaries such as the agronomist
Léonce de Lavergne or from aggregate statistics together with studies
of individual estates.[54] The task is not lightened by the great variations
in terrain and climate within France.
   As H. D. Clout's *French Agriculture on the Eve of the Railway Age*

pointed out, historical studies of French agriculture have been frag-
mented by concentration on the department or region or on the individual estate.[55] This resulted from the inaccessibility or unwieldiness of
information dealing with agriculture at a national level. The nineteenth
century saw the emergence of national statistics in a more usable form,
and Clout himself made exhaustive use of the enquiry of 1836. At that
time the land survey (cadastre) initiated by Napoleon 1 was still incomplete. The cadastre was also department-bound and could not express the elaborate network of holdings that made up the collective
property of noble families. These were linked together by obligations in
marriage contracts on properties held in other names than that of the
male head of household. They were also linked by a sense of obligations
other than those spelled out by the Civil Code, as in the example given
below of a bachelor on the maternal side whose death so handsomely
contributed to the prosperity of the Raigecourt family. His own family
name being on the verge of extinction, since he was without progeny, he
passed his property on to a male in another family to whom he had only
collateral obligations. As the social category most likely to have properties in scattered parts of France, the nobles, particularly at the
wealthiest levels, were least well portrayed in the aggregate statistical
compilations drawn from local studies of the cadastres.

The electoral lists (and those of the various enumerations of notables)
of 1800–1870 cannot adequately overcome these obstacles. They were
of uneven quality. Historians have made the greatest use of those dealing with the constitutional monarchies. In 1937 Sherman Kent pointed
to the imperfect picture given by the focus on a single jurisdiction, the
exclusion of wealthy women (although widows and other women of
means not blessed with a mate could designate a family member to
represent their property; however, there was no evidence of this on the
list), and problems involved in calculating the real wealth represented
by the sums of taxation printed on these rolls.[56] With these reservations
in mind, a variety of insights can be gleaned from electoral lists. For
agricultural history, however, there is a serious flaw in that many historians refer to the land tax, the predominant part of the totals for eligibili-
ty as elector or deputy (the *cens*), as though it were everywhere taken at
a standard rate. The late Albert Soboul does this in his magisterial
chapter in the *Histoire économique et sociale de la France* when he
discusses the impact of the Revolution on land ownership. It is important to realize when drawing national conclusions that this was not the
case, although it is not easy to recalculate the statistics.

Set up during the Revolution under the impulse of physiocratic notions, the *foncière* provided some two-thirds of the total of all direct taxes
during the July Monarchy and over a quarter of the kingdom's annual

revenue.[57] Kent deduced from an examination of statistics that 79 percent of the *foncière* on average was derived from land but that only 21 percent was derived from the buildings, barns, houses, bridges, and so on, to be found on the property. By using an estimate of net average income to landowners in France of 40F per hectare, he advanced that the land tax took 12.5–14.3 percent of net income. Kent readily admits that these are notional figures, especially to the extent that the net yield per hectare is the residue of the gross after the deduction of costs for seed, cultivation, harvesting, and the expense of maintaining farm animals. Thanks to Clout, we now have a map of average yield per hectare by arrondissement calculated from the 1836 statistics; it shows the considerable gap between levels of return.[58] At various times under the Empire, the Restoration, and the July Monarchy, voices were raised in protest against the inequities of taxation of this varied agricultural production. However, the chorus of unhappy landowners never swelled sufficiently to overturn these differences, differences that had actually been increased by bureaucratic adjustments in the 1820s as prefectural staffs tried to manipulate tax assessments of landowners according to their political sympathies. The amount of *foncière* to be paid was fixed for each department, and each then subdivided the assessment among its cantons. To Paris, the status quo was preferable to reform, which would inflame jealousies. One generally overlooked calculation after the Revolution of 1830 emphasized inequities in levels of land tax. This was the work of an individual and may be exaggerated, but it suggests the need to correct nuances in earlier accounts (see appendix 1).

Some nobles farmed their properties directly, but it was more usual to have one of the three main types of tenant farmers, just as in the eighteenth century.[59] A widespread method of managing property was to lease land to tenants, in either sharecropping units (*métairies*) or small farms to families, who cultivated the land for an annual rent under the surveillance of the *régisseur*. The total area of leased land was usually less than 25 hectares but might reach 50 hectares. Another type was the large-scale tenant, almost exclusively from the Paris Basin and northeastern France and specializing particularly in wheat production for an accessible urban market. He was thus in direct contact with production and marketing, or what in our own century might be called agribusiness. His lease was often for nine years or longer. Finally there were *fermiers généraux*, who collected rent from up to a dozen or more subtenants, who might pay their dues in produce or cash. Leases were usually of six to nine years. Before the Revolution, the biggest landowners and aristocrats had preferred this form, and they continued to do so afterwards. Longer leases were assumed to stimulate innovation. The large landowners of the 1787 Assemblée provinciale of Melun protested against three-year leases as too short. A deputy from Meaux, in the same wealthy agricultural region, was behind the 25 May 1835 law permitting communes and hospitals to lease their property for as long as eighteen years.[60] The *fermiers généraux* were common along the Saône and Rhône valleys, in Maine and Anjou. The *fermier général* was often involved in lending and rural credit. Tenant hostility was more likely to be against him than the noble landowner, who, for his part, at one remove from the peasantry, was content to receive a regular and, he hoped, trouble-free income.

THE EFFECT OF THE FRENCH REVOLUTION ON NOBLE LANDOWNERSHIP

The nobles' place in nineteenth-century French agriculture can be surveyed in order to comprehend better both continuities and change, but to do so requires brief consideration of the lasting effect of Revolutionary legislation on the property of the former *noblesse*. It is well known that before 1789 everywhere in France, although to differing degrees, the proportion of agricultural property belonging to nobles exceeded their proportion in the national population. This was truest in northern France, especially near Paris, where nobles owned the best arable land. In the south, estates were generally smaller, but the nobles possessed from 20 percent to a third of the agricultural land, usually the best arable land, as in Aquitaine. Often described as an attack on seigneurialism, the Revolution brought to an end many financial and feudal exactions on tenants. The confiscated property of noble émigrés was put up for sale. To inquire into the economic and social consequences of the sale of the *biens nationaux* a commission was established under the Third Republic. The commission reported in a series of publications that traced the extent of land transfers; analyzed how confiscated property, both ecclesiastical and individual, was sold; and examined the results of the property confiscations of émigré nobles. The investigations usually revealed buyers to be predominantly urban office holders, mostly lawyers and petty bureaucrats, together with speculators, merchants transferring paper profits into real estate, and the richer peasants. Large commercial estates in the modern sense rarely emerged, reflecting that the lots were often small: in the Toulousain the average purchase was seven and a half hectares.[61] When larger estates were assembled, it was generally from clerical property, which in the Meurthe and other places sold more cheaply than noble property. Perhaps the cheapness resulted from the absence of the agents or relatives of the despoiled, who made 16.7 percent of the total purchases in that department in salvage operations of family estates.[62]

A growing body of historical evidence questions the lingering idea that the Revolution saw a lasting spoliation of nobles at large. Some sales were simply never carried out. Adroit nobles in touch with local politics and administrators were often in the best position to set in motion a whole network of complicities to defend their patrimonies. Nobles had not lost the Old Regime taste for litigation, and so the French archives were bequeathed a rich harvest of account books, receipts, leases, bills, and, on occasion, vituperative pamphlets directed against tax assessors. During the Revolution the nobles who remained at home, or at the least the elderly men and women of the family, spurred on by family legends of tax gatherers confounded and lawsuits that had lasted for generations and aided by the faithful (or so they hoped) notary, who often enough under the Revolution found himself a municipal official, used every procedural device to stave off confiscation and exactions on the family property.

Marquise du Hardas de Hauteville requested and obtained legal separation of property in 1792 after her husband's emigration in order to save her dowry: a château and estate that had been in her family for two centuries. Subsequently she divorced the marquis and successfully reclaimed part of her dotal property. At this point the counterrevolutionary activities of her sons posed a new threat to the estate, but she showed admirable tenacity in warding off confiscation of the presuccession on her twelve farms, a walled garden, two mills, and a château, property that had been evaluated at a half-million livres in 1789. After 1800 she recovered in her husband's name some portions of the sold property. On 18 nivôse XI she repurchased the splendid new château which they had constructed just before the Revolution. In 1825 the properties were producing an annual revenue of 9,442F, indicating recovery of about half of the pre-Revolutionary value. In 1827 the marquis was awarded an annual *rente* of 14,558F, for a total indemnity of 485,283F in the Emigrés' Billion. The family had, after many vicissitudes, survived quite well financially, thanks largely to the efforts of the marquise.[63] To the south Christine de Fleury saved her family property from confiscation by ten years of unremitting legal chicanery to hold on to the hot springs that provided the bulk of her family's income in the nineteenth century.[64] Among the court nobility similar prodigies were to be found. The wife of one of Louis XVI's bankers, Laborde, saved for her son's return from Austrian emigration what contemporaries called the considerable remains of a colossal fortune.[65] With Napoleon's advent as first consul, the women showed an equal diligence in requesting the removal of names from the lists of proscribed émigrés in the event that there were any among their kin. The documentalist mania of the French bureaucracy was plaited into a protective cocoon around the family property.

If the majority of noble families preserved the bulk of their wealth, a minority did suffer grievous losses. As a rough rule to which all kinds of exceptions can be made, the principal losers among the nobles were the poorer *noblesse* (represented especially heavily among the military officers who left France to continue to support the princes and then, as often as not, younger sons) or those from areas closest to the frontiers, such as the shabby gentry of the Pyrenean valleys. More spectacular losers were found among the rich aristocrats. They were in evidence at Versailles and in fashionable society, habitual absentees from their properties, especially vulnerable to a vengeful *société populaire* or a greedy overseer, although the Saulx-Tavanes were very lucky in their estate manager. The losses even for the court aristocrats should not be overstated. Of fifty-one hereditary ducs at the outbreak of the Revolution twenty emigrated, but at least twenty-seven stayed in France and were in a position to protect some, if not all, of their interests.[66] Of the peers on 1 January 1825, 121 received indemnities from the Emigrés' Billion.[67]

The majority of nobles followed the dictates of prudence in as self-effacing a way as possible in the hope of avoiding confiscation or exactions. Indeed, for many of them the Revolution brought immediate material advantage, at least in those places where the profits of seigneurial dues represented a small proportion of income. Abolition of the tithe more than compensated for the losses of seigneurial payments. Of course this was untrue of those provinces such as Burgundy, where feudal exactions exceeded the tithe by quite a lot, but the observation serves to remind us that when we look more closely at the actual conduct of the nobles and the various means used to avoid punitive legislation, we are far from encountering a ruined or spoliated class. A resident nobility that survived the Revolution relatively unscathed thanks to submission to the local authorities and ingenious legal pettifogging was scarcely promising material from which to manufacture a mythology of modern Bayards. As a result, right-wing historians found no reason to quarrel with the judgments of their republican colleagues about the serious wounds inflicted on the privileged. To do so would have detracted from the martyrology of the Revolution that they wished to promote. Conservatives and republicans agreed, then, in stressing the damages sustained by nobles, but what were the facts of the matter?

Conclusions derived from the sale documents of the *biens nationaux* may sometimes be questioned. The main criticism of histories based on the documentation of the sales is that they almost never follow what happened to the property afterwards. Transactions were rarely permanent. Often they represented no more than a speculative purchase for quick resale within a year or two. Property changed hands frequently at the beginning of the nineteenth century, as shown in a study of the search for tangible assets in an economy as volatile and inflationary as that in Paris between 1795 and 1803.[68] A variety of investigations have shown that nobles remained in a leading place among post-Revolutionary landowners. In the Laval district of Mayenne 26 percent of émigré property was sold, but of that as much as 62 percent was repurchased by relatives or returned émigrés. In consequence the permanent property transfer from the former owners to another family was a scant 10 percent.[69]

Of course, in that situation the poorest nobles were most vulnerable, for they could not command the credit (even in depreciating *assignats*) to pull off such deals. In western France the Sarthois *noblesse* at least partially recovered their hold on local property, despite the sale to commoners of almost 200 châteaux during the Revolutionary period.[70] Paul Bois claimed more boldly that after the Revolution as before, local nobles owned about 21 percent of the Sarthe.[71] A study of the Loire-Atlantique estimates that the nobility lost at least 20 percent of their pre-Revolutionary holdings—a heavy blow but in no sense a complete spoliation.[72] In neighbouring Mayenne, however, only 24 of the 250 existing châteaux, or less than 10 percent, were sold.[73] A study of landownership in the Nivernais in the period 1830–40 showed that nobles possessed 26.5 percent of the surveyed area, and this in the largest estates, which allowed the author to write of "true latifundium."[74] Property sold and repurchased, property never put up for sale in fact, and property protected from confiscation by a host of legal strategems, especially delays of sale, help to explain the success of the majority of the nobles in warding off ruin.[75]

Aggregate statistics giving the location of the largest estates and statistics drawn from the electoral lists may be usefully compared. In 1862, 53,000 out of 11,511,841 landowners in France paid over 500F in *foncière;* put another way, the richest 1 percent of all landowners generated some 20 percent of the tax revenue. By contrast, in the largest category of tax-paying landowners, 77 percent of the total, the mean land tax paid was less than 20F.[76] One study of the electors in the 1840s showed that nobles whose title figured on the lists paid a mean land tax of 2,050F. Those whose name contained a particle but without mention of a title paid a mean tax of 871F. The vast majority of the electors with neither title nor particle paid a mean tax of 380F. Moreover, 85 percent of those with a title paid more than 500F in *foncière* even though they numbered only 1.5 percent of the electorate. Of those with a particle, 59 percent paid more than 500F in *foncière* while making up 1.7 percent of the electorate; 23 percent of commoners paid more than 500F in *foncière* while making up 96.9 percent of the electorate. From the two sets of figures we deduce that nobles were very heavily overrepresented among the 53,000 wealthiest landowners.[77] Such calculations are less easily made for the period after 1848, since the nature of the electoral rolls changed, and we need to find another measure of the evolution of noble landholdings through the 1860s. However, a survey of agricultural tax statistics for the decades from the 1850s to the 1880s made plain those regions in which large-scale property predominated. Joined with the earlier deductions, it permits a crude but fair contrast between wealthier, northern nobles with large estates and less successful, southern counterparts, despite notable exceptions such as the sizable Gramont-Caderousse estates in the Vaucluse and Gard described earlier.

Ultimately, however, the success or failure of the noble landholder, wherever his lands were located, depended on family strategies. Not all nobles behaved in the same way—a statement that is self-evident save to those who deny the noble capacity for change. This is shown by two examples completely at odds but both drawn from estates in the Saône-et-Loire. The comte de Rambuteau at Chaunay had an estate of over ninety-five hectares in size until 1873, at which time it was sold to his grandson, Lombard de Buffières, a baron and *avocat* at Millassière who was married in that year. The latter demolished fourteen cottages belonging to vintners in 1882 and sold off almost fifteen hectares in 1896 but promptly bought another sixteen. There was no further change until 1912. Despite the change of ownership between nobles, albeit that the *avocat* carried a less famous name than the former peer of France, this property remained in the hands of the titled for a century. By contrast, comte de Noaille's estate near Mâcon (Senozan) steadily wasted away as small lots were sold off, going from 119 hectares in 1826 to 80 in 1834, 62 in 1842, and 54 in 1857. By 1857 this steady attrition had reached its term, at least until 1906.[78] The first estate could be cited for the stability of noble property, and the second for its relentless decline, but neither makes much sense unless we can recreate the overall evolution of the Rambuteau and Noailles fortunes. We need to know the location of their land and real estate holdings throughout France, as well as their choice of other investments.

Sales and exchanges of land by Parisian residents were particularly numerous and affected limitrophe departments. A rather detailed example of the changes in one estate, Gineste in the Montfort commune near Rambouillet (Seine-et-Oise), illustrates the recent history of a piece of property in the radius of highly desirable properties close to Paris. It was sold in August 1808 for 161,000F, of which 60,000 was paid in cash, with the remainder, plus 5 percent interest, due a year later. The sale act traced the ownership for the preceding thirty years, covering the whole of the Revolution:

From	Adjudicated to	Date
Bouillé	Simon	July 1775
Simon	de Chavigny	August 1778
de Chavigny	d'Espagnac	January 1786
d'Espagnac	Allemand de Champier	February 1792
de Champier's widow	de Gricourt	August 1808

The property was described as having been before the Revolution of 46 percent *biens nobles* and 54 percent common (*rotures*), complete with château, but in 1808 de Champier's widow, now married to a commoner, described the "maison de maître" with its variety of rooms, including a fine billiard room, four servants' rooms, and stables with space for six horses, four carriages, and sleeping for two coachmen. The furniture was included in the sale and estimated at 3,000F. The estate boasted five houses, a small vineyard of 48 ares, a watermill and its dependencies, 29.5 hectares of arable land, 7.6 hectares of meadow, and 29.5 hectares of woodlands.[79]

The purchase and sale of châteaux and estates continued at a steady pace throughout the century, and just as much as property transfers resulting from dowries and wills, this commerce altered the noble place in the countryside more than the legislation of the Revolution had. Nobles, particulary Parisians, often made transactions outside their department of residence. On 2 November 1850, to take two examples among tens of thousands over the century, M. Joseph de Monicault, a prefect under the July Monarchy now dwelling on the quai Voltaire, and his wife sold to a sapper captain's widow who lived on the unmodish boulevard Gobelins a farm in Coulommiers arrondissement (Seine-et-Marne), with a total area of 234 hectares, for 260,000F. On the same day the notary exchanged various parcels of land in the Pontoise arrondissement (Seine-et-Oise) between an *avocat* and César de Choiseul, who lived on the fashionable rue de l'Université.[80] A few months earlier he had acquired for 300F a small field of just 38 ares in Cosne arrondissement (Nièvre) from Clerel de Tocqueville, who owned it as a result of a four-elevenths claim as the nephew of M. de Damas-Crux on the estate of his widow. The plot of land was surrounded by Choiseul-owned fields.[81]

These continual transactions in different departments incite considerable caution over conclusions based on the study of mini-regions on the turnover of property, as in the Saint-Léon near Toulouse: "During the eighteenth century property of under 5 hectares stagnated, that of 30 to 60 receded, while there was an advance of large properties of over 60 hectares which made up 10 estates in 1830 instead of only 8 in 1730. From 1830 to 1885 massive advance of small and medium property, collapse of the large. The four domaines of more than 100 hectares disappear."[82] The historian of a noble family would wish to complete strictly localized information by a study of whether the lineage dwindled in wealth or whether the property was sold in one place and the money reinvested elsewhere. One division of property in the Basses-Pyrénées, not far from the Spanish border, in 1839 revealed a military noble family's widely scattered property, including a Parisian house, a flour mill in the Lot-et-Garonne, woods in the Oise which had provided a seigneurial title to the grandfather before 1789, as well as lands from Calvados which figured in their father's 1810 *majorat*. Girardin property was thus in five departments and two different regions, as well as in the capital. The dispersal of the properties means that any conclusions about the economic situation of nobles drawn from regional studies, let alone those of departments or small towns, do not necessarily apply to that aristocratic family.[83] This point has been made forcefully by Clout in his discussion of the effects of the monographic tradition in studies of French agricultural history on the eve of the railway age.[84] The noble family strategy in agriculture lies between aggregate statistics and those of the department or agricultural regions.

Economic decisions by noble landowners were crucial to their success at a time of real change in French agriculture with the evolution of regional specializations—such as the wine of the Midi, the northern sugar beet, wheat growing in the Paris Basin, the Massif Central's changeover to rye—which were marked by the time of the agricultural enquiries of the 1880s and sounded the death-knell of the diffuse and often ill-adapted polyculture of pre-railway days. However, it was simpler for nobles, and anyone else who thought that long-established big landowners were stabilizing "tradition-carriers" in the countryside, to find a scapegoat in the Civil Code. They preferred to believe that the Revolutionary laws had sapped the moral basis of monarchy in the countryside rather than to accept that a commercial rationalization of agriculture affected even nobles. Napoleonic inheritance laws splintered property, and in turn this produced the collapse of family solidarity—so ran the conventional wisdom in the salons of Norman châteaux or the dining room of Gascon manors. Robert-Trancrède de Hauteville in an 1862 pamphlet made a typical lamentation about the "new legislation": "One cannot ignore the unfortunate results produced daily by its application. Not only does it have as a consequence this unlimited parceling out of landed property which puts such regrettable obstacles to agricultural progress but, even more, this perpetual turnover of estates tends to weaken without ceasing the bonds of the family, to efface its traditions, and to thus shake the very bases on which it rests."[85]

In general one can say that nobles preferred moral explanations of their changing circumstances to any appreciation of economic innovations. However, a few candid nobles voiced the truth. Martignac coolly appraised myth and reality in the chorus of noble groans about their spoliation during the Revolution:

> Of émigré property only a billion was sold—exactly 987,819,968F96—and most of that billion was restored to those who were entitled by the indemnity law of 17 April 1825. Even among the goods sold some had been bought covertly by the families of the émigrés or by go-betweens; others were voluntarily sold by those who acquitted them freely, by legal agreements, by wills, by exchanges, or by the reimbursement of all or part of the price. The true dispossession has not exceeded three or four millions, and the equivalent of that loss and beyond having been recovered by marriages, one would probably find, if one looked closely, that the majority of the families that the Revolution believed it had ruined are richer today than in 1789.[86]

Léonce de Lavergne, a prominent member of the Société centrale d'agriculture under the Second Empire, took up the same refrain in his book about French rural economy, republished on various occasions between the 1850s and the 1870s, saying that nobles were wealthier in the mid-nineteenth century than on the eve of the Revolution.[87]

In the crucible of productivity changes and the new crops introduced into French agriculture a new taxonomy emerged among nobles, more significant by far than former distinctions between robe and sword, *noblesse* and *titré*, Legitimists and those who served the government of the day: by 1870 the major stress line between nobles was that which separated landed families of real means from those who no longer found, in the countryside, adequate revenue for their pretensions. The wealthiest noble landowner in France during the first half of the century was probably the duc de Choiseul-Praslin (whose family property is discussed in chapter 3).[88] A little later the closest rivals in point of wealth were the marquis d'Aligre, of an Old Regime robe family, and the duc de Crillon.

An estate's profitability certainly depended more on location than on the gentility of its owner, and despite notable exceptions, there seem really to be no grounds for arguing that there was any appreciable difference in farming skill between nobles and commoners with estates of similar size. In any event, the different ways of running an estate were found side by side. In mid-century Loir-et-Cher there were châteaux whose immediate environs were cultivated by gardeners under the eye of the owner, while adjacent farms on the estate were leased; estates where all the land was leased, with the interests of the owner being watched over by a *régisseur;* and even a few estates like that of the mayor of Launay, de Brunier, who himself managed the large farms.[89] Comte de Falloux took great pride in the consolidation and profitability of his Angevin estate at Bourg d'Ivré, to which he devoted all his energies after his withdrawal from active politics at the advent of the Second Empire.[90] However, despite individual exceptions—and the historian is generally better informed about the successful and dynamic farmer than about the slovenly and incompetent one—all indices reveal that northern agriculture improved at a faster rate than did that of the south.

Great landowners in the departments near Paris emerged at the pinnacle of wealth among nobles now more rarely funded by the profits of state service than from the commercial agriculture of the Seine-et-Marne, Seine-et-Oise, Eure, and so on. In 1822 Harcourt noted with satisfaction the decline of the triennial rotation and other pernicious agricultural practices in the progressive northern departments, although one can recall that the elder Villèle in the southwest was just as eloquent on this topic under the Empire.[91] The marquis de Chambray, a graduate of the Ecole polytechnique, wrote in 1831 of the agricultural improvements possible in the Nivernais while excoriating the sharecroppers for their backwardness. He told his readers that far too many buyers of land were careless about the true value of what they purchased, and he told of selling for almost 100,000F in small lots a property that did not bring in 1,200F in revenues.[92] The north-south contrast in France was evident to contemporaries such as Léonce de Lavergne, who compared the feudal law, large properties, work done by horses, leased farms, and triennial rotation of the north with the Roman law, small properties, work done by oxen, sharecropping, and biennial rotations of the south. He perceived that these characteristics linked together to produce an agriculture not solely because of climate.[93]

A historic turning point in French agriculture occurred between 1850 and 1860 when the total area of arable land in wheat began to shrink from the high point of 58.8 percent (of eighty constant departments). For the first time in more than a thousand years the pressure to sow ever more land in wheat ended, despite the rising national population and a generally better-fed one. The reflux was owing mainly to the approximate doubling of wheat yields during the century but also to improvements in the transport of grain by both ship and rail, which caused landowners to give up wheat cultivation on marginal or unsuitable soil. Instead, wheat cultivation became increasingly a speciality of the northern lowlands and the environs of Paris—the Beauce, the *pays* Chartrain, Champagne, the Brie, Picardy, Flanders, and Upper Normandy. This was the area preferred by the court aristocracy with large northern estates. By contrast, nobles sowed fewer potatoes, another crop that dramatically increased its yield during the nineteenth century. The new crop of sugar beets took only 1 percent of the cultivated arable land but predominated on the northern plains. The mildew crisis of the vineyards permitted rapid growth in industrial production of sugar-beet alcohol, while waste pulp could be used economically for feeding slaughter cattle. Great fortunes were to be made in the drink trade, as the English "beerage" attested, and the aristocrats in France reaped some profits from distillation.

At the same time that urban requirements and new crops offered great possibilities, other traditional crops dropped out of favor, either because of a collapse of demand—as when madder was replaced by a cheaper, metallic dye—or because of changes in consumer tastes. Market gardening provided bounding profits for suppliers of the burgeoning cities. Increased beef and mutton consumption considerably stimulated new animal husbandry methods adapted to large farms with plenty of stables and pasture. The dairy industry offered increasing rewards thanks to rising demand for butter and cheese. Speaking loosely, farmers in northern France profited from the structural changes in agriculture that took place during the nineteenth century. The Midi saw its traditional polyculture collapse, just as the silkworm diseases, maladies of the vine, the demise of dye plants such as woad and madder, and the inauspicious terrain and climate for the production of the fleshy sheep and cows sought by the hungry towns all heightened the contrast.[94]

One must bear in mind that a map of noble rural residences in the nineteenth century tells us little about comparative land values. For example, an 1807 report on the average *per hectare* price of top-grade land in adjacent arrondissements of southwestern France indicated the following: 2,800–3,200F (Castelsarrasin), 2,200–2,400F (Toulouse), 2,000F (Villefranche), 1,500F (Saint-Gaudens).[95] In the 1850s a hectare on the Limagne Plain, close to Clermont (Puy-de-Dôme), perhaps the richest soil in France, sold in the range of 5,000–10,000F. Theoretically, a regional study would thus show that a noble estate near Castelsarrasin under the First Empire could be half the size of one in the foothills of the Pyrenees, close to Saint-Gaudens, and represent the same level of wealth. A similar, even more dramatic contrast could be drawn between a noble family owning a Bordelais vineyard and an impoverished Landais petty noble family owning fetid ponds and salt- and sand-blown fields of almost sterile earth. Obviously, estimates like that provided by Lesur in *La France et les français en 1817*, which gives the national average gross product of one hectare as 110F per annum, or that of Lullin de Chateauvieux in *Voyages agronomiques en France* (1843), giving 40F as the average net income per hectare (that being the gross minus costs of seed, planting, cultivation, harvesting, and draught animals), are of little precise use.[96]

Pressures generated by the short-term crises of 1847–52 and 1853–57, together with bigger structural changes in techniques and the increase in the number of mini-properties, were not fully understood by contemporary nobles. The most disquieting effect was the rural exodus, blamed more on the insidious attractions of vice-ridden, drink-sodden towns than on the stricken condition of landless *journaliers*.[97] During the 1840s the depopulation continued apace, and the first signs of the demographic consequence of the definitive migration of younger adults appeared: aging field hands and fewer births in the villages. The noble landowner became as conscious as his untitled neighbor that he had fewer sharecroppers to choose among and that workers asked for more. Cardevac d'Havrincourt found with great satisfaction that women could do many of the traditionally male jobs on his big estate near Arras, and this stopped the pernicious tendency to take up embroidery.[98] Cheap labor had been important to the recouping of noble prosperity in the Empire and the Restoration in the absence of innovation in crops or techniques, but now the situation reversed as urban growth offered refuge to the victims of the driving exploitation of the landlords, noble and commoner alike. Doubtless the improved mobility introduced into France by the railway quickened traditional migratory flows such as that from the poorer soils of the Yonne. Local nobles found that the peasants were attracted away by the prospects of higher wages. The railway that carried them ruined traditional transport-associated industries (carters, innkeepers, rivermen-boatmen) which earlier had provided a supplementary income to local peasants. All over France the increased mobility and urban growth upset traditional economic arrangements and set the feet of the excess rural population itching to escape their often insufferable conditions.

Literary testimony by observers of the aching misery of the poor concord with the more rebarbative but equally damning statistics of the *enregistrement,* which charted the growing destitution of the bottom echelons of rural society, landless day laborers, called by a host of names according to region but everywhere the victims of an agricultural society sloughing off the last vestiges of communal and village rights.[99] The bold assertion that rural poverty excited special compassion among nobles was, alas, not wholly true. Nobles could scarcely overlook the fact that poverty, at least in the short run, guaranteed a source of servile cheap labor. Tenant farmers relied on the inexhaustible supply of poverty-stricken migrants from the Massif Central for whatever extra hands were needed and usually paid starvation wages. To judge from random evidence, tenants themselves took increasing profits: in Mees (Mayenne) a noble rented farms on a nine-year lease without changing the conditions between 1819 and 1828, while the tenant's livestock rose in value from 2,254F to 5,671F.[100]

It is difficult to know how many noble landlords were also good managers and farmers. Did nineteenth-century nobles show a particular bent for innovation in agriculture, by contrast with their traditional methods of precise bookkeeping, but little technical renovation? The question is worth posing, since historians have noted that before the establishment of training centers such as the Institut national agronomique (1876) farmers learned mainly by example. Training in new agricultural techniques at the handful of privately funded schools— such as Grignon (Seine-et-Oise), which was founded in 1827 on a property provided by Charles X (and became a public institution in 1848), or the model farm of Grand Jouan, near Rennes, founded in 1830—was not sufficiently widespread to counteract the traditional and less productive methods employed on many family estates. Views on the merits of rye or sugar beets, or on the merits of one breed of pig or cow over those of another, were most frequently transmitted from father to son.

Nobles were, of course, prominent on the membership lists of many agricultural societies, but it remains to be investigated how assiduously they attended meetings. Article 8 of the royal ordonnance of 28 January 1819 had stated that corresponding members of a national agricultural council would be chosen by Paris after nominations by the prefect of each department of those most active in those pursuits. The accompanying circular made plain that these individuals should not only be sufficiently rich to afford a slow return on investment but, even more important, have the personal reputation and the honorable renown that would cause others to follow their example. Each departmental correspondent was, rather optimistically, supposed to donate a piece of his property for instructional purposes. Some months later a clarification followed to say that landowners would not lose the profit from those experimental lands and to add that all the nominees would be named correspondents (to assuage any jealousies that might have arisen). The vocabulary used was a set of code words encouraging the landed gentry to collaborate with commoners, and they were reminded that without doubt the encouragement most likely to stimulate them to further exertions was the likelihood of being useful to their *pays*, as well as drawing "a benevolent look from His Majesty."[101]

Certainly noble participation in local agricultural societies was greatly increased. In the Yonne the prefect nominated two nobles and two commoners: one of the latter was chosen, but he joined to his other merits the fact of being a councillor at the prefecture. The Tonnerre subprefect nominated marquis de Tanlay, who possessed in the Yonne, Aube, and Côte-d'Or domains with an annual revenue of 60,000F from a variety of terrains, fields, vines, meadows, woods, and gorse. He also owned a flock of 150 merinos descended from the first animals imported from Spain in 1777. The total value of his properties was over 1.5 million francs. The marquis spent most of the year at Tanlay, where he himself oversaw some 60–70 hectares of good soils on his property that he was prepared to donate to experimental agriculture.[102]

Of the 288 French members the leading figures were the duc de la Rochefoucauld, baron Morel-Vindé, and comte Chaptal, all peers of France. There were also baron de Ramond, like Chaptal a member of the Académie des Sciences, and comte de Lasteyrie as secretary. Taking the membership at large, 18 percent were titled, and a further 21 percent had a particle in their names.[103] Examination of the 136 members of the Nièvre agricultural and industrial society in 1839 showed 11 percent titled and 24 percent with a particle.[104] The publisher of Lullin de Chateauvieux in 1843 noted that in 86 departments there were 157 agricultural societies; 22 model farms, of which some had schools associated with them; a further 15 schools and chairs of agricultural science for prisoners; and another 664 *comices agricoles* or *comités d'agriculture*.[105] The membership lists of these agricultural societies showed variations in the number of noble members but also a continuing aristocratic taste for the mysteries of drainage, irrigation, and crop improvement.

Besides knowledge of new advances in crops, there was also the issue of what might be called management attitudes. In 1822 Harcourt summarized the economic outlook necessary for being a successful farmer in terms worthy of modern agribusiness: "The same precision and spirit of order is needed, the same symmetry in every part of a rural establishment, as in a factory, which only prospers thanks to the strictest economy in the making of its products; and it is that which makes agriculture really profitable."[106] Those attitudes seem to have found an attentive ear in comte Charles de Polignac, so celebrated for the large flock of merino sheep that he carefully supervised on a Norman estate. At his death in 1830 he owned nearly seven thousand purebred animals bearing the prize-winning wool. He explained that the sheep were

> placed with local farmers, who are charged to nourish and care for them according to uniform conditions laid down by printed leases renewed annually from one Saint Michael's Day to the following. The landowner pays 9F 50 a head for the animal that does not produce and 16F 50 per ewe with lamb. . . . All the expenses, even the shepherd's wages, food, and that of their dogs, are at the expense

of the farmers. . . . I never change my farmers unless they force me
into it by negligences or other reprehensible acts. In this way I keep
them very mindful of their obligations.[107]

Havrincourt also was concerned about the surveillance of agricultural
workers in the Nord. He thought them bad, "the enemy of all order and
arrangement, of all accounting and innovation, and there is no sort of
malice that he does not employ with an incredible perseverance to
demonstrate the uselessness and the inconvenience of any new tool or
procedure. This is the character that gives the agriculturalist who wishes to improve his crops and to have a regulated accounting the most
difficulty, for each day he has to struggle much more against his employees than against the sun and the bad weather."[108] At the same time,
Havrincourt wrote of feeling obligations to farmers whose families had
been tenants of his own for centuries.[109]

One may note Polignac's reference to keeping tenants on, which was
the usual practice across the Channel in England at the time. This has
been seen as an important difference between English and French
agriculture in the eighteenth century; in France there was not only a
steady series of rental increases but also a constant turnover of tenants.
Robert Forster emphasized the positive aspect of the English practice of
not pushing tenants so hard as to stifle initiative.[110] Constant turnover
of tenants was not everywhere the case, of course. In his study of the
Old Regime Vannetais Le Goff discovered that family tenancies held
under the *domaine congéable* often lasted as long as ninety years, apparently more because of the expense of changing the leases than because
of enlightened agricultural policy. That regional stability was perhaps
continued into the nineteenth century.[111] As will be seen below, even
the avaricious M. de Fleurigny had maintained the Bourgeois family
through a number of leases on his estate.

A famous estate of the 1820s and 1830s was Roville (Meurthe-et-
Moselle), celebrated in the often reprinted *Annales agricoles* of M. de
Dombasle, which sang the praises of the plough he had invented. In
order to keep up the exemplary estate at Roville, Villeneuve-Bargemont,
then prefect of the Meurthe, organized a subscription, to which
Choiseul, Decazes, Durand de Chagny, Hunolstein, Pange, and a galaxy of other titled individuals subscribed.[112] Falloux in Anjou spent
heavily on improving bloodlines and increasing yields.[113] Lorgeril in
the Ile-et-Vilaine was the first in his area to demonstrate the utility of
large-scale liming.[114] Comte d'Angeville, a retired naval officer, stimulated his neighbors in the Ain by his agricultural experiments.[115] In the
Loir-et-Cher in the 1840s Vibraye and Périgny were the best-known
among twenty-eight nobles who made up a quarter of the agricultural

society.[116] In the 1850s and 1860s Havrincourt, a former polytechnician who became president of the general council of his department and a chamberlain to Napoleon III, was considered a model farmer. In 1867 he published a monograph recounting his techniques of estate management developed during the years since he had left the artillery in 1834. He reduced the number of small lots on his estate, started a successful sugar mill using a coal-fired pump to provide the necessary water, and strove to pay his workers at an hourly rate rather than by the day, and this in combination with piecework.[117]

Badly run farms, naturally enough, were less often found in the hands of latter-day agronomists. Some nobles were maladroit, for example, Charles-Théodore-Antoine-Palamède-Félix de Forbin-Janson, owner of extensive properties in the Durance Valley, who attempted a series of unfortunate experiments. He put blood on his fields but found that any fertilizing effect was offset by the attraction to wolves. He unsuccessfully attempted large-scale sugar-beet cultivation. Despite hiring an engineer and making an investment in factory building, he had not correctly estimated the cost factors of production. The Villelaure sugar factory, the rental value of which was 11,290F paying a *patente* of 1,760F—an amount unmatched by any other local establishment—was forced to close and precipitated Forbin-Janson's bankruptcy.[118] From his records it was possible to reconstruct his misfortunes, but the hallmark of the incompetent farmer was inadequate estate records.

The smaller the estate the easier to follow in an unthinking way the traditional routines. The difficulties of one petty *noblesse* family, the Puybusque-Toutens, shone through the saccharine evocations of an early twentieth-century genealogy. Soon after his 1826 marriage, Ferdinand overreached himself in rebuilding the Toutens château (Haute-Garonne) with cash raised from a very heavy mortgage on his property. Later he saw the château and its lands slip out of his grasp and pass to a commoner. In 1848, with four children and a wife to support, desperate for money, he enlisted the sympathy of a relative, who gave him in return for annual dues the produce of properties at Villate, near Muret. The family settled into the long uninhabited château of Lacombe, where they spent about twelve years, during which "numerous births arrived to augment the lineage."[119] Puybusque-Toutens fell out with his benefactor, who had obviously sized him up shrewdly enough and who wanted to change a situation that was "from all points honorable" to that of a "mere manager" (*simple régisseur*), whereupon with his wife and eight children Ferdinand took himself off to stay with his grandmother. At this point some inheritances and the economy of living off the old lady gave the family, or at least Ferdinand and his wife, the wherewithal to frequent good society in Toulouse. At this point Ferdinand again revealed his inability to estimate his situation correctly and took loans far beyond the capacity of his income to repay. Even with stringent economies, he was unable to balance the family budget. Meanwhile one son made a successful military career under the Second Empire, like so many other members of the southern and Breton *noblesse,* and he received a *dotation* from Napoleon III. This son tried valiantly to pay off a variety of debts weighing on the family, but the fall of the Second Empire cut off his income. By this point there had been an (unexplained) rally in the family fortunes, although it was perhaps put in jeopardy by Ferdinand's excessive preoccupation with his unpublished verses in French and Occitain, which, the genealogy assured posterity, were "vraiment remarquables."[120] A branch of the Hautpoul family in the nearby Aude displayed similar uneven revenues and misfortunes.[121] Examples of other poorly managed small estates could be cited from all over France.

The causes behind success or failure in agriculture were thus numerous and could range from poetry to fertilizers. However, land rents rose more rapidly than salaries in nineteenth-century France, at least in the first four decades.[122] On the one hand, the rural proletariat remained pauperized, and on the other hand, landowners in general saw little reason to seek for improvements in their agricultural technology. Certainly, better iron ploughs and new seeds made progress, but one can scarcely speak of a period of rapid innovation. Nonproductive, status elements of noble estates were a burdensome imperative, especially the wasted space of hallways, reception rooms, and driveways, or the crumbling vestiges of feudal *donjons,* or other architectural follies constructed if there were no genuine relics on the property to attest to family distinction. Only forest land could match its ornamental purposes with economic utility, as a source of wood for building materials, fuel, and cover for game. To sacrifice these symbolic dispositions of rooms and land, to plant the park with cabbages, so to speak, sacrificed status irrevocably. Exterior, visual, observed aspects of rural life were least open to change. If financial need ground landowners down to the point of selling the château and its lands, they chose to flee to urban anonymity rather than to remain diminished in the eyes of country neighbors.

The position of nobles in French rural society evolved at different rates in the partially independent regions and communities, each one with its own ethos and economy, in the years before and immediately after the advent of the railway. Some parts of France, such as Velay in the Haute-Loire, saw a precipitous decline from the numerous monastic estates and noble holdings of 1789 to what Lavergne called the

TABLE 4. Average Value of Gross Product Per Hectare in France, 1859

	1789	1815	1859
Landowner's return	12F (100)	18F (150)	30F (250)
Tenant's profit	5 (100)	6 (120)	10 (200)
Extra costs	1 (100)	2 (200)	5 (500)
Land tax (and tithes for pre-revolution)	7 (100)	4 (57)	5 (71)
Salaries	25 (100)	30 (120)	50 (200)
Total	50F	60F	100F

Source: Léonce de Lavergne, Economie rurale de la France depuis 1789 (Paris, 1860), 59.

Note: 1789 is the base year. Increases are shown in parentheses.

"rural democracy" of small holdings by the 1850s. By contrast, in the pays de grande culture, the Beauce or the unhealthy Sologne, lying between Loire and Cher, saw a continuation of many properties of over two hundred hectares in size.[123] In addition to estate size, proximity to urban markets, access to investors, and individual skill in farming, whether on poor land or good, on vineyards, meadows, or deep-ploughed fertile soil, determined profitability. Each estate had its specifics, and enough has been said to show that any claim that nobles as a social category had particular skill as farmers is highly dubious. Contemporaries preferred to make general estimates, such as that of Léonce de Lavergne comparing the landowners' situation in 1789, 1815, and 1859 (see table 4).

The Lavergne figures show that the landowner improved his position vis-à-vis the tenant. Lavergne's generalizations were based on a past time of agricultural prosperity propitious to landowners revealed by the tax returns on the electoral lists of the constitutional monarchies, 1815–48. Some modern historians propose a different picture.[124] They emphasize that if landowner profits rose, tenant revenues rose even faster. Easier profits could be made from urban real estate in the frenetic speculations of the 1860s, secure bonds with trouble-free returns, and industrial investment. Large landowners were more disposed to sell land, just as tenants could accumulate the capital to buy. New pressures during the 1850s and 1860s were particularly deleterious to those aspects of country life most prized by nobles. Servants and fieldworkers became ever more expensive with the ravages of the depopulation. The subprefect at Joigny (Yonne) replied to the 1856 enquiry into the flight of agricultural workers from the land with a warning against official tampering with conditions of employment: "To intervene in such a delicate matter, to wish to regulate salaries and land rentals, would overthrow, to the detriment of the interests that one is trying to serve, the natural and necessary relationships that must exist between master and worker, between the landlord and his farmer."[125]

In fact it was the agricultural crisis of 1846–47 that sharply drew attention to these developments. Léonce de Lavergne described it as closing "the grand epoch of the national agriculture" and summarized the difficulties as follows: "From 1846 a mysterious malady attacked the potato. . . . The same year saw a bad cereals harvest which produced the 1847 dearth. Then we saw, successively, the political crisis of 1848, the bad crops of 1853 and 1855, the war of the Orient, the cholera, the Italian campaign, the special construction in Paris and in some other large cities which drained the countryside of a great number of workers—all being circumstances that were very little to the advantage of agricultural development."[126]

Although the process of change was less abrupt than Lavergne believed, and the national increase in the number of small properties did not reveal its full extent until after 1880, it remains true that the golden period for the landowner, titled or not, during the first half of the century was evanescent. Increasingly heavy demands were made on the landowner to respond to a new situation; in the north the largest estates emerged from the trial strengthened and prosperous, but others splintered. The statistics of the subdivision of land show an increase in the number of smaller farms and a slight drop in the average size of the largest estates.[127] This resulted partly from a fall in the rural population, which put those rural workers who remained in a better bargaining position. The markets for their produce had much increased in the towns. Those vestiges of Old Regime rents in kind (*suffrage*), which evoked feudal payments—of eggs, poultry, butter, cartage services, and sometimes even a promise of a day or two of work on hedges or other chores—although encountered in some post-Revolutionary leases, became much rarer after mid-century. The widow de Gussy was harking back to an earlier age when in 1839 she leased for nine years two small estates, one of under eleven hectares in sixty-eight pieces, another of sixteen hectares in seventy-one plots, for the money rental, quantities of good-quality wheat, a "plump, lively, and feathered" pair of chickens, as well as twelve kilos of fresh butter, to be delivered to her at her house in Sens.[128] Everywhere in France the trend was away from these details towards an impersonal, commercial practice. Terms of leases appear to demonstrate a widespread similarity to what has been found in a part of Provence: a veritable collapse of "landlord power" between 1870 and the 1890s.[129]

Noble-owned properties fitted firmly within the general evolution of nineteenth-century French agriculture. Moreover, four-fifths of French nobles lived in an urban setting for part of each year. Indeed, they were more urban than French people at large while still looking to the countryside for the bulk of their income.[130] Those with smallish estates and hence least capable to afford the additional symbolic expenditures that would set them off from untitled neighbors with similar incomes were most likely to display aggressive endogamy, to cling to pride of family, which distinguished them from commoners, and to maintain "service" clauses in leases, which might seem a faint echo of vanished feudalism. However, the Parisian aristocracy drew their wealth from commercial estates situated mainly on the northern lowlands. They saw the value of their large estates rise steadily in net worth.[131] While they shared a symbolic discourse with the petty *noblesse*, aristocrats also understood a more contemporary idiom of enrichment and power.

3

Three Family Profiles, 1800–1870

A nobility, at least in the estimation of its members, is an elite that draws cohesion from a historical sense of family achievements and glories. For those with a scarcity of ancestral magnificence or accomplishments there was more likely to be an exaltation of a genteel way of life sustained by the family for generations. Since the telling of family history is one of the most ancient forms of historical discourse, it may appear to be a primitive, almost childlike approach to the past. When recounted by nineteenth-century French nobles, it was also a narrative about a family name transferred in the male line, with much less attention to the female descent. Properly conceived, family history must establish whether this assumed and theoretical solidarity with blood relatives ("family spirit") in fact existed in tangible forms, particularly economic.

The historian of French nobles cannot limit his curiosity to a sympathetic hearing of stylized family chronicles. Can we speak with any precision about the family wealth over time rather than the worth of individuals? Was the lineage rising in the social hierarchy or sliding down? Can we speak of family changes in religious, political, or professional attitudes? Any investigator faces a host of difficulties that are themselves conditioned by historical events, as in the case of those nobles whose property was confiscated and sold during the 1790s. Robert Forster's work on the Saulx-Tavanes family from Burgundy and the Depont family from La Rochelle has shown the wealth of insight that can be drawn from a fully elaborated study.[1] To establish what is the worth of a family at different moments in the nineteenth century, and what the outstanding claims of family members on the patrimony, is the first step towards setting the markers of success, but it is extremely difficult to do so. Information is almost always fragmentary about the varied forms of income and revenue, the costs of education, the liabilities for medical care or pensions, the level of charitable donations, the wages of servants, the burdens of living in the style expected by other nobles, and so forth.

These difficulties are evident in the following sketches of the wealth and strategies for its management followed by three families in the nineteenth century. Those "plans" to maximize prosperity, prestige, influence, and social authority of family members were, in each case, deflected or disrupted by unforeseen disasters: in one case by scandal, in another by want of heirs, and in the third by the July Revolution. All three can inform us about getting and keeping a foothold in the national and local elites in France. First are the Choiseul-Praslins, the wealthiest branch of the house of Choiseul, with its ancient and aristocratic attachments to the court. They traversed the Revolution with an adroit avoidance of serious economic loss. Second are the Raigecourts, an old, pious, wealthy family of Lorraine that only "arrived" at court in the 1780s with a marriage to a favorite lady-in-waiting of Mme Elisabeth de France, the devout, spinster sister of Louis XVI. The Raigecourts suffered grievously from Revolutionary confiscations and exactions. In 1789 the third family was respectable, but of obscure provincial *noblesse*, without court connections, and with only a modest income by Versailles standards. Their patrimony was not confiscated during the Revolution. Thanks to the brilliant powers of organization and conciliation of the head of the family, Joseph de Villèle, by 1830 he was a comté, peer of France, and member of the Order of the Holy Spirit. A number of his relatives and friends were to profit from his political rise by being named to a variety of local and national posts, most of which they lost after 1830. Each family moved along a different trajectory within the universe of noble aspirations, but each exemplified facets of noble life.

THE CHOISEUL-PRASLINS

The Choiseul-Praslin family was but one of several branches of that illustrious and ancient house in the nineteenth century, but it was the richest.[2] Its structure and wealth are harder to discern than the Raigecourt family's because of the numerous collateral branches, which complicated all estimates of worth at any given time. There were larger numbers of males heading new collateral lines, and more offspring. Antoine-César, at the twenty-third degree, was born in 1756 and became a colonel in the Lorraine infantry regiment and a *maréchal de camp* in 1788. He represented the nobility at the Estates General in 1789, when he sat as a deputy for the Maine *sénéchaussée*. However, by accommodation with the course of Revolutionary politics and not emigrating, he successfully safeguarded his fortune. His son studied at the Ecole polytechnique in the year IV of the Republic, entered the school of military engineering in the year VII, and was a sapper lieutenant by the

TABLE 5. The Landed Succession of Renaud-César-Louis de Choiseul-Praslin (1735–1791), 1797 (30 thermidor V)

Customary Law Governing the Properties	Percentage of Total Fortune	Values in Livres*
Paris	15.0	1,922,948
Melun	27.0	3,288,995
Anjou	8.7	1,073,524
Maine	18.3	2,255,966
Touraine	6.0	737,720
Poitou	7.1	875,696
Bourgogne	4.0	493,051
Auxerre	3.9	486,190
Nivernais	9.2	1,136,754
Total	99.2	12,270,846

Source: MC LVIII 597(bis): "Tableau des droits actifs de chacune des parties dans chacune des diverses coutumes qui regissent les biens."

*The notaries observed that 5 deniers (!) in these calculations of over 12 million livres had been "perdu par les fractions." Numbers are rounded to the nearest livre.

year ix and a captain in the year x. Antoine-César remained the wealthiest landowner in France at the dawn of the nineteenth century.[3]

The extent of the family properties is revealed by the *partage* of the landed properties of Antoine-César's father, Renaud-César-Louis, which took place on 30 thermidor v (12 July 1797). His marriage contract had been one of *communauté des biens*. The properties were worth over 12 million livres (see table 5). Such a division represented one of the rare occasions in each generation when an attempt was made to put a cash value on the family properties with a view to bequests. The documentation was so considerable that the notary bound it into a separate volume complete with an alphabetical index: "H: Habitation à Saint Domingue," (bought in 1765 for 150,000 livres), and so on. Particles were dropped from the Choiseul-Praslin family signatures, although Amédée d'Hautefort used his. The table drawn up to show the claims on the estate according to the different customary laws shows the spread of the properties owned in France (see table 5). It also revived a flicker of Old Regime legal practice, since Antoine-César, normally resident at Auteuil, claimed that the entailments (*substitutions*) set up in his favor by his father remained valid, for his father had died on 5 December 1791, while the abolition of that legal procedure had taken place according to decrees of 25 October and 14 November 1792. In April 1791 his father had bought up church lands of the former Abbey of Our Lady of Evron, so that the *partage* reflected advantages to be gained both from the old inheritance laws and from the new laws introduced since the Revolution. The senior heir, Antoine-César received 46.7 percent of the properties, while each of the three living siblings, together with the heirs of the fourth, received 8.9 percent.

This giant fortune had at its fulcrum the splendid château of Vaux-Praslin (today Vaux-le-Vicomte), which the Choiseuls acquired in the mid-eighteenth century and held until they sold it to a rich sugar refiner in 1875. For a century the family found a setting in rooms first built for the seventeenth-century financier Nicolas Fouquet. They would certainly appreciate his choice of a squirrel motif to represent the nimble movements required to keep and gain money: their own motto was "Success accompanies courage."

In 1802 Antoine-César became a member of the Sénat conservateur and remained a member until his death at age fifty-two. In his will he expressed the hope that his children would share equally his properties as during his life they had shared his *amitié*—a characteristically restrained statement of affection in the aristocracy.[4] They were, as the Michaud biography correctly put it while confusing father and son, destined by family tradition to power ("Voué par tradition de famille à la puissance de fait"), and indeed the Choiseul-Praslins survived and flourished under all regimes.[5] Antoine-César's wife was Charlotte-Antoinette-Marie-Septimanie O'Brien de Thomond, daughter of a marshal of France. She also died before the end of 1808, and this led to an informative family *partage* in August 1810.[6] There were two heirs of Antoine-César, his son Charles-Raynald-Laure-Félix (1778–1841), at that time "comte de l'empire chambellan de S.M. l'Empereur et Roi," and his daughter Lucie-Virginie (1795–1834); two boys and a girl had predeceased them. Félix's brother-in-law, Emile Le Tonnelier de Breteuil, also a graduate of the Ecole polytechnique, had become a diplomat and was made a baron of the Empire in 1810 amidst protestations of love and respectful devotion to the emperor and of his intent to marry and found a family. The weaving of the web of useful connections continued, whatever the regime.

Antoine-César's fortune later included one-fifth of his mother's estate (she died on 26 February 1806 at Courbevoie in the Seine department, where she lived with her married daughter, Mme de Grollier), which later passed to her grandchildren from César. The remaining four-fifths were split up in a complicated way among further relatives: three-quarters of another fifth went to the surviving children of her son Hippolyte (1757–93), whose wife was still alive, and the remaining quarter was shared between her daughter Bonne-Désirée (1775–1865), who had married comte de Grollier in 1797, and the surviving daughter of Julie-Alix (b. 1777), who had married Amédée-Louis-Frédéric-Emmanuel, comte d'Hautefort. Three full fifths were to be left to her son, daughter, and granddaughter. The exactitude of this arrangement is easily understandable if we note that the estate of the old lady was worth 3,233,371F, enunciated in sixty-three articles in the inventory. This was reduced by claims on the estate of almost a million (980,704F). Among the debts, for example, were three fractions of *rentes* set up between 1768 and 1777 for Mme de Querhant and worth a capital of 98,000 livres which had come into the possession of Choiseul-Praslin's widow. On that sum Jean [de] La Rochefoucauld [-Bayer] had a claim of 65,000F recognized by law in 1806 and 1807, in partial payment of which he received in January 1810 the sum of 34,417F from a professor in the Paris Medical School for an estate at Beaumoulin, Seine-et-Marne.[7] The remainder included estates and four châteaux—in the communes of Randan (Puy-de-Dôme), purchased in 1781 for 920,000 livres; Quintin (Côtes-du-Nord); Lorgues (Côtes-du-Nord); and Brie (Charente-Inférieure)—plus the mere "habitation" at Beaumoulin (Seine-et-Marne). The furniture of the place where she died was valued at 55,589F. The entire estate was parceled out in the form of shares of both assets and liabilities to six family members, leaving one more, Mme de Grollier, with an unencumbered legacy of 520,471F. A further 283,371F was to be paid out to individuals without direct family ties. The undischarged liabilities were to pay an interest of 5 percent per annum. The assets immediately flowed into new obligations, as in the 21 June 1807 *communauté* marriage contract between her granddaughter Apollonie and Charles de Talleyrand de Périgord, both minors (see the discussion of marriage contracts in chapter 7). The future groom brought a promise of a quarter-million francs in due course, and Mlle de Choiseul-Praslin produced from the inheritances of her father, grandfather, and grandmother an estate in Mayenne (678,863F) and a capital of 298,633F, plus two annual revenues totaling 2,600F and a trousseau of 25,000F.[8]

In 1810 the senator's sister sold the *biens nationaux* that had come from the Abbey of Our Lady of Evron (Laval arrondissement, Mayenne), which she had acquired in the family apportionment of 30 thermidor V.[9] Now living either in Paris at 128, rue du Bac or at the Montgoger château in the Indre-et-Loire (itself an inheritance from a female relative *née* Elisabeth de Beauvau), she decided to sell the property to André Guillet de Préau for the sum of 29,629F, and her brother, César-René, acted on her behalf in the sale.[10]

Another wing of the family drew up its accounts when the surviving children of Hippolyte entered their inheritance of 1,080,915F each.[11] His son Albéric was bequeathed a château and estate worth over 1 million francs at Chassy (Loiret/Yonne) plus two farms and a large house on the rue de Reuilly, not far from the Bois de Vincennes. This had been rented to a commoner since the year XIII, and the 1811 renewal of the lease for six years was to bring in 2,400F annually.[12] In 1829 the same Albéric-César-Guy Dechoiseul [sic] was listed on the electoral roll of the Nièvre as a peer of France with a political residence at Couloutre (Nièvre) and paying in that department a tax of 4,224F.[13]

The Choiseul-Praslins were an exceptionally wealthy and numerous house. The successive heads of the family were, at the twenty-third degree, Antoine-César (1756–1808) with four siblings; at the twenty-fourth, Charles-Raynald-Laure-Félix (1778–1841) with four; at the twenty-fifth, Hugues-Charles-Laure-Théobald (1805–47) with five, and at the twenty-sixth, Gaston-Louis-Philippe (b. 1834) with eight. The various relations constituted a network of credit that involved legal transfer of claims back and forth between them and their children. Félix, for instance, was paying a life annuity of 3,000F per annum to his younger brother Gilbert at the time of the latter's 1806 wedding, as well as recognizing his 35,000F claim on the Praslin townhouse in Paris.[14] As figure 3 shows, the Choiseul-Praslins had far more marriages (twenty-one) in the direct line than the two other families considered in this chapter. There was an incessant recourse to the notary by the Choiseul-Praslins which showed that they relied more on precise legal terminology than on the spirit of family solidarity. Or perhaps it is fair to say that their family spirit was corseted by the notarial precision. In May 1843 Jean-Baptiste-François-Sales-Ambroise-Félix, comte de Choiseul d'Aillecourt, gave his legal permission for the enactment of the will of Félix de Choiseul, after deduction of 391,379F for the liquidation of the société des acquêts (common property of a married couple) in his marriage contract.[15] Money entered from dowries, as in the case of César-René's second wife and mother of three additional daughters to join the two with whom he was already blessed and his solitary son. In 1838 the second wife brought in her share of her mother's (née de Lignérac) succession, which amounted to almost one and a half million francs.[16]

These lateral exchanges were sometimes within the family. César-Hippolyte had married a cousin, Choiseul d'Esguilly, in 1780. Forty-six years later she died, on 1 June 1837, and the following winter division was made between her son and daughter of the 320,989F of the estate not already paid out in dowries and legacies. The properties in question were estates, buildings, French and English investments, and individual debts to her.[17] In May 1837 there was a marriage (dotal contract) between comte Louis-Jean-Baptiste-Léon de Choiseul d'Aillecourt and

FIGURE 3. Succeeding Generations of Three Noble Families in the Eighteenth and Nineteenth Centuries

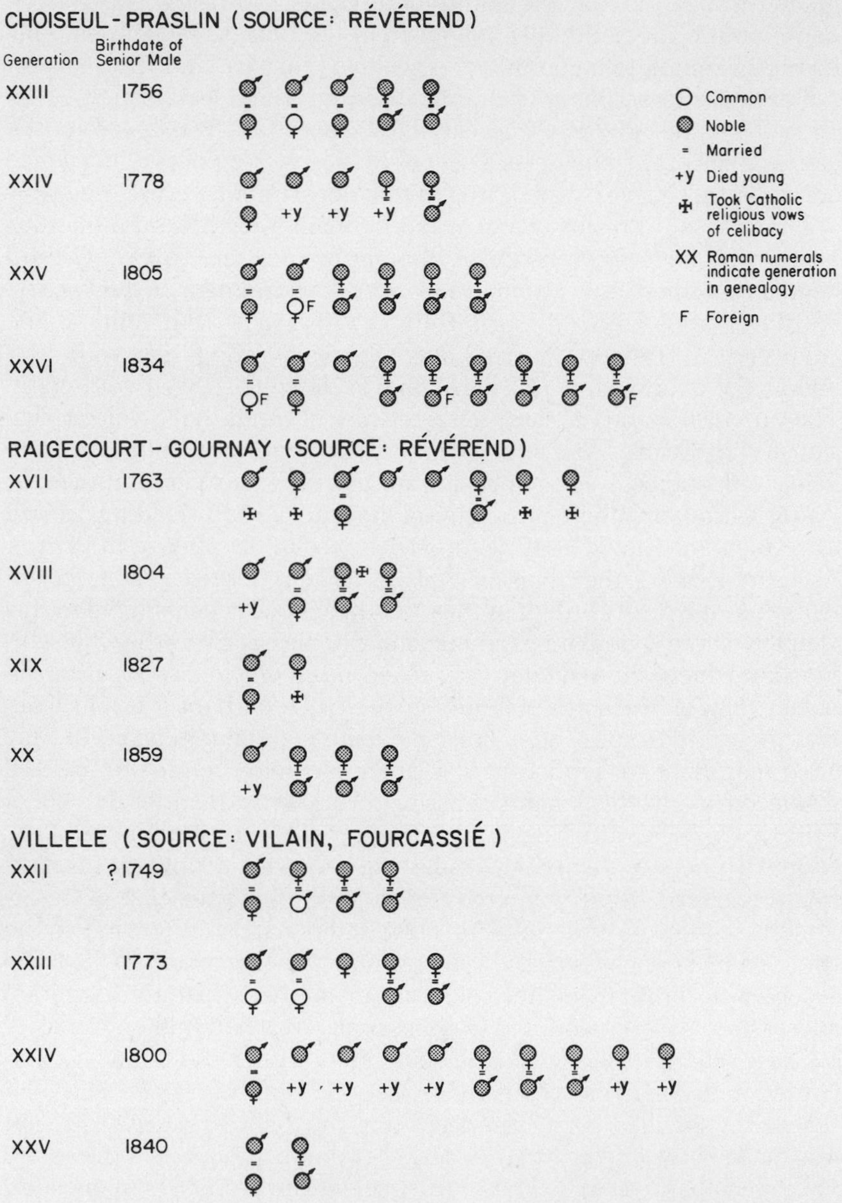
CHOISEUL-PRASLIN (SOURCE: RÉVÉREND)
Generation
Birthdate of Senior Male
XXIII
1756
XXIV
1778
+y
+y
+y
XXV
1805
F
XXVI
1834
F
F
F
RAIGECOURT-GOURNAY (SOURCE: RÉVÉREND)
XVII
1763
XVIII
1804
+y
XIX
1827
XX
1859
+y
VILLELE (SOURCE: VILAIN, FOURCASSIÉ)
XXII
?1749
XXIII
1773
XXIV
1800
+y
+y
+y
+y
+y
+y
XXV
1840
Common
Noble
= Married
+y Died young
Took Catholic religious vows of celibacy
XX Roman numerals indicate generation in genealogy
F Foreign

Note: Individuals are not listed in order of birth.

Léa-Marie-Régine Choiseul-Praslin.[18] The property of the groom came from the *partage* of his father, composed of fractions of lands in the Orne (one third), mills (one sixth), and Seine-et-Oise lands (one third), as well as 1,000F *rente* in 3 percent, and six shares in the Banque de France, while from his mother, with whom he lived in the noble faubourg, came diamonds, furniture, a horse, and an annuity of 4,000F, as well as another income of 5,000F on a capital of 100,000F. These arrangements would thus yield annually at the least 10,000F without diminishing the value of the properties. His bride had farms and lands near Cherbourg and Valognes (Manche) which had been divided between her brother and sister from the *premier lit* by an agreement of 9 April 1834, an annual income of 1,350F in unspecified grains, and a one-third share with her brother and his wife of the inheritance of one-third of the estate of M. et Mme de Mauconvenant de Sainte Suzanne, their maternal great-grandparents. She further brought an annual 2,000F *rente* at 5 percent, 10,000F in cash "derived from her savings," one-sixth of her rights to another estate (Fresnes), a listing of revenues amounting to 13,000F annually, diamonds worth 4,000F, an annual *rente* of 5,000F from a capital of 100,000F, and a trousseau worth 12,000F. In short, the couple had available in 1837 annual revenues of, at a minimum, some 32,000F, with additional wealth invested in a variety of lands and movables. Both were mature adults, and they seem not to have had children, so all this wealth would in due time return to the general family fortune.

In 1865, seven months after his wedding, a young sublieutenant in the second cavalry regiment garrisoned at Chartes, comte Horace de Choiseul, who lived at 42, rue Saint-Pierre with his young wife Joséphine-Béatrix, *née* Beauvau (1844–95) (who signed herself Beauvau, C^esse H. de Choiseul), sold her lands in the Seine-et-Marne as a reinvestment of inalienable dowry funds for the sum of 350,000F.[19] Later he served as mayor of Maincy and member of the Seine-et-Marne general council and stood for election in 1869, when he told the electors, among other things, that he would not forget that agriculture lay at the base of public prosperity and that as their representative he would concern himself above all with the rights and interests of those who produce and those who work.[20]

Money, of course, flowed out and in, and sometimes across national borders. In September 1839 the sister of Régine, also adult, married a Belgian noble who lived near Tournay.[21] He had a revenue of 3,000F on lands near Lille (Nord) and more in Belgium, as well as 5,000F on 100,000F held at 5 percent. For her part, she brought lands from the Manche, 5,300F annual revenue in 5 percent *rente,* 141F annual *rentes* in grain and money, one-third of the heaths owned in Seine-Maritime at

Vatteville and those at Heauville (Manche) together with a *rente* of 1,100F at 3 percent, 32,000F in cash, and diamonds worth 7,000F. The couple thus disposed of an annual revenue of at least 16,000F for life in Belgium. The marriage of Edgard-Laure-Charles-Gilbert to the daughter of a Prussian businessman, Schickler, brought the new family far higher rewards. The dowry provided some half a million francs to help with the expenses of their home at 17, place Vendôme, and at the death of Angélica Schickler nine years later the inheritance passed on to her surviving spouse and children was more than one and a half million francs.[22] Several of Théobald's children, including the heir to the title, married and lived abroad. His eldest son wed Miss Forbes in Geneva in 1874 and subsequently lived on the Isle of Wight, off the south coast of England, for much of the time. Théobald's last child, a daughter, married in 1858 (*régime dotal*) the Italian cavalry officer marquis d'Adda Salvaterra and lived in Milan. In 1863 she exchanged some dowry property which was inalienable, woods in the Aisne department, and *rentes sur l'état* for a house at 46, rue Jacob in Paris, purchased for 420,000F.[23]

The fundamental underpinning of this family lay in land, mostly in the northern half of France in departments not far from the capital, especially Seine-et-Marne but also Côtes-du-Nord, Charente-Inférieure, Seine, Manche, and Seine-Maritime. Puy-de-Dôme was the most southerly location in 1800. How did they administer these far-flung properties? Essentially they relied on managers (*régisseurs*), who oversaw relations with tenant farmers, who were responsible for the fine details of running the property. Less than a month before her death the widow of Antoine-César, together with her son, dating the procuration 27 April 1808 at the Hotel de Praslin, at 79, rue de Grenelle in Paris, gave their instructions to the *régisseurs des terres* of Praslin (Seine-et-Marne), Gery (Nièvre), Thoisy (Nièvre and Côte-d'Or), Hardenges (Mayenne), and St. Denis d'Orques (Sarthe) reminding them that they could undertake new buildings "only upon written instructions from Paris" and added that they could neither ask for nor receive for any cause whatsoever any gratuities (*pot de vin*).[24] Management of the Choiseul-Praslin estates was thus heavily dependent on written instructions and the obedience of subordinates to them. A lease from a large, 216-hectare farm in the Choiseul-Praslin network of properties drawn up in 1844, not too distant in either time or place from that of M. de Fleurigny discussed below in the section on the Raigecourts, provides a number of clues.[25]

César-Corentin-Ferri, vicomte de Choiseul-Praslin, described as a landowner (*propriétaire*) dwelling on the rue des Saints-Pères (in the noble faubourg of the left bank of the Seine) made a nine-year lease to

begin after Easter 1848 with M. Dosne, "cultivator," and his wife
(named as *dame* rather than the *Madame* of the document when speaking of the vicomtesse). Dosne and his wife accepted joint legal responsibility for the lease of the farm in Andonville commune, canton Outar-
ville, in Pithiviers arrondissement in the Loiret department which
actually belonged to Mme Jeanne-Adélaïde-Valentine de la Croix de
Castries, wife of the vicomte. The couple had no posterity. From the
detailed description, we know that the property included a house with
lofts, barns, stables, sheepfolds, cattle sheds, pigsties, yards, gardens,
and other "facilities and out-buildings" and a further 216 hectares 97
ares of arable land and woods. Dosne accepted that he did not need a
more precise description than this, since he lived together with his
father-in-law, "M^r [*sic*] Louis Laurent," who had the enjoyment of the
property in virtue of a lease (made by the same notary on 5 January
1837) which was to run until the beginning of the present agreement.
The lessees agreed to execute in full the terms of the lease and to
renounce any right to claim for a diminution of *fermage*. The terms
provide a good overview of the links between Paris noble and provincial
tenant and are quoted here *in extenso:*

1º De fixer leur demeure et résidence habituelle dans les bâti-
ments de la ferme louée, les garnir et tenir garnies de meubles
meublans, ustensiles de ménage, effets, bestiaux et attirails de
labeur nécessaires et en quantité suffisante pour l'exploitation, et
pour répondre du loyer ci-après fixe, faire aux bâtimens les mémes
réparations locatives suivant l'usage, souffrir faire les grosses en cas
de besoin; faire avec leurs chevaux, harnois et voitures l'approche de
tous les matériaux nécessaires pour les dites grosses réparations et
même fournir tout le chaume qui sera nécessaire pour l'entretien
des couvertures des bàtimens et murs.

2º De bien et dûment labourer, fumer, cultiver et ensemencer les
dites terres en temps, soles et saisons ordinaires, sans pouvoir les
dessoler, refroisser ou désaisonner et les rendre en fin du présent
bail en bon état de culture et en trois soles égales.

3º De resserrer dans les granges et batimens de la ferme tous les
produits des terres, sans pouvoir les mettre ailleurs, de convertir en
fumier toutes les pailles et fourrages provenant des dites terres, pour
les enfermer et non d'autres et la dernière année du bail laisser dans
les cours et batimens de la ferme les pailles et fourrages de la
dernière récolte et même confusion de l'avant dernière sans pouvoir
en enlever ni brûler ni divertir aucune.

4º De veiller à la conservation des biens loués, s'opposer à ce qu'il
y soit fait aucune entreprise, ni usurpation et dans le cas où il en
serait fait, d'en prévenir les propriétaires ou leur fondé de pouvoir
dans la huitaine, à peine de dépens, pertes, dommages et intérêts.

5º De ne pouvoir prétendre aucune indemnité ni diminution de loyer pour cause de grèle, gelée, sécheresse, incendies, stérilité, inondation, et d'autres inovation, et autres événemens de force majeure prévu et imprévu.

6º De faire en l'acquit et décharge de Mr et Made de Choiseul sur les chemins et routes qui peuvent traverser les terres de la dite ferme, les longer et y aboutir, toutes les plantations qui pourront être ordonnées par la loi ou par le gouvernment à leurs frais et de les entretenir, aussi à leurs frais et sans aucunes répétition contre les propriétaires en diminution de fermage.

7º De payer et d'aquitter annuellement pendant le cours du présent bail, en l'acquit et décharge de Mr et Made de Choiseul sans aucun recours ni répétion contre ces derniers, ni diminution de loyer; les contributions foncières et accessoires, tant de propriété que d'exploitation dont la dite ferme de Gondreville et toutes les terres et bois en dépendant, sont et pourront être chargés, en principal, centimes additionnels, taxes, subvention et à tel titre et sous telle dénomination que ce puisse être, à telle somme que le tout puisse monter et en quelque nature et valeur que l'acquit doive en être fait, en sorte que le prix du loyer de la dite ferme reste franc et sans aucune déduction à Mr. et Made de Choiseul et de justifier annuellement de l'acquit des dites impositions par le rapport des quittances.

8º De fournir aux propriétaires, à leur première réquisition pendant le cours du présent bail, une déclaration exacte des biens loués par consistence de chaque pièce, nouveaux tenans et aboutissants dûment certifié véritable.

9º De ne pouvoir ceder leur droit au présent bail ni sous louer en tout ou en partie sans le consentement exprès et par écrit du bailleur.

Outre ces charges, le présent bail est fait moyennant la somme de huit mille francs de loyer et fermages annuel que le Sr. Dosne s'oblige et oblige la dame son épouse solidairement avec lui, à payer à mr. et made de Choiseul en leur demeure à Paris, ou au porteur de la graphie des présentes et de leurs pouvoirs en trois termes et paiements égaux les jours de Noël, Pâques et Saint Jean Baptiste de chaque année. . . .

Par ces mêmes présentes M. de Choiseul donne pouvoir au dit Sieur Dosne son fermier de veiller à la conservation de la ferme présentement louée et ses dépendances; empêcher et réprimer tous empiètements et usurpations; faire procéder et assister à tous arpentages et bornages, faire dans le cours de ces opérations tous dires, observations et requisitions dans l'intérêt du mandant; former et défendre à toutes demandes, citer et paroitre sur toutes citations en justice de paix, se concilier s'il y a lieu sinon suivre devant les juges compétens, faire executer tous jugemens.

Fait et passé à Paris en l'étude de M Fourchy l'an mil huit cent quarante quatre le vingt sept décembre.

Twenty years later the same lessor, still signing himself with the abbreviation of his title just as it appears on the earlier document—"Vte de Choiseul"—and still living on the rue des Saints Pères, made another arrangement to oversee his properties, this time not with the actual tenant.[26] He empowered a fellow noble, Edmond-Maximilien Des Portes de Linières, mayor of the commune of Clermont Gallerande (Sarthe), who was also a director of the local agricultural insurance society, to regulate and administer Choiseul properties in the la Flèche arrondissement of the same department. He could make, renew, and cancel all leases with the price, clauses, and conditions that he thought suitable and repress all hunting offenses.

Both documents reveal that the vicomte himself took no part in the close, day-to-day running of his estate. His agricultural endeavors were seemingly limited to studying the clauses of his leases. Whatever agricultural innovation took place was here more in the hands of the tenant farmer than in those of the owner.

Enough has been said to indicate the complexity of family obligations among the Choiseul-Praslins. Family members lived in scattered locations. When the fortune of the dowager duchess was divided in 1861, it was split between five males and five females living in Paris, a further eight family members six of whom were scattered among the departments of Manche, Eure, Seine-et-Marne, Haute-Savoie, Bouches-du-Rhone, and Aude and two more in Italy.[27] Their homes, châteaux, and estates comprised a kind of collective wealth, a lode that sustained these aristocratic individuals during their lifetimes. Theirs was a model that other rich aristocrats in the period 1800–1870 emulated, just as it was one to which poorer nobles wistfully aspired.

THE RAIGECOURTS

We are quite well informed about the landed wealth of the Raigecourt family, a lineage that disappeared during the nineteenth century.[28] They sprang originally from Metz. Numerous members of their family had held municipal office there, and in 1375 one *maître-échevin*, seigneur of Ancerville, was a chamberlain of the duc of Lorraine. From his progeny derived three branches, of which one continued into the nineteenth century.

Born at Nancy in 1763 to the second of his father's three wives (all of whom produced children, to a total of eight), marquis Anne-Bernard-Antoine de Raigecourt-Gournay was at the seventeenth degree of his line. (An older brother from the first union took orders and outlived him, serving as the superior of the Rheims seminary.) The addition to the family name had been a condition of his grandfather's wedding with the only daughter of the comte de Gournay. This was not the first time that they had taken on a seigneurial name, for *Spincourt* had been added earlier; nor would it be the last, for they added that of Fleurigny in the nineteenth century. Anne-Bernard-Antoine, sublieutenant in the Royal Allemand regiment before the Revolution, in line with the strong military traditions of his family, married at age twenty-one in Paris on 28 June 1784 a woman five years his senior, Louise-Marie de Vincens de Mauléon, daughter of a marquis and a lady-in-waiting to Mme Elisabeth de France. This meant that she had an annual court income of at least 4,000 livres, not to mention income from her properties.[29] She was at that time a *dame chanoinesse* of the chapter of Saint-Louis de Metz, recruited exclusively from noblewomen. He took an interest in public affairs and was a substitute deputy of the Nancy *bailliage noblesse* to the Estates General.

With the advance of the Revolution, he found himself at odds with the new order. The family motto was "With honor," and like others with courtier connections, he quickly emigrated and saw service against the Revolution with the Condé army. The liberal publication *Biographie nouvelle des contemporains* (1824) mentions an émigré M. de Raigecourt arrested near Valenciennes "weapons in hand" and executed on 1 vendémaire IV (23 September 1795), but I have not identified this individual.[30] Anne-Bernard-Antoine became an aide-de-camp to the comte d'Artois.

At that time both he and his wife corresponded with the pious marquis and marquise de Bombelles; those letters were published at the end of the nineteenth century and revealed the sordid squabbles among the exiles. By 1792 Mme de Raigecourt saw the misfortunes visited on French noble exiles in biblical terms, comparing the nobles to the Jews stricken by divine anathema and adding that both were guilty and impenitent.[31] Raigecourt became completely disillusioned with the possibility of returning as a member of a victorious army. His wife returned home in 1797 and tried without success to have her husband's name removed from the list of émigrés. He came back in 1800, like so many others, in a chastened and constructive mood and was taken off the list without mishap.

He was now confronted with the realities of rebuilding the shattered family finances after the loss of his and his wife's properties. He also had obligations outstanding to his half-brothers and half-sisters from his father's first and third wives. Those who had taken religious vows renounced their claims on the paternal estate but still expected an annual *rente,* and the widow and son in Vienna also expected annual payments. Only scraps of the landholdings in Lorraine had not been sold, mostly woodland, and most of this was sold off by 1810. Again like so many others, he served Napoleon as a mayor.

At the time of his daughter's wedding in 1809 the Raigecourts were living in the Saint Germain district (rue de Sèvres), and henceforth they were Parisians. They sought to acquire land close to Paris and in 1816 made their first major purchase in the fertile agricultural region of the Niévre. Anne-Bernard-Antoine's service as a mayor under the Empire was not held against him under the Bourbons. In August 1814 he became a *maréchal de camp.*

In 1816 he was named a peer of France, and he promised to set up a *majorat.* A reference to him in the biography of the peers compiled by Lardier says that he rarely took the podium. However, in March 1816 he opposed the continuation of ecclesiastical pensions to priests and nuns who had married or taken other professions since the Revolution. Ten years later, in April 1826, he opined against the form of the indemnity proposed for Haitian planters on the constitutional grounds that the king could not undertake its payment without the approval of the Chambers. And he delivered other speeches that showed that he had distanced himself from the ultraroyalists.

In 1824 he made over his pension as a peer in place of the *majorat,* an option taken by a number of members of the upper house. He had regained sufficient property to live in style. He would receive one of the larger indemnities of the Emigrés' Billion, approaching 1 million but still not a true compensation for what had been lost, mostly in the Meurthe and Moselle departments. He protested against the fatuous undervaluation of the château at Friauville, which had been much dilapidated by its first owner after its confiscation and sale but which he believed was certainly worth more than the appraised 412F 50.[32] Other property not regained by the Raigecourts included their townhouse on the rue Callot in Nancy, which in the nineteenth century was the property of the teaching order of the Brothers of the Christian Doctrine.[33]

The Raigecourts retained a certain prestige in their ancestral city of Nancy, as was apparent in the November 1826 ceremony for the reinterring of the remains of the dukes of Lorraine dispersed during the Revolution. The pallbearers were representatives of the leading old families of Lorraine, who marched in a procession with drawn swords: one of them was the marquis de Raigecourt, together with the marquis de Lambertie, the comtes de Ligniville, de Ludre, d'Ourches, and de Mitry, and others. The ceremony must have had a certain pathos for Anne-Bernard-Antoine, since by then the family had in large measure relocated its landholdings in Burgundy.[34] He had other relatives in the upper house. His wife's brother, vicomte Vincens de Mauléon de Causans, took his seat in the same chamber in 1827, but he would be unseated in 1830 as one of the appointees of Charles x. Anne-Bernard-Antoine for his part was among the 210 peers named by the Bourbons who accepted the Orleanists. The news of 1830 was perhaps not a complete surprise to a man who had seen the comte d'Artois in youth as well as in age. His pious wife died at Draveil (Corbeil arrondissement, Seine-et-Oise) in March 1832, and he followed her to the grave in December 1833.

Anne-Bernard-Antoine had four children: his first son, born in 1790, died while still a child, and his second son, Raoul-Paul-Emmanuel, was born in Paris on 27 January 1804 after their return from emigration, when they lived on the rue des Saints Pères, Division de l'Egalité. His eldest daughter, Hélène, was born on 23 May 1791 and was baptized with royal godparents (Mme Elisabeth de France and the comte de Provence). The second daughter, Ernestine, was born on 13 March 1795. His only son had a military career during the 1820s and would inherit the titles and take public office (see below).

Hélène married on 6 April 1809 (with a marriage contract on 27 March 1809) Charles-Louis-Modeste de Beufvier de Paligny, a former naval officer and widower without children.[35] His second marriage was also childless. She promised 50,000F payable at the first death of a parent, although in fact this sum may never have been paid, since she was separated from her husband by 1817. He brought to his second wedding "tous les biens, meubles, immeubles et droits à lui appartenant," notably the La Sécherie château in Vendée, although in his 1811 will Charles spoke of the building as "my house de la Sécherie." He also spoke of the "good and sincere friendship" that he felt for his wife and asked for four Masses to be said, and twelve paupers to be dressed in woolen cloth, immediately after his death, which ensued twenty-seven years later, in December 1838.[36] In his mother-in-law's 1817 will there were pointed allusions to her daughter's great misfortune to be married to such a man, and she left a picture of her daughter's godmother, Mme Elisabeth de France, who had been guillotined during the Terror, with the wish that it would inspire in Hélène the courage and resignation needed to endure her unhappy lot.[37] The couple lived apart for many years, but during that time Beufvier felt no need to change his will's provisions of 31,000F in cash (*francs d'argent*), which is to say real rather than paper money, that enduring phobia of the possessing classes who had known the ravages of *assignats* and *mandats territoriaux* during the Revolution. He bequeathed to his widow for her life the enjoyment of half his property.

After his death, Hélène de Beufvier in fact became a hospital nun of Saint Thomas of Villeneuve, although she lived either at home in Paris at 27, rue de Sèvres or at Draveil (Seine-et-Oise). Three of the four generations of the Raigecourt family shown in figure 3 included family members who took religious vows, whereas in the Choiseul-Praslin and

Villèle family branches discussed in this chapter nobody did so. Indeed, we can surmise that these vocations contributed to the extinction of the Raigecourts family name.

Ernestine married in 1816 marquis Stanislas de Las Cases, a member of the royal bodyguard. If Beufvier was reproved in his mother-in-law's will, Las Cases was praised as being virtuous. The couple had six children. He was given permission to set up a *majorat sur demande* in June 1830 entailing his property in the Gironde. Ernestine died there, in the Léoville château, in 1872, eight years before her husband's death.

Hélène's share of the family wealth would pass through a donation she made to Ernestine's daughter Esclarmonde, who married Athanase, marquis de Retz de Mallevielle. This transfer was not made without some litigation over a bequest from an aunt, Alexandrine, who was a half-sister to Anne-Bernard-Antone, which was most instructive about the arrangements with her niece. Mme de Beufvier, now a nun, had opposed the bequest of 40,000F to her own sister's daughter. As a result of bequests from half-brothers and half-sisters of her father, various sums were owed to Mme Beufvier by her niece (as transacted before the notary Julia in Albi on 4 March 1840), and she was permitted by decision of the Seine tribunal to receive the amount of 14,739F cash, as well as various treasury bonds—"au grand livre de la dette publique"—directly from the hands of Raoul, and payment was made on 29 March 1844. Years later she declared that her intention had always been to make a donation of the amount of 40,000F specified by Alexandrine, or even more, to her niece. In August 1851 she enacted an outright gift of the estate she had bought in 1845 located in the Var. It yielded an annual gross revenue of 3,350F. This present was made on condition that it provided her subsistence ("ses faits personnels, à titre alimentaire"):

> 1° D'un grand domaine rural proprement dit le Domaine de Bénat, situé sur le Territoire de la Commune de Bormes [arrondissement de Toulon] départment du Var, quartier de Bénat, consistant en Vignes, Oliviers, collines agrégées de pins, chênes-lièges, chênes-verts et autres essences de bois essarts, terres incultes et laborables, *avec bâtiment de maître ou château,* [my emphasis] Chapelle, Moulin à huile, logement de fermiers, hangar, écuries, bergerie, Cour et parc, fontaine, bassin, lavoir, jardin d'orangers et autres dépendances; le tout formant une contenance de deux cent soixante dix neuf hectares soixante deux ares soixante quinze centiares en y comprenant le bâtiment sur le bord de la mer et la partie de terre dite L'Acapte. . . .
>
> 2° Et d'un Pré sec situé aussi sur le Territoire de Bormes . . . de la contenance de vingt trois ares trente centiares . . . les dits

> biens . . . ont été aquis par made de Beufvier . . . vingt-sept mars
> mil huit cent quarante-cinq . . . compris tous les capitaux de
> bestiaux, charettes et instruments aratoires servant à l'exploita-
> tion du domaine de Béna . . . acquisition de . . . M. François
> Vidal, Capitaine d'Infanterie en retraite, officier de l'ordre de la
> Légion d'honneur, demeurant à Bormes . . . moyennant la
> somme de soixante-douze mille francs de prix principal. . . .[38]

This was certainly a handsome restitution of the 40,000F which had been sequestered from the estate. Hélène de Raigecourt, born in emigration in 1791, would not die until January 1884.

All of the family's hopes for the perpetuation of the Raigecourt name were concentrated on Raoul-Paul-Emmanuel. His very pious mother's will of 1817, written when the boy was thirteen, exhorted her children to walk in the path of virtue, to help and care for one another, and to uphold fraternal harmony while always remembering that true tenderness cannot be separated from "the politeness and urbanity which is a part of Christian charity." Among other bequests to her son she included a "true cross" mounted on an ebony pedestal which she hoped would give the boy the strength to resist "the torrents of the world and to master his passions," just as his father had done. She added that he should remember that "the finest titles that his ancestors have left him are those of a virtue and integrity which made them the arbiters of their neighbors. True pride is neither in haughtiness nor touchiness."[39] Following in his mother's family traditions of service at court, he became a page of Louis XVIII in 1820. He was an infantry officer at age 18 in 1822, he took part in the 1823 Spanish campaign, and he was in the dragoon guards in 1825. He married for the first time at age eighteen in Paris (21–22 November 1822). He brought to the marriage the gift from his parents of the 435-hectare estate of Germancy, near Nevers, in an area of large properties lying alongside the canal du Nivernais. There were a château, its adjacent buildings, and courtyard, as well as gardens, vines, barns, stables, meadows, ponds, heaths, and several farms and woods. The revenue from these properties was spelled out in more detail by the marriage contract:

> plus deux rentes ou redevances annuelles dues par les nommés
> Perrin et Ve Hugot et toutes autres redevances qui peuvent être dues
> par les autres habitans des Bruyères de Lancy . . . ainsi que cette
> terre et ses dépendances se poursuivent entendent et comportent
> avec les fonds de cheptel, emblavures, empoissonnements et foins de
> reserve auxquels les propriétaires ont droit en vertu du bail cy après
> énoncé; sans par les donateurs en rien excepter, retenir ni reserver.
>   Cette terre est affermée (à l'exception de quelques reserves faites
> par les propriétaires, notamment l'habitation d'une partie du château

et la coupe des bois taillés) à Bernard Geraud M^d de Bois et Jeanne
Françoise Campanel sa femme pour douze ou seize ans, au choix
respectif des parties, à compter du onze novembre mil huit cent
vingt un moyennant un fermage annuel de six mille deux cents en
numéraire payable en deux termes égaux les onze mai et onze
novembre dont le premier paiement a eu lieu le onze mai mil huit
cent vingt deux, et les fermiers sont chargés en outre du payement
des contributions foncières, le tout aux termes d'un bail passe devant
Decray notaire à Decize le dix septembre mil huit cent vingt un,
Enregistré[40]

In fact this estate was a recent acquisition and was thus a "conquest" of
the legal community of property between the two Raigecourts. They
had bought the Germancy estate in the name of their solicitor at a public
auction at the Seine civil tribunal in the summer of 1816 which had
been held at the demand of the Territorial Bank's creditors. These creditors wanted to liquidate the assets, which included this property which
had come into the bank's hands because of a foreclosure on Jean-Joseph
Sallonyer de Taunay (?Camnay) and his wife, Jeanne Prévost de Germancy, in early January 1804. Of the 140,000F purchase price, all save
18,742F 60 had been paid off by the Raigecourt parents at the time of the
wedding. This valuable property had thus been acquired by the elder
Raigecourt as an indirect result of the financial difficulties of the husband of the lady whose maiden name had been that of the seigneury
(Germancy) before the Revolution.

Raoul's wife, Louise-Françoise-Lucie de Leusse, brought a large dowry of 150,000F, to be paid in stages.[41] A sum of 10,000F was handed
over immediately; a further 40,000F came from the comtesse de
Bézieux, who paid on the last day of 1825 to discharge a price of sale;
and the remaining 100,000F were promised (and paid) within a year.
Moreover, the marquis de Leusse made a "donation between living
individuals as an advance of inheritance" to his daughter or to her
descendants of the Poussery estate (Nièvre), although reserving to himself the usufruct during his lifetime (he died in October 1829). Through
this Raigecourt-Leusse marital link to his mother-in-law, the 178-hec-
tare Fleurigny estate (located in Sergines canton, near Sens, and worth
192,886F in 1854) came into the hands of the son of the Raigecourt-
Leusse marriage via a bachelor uncle, the last of his line, whose will was
made between 1839 and 1843.[42] Once it was theirs the Raigecourts
preferred the Fleurigny château to their other properties and thence-
forth made it their principal estate.[43] Hortense, sister of Lucie, who
married a commoner, was scarcely remembered in the Fleurigny will,
save for a few family trifles. Lucie had died within three years of her
wedding day, but directly or indirectly, the union brought 1,605 hec-

tares of prime agricultural land to her son by the time he came of age in the 1850s.

Uncle Leclerc de Fleurigny was a frugal man who, according to the inventory made after his death, had an apartment in Sens at 16 rue de la Charte which he rented for 500F per annum and the château at Fleurigny which the family had owned for three centuries.[44] At his death he had 8,400F deposited with the Sens *receveur particulier des finances* and a further 47,705F in treasury bills, which with back interest at 3 percent amounted to 56,105F. It was from those sums that his legacies were paid, after which 15,461F remained. Marquis de Fleurigny also owned 165F in revenue from 5 percent bonds, of which 60F was bequeathed to the church in his own village and that at Fontaine-la-Gaillarde, so that 105F income reverted to young Raigecourt. The furniture in Sens was valued at 2,620F, and that of the château, at 20,861F. This property had come to Fleurigny because of an act passed:

> devant Me Anjubault, notaire à Paris, le trente un mai mil huit cent six et contenant partage entre M. de Fleurigny et M. et Made de Leusse de la succession de M. Antoine-Claude-Edouard Leclerc de Fleurigny, leur père et beau-pere. [Inventory had been made by Bellaguet, notaries at Sens, 4 July 1778.] Par cet acte, pour fournir à M. de Fleurigny le montant de ses droits dans les biens compris au partage, il lui a été abandonné, entre autres choses, le château de Fleurigny et dépendances, la ferme de la basse cour du château, et différentes pièces de terre et de pré. One été laissées en commun cinq cents hectares quarante huit ares soixante centiaires de bois sis aux finages de Fleurigny, Vallières et Villiers Romeux.

In the quite recent past there had been additions and subtractions of parcels of land to the property. In April 1791, represented by a wood dealer, the widowed mother of M. de Fleurigny purchased for 1,325 livres some nine and a half arpents, or approximately 4.72 hectares, of property confiscated from the former curé of Fleurigny. Some years later, in 1796, the wood dealer was described on a sale document as a landowner and cultivator when he bought the former priest-house, this time presumably for himself, while the widow Leclerc de Fleurigny, now noted as an émigrée, had ten arpents confiscated from her. They were sold off for the sum of 1,224 livres to a clockmaker from Sens.[45] Thus in the early years of the Revolution the family followed the example of those who, like Marie-Antoinette, purchased church lands that had been put up for sale, but later on in the Revolution they suffered some losses themselves.

However, the property division of 1806 between Fleurigny's heirs makes plain that this was very far from a spoliation of the family. In 1809 he was among the wealthiest fifth of the eighty nobles in the Sens arrondissement.[46] Young M. de Fleurigny also carried out adjustments to the surface extent of the estate after he took over, notably the acquisition of 15 ares 24 centiares, the exchange of 15 ares 81 centiares for 6 ares 96 centiares, and the purchase of a fragment of property measuring 5 ares 27 centiares, resulting in a slight extension of the estate by 11 ares 66 centiares. The uncle was a fastidious manager who kept good records, as can be seen from item 40 of the inventory: four documents dealing with an account between M. de Fleurigny and M. Chevillot about the sale to the former by the latter of potato crops and a colt. He preserved with equal care the papers proving the pre-Revolutionary noble status of the Fleurigny property, as well as information on the building of the chapel. The 1843 inventory noted that he had not paid an attorney who had acted on his behalf nine years earlier in a dispute with the commune of Fleurigny which unsuccessfully claimed a piece of land located on the limits of Saint-Martin-sur-Oreuse. He clearly felt a strong attachment to the family château which had come to the Le Clerc family in 1513. This moated, three-sided château with a chapel in the east wing was entered via a bridge to the north façade; the south was open. The moat was shown as filled with water in an 1838 illustration of the château. The desire of M. de Fleurigny to control his château beyond the grave was shown in his will: he specified that all construction under way at the time of his death should be carried out according to his instructions. His executor, L. B. Garsement de Fontaine, an old friend and noble who lived nearby in Sens arrondissement and who, like the deceased, was a former *garde du corps* of Louis XVIII who had refused to take the oath to Napoleon in June 1815, doubtless understood his sensitivities.[47] So too did Gustave's father, who in a letter of March 1841, two years before the old gentleman died, wrote to him that he agreed with all his heart that his own son should add the name and armorial bearings of Fleurigny to their own. "This name is too fine and too honorable for you not to wish that it be continued after you."[48] M. de Fleurigny's body was interred on the château grounds in a funeral chapel blessed by the archbishop of Sens in 1844. (The Raigecourt nephew in 1863 requested imperial permission to add his maternal uncle's name to his own, so that henceforth he was de Raigecourt-Gournay de Fleurigny.)

From the estate records of Fleurigny presented in the accounting of tutelage (*compte de tutelle*) by M. de Fontaine, the executor—since the heir was not an adult at the time of entering into his inheritance—we can tell something of how a noble estate in the Yonne was operated around 1840. Annual payments had to be made on the rambling château with its moat and steep slated roofs: 150F annually to a roofer in Sens to keep it watertight, another 125F for leaf-raking and weeding in the garden alleys, and 28F for insurance on the château farm against fire. At his death various repairs to the château, built at the time of Francis I on the site of an earlier château, were under way. Venetian shutters were being placed on windows, fresh paint applied, bannisters replaced, flagstones newly laid, and a parquet set in the study. Cosmetic touches were indulged: a new billiard table was ordered, ebony furniture was sent for fixing, and 1,530F worth of silver repairs were outstanding. Some of this may have been posthumously arranged to reduced the amount open to taxation. Or perhaps one can imagine the old bachelor sprucing up his château so that it might pass worthily to the young man who was to take his name. At all events, the executor had a cash account of 110,274F 92, of which he contrived to spend 107,102F. This left less than 3 percent of what had been on hand at the marquis's death.

The agricultural yield of each hectare "cultivated as a garden" according to the 1839 estimate showed the arrondissement of Sens, where the château was located, as the richest in the department (Sens 1,800 F, Tonnerre 1,300F, Avallon 700F, Auxerre 550F, Joigny 500F).[49] The kind of arrangements made with tenants can be seen from the nine-year lease concluded for the period beginning 23 April 1838 (St. George's Day)—although for a meadow and woodlands to be cleared beginning 15 February—with M. and Mme Bourgeois for the farm of the backyard of the château, with its dwelling and work buildings. (By the end of the century this had been grassed over with flowerbeds as the main courtyard.) The property comprised 122 hectares 74 ares 84 centiares in forty-two pieces, as well as a further half-hectare governed by the usages of the commune of Fleurigny (and of which the enjoyment was to cease if the lessor died) and almost 15 hectares of woodland and meadow. The rental for this arable land close to the château buildings was the substantial amount of 2,840F in cash, to be paid to the communal tax collector on the first of each month against the tax bill of M. de Fleurigny, and after that was satisfied the surplus was to be paid to M. de Fleurigny. Also specified were the dates of payment of the noncash items of the lease, which included interestingly, a wide variety of other produce:

19.25 hectoliters wheat	24 chickens
44 hectoliters oats	5 turkeys
13 hectoliters rye	4 geese
775 bales grass fodder	4 ducks
400 bales wheat straw fodder	8 days' cartage (4 horses)
40 kilos butter	15 kilos white wool
80 dozen eggs	3 hectoliters walnuts

In addition to the big property, there were other nine-year leases, such as that on 14 hectares 70 ares 92 centiares of arable land in forty-three pieces in the Vallières commune for an annual rental of 48F, 8 hectoliters of wheat, 10 hectoliters of oats, 30 kilos of butter, and 24 dozen fresh eggs. There was a lease of 1839 for 8 hectares 70 ares 23 centiares in thirty-one pieces for 25F and 7.5 hectoliters of oats and the same amount of wheat, 2 kilos of butter, and 6 chickens; and another on 6 hectares 53 ares 79 centiares in ten pieces for 60F, 5 hectoliters of oats, and 4 chickens. When the lease on the largest property was renewed in 1846, the father of young Raigecourt kept on the old tenants but also enumerated the twenty-nine specified subtenants and the rents they were to pay, all for a period of twelve years and for a rent substantially higher than ten years earlier—5,416F—but without the supplies which had been so considerable a part of the leases of M. de Fleurigny.

Fleurigny had also subdivided the estate woodlands into eighteen "cuts" of equal size: 5 hectares 6 ares 40 centiares, and another section of 82 hectares 22 ares divided into an additional ten "cuts." The Nivernais had long found the provision of firewood for the capital to be extremely lucrative. Sixteenth-century letters from the Sens master of the woods and forests spoke of the woods of the community of inhabitants of Fleurigny.[50] In 1843 M. de Fleurigny was selling the trees massively at high prices: on 4 hectares 22 ares, 1,600F; 187 trees, 325F; and the large 14,000F sale with the additional delivery to the château of 24 cubic meters of firewood, 700 tiles, and 100 bundles of laths. There was the sale of 163 poplar trees along the river for 1,650F plus the delivery to the château of 150 staves. More trees in the park and near the château were sold for 1,944F. Such a heavy logging seems to be the stripping of the estate by the last of the Fleurignys before it passed to the Raigecourts, for since 1840 the old man had received from them a *rente viagère* of 2,400F.

The estate yielded other produce after the death of M. de Fleurigny. The château gardener, who was paid 50F a month for his work, was steadily selling vegetables in 1845, while the maid Babet did washing and sold young pigeons. Extras were reported as coming in from the farms where the widow Bourgeois was responsible for the payments.

Emmanuel's young wife Lucie had died in October 1828, two years after giving birth to her daughter Marie-Eléonore, who became a nun and whose will is discussed below, and to Gustave-Emmanuel-Louis, born in 1827. The family then lived in an apartment on the decidedly unfashionable rue Pot de Fer in Paris. Lucie's will, which predated her death by just a few days, noted that she had 9,500F cash on hand and debts outstanding totaling 3,700F—500F to one tailor and 100F to another, 100F to a carriage painter, 2,500F to a harness maker, and 500F for various provisions. No mention was made of her dotal property, which, in any event, now passed to her husband to manage in their children's interests. After various deductions, the father's responsibility to his children was fixed at 130,000F.[51]

That dowry included the estate of Poussery in the *pays Morvan* (Nièvre), which enjoyed local renown during the nineteenth century as a model farm, a breeding center for livestock, and an orphanage to train "petits Paris"—parentless children from Paris—for agricultural life. The departmental agricultural society reminded readers in 1846 of the reason why it had decided to set up the model farm on Raigecourt property, 58 kilometers from the city of Nevers, even though many farmers subsequently complained that this isolation weakened the pedagogical value of the farm. When the idea was still in the planning stage and attracting only decidedly lukewarm support, marquis de Raigecourt had come forward and offered a reasonable annual lease of 11,500F without asking for a deposit, together with cattle valued at 25,000F. Nor was this all: he further undertook to build a sheepfold, a piggery, and an oven for preparing lime, as well as to pay half the price of any further buildings needed, a promise pregnant with future expense, since there was already talk of a school, a cowhouse, and the orphanage. The château needed repairs, since it was first built from the fifteenth to the seventeenth centuries. The marquis also subscribed 9,200F in shares towards the total 30,000F initially proposed to be raised to fund the·school, of which only 116 shares at 100F each had been taken by other investors.[52]

Raigecourt's attitude contrasted strikingly with the caution and hypercritical attitudes of other landowners. Indeed, with his open-handed approach which permitted the establishment of the model farm, his example brought about a change of heart among the other landowners, and additional shares were purchased by them. For his limitless confidence in the project and his personal financial sacrifices for it, Raigecourt was cited as the very model of a concerned landowner. Although the fulsomeness of the version of how the model farm at Poussery was begun may seem rather excessive, it attests to a readiness to invest and show support in local agriculture by an aristocrat who sat on the departmental general council.

Emmanuel's second marriage, on 18 June 1835 also at Paris, was to Mlle Lefebvre de Balsorano, daughter of Charles, who subsequently became comte de Balsorano, but there was no issue from the union. She died in Naples in 1843. He took his seat as a peer of France (19 May 1845) and lived on the rue d'Astorg in Paris, close to the Elysée Palace. In 1854 the twice-widowed Emmanuel made an accounting of his stew-

TABLE 6. The Fortune of the Raigecourts, 1800–1870: Major Inputs and Outputs

Date	Male Side	Female Side	Debit	Credit
1800	Unsold woodlands			49,127F
1800		Unsold woodlands		70,000
1809		Beufvier dowry	50,000F	
1816		Las Cases dowry	100,000	
1825		Leusse dowry: cash & income		50,000
1825		Leusse dowry: Poussery estate (Nièvre)		100,000
1825	Raigecourt-Leusse dowry: Germancy estate (Nièvre)			140,000
1826	Indemnity award for confiscated property to marquis and marquise de Raigecourt			835,103
1826		Legacy from second wife of M. de Leusse promised		30,000
1832		Legacy to Prince de Croy	33,528	
1834		Leusse legacy*		235,784
1843		Fleurigny legacy		192,880
1851		Retz gift	40,000	
1855	Raigecourt-Caumont de Laforce dowry			?150,000
1855		Caumont de Laforce dowry		?250,000

Sources: MC CXI 513, LVIII 731, 822; A Gain, *La Restauration et les biens des émigrés: La Législation concernant les biens nationaux de seconde origine et son application dans l'est de la France, 1814–1832,* 2 vols. (Nancy, 1928); Decise cadastre.

*"Consistant en un château avec cour, Jardin et dépendances, moulins, terre labourable, prés et bois appartenant à Mr le Mis de Leusse au moyen de l'acquisition qu 'il en a fait . . . de L. A. François Bruneau, Marquis de Vitry tant en son nom que comme mandataire de made Gabrielle de Reugny sa mère épouse séparée quant aux biens de Mr Pierre Etienne Bruneau" (see purchase, MC CXI 455, 22 August 1810).

ardship of the property of his children.[53] The very detailed accounting ("Mr Gustave de Raigecourt: recettes et dépenses faites pour lui comme légataire universel de M. de Fleurigny depuis l'ouverture de la succession jusqu'au treize décembre mil huit cent quarante cinq, époque à laquelle il a accompli sa dix-huitième année") also included a "Compte de tutelle par M. le marquis de Raigecourt à ses enfants," notification of a reduction of rente at 4.5 percent, and the "partage, licitation et arrangement de famille entre le marquis de Raigecourt et ses deux enfants." This latter included a detailed valuation of lands. The Fleurigny, Pouligny, and Poussery estates totaled 1,378 hectares 33 ares 55 centiares, with a gross revenue of 40,053F 04; the net revenue after deduction of tax paid, upkeep (mostly the responsibility of the tenant farmers [bailleurs]), and guard was 32,553F 90. The land value alone was 954,070F; with the cattle (40,000F) and interim improvement (mise en état) it was given as worth 986,490F. These can be regarded as highly conservative figures drawn with an eye on the tax assessor.

Gustave, born in 1827, was at the nineteenth degree of his line. As an adult he lived on the Fleurigny estate and also in Paris, at 131, rue St. Dominique, in the heart of the noble faubourg. We can tell something of his adolescence from the accounts of his expenses: he traveled to the United States and Italy and took private lessons from a professor as part of his education. (His sister for her part had a governess). On 3 November 1855 he married the daughter of senator and duc Caumont de Laforce. I have not yet located the marriage contract, but we can be fairly confident that it was substantial, in the 250,000F range on each side. From this match he had three daughters but only one son, Emmanuel-Ghislain, who died before his tenth birthday, the last male in the direct line of descent. At the child's health the dispersement of the properties held by the Raigecourts would begin, passing through the dowries of the surviving sisters, who in the 1870s and 1880s married active or former cavalry officers all of whom were noble. It was the youngest of these sisters who wrote a brief note of the history on the maison de Raigecourt.

Table 6 is an attempt to summarize the post-Revolutionary development of the family fortunes.

THE VILLÈLES

Several books by members of the local gentry from the fertile wheat-growing Lauraguais region, to the southwest of Toulouse, describe the running of estates during the first half of the nineteenth century. That by Picot de Lapeyrouse was translated into English in 1819, and that by Louis Théron de Montaugé appeared in 1869.[54] More renowned among the local noblesse was Joseph de Villèle, who had a brilliant but short political career under the Restoration, when he made a profound and lasting impact on the organization of the national financial machinery of France. Here the aim is to sketch the cadet Campauliac branch of this seigneurial family as noble landowners on their property in the Caraman canton of the Haute-Garonne from the Revolution to 1870.[55]

At the mid-nineteenth century the local nobles were the richest social category in the canton: Villeneuve-Crossillac at his death, at age 81, was declared to have a revenue of 28,613F, Marguerite de Beaumont at age 85 was declared to have 18,600F, and Joseph de Villèle was declared to have a mere 6,500F. Some commoners had incomes on that scale, such as Blanc, with 7,976F.[56] These declared revenues were well below the true income. The remarkable thing about the Villèles, however, was their fixity on the same estate by contrast with the rapid turnover of the aristocratic Choiseul-Praslins and Raigecourts. As the century progressed, so, too, did the number of artisans and shopkeepers who bought a small sharecropping farm (or *borde*, as it was known locally), but the Villèles did not sell their lands to such newcomers to the canton. They were still managing their own property in the 1980s. In local agriculture wheat and maize cultivation predominated, whereas in the nearby environs of Toulouse and Muret a mixed cropping pattern was found—wheat, oats, barley, rye, maize, wine, and meadows. The Villèle properties lay in the most commercialized area of local agriculture, that with the best return of crop to seed in the department but with the worst wine.[57]

The father of the future statesman, Louis-François-Joseph de Villèle, seigneur of Mourvilles, de Fourtonnens, et de Campauliac, could properly be called an *agronome* with an ongoing passion for agricultural improvement. In May 1777, five years after his wedding to the daughter of an *avocat* in the local *parlement*, he purchased the château of Mourvilles-Basses from the widow of the previous owner, who himself had bought it in 1770. The bill of sale stated that "la dite terre et seigneurie vendue consistant en la justice haute, moyenne, basse, directe et foncière, du droit d'établir le juge et autres officiers pour l'exercice d'icelle, rentes, cens, et en grains, argent, volaille, droit de lods et ventes, préstation et autres droits et devoirs seigneuriaux, droits utiles et honorifiques en dépendant."[58] The new château itself lay over the hill from the Campauliac château, near Labastide de Beauvoir, where he had been brought up, and was a large building in the characteristic rosy brickwork of the area, halfway up a small hill overlooking another rise of ground in a gently rolling landscape. There were numerous outbuildings, a windmill, a forge, and a place to make tiles, as well as living accommodations for the workers.

He never left France during the Revolution, but he had his own grievances. He was imprisoned in Toulouse from August 1793 to October 1794. As a model farmer he had further reasons to be against social upheaval, as he made clear to Fouché, then minister of the interior, in a letter written from his house in Toulouse on 15 August, 1799 in the aftermath of the insurrection of the year VII. This was a year later than the establishment of the departmental society of agriculture of which he was a founder member.

Citizen Villèle was a government agricultural correspondent and unlike in his last letter, which had dealt with the use of plaster as fertilizer, he was now denouncing an uprising that he characterized as the result of an "invisible and infernal outlook" resulting from Jacobin intrigue, as well as the "credulity" of the royalists, which had caused the local farmers to abandon their family and harvest and to converge on the largest communes or the chief places in each canton, against which they harbored resentment ("dont ils croyoient avoir à se plaindre"). He claimed that as a result of these insurrections he himself had been menaced by the insurgents, whereupon he had fled to Toulouse, but in that city he was pursued by calumny and animosity on the part of "some exclusivist and exaggerated men who claim to be patriots, and against whom I have resisted for ten years, laws and constitutions in my hand, to prevent them from ultra-revolutionizing the area [*d'ultrarévolutioner le païs*] and establishing themselves in the place of the landowners."[59] Doubtless he was thinking of his petition of 28 October 1791 against the crowd of armed men led by a local municipal official which searched the château and house at Campauliac, or the hunt for arms at Mourvilles on 25 September 1792 and the dispute over taking down the weathercock, which was there displayed as a sign of privilege. He successfully defied the erstwhile egalitarians.

For his part he wished to work quietly on the materials he had been collecting for three years on the subject of the diminution of fodder by dessication and by the debris that are lost during haymaking, but he was arrested by a local official, the *directeur du jury,* and had his papers seized in the hope of compromising him "in order to apply to my much-envied properties the dispositions of the new law [punishing royalist insurgents]." At this point his wife and daughters fled from the Mourvilles-Basses château, where they had remained, despite the precipitate flight of the workforce, lamenting the unfortunate results that the workers' departure might have for their persons, as well as regretting the bad effects on the crops of the land owner—if Fouché read this letter, this must have caused him an ironic smile—and Villèle protested that "at that time only the big landowners were threatened and the most peaceable were not distinguished from the guilty."

Mourvilles had been plundered on 25 thermidor VII (12 August 1799) by a hundred men of the Tarn detachment of troops under General Vicose, who were moving from the villages of Caraman to Baziège. They were, observed Villèle, "doubtless excited by someone from Caraman." Oxen, prize bulls, heifers, and sheep waiting to be leapt by merino rams which the ministry intended to import from Spain were taken, and his furniture and prize agricultural specimen collection were damaged. He asked for an end to the plundering of his property. The minister of the interior was in fact sympathetic to Villèle and argued on his behalf.[60] So, too, did the celebrated agronomist Parmentier, who described him in October of that year as a leading propagator of the potato in the Midi and asked the minister to allow the elder Villèle to return to his stubble fields and flocks. However, when the family returned home on 1 fructidor (18 August), worse was to follow, for the next day the house was violently searched by *commissaires,* who ripped open feather mattresses, smashed furniture, casks, and clocks, stole the kitchen copperware, and threw medecines—"so precious in an isolated country district"— on the floor. The library was also damaged. Villèle was a past master of written complaints, but even making allowance for possible exaggeration, there is a clear echo here of the sense of grievance among large landowners against vengeful arbitrariness on the part of small-town officials.

Villèle's prestige among his fellow landowners was revealed in a letter from his country neighbors who also lived part of the year in Toulouse. In a letter of 1 ventôse XI (20 February 1803) they proposed him as the president of the Caraman electoral canton assembly and emphasized:

> Possibly citizen Villèle has been thought to live in Toulouse because he goes there sometimes and has a lodging; however, he lives and pays personal taxes at Mourvilles-Basses in Caraman canton, where he pays the highest tax and is one of the most zealous defenders of the interests of agriculture and the countryside, he who best knows the potential of the arrondissement [*les forces contributatives*] and who has drawn up and presented the best plans for assessment, and he is doubtless the best known under all these aspects in your agricultural and arts council and in the offices of the Ministry of Finance.[61]

The brothers Martais thought it worthwhile to mention that young Joseph at the colony of La Réunion had victoriously combatted "the disorderly party of the independentists and the traitors who wanted to turn the island over to the English." This official correspondence relating to Villèle senior shows something of the concerns of noble landowners in the southwest at the dawn of the nineteenth century. So, too, did his 120 contributions on the subject of local agricultural conditions to the *Journal des propriétaires ruraux* from 1805 until his death. This

TABLE 7. The Declared Revenue of Joseph de Villèle, 1816

Property	Revenue	Tax Paid
Commune de Mourvilles-Basses, Caraman	3,271.99F	2,497.10F
Canton	108.05	82.46
Château de Villèle		25.46[a]
Château de Campauliac		19.10[b]
Commune de Caragoudes, Caraman Canton	628.60	29.26
Commune de Varennes, Montgiscard Canton	545.25	297.29
Commune de La Bastide-Beauvoir, Montgiscard Canton	211.65	189.32
Toulouse		36.58[c]
Total	4,765.54F	3,176.57F

Source: AN C 1215A (52), elections, 1816.
[a]Tax on 24 doors and windows. The doors-and-windows tax was a small payment based on the number of doors and windows in a house.
[b]Tax on 18 doors and windows.
[c]House tax, a small levy on the rental value of a dwelling.

publication was the organ of the Haute-Garonne agricultural society and was read by the most influential and substantial landowners of the region. The society had a number of nobles who served as presidents during the first half of the century. If they were much less wealthy than great aristocrats like the Choiseul-Praslins or even the Raigecourts, they were more closely involved in agriculture and the local community. They were also conscious of the place of the gentry in national agriculture. The elder Villèle was an active correspondent of the agricultural society of the Seine; in 1812 he was discussing articles to be sent for publication.[62]

The election of Joseph de Villèle gave rise to a formal estimate of his tax and revenue in 1816. (The breakdown is shown in table 7.) This statement of income is very much lower than the real values of farm income found by Fourcassié, which explains the astonishing ratio of revenue to tax.

In August of 1817, the year following the famine, the 340-hectare Mourvilles-Basses estate, with its fields, meadows, woods, and vineyards divided among fourteen métairies, was one of four proposed for the Haute-Garonne in a national competition to identify the best-run properties in each department. As a result we have a fairly complete description by the commissaires made at the same time as the tax declaration given above. This was published in the journal to which the

elder Villèle had been such a prolific contributor, and at a time when his
son was in the ascendant as mayor of Toulouse and a member of the
general council of the department and the Chamber of Deputies in
Paris.[63] The account enables us to see something of the noble landowner's view of labor relations at a time when the rural population was
increasingly sharply.

Both father and son insisted on cultivation by *maîtres-valets*, by sal-
aried workers rather than sharecroppers. The *commissaire* wrote of
"the profound conviction of the owners that one cannot obtain good
cultivation by sharecroppers or *colons partiaires*." They added that the
buildings of the *maîtres-valets* (resident wage laborers who received
lodging and fixed quantities of produce) were well-made and healthy.
For his part the elder Villèle described how the *maîtres-valets* should be
employed as family units of one, two, or three paid men to work especially on cartage and plowing, with a pair of oxen for each, while
adding that "one should try to have always, insofar as possible, a super-
numerary member of the family who is unpaid."[64] Those who were paid
(*gagés*) each received four hectoliters of wheat and four of maize per
pair of oxen, with further arrangements for the product of the poultry,
piglets, and so forth. The Toulouse agricultural society had set up a
system of prize medals for *maîtres-valets* who had worked on the domaine for at least ten years, who were of unquestioned honesty, and
who were extremely careful with the livestock. Two families at Mourvilles-Basses received medals (in 1809 and 1813). Joseph's oldest son
took over the management of the estate when his father became elderly,
but he was a much less talented man than either his father or his
grandfather. However, in his own way he exemplified the patience
vaunted in the family motto which stated that all comes to he who
knows how to wait. He did not dissipate the properties that he had
inherited. Over three generations and at a time of radical political os-
cillations in France, the Villèles retained their lands and their château at
Mourvilles-Basses.

In the 1772 marriage contract Jean-Baptiste-Guillaume de Villèle
(1708–78), at the twenty-first degree of the Campauliac branch, gave to
his eldest son, the future groom, Louis-François (?1749–1822), "pour
témoigner le plaisir qu'il prend du présent mariage" to a "noble demoiselle" an irrevocable gift of all his possessions—under the reserve that
he was to retain their enjoyment throughout his life.[65] Nevertheless, we
see here something that the Villèle family repeated in the period that
concerns us: the father gave to his eldest son the management of affairs
before his own death. The 1772 contract spelled out different obligations for Louis-François. Unlike the Montesquieu branch, the Campauliac branch had not slipped into a large number of weddings with

commoners, and they had sufficient male heirs, which was not the case with the Caraman branch. The 1772 marriage had transferred responsibiility to Louis-François and five years later he bought the Mourvilles-Basses château, which remained the family seat at the time of this writing.[66]

In 1799 Joseph (1773–1854) married (*communauté* marriage contract) at the Island of La Réunion the eighteen-year-old daughter of a wealthy planter, and this without the approval of his father, for which he felt the need to apologize profusely. He had made an excellent match, however, and he returned to France a great deal better off than when he had left. This was important for the 1807 *partage* sale, when Louis-François passed responsibility to his eldest son.[67] Joseph's younger brother joined him soon after the wedding, fleeing from conscription, and that young man soon married into his sister-in-law's family. The younger man remained in the colony when his brother returned to France in 1807. In later years he made some bad investment and business decisions and greatly diminished the Villèle colonial holdings by 1820. Meanwhile, in France Joseph advanced his political career while never losing sight of the details of his financial interests. In May 1817 he drew up a memorandum of money deposited with the Protestant banker Courtois, in Toulouse, and in February 1828 he took out fire insurance on his house on the rue Vélane in the city.

In 1829 it was time for Joseph's eldest son Henri to marry. Arrangements were again made to begin the property transfer. An important new aspect of this marriage contract was that of the *majorat* for the title of comte which been set up by Joseph and which was to pass to his son with the hereditary title. Article 6 of the marriage contract specified that if his mother survived his father, the revenue of the Campauliac château was to be hers for the remainder of her life. Henri's parents were thus speaking of their "intention to advantage him" but at the same time were maintaining the web of obligations between all family members. At the time of his 1846 will Villèle reviewed the financial advances made since he had received the management of Mourvilles-Basses. He calculated that he had increased his fortune by 901,025F and that the total worth of his fortune, including the dowries paid for his daughters (*régime dotal*), was 1,370,000F. Joseph observed that, after God, the family owed this good fortune to "the moderation and simplicity of our tastes, to the exactitude and orderliness of our conduct . . . and to the kindnesses and the confidences with which I was honored by the two kings whom I have had the happiness to serve."[68]

Henri was a less able manager and farmer than his father or grandfather, and he also kept out of politics. "The desire to augment his revenues was not, in the management of his estates, his principal concern" was how his 1883 eulogist put it. One can scarcely imagine such a remark being made of his father or grandfather! The eulogy continued that the key to his character was "the extreme modesty which throughout his life was the essence of his character and which always prevented him from having any desire to play a public role at any level."[69] Yet if he did not augment the family wealth, neither did he squander it, and at his death he passed on the same patrimony that he had received. Indeed, changes in the inheritance law notwithstanding, the Villèles kept the Mourvilles-Basses estate intact during the period 1800–1870. The head of the family recognized his debt to siblings, and for their part they did not foreclose or demand immediate payment of what was owing to them. The Villèles illustrated what such family forbearance could achieve.

The three rough outline sketches in this chapter suggest factors affecting how marital links and bequests moved property among nobles. All three families examined seem to have increased their net worth substantially after 1800, especially the Raigecourts. Less wealthy nobles were nearer to the details of field and farmyard than aristocrats. The elder Villèle moved between Toulouse and Mourvilles-Basses and Campauliac, the bachelor Le Clerc de Fleurigny between Sens and Fleurigny. Their knowledge of local conditions and personalities was more finely grained than that of the Parisian Raigecourts or Choiseul-Praslins. Yet all nobles venerated the rural basis of their social position. One recent study has aptly advanced the idea that the economic outlook behind the management of large noble estates could be characterized as a continuation of a physiocratic outlook in an age of nascent capitalism.[70] Not all nobles were equally close to peasant life, as we saw in reviewing their residence patterns. Yet Parisian aristocrat and country gentleman alike had the same respect for land as the most valuable form of wealth, not necessarily in its cash value, but in its worth as the necessary sustenance of hierarchy in society.

4

Noble Wealth

Despite the best efforts of historians since World War II, it remained possible for a 1983 textbook survey of French nineteenth-century history to insist that the 1789 Revolution resulted from the constraints on a dynamic and capitalist bourgeoisie and to see the nineteenth century as the era of triumphal implantation of the power of that class.[1] Clearly, still more information and analysis is required to deepen our understanding of the alleged clash between, and knowledge of, those clusters of social power labeled, respectively, bourgeois and noble. The dichromatic contrast between bourgeois and noble may be seen as still too crude, since it does not distinguish between the interconnections of the financial, industrial, and commercial realms. How capitalist were the bourgeois, and how feudal the nobles? How rich were both sets of people, and what ranges of wealth were involved? While we are still far from satisfactory answers to these questions, we must survey what investigations have uncovered about the post-Revolutionary prosperity of *noblesse, titrés,* and aristocrats if we are to examine their political outlook and activities with any sense of their relative socioeconomic standings. Too much economic history of nineteenth-century France is written from aggregate statistics unconcerned with the collective attitudes towards economic activities among the population, especially the nobles. The historian is reduced to a rather thin harvest of individual biographies or studies of particular enterprises when he explores the motor relationship between social rank and economic dynamism in nineteenth-century France.[2]

Is it possible in even a crude way to equate the local presence of nobles with industrial activity? Almost all of the seventeen departments with the highest indices of industrial activity in 1836—the greatest number of forges and mines, of electors paying the business premises tax (*patente*), and that at its highest amounts—as calculated by comte

d'Angeville, lay to the north of the Saint-Malo/Geneva line.[3] Of the top
20 percent of departments with the most nobles, almost as many lay
below that line (Ille-et-Vilaine, Loire-Inférieure, Maine-et-Loire,
Gironde, Haute-Garonne, Hérault) as above it (Calvados, Orne, Loiret,
Seine, Seine-Inférieure, Seine-et-Oise, Somme, Pas-de-Calais). While
residence in one department was no obstacle to heavy investment in
another, there seems to be no grounds to suppose that at the national
level the mere presence of nobles stimulated industrial advance. Did the
more wealthy nobles, those with big landholdings who also, according
to Mlle Daumard, invested in the most secure and profitable holdings on
the stock exchange, show a special interest in capital investments?[4] In
the current state of knowledge those individuals are more easily generalized about than identified in any numbers.

THE WEALTH OF THE NOBLES

To the present day it is notoriously difficult to estimate accurately the
distribution of wealth among the different social categories in France,
and in their efforts to do so even for the recent past historians have been
perplexed. In the case of nobles and bourgeois included among the
wealthiest 5 percent of adult males between 1800 and 1848, the lists of
notables and voters for each department provide the best readily available source, at least until a complete analysis of the *mutation par décès*
and notarial records is completed. That enormous enterprise is still so
remote as not to detain us further now.

Yet, under the Empire the lists of notables were always partial and
inaccurate. The notable lists envisaged by the Constitution of the Year
VIII (the 600 highest taxed; and departmental lists of notables) excluded those in political bad odor, but they provided only a rough guide
to levels of wealth. The Seine department lists of the 30 highest taxed in
1806 and 1812 carried such indisputably aristocratic names as de
Luynes, Choiseul-Praslin, d'Harcourt, d'Aligre, Lefèvre d'Ormesson,
and Talleyrand-Périgord but no noble "representative of active capitalism," to use Bergeron's terminology for those whose wealthiest representative was a merchant goldsmith paying 27,431F in tax.[5] Those
aristocrats were from liberal families at the end of the Old Regime who
participated in capitalist ventures, with families not averse to inter-
marrying with the offspring of financiers. Their names are not those of
the petty service *noblesse*, scrimping to make ends meet and necessarily
restricting their ambitions to military service and estate agriculture.
Farther afield from Paris at the start of the new century we find less
celebrated patronyms on the lists (whose fortunes, estimated by officials, were given as rounded figures). For example, on the Indre electoral list of 1809 are d'Aubert, "student, landowner" with a fortune of

100,000F; a retired major, Depoix, a landowner with 400,000F; and Crubelier-Chandaire, former *trésorier de France* on the departmental general council, with a 1,000,000F.[6] The 1810 electoral colleges' lists of the arrondissements throughout the Empire were only a little more precise.[7] One recent examination of 100,000 notables identified the annual revenues from real estate of 44,079 residents of the 1792 departments that were under 1,000F (27 percent), 1,000–4,999F (58 percent), 5,000F–19,999F (13.9 percent), and 20,000F or above (less than 2 percent).[8] Nobles were scattered throughout this corpus but were most likely to be encountered in the top third.

Under the constitutional monarchies, particularly after 1820, the accuracy of reporting tax paid improved dramatically. The lists were open to genuine public scrutiny, and the opposition took a keen interest in their contents. As was intended, the lists systematically favored landed wealth and underrepresented commercial and industrial revenues. Electoral lists excluded minors, of course, and, what is more important, single or widowed women of rank who paid the land tax. The lists omitted adult nobles who did *not* pay the minimum tax required to figure among the electorate, which was 300F until 1830 and 200F thereafter.

Less often appreciated were the differences between departments when the 300F was expressed as a proportion of the net landed revenue (see appendix 1). The investigation by Allard from Carcassonne in the early 1830s, based on calculations from the July 1821 finance law shown in appendix 1, claimed that the range varied from a low point in the Seine (1,573F), followed by the Loiret (1,769F), and rose to the Ariège (3,260F) or Basses-Pyrénées (3,478F) in the eighty-sixth and last place of the French departments in 1830. He provided a theoretical example from his own department, the Aude, and Ariège, which was its neighbor, when he asked: "What would one say to an Ariègeois landowner who says that with my 2,150F revenue I am not able to be an elector, while my neighbor in the Aude, whose estate is not separated from mine save by a river or a path, is an elector with a revenue of 1310F?"[9] Despite all these weighty reservations about treating the electoral rolls as a standard or complete source on noble wealth, recent quantitative studies based on them reveal that the nobles were the wealthiest social category among Restoration and July Monarchy voters. Moreover, when examining the *patentés* in the electoral documentation of the 1830s, Beck concluded that noble participation in business was inconsequential.[10]

We are less well informed about the relative prosperity of the nobles as a part of the French population during the years of the Second Empire. The electoral system changed drastically; the rolls did not give the tax paid. It thus is hard to know whether a higher proportion of nobles paid the *patente* tax at ten-year intervals as time passed. The question is thorny because nobles, and especially noblewomen, still affected a ritual disdain for the attitudes of the businessman despite the natural attraction for cash. Writing from his impressions, Beau de Loménie thought a significant percentage of all nobles turned to business after 1875, and future research may sustain that intriguing suggestion. However, between 1800 and 1870 the new forms of industrial and commercial activity had less influence on the wealth of French nobles than, perhaps, at the end of the Old Regime and than in the twentieth century.

NOBLE ATTITUDES TOWARDS ECONOMIC ACTIVITY, 1770–1870

Nobles liked to imply that generosity, flair, and a chevaleresque disinclination to count the change characterized their attitude towards money. These quaint ideas suggesting that nobles managed their finances in an archaic way were popular with the readers of romantic novels and perhaps with those engaged in squandering their patrimony. If there was a collective archaicism, it was hardly in the direction of extravagance. The nineteenth-century noble could in fact invent and make shrewd investments; he could work for the state (from the army to the Post Office) or even run a suitable business, particularly the sale of agricultural produce. The noble was unwilling, however, to rub shoulders at the Café de la Bourse, to haggle over discounts, or to discuss deals freely with business equals. To nobles the "grocer mentality" was vulgarity personified, or so it was widely believed. Yet nobles were obviously eager, and indeed constrained, to secure sources of rising revenue.

The public hostility of nobles to business ethics and activities under the Old Regime was often commented upon, although research revealed that a minority of the Second Estate was not prevented by those ideas from entering into business and capitalist activities.[11] The indemnification records compiled from 1826 of losses suffered in Louisiana and Santo Domingo show something of the extent of overseas investment by nobles before the Revolution. The established view that nobles sought distinction, not lucre, and that they were opposed to the rise of capitalism during the eighteenth century has been vigorously attacked by Chaussinand-Nogaret, who went so far as to write that "among the economic elites the nobility, who in political terms represented one of the lines of resistance to kingly absolutism, stood in the first rank of the most dynamic minorities, and in terms of innovation and modernization nobles were among the leading activists." A little later he added that if nobles did not like to run family businesses, they were of qualitative importance "wherever the early forms of modern high capitalism were emerging. There they enjoyed a sort of monopoly."[12] More remains to be said on that score for the Old Regime. The political shocks of the Revolution slashed the profits of many pre-1789 enterprises or brought about their collapse. Emigration trampled down the earlier growth.

Historians of both the eighteenth and nineteenth centuries investigating the noble influences on the French economy have usually addressed one of two questions pointing in different directions: on the one hand, Who were the *noblesse* who wanted to engage or invest in commerce or industry? and on the other hand, Who were the businessmen who wanted to climb socially, either by stopping the activities that made them rich or, more unusually, by continuing them as *titrés*? The debate over the place of French nobles in business had gone on at least since the publication by abbé G.-F. Coyer of his *La Noblesse commerçante* of 1756. Much obscurity remains over the extent of the changed noble attitudes towards capitalist operations and trade during the nineteenth century. And how representative of businessmen was Ruinart, a wholesale merchant who from 1820 to 1828 was mayor of Rheims as well as a member of the departmental general council, or was he exceptional in his search for rank? Ennobled in 1817, he was made an honorary gentleman-in-waiting to the king and in 1825 became a vicomte, which was raised to a hereditary title in 1827 when he declared an annual revenue of 45,000F, drawn from land.[13]

In proportion to their numbers in the population, did nobles take advantage of openings in an expanding economy at least as frequently as commoners? This was perhaps the case, but the statement needs qualification. Among the vast majority of bourgeois, few had the capital and skill to invest in the stock market or to set up new companies. The difference between the economic attitudes of the titled and those of the untitled was not that between landowner and capitalist but rather one of behavior and ethos. It flattered the urban shopkeeper or clerk without a share to his name to feel akin to the freewheeling investor who made a fortune. Such an individual certainly knew that he was not rich. He could scarcely convince himself that he belonged to the same social family as marquis de Dreux-Brézé. Conversely, the marked regional differences in the average wealth of noble families made the poorer all the more likely to stress what conjoined them to the richer aristocracy: the intangibles of a shared sociocultural heritage. In the nineteenth century, then, a noble like Greffulhe, with great wealth made in finance, was respected and easily accepted by the antique aristocracy, but a member of the provincial *noblesse* who tried and failed in either finance, commerce, or industry was somehow reproved by his fellows. The loss by Henri de la Broise of nearly his entire personal fortune in the collapse of a mechanized weaving factory near Laval was interpreted by some of his neighbors as the result of a *dérogeance*.[14] The signpost that read *dérogeance* pointed only down the hill of society, not to the ascent.

NOBLES IN THE FRENCH ECONOMY

During the slowdown in industrial development brought about by political upheaval, inflation, and war from 1790 until the end of the Napoleonic adventure in 1814, only cotton spinning made much progress, as a result of strenuous French efforts to service European markets now unsupplied by Britain. Apparently, this was not attractive to aristocratic investment. In the aftermath of the emigration that had touched one in twenty of the former second estate, real property seemed by far the safest place to put funds. One might speak of a real psychological falling back on landownership. In the provinces, hoarding of noble cash was noted by sharp-eyed contemporaries such as the Toulouse merchant who in February 1800 said that the peculiarly long-lived local Jacobin ascendancy had prejudiced both commerce and industry by frightening the nobles into living with the utmost frugality and into clinging onto their money, so that it went out of circulation.[15] Moreover, the profits in agriculture appeared to justify this caution. In the present state of knowledge it seems wrong to speak of heavy aristocratic investment in capitalist enterprises under the First Empire. Recent experience made them wary. In its disruption of the national economy, the Revolution affected particularly the great seaports and shipowners. In the collapse of the old credit mechanisms, many aristocrats lost investments, and so did members of the provincial *noblesse* with interests in the Atlantic trade in places like Nantes, La Rochelle, and Bordeaux. Landed nobles were generally more fortunate than the leading Old Regime businessmen, many of whom were ruined and whose trade did not survive the chaos. The exceptions were those in finance.

The old business elite was largely replaced by men with new fortunes made from speculation, especially in real estate. Some of those with new fortunes became nobles after 1810. Louis Bergeron's study of the Parisian bankers, businessmen, and manufacturers at the turn of the century informs us about fabulously wealthy men who themselves, or whose sons, became *titrés*, among them Greffulhe (comte, 1818), Seillière (baron, 1814), and Delessert (baron, 1810).[16]

The Greffulhe family represents a particularly fascinating social trajectory for the subject concerning us as we examine the economic attitudes and permeability of rich bourgeois and nobles from the eighteenth and nineteenth centuries. A Greffulhe (pronounced *Greffeuille*, and there was no particle in the name) provided Proust with the model for his character Guermantes, and he can be seen in the Paul Nadar photograph, staring into the camera with cool condescension.[17] The Greffulhes originated in Languedoc, but the banker Louis at the root of the family rise to fortune was born in Geneva. His second wife was noble, Mlle Randon de Pully, of a family from Languedoc with various branches, all of which had prospered in the eighteenth-century financial system. Her father served throughout the Revolution (he was a divisional general in March 1793) and became a comte under the Bourbons in January 1815. Louis Greffulhe married her in London on 14 October 1793 and found the new family links highly useful. His son and heir Jean-Henri-Louis was born of his first marriage in Amsterdam in 1764. Jean-Henri-Louis already turned aside from the ruthless sharp dealing that had made his father so wealthy. He was mayor of his commune in the Seine-et-Marne and became a peer of France in 1818. He received almost 50,000F indemnity in the Emigrés' Billion for property mostly located in the Var. He married Mlle Vintimille du Lac in 1811, the year after his father's death. Their eldest son, Louis-Charles, born in Rouen in 1814, also sat as a peer of France and married into a ducal house, the La Rochefoucauld d'Estissac. In turn his son, Henri-Jules-Charles-Emmanuel, born in Paris in 1848, was the man whom Proust idolized. This brief outline of family history shows the eighteenth-century movement through Protestant commoner and commercial Europe to a nineteenth-century focus on high decorative office and luxurious living in Paris.[18]

The Seillière family, originally from eastern France (Meuse), showed a parallel rise from banking and business to status. They included in the nineteenth century a member of the national Conseil général des manufactures, an advisory council on industrialization; a banker; and the president of the Salt Company of Eastern France. More than three-fourths of the descendants of the commoner couple who founded the lineage married nobles over the next two generations, with three weddings to commoners (14 percent) and two bachelors (9.5 percent). In Bergeron's consideration of "the remodeling of the French economic space" during the early years of the nineteenth century, when the Parisian concentration of capital and entrepreneurs was obvious, more even than the emergence of Swiss and Protestants into the Haute-Banque, so also was the absence or feebleness of those Old Regime business nobles identified by Guy Richard.[19] Their families did not—with a few obvious exceptions, such as the Solages family near Albi or the Wendel in Alsace—continue on the trajectory of commercial and industrial ventures started before the Revolution. The financiers and bankers showed most ability to prosper and to blend into the greatest families in the court aristocracy, just as they had done before the Revolution.

In 1814 the nobles began insistently to pursue the search for a political response to the economic needs of their despoiled members. The most straightforward demand was for indemnification of émigrés whose former property had been sold. At the Chamber of Peers on 3 December 1814 *maréchal* duc de Tarento suggested an annual indemnity payment of 12 million francs to compensate those émigrés whose property had been auctioned off. This pleasing prospect was obviously impractical in the tight postwar financial situation. A decade later the Villèle ministry tried to end continuing resentment over the losses caused by fidelity to the Bourbons—or simple bad luck—by introducing the celebrated Emigrés' Billion project. The political storm of opposition to a measure that had the laudable aim of assuaging bitterness among the victims of Revolutionary confiscation seemed to the *noblesse* convincing proof of liberal malevolence towards them. The funds actually paid out were used largely for the rental of urban real estate. In any event, the Emigrés' Billion did not radically alter the collective economic situation of nobles, although it provided compensation for individuals.

With the general peace from 1815 to mid-century, France resumed the economic growth so brutally stopped by the upheaval of the Revolution. Complaisant governments looked benignly on the search for profits by the political class that made up the electorate. Roads, canals, and stone and iron bridges yielded good profits at first, and from the 1830s the railroads became important motors of development. There were also opportunities abroad in which to invest as Algeria was taken over. Economic historians have pointed out how under the July Monarchy even agriculture became more businesslike, with an emphasis on lands as a commodity rather than an heirloom, stress on grain as a cash crop, and an indifference to customary and communal rights that were vestiges of another age. Nobles with the security of large estates were in a position where they too could dip into alternative sources of wealth with other shrewd investors.

Over the whole process of French economic growth, however, lay the pall of an inadequate supply of risk capital, as Fohlen and others have argued, which was only resolved with the rise of a banking system that combined the innumerable deposits of small savers into the large units of capital required for major investments. In 1847 the first bank notes of under 500F were circulated. During the Second Empire, with the vulgarization *strictu sensu* of banking, giant strides were made, but not by nobles. If nobles had a leading place in the old court capitalism, they were slower to find a niche in the new demotic capitalism of the nineteenth century. During the fifty years after 1800, nobles increased in per capita worth at a faster rate than other large categories in French society even as they fell in their absolute numbers. After 1850 their wealth was not directed into new investments on a sufficient scale to keep their favored position as their numbers fell relative to the number of commoners with large and growing fortunes.

In the remainder of this chapter I touch on noble economic activity beyond that based on land. Of course, to separate noble economic activity from agriculture is artificial, since landed wealth lay behind almost all nineteenth-century nobles who ventured into other economic realms. This is well exemplified by the liberal aristocrat duc de La Rochefoucauld Liancourt, the former grand master of the wardrobe, knight of the order of the Holy Spirit in 1786, and as close to being a friend of Louis XVI as a cautious king may permit a courtier to be, who found himself in 1802 after his return from emigration plowing up the parkland around his château and introducing English equipment from Suffolk to increase crop yields. He was also involved in the production of carding machines, currying leather, and wire-drawing machines, and in 1806 he was named inspector general of the Ecole des arts et métiers. He later became a member of the Conseil général des manufactures, and in 1818 he joined with baron Delessert in setting up the caisse d'epargne before being stripped of his numerous charitable, local, and other appointments in 1823 as punishment for his liberalism. In 1826 he composed the *Statistique industrielle du canton de Creil*. In 1827 his coffin was carried by pupils of the Châlons Ecole des arts et métiers; indeed, they dropped it during a scuffle with police. This great liberal seigneur and *agronome* of the Old Regime had thus shown after the Revolution an intense interest in new ways of making money and of assuaging poverty by providing employment. In his last writings he was at pains to underline that industrial innovations did no harm to agriculture but actually permitted thrifty workers to buy small allotments where their wives could cultivate food. Recent studies of La Rochefoucauld Liancourt have cautioned against some of the more enthusiastic and partisan contemporary praise, but they depict him as a man of practical intelligence who achieved a modicum of success.[20] However, the revenue from his estates was always the real source of his affluence.

The most evident place to begin to search for revenue over and above land produce often lay close to the family château. Le Tellier de Souvré, marquis de Louvois and peer of France, constructed in his château park at Ancy Le Franc (Yonne) blast furnaces to produce high-quality iron, as well as a flour mill and a sawmill. He was known for a keen interest in railway technology, and in 1837 he took a patent on a method of navigating rivers at low water. Describing these achievements, an admiring baron Chaillou des Barres stressed the contrast between the "almost feudal manor house" and the great lord ("if such there are any left"), who in the nineteenth century applied his thought, his leisure, and a part of his fortune to "the extension of social riches and of the well-being of all."[21]

Manufacturing initiatives that combined familial resources with seigneurial responsibilities were eminently respectable. Their localism and proprietary aspects of being linked to an estate made them very different from the predatory search for profit of mature capitalism. The marquis d'Hautpoul recalled his pleasure at combining the resources of his estates and the work provided for women and children of the neighborhood when he established in 1829 at Saint-Papoul (Aude) "a factory of common earthenware, yellow and brown, which would retail easily because its products were to be used by the lower class."[22] In the 1850s Alfred de Vigny marketed *eau de vie* from his properties, and other nobles dabbled in similar ways.

Such additional revenues among nobles were probably as important as salaries or dividends received. In the provinces during the first half of the century only rarely were investments other than in property to exceed 5 percent of the total value of the largest noble patrimonies. This seems to have been the norm. In Mayenne the rise has been calculated as from 3.1 percent to 4.7 percent between 1800 and 1870.[23] The generalization is less true of Paris, where northern nobles tended to establish their principal residences. They found more opportunities for placing the wealth accumulated from successful agriculture. The 1807 Commercial Code regularized the joint stock company and created the Société anonyme. Such vehicles made it easier for nobles to invest liquidity indirectly through the family notary. Probably the Parisian nobles (and perhaps those in more economically innovative cities) were always in advance of somnolent provincial cousins, particularly in the south. Much more study is needed to settle this point. The most reliable statistical source for measuring the proportions of real property to other forms of noble investment would be a large-scale use of the *mutations par décès* registers, although many studies already undertaken did not distinguish nobles as a separate category in the general population.[24] This prevented observation of the difference in wealth levels between nobles and non-nobles and left untroubled the Marxist paradigm of social change.

In the absence of large-scale statistics, we must retreat to some exceptions: better-known nobles whose property other than real estate (*mobilier*) exceeded the 5 percent here suggested as the mean. The Aligre fortunes could perhaps be traced in British bank archives. Etienne-François, who had long presided over the Parlement of Paris, emigrated in 1789, having already transferred funds to English banks. Later he returned to the Continent and died at Brunswick in Germany in 1798, leaving what was described by contemporaries as "a colossal fortune which his extreme avarice prevented him from enjoying." His son Charles (1770–1847), who entered into this inheritance after 18 brumaire, was Princess Murat's chamberlain and from 1803 to 1820 a member of the Seine general council. The Restoration made him a peer.[25]

More detailed information has been amassed on how funds were protected by foreign bankers for baron Auget de Montyon, the celebrated miserly philanthropist and former intendant of Auvergne, Provence, and La Rochelle who died in 1820. He left a giant fortune of almost 7 million francs to various academies and the hospitals of Paris. Before the Revolution he had owned considerable estates close to Meaux (Seine-et-Marne), and until 1793 he continued to purchase new properties with *assignats* as he steadily expanded his estates. He made numerous loans to other nobles, although he suffered the misfortune that many of these were repaid in devalued *assignats*. He also had the foresight to transfer very large sums of money to foreign bankers. This permitted him to continue to invest from the comparative safety of a village near the Swiss border, but he was forced into definitive emigration and was officially declared an émigré in February 1793. He lent large sums of money in Switzerland, which provided a revenue but also caused a lot of litigation over repayments. Late to emigrate, he was also late to return, arriving after Louis XVIII in 1814. He was given a posthumous award of 815,292F in the Emigres' Billion. Inside France his properties, investments, and the indemnity made up a total of 3,185,102F, but his *foreign* assets were still more considerable, attesting to his shrewd management of funds while in London exile. His executors reported the following assets:

England	32.58%
Lubeck	Insignificant
Netherlands, Russia, Louisiana	6.80%
Saxony, Prussia	1.57%
Switzerland	0.90%
Tuscany	2.40%
United States	8.89%

Auget de Montyon was extremely careful in the management of his wealth, personally frugal to the point of tight-fistedness and industrious in watching over all of his interests. The loss of his government positions brought about by the fall of the Old Regime, the confiscation of his patrimony, and his exile first to Switzerland and then to England seem if anything to have stimulated him into still more financial exertions. Upon his return to France he repossessed some scraps of his family property that had not been sold and wistfully surveyed the château that he loved so much but would never regain, even though he engaged a local notary to investigate whether it could be repurchased. He was a bachelor and produced no heir to his fortune, which was all to the advantage of the poor and the sick of Paris.[26]

The governor of Vincennes château under the Restoration, marquis de Roux de Puivert, son of an Old Regime judge of the Parlement of Toulouse, held property in the Aude and Dordogne, various state bonds, investments in the insurance companies that attracted many nobles, and a share in a company that constructed iron ships. Some 63 percent of his income was drawn from property, but the remainder came from investments, so that his concerns were far from exclusively those of the soldier and landowner.[27]

Later in the century we find some other examples of the balance between land and other investments in noble fortunes. The 1853 share-out of the property of Numance de Girardin, a former cavalry officer, revealed that of a total of 843,942F, 6.5 percent was in land, 2.3 percent in houses, 54.5 percent in loans and other properties, and 36.5 percent in investments in railways, coal mines, and above all gaslight (217,600F).[28] The share-out of the duchesse de Maillé's property in 1852 revealed a different configuration. Of a total of 2,476,828F, 45.6 percent was in land, 9.9 percent in houses, 20 percent in loans and other properties, 17 percent unpaid legacies owing from her late husband's estate, 6.64 percent in French and American bonds, and only 0.2 percent in commercial investments, in her case in the new form of urban transport, omnibuses.[29] Two years later a noble spinster in much less opulent circumstances left her nephew in Toulouse an inheritance of 75,762F, of which 12 percent was in land, 46 percent in a house in the best district of Toulouse, 33 percent in loans and interest, and 8.2 percent in furnishings.[30] The impression from a limited sample of ninety-three wills is that the number of Parisian nobles who held interests on the stock exchange or who put funds into banking probably increased during the century. However, the transfer of liquid assets to relatives often took place before death. At least one historian has suggested that the process is better traced in marriage contracts than in legacies.[31]

Although the *majorats sur demande* of the Restoration established the entailments of their new titles on land, real estate, and *rentes*, a few of them gave information about other economic activiites. Among the *noblesse* were T. G. C. Boissel de Monville, the political economist from a Norman family of the robe who owned a sheet manufactory in Elbeuf, and Riquet de Caraman, with two soap factories in Marseilles worth 121,422F (which included the equipment). Cazin de Honinchun had a quarter-share of the mines and glassworks of Hardinhem, while Posuel de Verneaux held forges at Varennes. Like Bellet de Saint Trivier, he also had shares in the Givors Canal, near Lyon, which although short made a good profit on coal, iron, and glass transportation. Mme Camus de Martroy had an interest in the Littry coal mines near Caen, worth an average return annually of 15,000F, which was mentioned as a component of her husband's declared revenue. Among commoners who were given new titles, one owned a third of the Poullaouen mines, near Carhaix in the Finistère, and another had a factory producing bathtubs near Epinal, with an annual revenue of 15,000F, as the largest component of an income that included 10,000F in 5 percent *rentes*.[32] Marriages also forged new links between old lineages and new money, like that of Choiseul with Fraulein Schickler, daughter of a wealthy Prussian magnate.

The nineteenth century thus saw an economic education of nobles that, like that for France in general, was slow and uneven but irreversible. What was rare was any willingness to *advertise* financial expertise, and it was even rarer to display commercial skills. The slave-trader Du Fou, the former mayor of Nantes (1813–15; 1815–16), descended from a family of Breton *noblesse,* was a distinct oddity when he gave his profession on the 1820 electoral list as "comte, wholesale merchant," in that order. He paid 3,152F 36 tax in total, which placed him among the wealthiest 10 percent of electors in France. The child of nobles, in 1791 he married a commoner, by whom he had five children. His offspring married nobles, each one with the handsome dowry of 120,000F. He also became a business associate of his own father-in-law's. Du Fou had acquired *biens nationaux* during the Revolution but was arrested in 1793. His departure from endogamy and his excursion into business followed that of his father, who in 1762 had married the daughter of a rich merchant. Du Fou was named a hereditary comte in October 1817. One of his sons became a consul at Bremen but also a merchant, while one daughter married a prefect of the Maine-et-Loire and another, an officer and municipal official. Here we see an individual strategy, that of Du Fou and his father, that enriched a family but did not divert it from its noble trajectory.[33] In notarized wills, marriage contracts, leases, sales, the *partages* of family property, and other documents there are sufficient indicators to permit the historian to see favored investments for nobles. Some brief observations are made here on metallurgy, glassmaking, transportation, and insurance, which especially attracted them.

TEXTILES

There was a striking absence of noble holdings in the flourishing textile business of nineteenth-century Paris, which has been described as the cotton capital of France because of the number of looms in operation under the First Empire in response to the embargo of the Continental Decrees. However there was a considerable noble activity in textiles in the Norman wool and cotton business, as we know from Richard's study of families in the first half of the nineteenth century of whom two-thirds had no links with commerce before the Revolution.[34] Twenty-three of sixty-four enterprises were in the valley of the Andelle, located at the intersection of the commercial zones of Rouen and Paris. Richard looked into the cases of "nobles converted to industry" compared with "bourgeois converted to industry before ennoblement" and deduced that a significant number of *noblesse* had turned to cloth production. There seem to be no other examples of such a decisive regional *engouement* for industry, although a number of nobles were interested in metal production.

METALLURGY

The pre-Revolutionary *noblesse*'s metallurgical investments were mostly small ironworks on properties with mines, woods, and watercourses. The Old Regime aristocratic investors in Le Creusot who had owned shares of 2,500 livres each were still untypical even after the Revolution. Miners and metalworkers on the noble estates usually found most of their livelihood in local agriculture or even the seigneurial estate. The metal production was subsumed under other peasant activities. The noble owners of the ironworks were prone to see them as a seigneurial adjunct to their estate and took scant interest in improving scientific technology or making a real effort to increase profits.[35] In part that was a natural consequence of the small scale of operations. As in other small businesses, the noble ironmaster could not concentrate sufficient resources to attempt research. The Revolution had not changed the situation of the small estate forges which had little or no rapport with the Paris Ecole des mines, and everywhere at that level technical advance was sluggish.

François-Godefroy de Saincthorent, a rich member of the *noblesse* who had been a deputy in the Conseil des Cinq-Cents, the political assembly created by the constitution of the year III (1795) and dissolved by the 18 brumaire coup in 1799, before his nomination as the Aveyron's first prefect (1800–1808), was unusual among his local fellows in his passion for factories, blast furnaces, and watercourses, an eccentricity described by local critics as his "minérogamie," almost as odd as his egalitarian outlook.[36] The ironworks near Bourges belonging to the de Vogué family was equally unusual in its search to improve methods. Generally the rural nobility perpetuated a semiartisanal production of "sylvopastoral" Catalan forges along the Pyrenees, which used local charcoal and ores like those from the open mine of marquis d'Angosse, peer of France, at Louvie (Hautes-Pyrénées). Nobles saw nothing peculiar in this, since neighboring commoner ironmasters were equally sunk in routine. The number of traditional Catalan forges along the Pyrenees increased from forty-three to fifty-seven between 1818 and 1848. The largest were in the hands of *noblesse* families such as the Saint-Jean de Pointis, the Astriés, the Gudanes, and the Thonnel d'Orgeix.[37] In the center of France there was a similar noble presence: in the 1820s Mme d'Osmond owned a furnace at Saint-Baudel, and Mme de Charost had five forges in the Cher.[38] Nowhere, however, did nobles take a lead in improving an industry in which they were, at first glance, well represented.

By the 1870s nobles were dropping out of the national iron industry. In the Cher the withdrawal was marked from earlier noble-owned ironworks at Mazières, Bigny, Chateauneuf, Mareuil, and Thaumiers.[39] At Chailland (Mayenne) the marquis de Chavagnac bought an ironworks in 1834 from a count at the Swedish Legation in Paris for 1,400,000F, which constituted the bulk of his unusually substantial payment from the Emigrés' Billion (his was the sixth largest award in the nation). He showed himself a bold exception by not following the usual tendency to place the money in real estate, land, or government bonds. Unfortunately for him, this venture turned out to be too risky. The Chailland works were persistently weakened by the same flaw as other smaller operations: dependence on charcoal. The ironworks survived for thirty years before its final closure, but it swallowed up de Chavagnac's fortune.[40]

In the Isère the Marcieu family regained in 1802 a blast furnace that had been confiscated during the Revolution, but despite their high hopes, it did not flourish under the marquis's poor management. Bad accounting, as well as high fuel costs, meant that the Marcieus did not achieve the economies of scale and technical efficiency needed to make the enterprise profitable. The business crisis of 1839 shook the family finances. Despite the introduction of improved bookkeeping in the 1850s, the last pouring took place in 1863, and eleven years later marquis Gaston de Marcieu sold the remaining mineral rights in his possession to the Schneider Company of Le Creusot.[41] Scattered evidence from different parts of France demonstrated continuing noble interest in metallurgy, but the enterprises were too small and cautious to achieve big success. The cheap imports allowed by the 1860 treaty with Great Britain eliminated a number of marginal producers struggling with the high costs of fuel and ores.

The decline of the small "sylvopastoral" ironworks brings into glaring contrast those few nobles engaged in large-scale industrial and capitalist operations. One outstanding titled entrepreneurial family of Lorraine, the Wendels, sprang from origins in the Low Countries.[42] Their forges prospered in eighteenth-century Lorraine, where they purchased a seigneury. During the early Revolution they stayed by the forges and did not emigrate, but after the execution for royalism of one of the family at Metz in 1793, the men left for Germany and Austria. Despite the prodigious efforts of the dowager Wendel to safeguard the ironworks by making them indispensable to the republican war effort, they were put up for sale, but in 1803 through a straw man (in the event a wholesale merchant of Metz) François de Wendel again took control of the forges. François profited from the Empire's demand for war materials, and the growing labor force indicated that the momentum built up during the war was carried over into the Restoration. In 1811 there were 180 workers, by 1820 some 2,000, and by 1825 about 3,000. In loose principle François, like most nobles, was royalist, but like so many others in 1807, he agreed to serve the Emperor as mayor of the village where his seigneury was located (Hayange), became a general councilor in 1808, and during the Hundred Days supplied the imperial armies with shells.

The Wendels were cosmopolitan in outlook, habitually speaking German with their workmen. They looked overseas to Britain for ideas on industrial innovation. In 1816 François visited Wales to examine metallurgical factories, and he lured some workers back to France. Charles, his son and successor, made a similar trip in the 1840s.[43] The Wendels were proud of their nobility and married into respectable *noblesse* families. Charles ran his forges with real attention to the operative's welfare; under the Second Empire he was a deputy. His son Henri de Wendel graduated in 1865 from the Paris Ecole centrale, an institution with the most advanced engineering training of the time. Despite his emigration and his genteel symbolic royalism, François seems to have been snubbed by the local upper crust, while Charles was too engrossed in his factories and business affairs to investigate how well he was regarded by his peers. The Wendels were nobles by inclination and in fact, but in a manner that made their fellows uneasy.

MINING

Delving into the earth of one's estate had long been acceptable to nobles. Baron du Bord, member of the Drôme general council, had quarries in the Montélimar arrondissement employing more than two hundred workers whence were transported by rail the stones used to pave the main street in Lyons during the Second Empire.[44] More widespread than stone or marble quarries were those of coal, sometimes associated with related metal industries. Such property was vulnerable to confiscation during the Revolution. As soon as he returned from emigration under Napoleon the marquis d'Osmond laid claim to his pre-Revolutionary ownership of considerable coal fields in the Loire estimated at sixty-eight square kilometers in 1786. His claims were upheld, and public authority aided him in reasserting his rights, but these were contested by the local people. In 1815 his agents were harassed by a demonstration of women led by the local curate and with the connivance of the tax collector. Local landowners also resisted mining activities. Doubtless the marquis felt relieved when he retreated from the most exposed position by relinquishing his rights to a new company called the Compagnie des mines de Roche-la-Molière. In return for a cash settlement of 132,000F and a share in the new company, in 1820 Osmond gave up any direct activity in the Loire coal fields. The company was then controlled by a former subprefect, a baron of the Empire disgraced for rallying during the Hundred Days who subsequently trained as an engineer: Jean-Jacques Baude.[45]

Similarly, in the Anzin coal company noble directors such as the duc d'Aremberg and the vicomte de Hocquart made only minor decisions, and after the withdrawal from management of the elderly and cautious vicomte Desandrouin in 1817 the other nobles, who constituted a quarter of the shareholders, were inactive in running the company. In 1833 more than a quarter of the shares were in the hands of nobles, among them Mme Mayneaud de Pancemont with 40,000F revenue in 1825 from her 1 12/19 share in the Vieux Condé shaft.[46] The company increased profits and was at the root of the prosperity of various families, but nobles such as Louis-Alexandre-César Taffin de Givency, for example, simply enjoyed their revenues without busying themselves about the company's management.[47]

The noble family whose long involvement in coal mining is perhaps best known is that of the Solages. Before the Revolution they owned the coal mines at Carmaux, 92 kilometers from Toulouse, and in 1810 the vicomte François-Gabriel de Solages set up the Compagnie des Solages with forty-eight shares divided among his two sons and three daughters. By the 1830s Achille de Solages realized the importance of a railway to ease transportation difficulties for the coal, and in March 1833 he was attempting to have a railway link Carmaux and Albi.[48] At the transfer of the company from a family property to a capitalized company in 1853 there were fifteen owners, the descendants of the original six, all noble, with a predominance of women. As the historian of Carmaux has pointed out, they had little to do with operations but had a keen interest in the maximum income from the property.[49] There was inadequate reinvestment or concern with capitalist enterprise. Administrators were selected on the basis of inheritance. After 1854, when the company had gone public, the head office was moved to Paris, nobles and commoners bought stocks, deputies were named to the board of directors, and the Solages became few among the stockholders. Only when the company was taken out of noble hands, despite the good endeavors by some of the family, was the mine managed more efficiently. Indeed, one may generalize that in the second half of the nineteenth century, when the demand for fossil fuel was advancing by leaps and bounds, nobles lost their prominent and leading role in the coal industry.

A number of Paris aristocrats invested in the gas lighting of Paris, which was a side product of the coal business. In August 1841 an engineer, Selligue, set up a company for the lighting by gas of Batignolles until 1863 that included among its shareholders (with limited liability) baron de Girardin, baron de Montmorency, marquis de Boissy, marquis de Tilière, and the comte de Tilière, as well as two commoners, an *avocat* from Paris and a Lyon landowner. The capital was 410,000F, of which more than two-thirds had come from the noblemen. In 1842 the same engineer set up a company in Paris, with head offices on the avenue de Clichy, to light Batignolles, Monceaux, Montmartre, and surrounding communes. Marquis de Boissy, peer of France and a member of the Cher general council, lent the sum of 160,000F at 5.25 percent.[50]

GLASS MANUFACTURE

The manufacture of glass continued to attract noble investment during the nineteenth century, less because of any romanticism about *gentilshommes verriers* than because of the linkage of bottles to vineyards. One such investor was the vicomte who possessed shares in not only the Carmaux coal mines discussed above and ironworks but also a glassworks on the grounds of his château at Blaye-les-Mines (Tarn). In 1810–11 the properties generated an annual revenue estimated at 20,000–60,000F.[51] In 1862 the glassworks was sold to Ferdinand de Rességuier. By the last third of the nineteenth century the Solages had essentially withdrawn from the more commercial demands of being active in the glass business to the station of simply owning shares in the Carmaux coal mines and being at the pinnacle of local society.[52]

TRANSPORTATION

Nineteenth-century nobles enthusiastically took part in the biggest single capitalist venture in France: the modernization of the transportation system. After Napoleon's fall the country was left with the dilapidated Old Regime roads, neglected for more than a quarter-century. Repairing and extending the network, lengthening the canals, and undertaking the laying down of national railroads (a task that took forty years) involved colossal investments but promised enviably generous profits. The possibility of garnering wealth from transportation and communications excited astute nobles as much as it did the Saint Simoniens. The ducs de Doudeauville and Fitzjames and the vicomte de Chaptal put money into canal construction under the Restoration. Marquis de Louvois invested heavily in railways and canals. Particular nobles developed an almost seigneurial interest in branch lines. Baron de Damas invested in the Fougères-Vitré line, marquis de Contades in that of Briouze-Macé, and Charles de Wendel had influence with the Eastern Railway Company, which was profitable for his forges. An 1844 pamphlet underlined noble involvement in transportation:

> Take two or three deputies, two or three peers of the realm; these are absolutely indispensable, since the best way to make sure of operating within the law is to enlist the support of those who make it. Add to these about fifteen administrators, preferably titled, because the nobility has never enjoyed so much prestige as it has since it lost its privileges; take an advertisement somewhere on the fourth page of various newspapers since the fourth page is always devoted to financial news, which is read by everyone, and which best sums up the spirit of the age—and you will have as much money as you want.[53]

Comte de Clermont-Tonnerre, son of a former student of the Ecole polytechnique and equerry to Joseph Bonaparte, as a member of the general council of the Eure agitated for a railway line between Beauvais and Amiens. In 1866 he published a pamphlet on the importance of this "chemin de fer d'intérêt local."[54] Not all noble investment in railways was limited to France: an adventuresome member of the Machault d'Arnouville family included in his portfolio obligations on the Egyptian viceroy, shares in the Orléans railway as well as in that of southern Austria, and investments in the Crédit Foncier.[55]

INSURANCE

In eighteenth-century France there was a growing knowledge of the actuarial principles behind the tontines, and the first insurance companies were set up against fire, hail, and death. The Revolution not only saw the collapse of the existing companies but enunciated a noisy disapproval of the substitution of (counterrevolutionary) calculation for the warm fervor of republican humanitarianism.[56] With the Bourbon Restoration there was a renewed impulse to set up insurance companies, starting most notably with a Parisian mutual company authorized against fire in 1816. Vicomte Pinon, comte Butler, and the marquis de Gontaut-Biron were the leading figures. In the following year the former émigré Breton noble Auguste-Casimir de Gourcuff, who had made a close investigation of the English insurance business, was associated with the foundation of a maritime, fire, and life assurances company.[57] The movement gained momentum. Nobles invested in the insurance companies of the 1820s and 1830s: the Soleil-Incendie (1829), the Fraternelle Parisienne (1837), the Etoile, and the Concorde, or such provincial enterprises as the Toulouse company against hail (1826) or the Dijon fire insurance company.[58] In 1836 Alfred Potier de Courcy translated Francis Baily's *The Doctrine of Life Annuities and Assurances . . . Investigated,* an earnest of his fascination with the mathematical theories of probability that lay behind the financing of the insurance business. His curiosity about this led him to produce a flood of publications, especially after 1860.[59]

While it would be too much to say that nobles dominated the insurance business, they were certainly quick to see its lucrative possibilities. Alphonse Roullet de la Bouillerie (known as baron because his father had received a nonhereditary title in May 1830) presided over a board of directors of the Providence Fire Insurance Company in the second year of its existence, 1839. Fellow directors included such nobles as the marquis de Dreux-Brézé, the duc de Mirepoix, the marquis de la Rochejaquelein, and a more recent addition to the elite, the marquis de Pastoret. As befitted the descendant of Norman tax collectors who numbered in their recent lineage a baron of the Empire who became an ultra deputy in the Sarthe and a peer of France in 1827, Alphonse de la Bouillerie was a success: in 1843 he became president of the Paris-based consortium of insurance company directors.[60] By 1847 the same company, with offices at 92, rue Richelieu, had a board of directors presided over by vicomte de Vaufreland, a former *avocat général,* as well as a duc (Mirepoix), two marquis (Barthélemy and Pastoret), four comtes (Hauterive, Pontgibaud, Biencourt, and Aubespin), two vicomtes (Saint-Priest and de l'Espine), two barons (Dudon and Frémiot), and two particles (de Bousquet and de Raineville). The other two individuals were MM. Roux and Arthaud-Beaufort.[61] In 1847 the Compagnie française du Phénix included on its board of directors the son of an artillery sergeant and peer of France baron Gabriel Neigre, Joly de Bammeville, comte de Montesquiou, Anatole de Montesquiou, and comte Dumanoir.[62]

Under the Second Empire more than half of the Imperial Insurance Company's eleven-member board were nobles: the duc d'Albuféra, baron de Bonnemains, marquis de Chaumont-Quitry, the duc de Galliéra, comte Frédérick de Lagrange, marquis de Talhouet, and the duc de Valmy.[63] Doubtless all these individuals represent the long-established fondness for *rentes viagères* in noble families' financial practice, together with the vivifying experiments by eighteenth-century financiers. Their activities were made possible by growing state benevolence towards their activities, especially under the Second Empire. If in 1819–20 insurances against fire emerged from under a cloud of official suspicion, again in 1864–65 there was a similar spurt of insurance against accidents. In 1865 a General Security Company against accidents was founded with fixed premiums; senator-baron Brenier presided over the board of directors, and comte Ferdinand de Lasteyrie, vicomte de Léautaud, comte Léopold Le Hon (deputy for the Ain department), vicomte de Villiers, and MM. Le Pelletier de Saint-Rémy (an administrator of the Colonial Bank), Besnier de la Potonerie, and others served with him.[64] The relative security of return and low risk doubtless attracted investors who wanted a steady and anxiety-free income. Like government bond issues, insurance demanded of investors no unseemly fiscal agility nor unremitting attention if managed in a conservative way. Moreover, insurance was concerned with the kinds of properties held by nobles.

NOBLES AND PROFESSIONS

Collective attitudes towards labor and economic activity have fascinated historians since the days of Sombart and Tawney, and work and entrepreneurial attitudes are at least as important as the availability of skills, materials, and capital in explaining economic success or failure. Nineteenth-century nobles have frequently been seen as somehow embodying Catholic, monarchical, and landed values at variance with Judeo-Protestant, egalitarian, industrial, and commercial ones. Some writers have seen the contrast in political alignments between liberals and Legitimists. An honor roll call of nearly one hundred individuals involved in the 1832 adventure of the duchesse de Berry when she tried to precipitate a Legitimist restoration listed the professions of those implicated: baron de Chaulieu, former prefect of the Finistère and the Loire; chevalier de Léspinois, a former subprefect; the vicomte de Suleau, a former *conseiller d'état;* vicomte de Puységur, a former *auditeur* at the Council of State; comte de Jouffroi, a former magistrate. The soldiers included comte de Grive, former general of the Jura national guard; comte Curial, who had served in the artillery during the Algerian campaign; marquis de Lentilhac, a General staff officer; and the chevalier de Forceville, a former bodyguard of the king. Among these Legitimist paladins only one wholesale merchant (*négociant*) was listed, with the commoner name of Lahirigoyen.[65] The assumption that business and moneymaking were, if not despicable, at the least sordid "bourgeois" pastimes, derided in literature from M. Jourdain to Ubu-Roi, was not restricted to the literati but was frequently found among, if

TABLE 8. Avowed Professions of Nobles, 1816–1870

Profession	Restoration[a]		1866[b]		1854–70[c]	
	Number	%	Number	%	Number	%
Agriculture	15	4.3	16	2.4	16	7.5
Town/village worker	4	1.1	—	—	—	—
Commerce/manufacture	8	2.3	5	0.7	5	2.3
Central administration	42	11.9	122	18.4	43	19.7
Local administration	24	6.8	130	19.6	34	15.9
Judiciary	42	11.9	68	10.3	17	7.9
Military	145	41.0	113	17.1	79	37.0
Government	14	3.9	60	9.1	8	3.7
Court	12	3.4	—	—	1	0.4
Liberal professions	20	5.7	116	17.5	9	4.2
Clergy	1	0.3	27	4.1	—	—
Deputies	25	7.1	—	—	1	0.4
Miscellaneous			3	0.4		
Total	352		660		213	

[a]AN BB²⁹778–84. This includes past professions (sometimes plural) by candidates for *majorats sur demande*: 218 individuals.

[b]Antoine Bachelin-Deflorenne, *Etat présent de la noblesse française, contenant le dictionnaire de la noblesse contemporaine . . . 1866* (Paris, 1866).

[c]Sample of 213 taken from Révérend.

not actually derived from, the nobles. At least until the 1870s and perhaps afterwards, noble reticence to take up wholeheartedly commerce and industry fettered French entrepreneurialism.

As France moved slowly from a primarily agricultural economy to a more diversified one, the demand for a host of new abilities increased. In practical terms the insistent question for any noble family, particularly the younger sons, was what professions were suitable for those unable to live from the produce of the family estate. This makes it instructive to look at the range of professions nobles followed after 1800. Table 8 contrasts the stated professions of three groups of nobles identified in the years between 1816 and 1870. The table permits us to say something about how nobles made a living. Agriculture is clearly the most deceptive category here. We know from chapter 2 the overwhelming predominance of noble income derived from land. Use of the term *landowner (propriétaire)* was by nature a redundancy in connection with other labels like mayor, judge, officer, or barrister. Indeed, among the aristocracy any professional label verged on the downright rude in good usage. To qualify one of the great names of France—particularly that of a family who thought they already possessed one—with an occupation was to imply that the latter was of equal importance to the name itself. That is why the term *landowner* is a redundancy, rarely used despite its ubiquity as the source of wealth. By contrast, we note the predictable prominence of military applicants for status under successive regimes; in 1866 it was double their presence among nobles at large.

One of the most durable effects of the Revolution was to initiate the process by which the French officer corps became increasingly lower-class, and the wars of the Revolution and Empire accelerated this, at least as much as the emigration of many officers drawn from the *noblesse*. Studying these changes in the social origins of French officers, one historian noted that "before giving ground to the thrust of the lower classes, the ruling classes put up a series of rearguard actions and long cherished the persistent hope of a victorious offensive return."[66] The continuing presence of the *noblesse* in the officer corps, although they almost never served below the rank of captain and remained for fewer years than did commoners, testified to the continuing prestige of the warrior rite of passage. It was also a station to be given up on the death of the family head, at marriage, or even in the face of a boring or unpleasant assignment. Among commoner officers there was a strong desire to gain a title to emulate aristocratic officers. The shrinkage in the number of nobles who entered the army probably paralleled but did not exceed the demographic weakening discussed earlier. On the other hand, there was always a strong demand for titles on the part of commoners in the armed forces.

Positions of authority in line with the service traditions of the *noblesse* were quite acceptable. Increasingly nobles were drawn to central and local administration. In 1866 nobles were listed as *conseillers généraux*, subprefects, mayors, and even municipality secretaries. State service remained the highroad to status. Other nobles held positions in the Ministry of Finance. There were various receivers and controllers of the direct and indirect taxes and indeed even mere tax collectors, as at Beauvoir (Deux-Sèvres). Haussmann was exemplary in his pursuit of rank. He began to ask for a position in the Legion of Honor as a young subprefect in the 1830s, received his baronial title when Seine prefect, and throughout his life was avid for foreign decorations and titles.[67]

Nobles were attracted by some completely new specialities, such as the postal service. In the 1866 directory of nobles we find the postal director at Alençon (Orne), the director of the Vannes (Morbihan) telegraph, and the much grander director general of the telegraph lines, vicomte de Vougy. Comte Ferdinand de Dürkheim-Montmartin was an inspector general of the telegraph service in the same period.[68] The postal service also gave noble spinsters positions, as in the case of the directresses of the post offices at Sap (Orne) and Petite Pierre (Bas-Rhin). Members of the judicial system were far less prominent than before 1789, their percentage falling steadily.

Medical practice was increasingly respectable to nobles, reflecting the rising prestige already obvious under the Old Regime. The king's First Doctor in the eighteenth century presided over the medical corps of the kingdom, enjoyed the title of comte which was attached to his functions, and lodged inside the Versailles château. One historian noted six families of royal doctors and surgeons whose members became active in the financial system of the *ferme générale*, thus making lateral linkages with financiers, another group entering the aristocracy by marriage.[69] Those doctors owed their status to their proximity to the body royal, but a century later there were many signs of the coexistence of distinction and medical practice. In the Bachelin-Deflorenne 1866 directory names of nobles such as de Beauvais, chevalier of the Legion of Honor and doctor on the Faculty of Medicine, or Besnard du Val, doctor at Rheims, appeared with some frequency. Scipion C. L. Corvisarts Desmarets, adopted son of the physician to Napoleon I who had been made an imperial baron, was himself "confirmed" as a baron in August 1859, and the title reverted at his death to his nephew Lucien, in turn physician to Napoleon III. Lucien's wife was a Mlle de Romain.

In chapter 5 ecclesiastical nobles are discussed at more length, ranging from the almoner at the Poitiers prison to the vicar at Notre-Dame de Bonne-Nouvelle in Paris or the bishop of Toronto.

Few men are listed in 1866 as having a position in the world of manufacturing and commerce—less than half of 1 percent—although many (almost 17 percent) were in the liberal professions. One of the few merchants was identified in capital letters—MARCHAND—and M. d'Auteville was dropped from the 1868 edition. *Négociants* were more acceptable, especially the small group of wine wholesalers. There were other noble *négociants* at Paris, Arras, Nantes, Nice, Réunion, and Martinique. None were listed with a title or a coat of arms. There were related professions among those given: business agent (*agent des affaires*) or salesman, as in the case of a "representative" for the Folembray glassworks at Rheims. About ten nobles were listed as representing insurance companies in different places. Closmadeu was a Nantes shipper. Chollet owned blast furnaces, as did Adelsward. Another was underdirector of forges at Guérigny, in the Nièvre. Another noble directed the Viroigne mines near Béthune in the Pas-de-Calais. Bernadières directed the Lorient gas factory.

Were nobles prominent among the inventors and technicians of the time? Comte Hilaire Bernigaud de Chardonnet, who invented artificial silk; Philippe de Girard, who designed a novel flax loom; and de Lesseps, of Suez Canal fame, spring to mind. Their careers can scarcely be said to reveal a specifically noble approach to technology; rather, the fundamental question was how nobles entered the entrepreneurial milieu as equal actors and how their elders and relatives viewed their aspirations. Without many more studies of family correspondence, it is hard to say much about this. Certainly one investigation of the Second Empire's leading corporate businessmen showed that prominent titled individuals sat on boards of directors: men like the duc de Galliéra, barons Rothschild, and many others on boards of companies of the second rank of corporate importance.[70]

One profession to which French nobles inclined in the twentieth century appears to have enjoyed less favor in the 1860s. This fitted into an evolution over centuries. Julian Dent argued that in the seventeenth century the financiers were separate from, and hated by, the feudal aristocracy. Towards the end of the century of Louis XIV the first marriages took place between financiers and nobles as the aristocrats pursued money. However, the *noblesse* continued to revile the "traitants" and to disdain commerce. In the eighteenth century, as Yves Durand stressed, there was an increasing number of marriages between financiers and aristocrats—usually the daughters of the former married the sons of the latter. Chaussinand-Nogaret, as mentioned above, saw the most capitalist and dynamically innovative economic faction in French life among the aristocracy that mixed with the Jacobites. The *noblesse*, however, still railed on against the financiers. The Revolution smashed the old "court capitalism," and Louis Bergeron's work seems to confirm that the aristocracy in the immediate post-Revolutionary trauma withdrew to the certainties of landownership. There was a timid continuation of the "proprietary enterprises" but no truly large-scale activity. *Titrés* for their part did not take noble titles as part of an industrial strategy: they were funded from state service and marriages. By mid-century the example of the peerage under the July Monarchy who invested heavily in the railways was timidly emulated by others.[71] There was also increasing interest in the actual machinery of finance. By the twentieth century the residual noble prejudice against financiers and banking had ended. A sociological investigation found that in 1954, 29 percent of the elite positions in insurance and banking were in noble hands; in 1964, 22 percent, and in 1974, 12 percent.[72] Indeed, a summer 1984 French newsmagazine identified the noble who then headed the International Monetary Fund as the most powerful Frenchman in the world.[73] In the 1860s there were apparently far fewer nobles in a smaller banking industry, and then almost never from the *noblesse:*

MM. de Boucheporn, Bouillerie, and Bovée; baron A. de Seillière, an administrator of the Crédit Mobilier; E. de Werbrouck, a Paris banker; and de Waru were noted as former bankers.

The tendency of nobles to enter banking and the high financial bureaucracy had not become as evident as it would a century later. In his memoirs the duc de Broglie recalled an émigré who became a banker, "exercising this profession with a lot of probity, intelligence, and success but with too much generosity and the habits of a gentleman to make a great fortune at it."[74] This judgment by so liberal and open-minded an aristocrat speaks for itself on the residual prejudice, at least in the noble-commoner contrast, that existed against the banking profession in the mid-nineteenth century. We may also emphasize that he did not *name* the individual. It could not be the Auvergnat artillery colonel, comte de Pontgibaud, who as an émigré was already a millionaire with a thriving business in Trieste when he traded cotton during the Continental Blockade, as well as provided banking services for a variety of émigré and Napoleonic clients. Pontgibaud had done much better in foreign business than he might have hoped to do in military service at home, and in fact he did not return to France under the Restorations, preferring to remain abroad until his death. His fortune permitted his son, Armand-Victoire, who was made a peer of France in 1827, to marry a girl whose mother was a Dreux-Brézé. The grandson of the banker lived as a rich landowner in Normandy, where in 1852 he took the place of Alexis de Tocqueville on the Manche general council and continued to be reelected until his death in 1892. Pontgibaud *père* in Trieste carried out all his commercial and financial activities under the name of J. Labrosse. His ultra brother, self-evidently a less astute man, was at great pains to stress that if the family wealth had been repaired at Trieste, the family name of Moré de Pontgibaud was unsoiled by the taint of business.[75] Only with the loosening of values under the Third Republic would this type of affectation change.

This cursory overview of professions exercised by nobles through two-thirds of the nineteenth century shows that nobles slowly changed. By 1866 they held positions hitherto unheard of, as well as hanging on to some old ones. Among those who ruled France, they held positions ranging from the presidency of the Corps législatif to the secretary-ship of an Algerian municipality. In law they sat from the Cour de cassation to the offices of barristers and notaries. In the Post Office their representation ranged from the director general of the telegraph lines to the spinster in charge of the district post office. They included the rector of the Bordeaux Academy and a librarian at the new Bibliothèque impériale in Paris. They were bankers and tax collectors. However, the distinct impression conveyed by the scarcity of commercial nobles in the Bachelin directory is that in the middle of the nineteenth century, business was still an unseemly label for the *bonne compagnie*.

The slow modernization of France has sometimes been blamed on the extreme division between capital and love of rural property, both typical of nobles as much as of the French middle classes. Nobles can scarcely be portrayed as the only obstacle to national development in light of similar conservatism found among other wealthy and untitled notables. What they failed to do was to link their leading place among the wealthy and best-educated element of French society before 1870 to an equally commanding place among the most innovative sectors of the emerging economy. One finds little of the daring, capitalist impulses that Chaussinand-Nogaret espied in the closing years of the Old Regime but, significantly, documented in large part from the papers dealing with confiscations preserved in the T series of the Archives Nationales. Nobles remained wealthy thanks to their land and intermarriage, but nonnobles became equally, and in time more, wealthy through success in business and manufacturing.

The uneasy relationship between nobles and businessmen is perhaps best illustrated by Ternaux, who actually rejected the title given to him by Louis XVIII, saying that he preferred to see his children follow an active, industrious life rather than emulate the useless laziness of the noble who looked down on commerce.[76] Ternaux was a remarkable man who learned the textile trade very early in his father's enterprises near Sedan, was forced to emigrate during the Revolution, and upon his return to Sedan in summer 1798 found the debris of his former business from which within twenty years he would have 1,100 looms in thirty factories employing 17,000 workers. One historian has estimated that at its height under the Restoration the Ternaux "empire" had some 20,000 employees at a time when Anzin had perhaps 5,000.[77] Ternaux's fortune was in part dependent on the dictates of court fashion: Napoleon had asked Josephine and her ladies to wear the shawls made of a mixture of fine wool and silk and known familiarly as "ternaux."

In 1803 Ternaux had bought the Saint Ouen château, where he gave sumptuous garden parties for what has been characterized as the *gratin* of the liberal high society. On his main driveway he used the shoulders of the land to plant wheat. He was active in charitable efforts and particularly obsessed with recipes for cheap but nourishing soup for the indigent. His enthusiasm for the Bourbons was cooled by anger at the sacrifice of the interests of industry to large property revealed by a protectionist customs policy on wheat. He ended a remarkable career in acute financial difficulties resulting from his daring innovations and the overextension of his finances. He died in April 1833. Dupin, himself an ennobled commoner, saluted him as the greatest *commerçant* whom

France had produced since Jacques Coeur. Here was a man who was sought out by the Bourbons in the interest of political reconciliation but who showed the limits of the honorific policy when it placed in oposition the commercial and capitalist interests of the time.[78]

The nobles' view on capitalism which set them apart from commoners was reflected in their collective loyalty to the obligation of maintaining family status. Zeldin remarked that the divergence between the economic and social conduct of noble and bourgeois has been overdrawn, but it is plain that he reached his conclusion from looking at similarities between the *haute bourgeoisie* and late-nineteenth-century nobles.[79] Beck's massive statistical labors on the July Monarchy's electoral lists showed that this was not the case for the different levels of participation in business during the 1830s. Detailed investigations of noble participation in business under the Third Republic which would show what changes had taken place are lacking. Of course the bourgeois had deeply-felt linkages to relatives but were free of the collective requirement to keep up the château, to support younger family members, and not to disgrace their ancestors. Nobles were trained in the correct ways of spending money even more than in getting it. As the task of getting money in the agricultural economy changed, and as the gap widened between the southern landowners and those of the northwest, more touched by the commercialization of French agriculture, nobles lagged in taking up new activities. As Beau de Loménie put it:

> It is certain that since 1830 the "gens de noblesse" have hardly
> created dynasties of financiers or industrialists. They do not become
> specialists, and their intrusion into the business world remains, in
> their eyes, accidental. The destiny of their race, its pride, its style of
> life is elsewhere. And in each generation their lineages traditionally
> continue to furnish a good number of soldiers, priests, diplomats,
> and country gentlemen.[80]

The evidence at present available for the period 1800–1870 seems to confirm that judgment in large measure. At the same time, the attitudes of *noblesse* and aristocrats towards capitalism and the professions were not immobile or monolithic. Yet their socioeconomic behavior affected them as much as the inexorable pressures of demography.

5

Nobles and Politics

The *dauphinois* liberal Barnave explained the 1789 Revolution as a struggle between, on the one hand, coastal, cosmopolitan, and trading cities and, on the other hand, interior, reactionary, and landed centers: a commercial class dominated the former, while the latter were in the hands of nobles.[1] After Sieyès's 1789 pamphlets and Revolutionary anti-noble legislation, it was all too usual to deduce political sympathies from class origins. The sweeping socioeconomic explanation of the Revolution first stated in the 1790s was continually embroidered during the nineteenth century. Soon after the 1830 Revolution the *Globe* newspaper observed, on 17 September 1830, that France's aristocratic rulers under the reign of Charles X had been replaced by "new patricians," numbered with curious precision as 22,000 bourgeois. During the discussion of the 1844 *patente* law a deputy used similar language when he said that a new aristocracy of finance and industry had arisen in France with businessmen for barons: they asked not for titles but gloried in the amounts of the business tax they paid.[2] Albert Maurin's *Histoire de la chute des Bourbons*[3] portrayed contemporary history as a losing battle fought by nobles in disarray before an all-conquering army of the middle class. Conservative political sympathies of nobles opposed to innovation were assumed long before Jaurès provided his majestic summation in the *Histoire socialiste* of the death struggle between the aristocratic and landed principles in France and those of capital and bourgeois egalitarianism.

Informed of these alarming notions by radical newspapers, books, and speeches, nobles were understandably in no hurry to quit the stage of history. They followed closely the enactment and implementation of laws affecting nobles after 1791: impediments on the use of Old Regime titles before 1814, the production of new titles when the March 1808 decrees were set in motion, and the nominations to the Chamber of

130

Peers by the constitutional monarchies. Nobles observed how opinion evolved during the great parliamentary debates on primogeniture (1826), in the comments on the compensation of émigrés, on the heredity of the peers (1831), and on the restrictions and then prohibition of new *majorats* (1835), as well as the brief but intense discussions preceding the 1848 abolition of noble titles. Nobles generally approved the restitution of titles by Louis-Napoleon "confirmed" to his loyal supporters.

In this chapter, however, our subject is not how nobles reacted to legislation about their use of titles (along with wealth the now supremely important attribute of their place in an elite) but the part nobles played in politics between 1800 and 1870. This is at once an immense and an elusive subject. Immense because nobles served every regime in France during the seven decades, and to trace only the leading ministers, senators, tribunes, peers, and deputies as they came and went would involve commentary on the parliamentary history of the century. Elusive since the various ducs, marquis, comtes, barons, vicomtes, and chevaliers were united in their pride of rank but not in a political union deriving from it. They never shared precisely the same outlook. Moreover, no political party (not even in the limited electorate of 1814–48) could be based solely on noble interests. That certainly included the Restoration ultras, as well as the Legimists, who after 1830 were increasingly affected by the "national" policy of Genoude and others, a policy that equated the monarchy with popular interests.

Nobles continued to set the tone of how to rule. The aristocracy had been attached to the court before 1789, and indeed the remnants of the "parti Choiseul" who reappeared in the corridors of power at the start of the nineteenth century continued that tradition. Napoleon encouraged the rally to him of former court aristocrats and hoped for an amalgamation with "new" families. When the Bourbons returned to power in 1814, it appeared to one journalist that presence at court was still highly indispensable to the ambitious noble: "A gentleman who does not show himself at court does not exist."[4] After 1830 it was members of the Old Regime liberal aristocracy who gave Louis-Philippe's court what style it possessed. Napoleon III dispensed benefits to courtiers often drawn from the opportunist and shabby southern *noblesse,* but aristocrats were prominent among the regime's supporters. Under successive monarchies court, politics, and rewards were conjoined. Nobles were indispensable to maintain the social forms in which French power was exercised.

By 1800 nobles were in an understandable state of confusion about their hopes to exercise any social power in post-Revolutionary France. The most widespread attitude was the least abstruse ambition: to cling to whatever remnants of the advantages that being of the *noblesse* had produced in the past. For nobles this meant conserving and regaining properties and what attendant deference they still enjoyed in the countryside. For those who wished to be left to the quiet enjoyment of their possessions and place in French rural society after the promulgation of the Constitution of the Year VIII the sensible course was to accept with as good a grace as possible the big legal changes introduced by the Revolution in matters such as feudal dues, communal lands, and special privileges while seeking to regain de facto small advantages by cajoling or browbeating the peasantry. This silent majority of the *noblesse* schemed for authority in the modest day-to-day life of rural France, particularly in the west, southwest, Brittany, and the Midi.

Their sphere of influence and aspirations contrasted with that of those descendants of the Versailles court aristocracy who lost none of their atavistic knowledge of the exercise of power, who took the view that the pursuit of great wealth and influence necessarily involved high risks, and who did not fear the public scrutiny involved in serving at court, in the high bureaucracy, and in the army. As for *titrés*, by definition they shared a symbiotic relationship with governments that decorated them. Despite rhetoric, members of the *noblesse* who wanted to escape genteel obscurity found themselves *titrés* as a result of participation in government, which in turn allowed them, if also rich, to enter the network of the aristocracy. This ladder of French politics which enabled French titled families to go up or down in the world remained in place throughout much of the century.

Royalism, however, like some varieties of Catholic thought, provided an arsenal, or refuge, of concepts and symbols to disguise the degree of collaboration with the new social realities. Very few nobles were openly aware of this function of their social discourse to provide an accommodation with the post-Revolutionary world. However, by the end of the Second Empire many *noblesse* had the same outlook as the marquis de Blosseville, a leading light on the Eure general council, or his friend, monseigneur de Bonnechose. They remained faithful to Legitimist doctrine, Blosseville's biographer observed, but they were absolutely against being lost in the political schemes propagated by the councillors of Henri V. This meant that they talked of guaranteeing the social order and of saving religion, but without having to compromise themselves as obdurate royalists.[5] Like so many others, Blosseville had before him paternal example, for his father, an émigré dragoons officer, had returned to France in 1797 and served as mayor of his seigneurial village from 1806 to 1830. If his father could serve a Bonaparte and still retain *noblesse* social values, so could the son. Nobles quite rightly objected that nineteenth-century conditions were hardly ideal for a Fronde or a crusade. In a sense the political theories most popular with the mass of the *noblesse* became an alibi explaining away their observable political passivity and resignation to the course of French politics.[6]

If we search for a national focus of aristocratic power in the nineteenth century, we must examine the French upper house, which existed under the constitutional monarchies and which, on the face of it, seemed a natural political focus for the nobles. The Chamber of Peers did not merely "royalize" the Napoleonic senate in 1814: it was the product of a continuing debate about the forms of parliamentary government that reached back for a quarter-century. During the discussion of provincial assemblies in 1788 the idea emerged of a second chamber in a representative system of national assemblies in France. No sooner had the National Assembly been constituted in 1789 than suspicions of the aristocratic designs of the proponents of separate assemblies were noisily voiced. That mistrust was dissipated by the invigorating experience of Revolutionary government. In 1795 the Conseil des Anciens was established, its very name a testimony to greybeards' caution. Composed of half the number of the Conseil des Cinq-Cents (the lower house), the Conseil des Anciens, married men of forty and over, was supposed to counterbalance the dangerously impetuous lower house. Between 1795 and 1848 and again from 1852 to 1870 France had a double tier of representative assemblies intended to prevent rash innovation or arbitrariness. From its inception in 1800 (3 nivôse III) the Senate included *noblesse*, but only one true aristocrat, the former duc de Choiseul-Praslin. A little later the duc de Luynes, de Viry, d'Aboville, and Eugène de Beauharnais joined its ranks.[7]

In what was called the nineteenth year of Louis XVIII's reign the Charter of 1814 replaced the Senate with a chamber of hereditary peers. In his self-important way Vitrolles was typical of the *noblesse* in his disapproval of the hereditary principle of the members of the Chamber of Peers. He described the nomination of new members to ensure a political majority sympathetic to the government as "this prostitution of the state's preeminent dignity."[8] In the autumn of 1815 the young Lamartine urged the suppression of noble privileges, while calling for "an elective peerage on the British [*sic*] lines."[9] In his memoirs Salaberry called the Chamber of Peers a bedlam (*pétaudière*) of former revolutionaries and members of the Convention, imperial senators and ministers deported into a modern Noah's Ark.[10] Even in retrospect the *noblesse* refused to find anything good about the institution self-evidently in the best position to advance their interests. No limit was placed on the royal right to name peers, but in practice the Bourbons, and later Louis-Philippe, kept it at around three hundred men. In 1826 there were 295, in 1830, 384, and in 1840, 306. With the exception of ecclesiastics, peers were required by an ordinance of 25 August 1817 to set up *majorats*. This was intended to ensure considerable wealth for the political peerage.

Many members of the Old Regime aristocracy, such as Raigecourt and Saulx-Tavanes, rejoined relatives who earlier had sat in the Napoleonic Senate. Presided over by a chancellor appointed for life, the peers deliberated secretly about laws brought before the Chamber of Deputies by the ministers and subsequently referred to them for an opinion. They also had to approve the budget, and they served as a court for high treason trials, as in the case of the duc de Berry's assassination in February 1820 by the stableman Louvel, or for crimes of their peers, like the celebrated murder by Choiseul-Praslin of his wife, *née* Sebastiani, in August 1847. The king's ministers sat either in the Chamber of Deputies or in the Chamber of Peers. The major offices of the Chamber of Peers were those of the grand referendary, the marquis de Semonville, who served from 1814 to 1834 and whose apartment was actually within the Luxembourg Palace, where the peers assembled, and those of the bureau—the president, vice-president, and four secretaries—which was charged with taking the views of the peers to the king.

Even during the Restoration the peers were never completely sycophantic in their dealings with the ministers. In the course of the struggle between Charles x and the liberals in the Chamber of Deputies many peers, especially those of the liberal court aristocracy under the Old Regime, showed themselves moderate. Decazes appointed eighty-odd peers in 1819, and Villèle appointed a further seventy in 1827, many of whom were former commoners. These promotions sufficed to win certain votes but not to ensure continuing obedience of the membership to governmental policies. In 1830 the peers reaffirmed loyalty to the Charter and survived the July Revolution, despite Lafayette's call for abolition of the upper house. The most important change in its practice was that debates were now public, and so speeches could be published. The *fournées* (appointments made to pack the Chamber with supporters to outvote the liberals) of Charles x were unseated. Article 15 of the Charter of 1830 stated that laws could be proposed not only by the king and the Chamber of Deputies but also by the Chamber of Peers. The king retained his right to name unlimited number of peers. In December 1831, however, after long debates the heredity of the peerage was abolished. Peers played a major role in the July Monarchy's political life. Great Old Regime names still figured there in the 1830s: Brissac, Noailles, Montmorency, and Crillon among others, together with Greffulhe, Albuféra, Roy, and other families first titled after 1800. The reputation of the peers was much soiled in the 1840s by the conduct of some of its members, and there was no public regret for the disappearance of the upper house. Napoleon III would return to a Senate, but one staffed with new men.

The year 1848 brought the Second Republic and ended the parliamentary system of the constitutional monarchies. The constitution hurriedly drawn up in the early days of 1852 named Prince Louis-Napoleon Bonaparte as emperor and returned to Napoleonic precedents. He appointed eighty supporters to life tenure in the Senate. They served without salary, although Bonaparte bestowed on them handsome dotations of 30,000F each. While the organization underwent various changes during the Second Empire, it remained essentially Napoleon III's creature. Vincent, whose grandfather had been ennobled in 1778, whose father was made a baron of the Empire in 1809, and who himself became a hereditary *baron-sur-majorat* in 1827 and a senator in 1859 symbolized the type of support the regime hoped for.

Senators rarely exceeded 150 in number, including *noblesse* and *titrés*.[11] According to Bachelin-Deflorenne, in 1866 the Senate was composed of 169 senators presided over by Troplong, Grand Cross of the Legion of Honor and first president of the Cour de cassation. There were five vice-presidents, a grand referendary, an unnamed secretary, and three princes of the imperial family who sat as members. If we count as noble those with a title or with a particle in the family name (Caignart de Saulcy, for instance), we have 98 individuals, or 58 percent of the total. In contrast, 71, or 42 percent, had neither title, particle, nor even military rank. Some names, such as Goulhot de Saint Germain, carried little prestige, but the lineage of an Elie de Beaumont could not be faulted. That there were few names of Restoration or Orleanist peers (Maupas, Ségur, d'Agusseau) in no way detracts from—indeed it emphasizes—the display by the senators of titles and noble-type names.[12]

Nobles rallied increasingly to the Second Empire. General d'Aurelle de Paladines, of a family of petty *noblesse*, boasted to Louis-Napoleon that he was the first to have acclaimed the Empire: "France awaits its salvation from the Empire: I take responsibility for Order!" The marquis de Chasseloup-Laubat, a *conseiller d'état* in 1828, deputy under Louis-Philippe, and at the Assemblée Législative of 1849, became minister of the Navy in 1851, an official deputy in 1852 and again from 1861 to 1867, president of the Council of State, senator, and again minister just before the Empire's defeat in 1870. Although somewhat unusual, he shows continuing noble participation in French political life from the Restoration crowned with assiduous efforts under the Second Empire and, indeed, afterwards: in 1871 he was elected deputy of the Charente-Inférieure.[13] A more notorious royalist showed equal flexibility: the marquis de la Rochejacquelin was republican in 1848 and died an imperial senator in 1867.[14] Great names from the Old Regime court at

Versailles, as well as resounding patronyms from the lesser *noblesse*, were to be found among the *titrés*.

Nobles also sat in the lower house throughout the period 1800–1870. Recent studies document their fluctuating presence in the successive assemblies but nothing to show any coherent political strategy. Noble deputies, of course, were never elected on a specifically noble program. In Haute-Garonne, one of the departments that most consistently elected right-wing deputies in the 1820s, nobles were found among ultra, ministerial, and liberal voters.[15] In the Corrèze, a department with a clear penchant for electing deputies well in with the government of the day, all the deputies were noble. Even so, Pierre-Joseph Bedoch, Chevalier of the Empire, Fouché, with an imperial title of duc, seven members of the *noblesse,* and Froment de Champ Lagarde, who passed for noble as the son of a former bailiff in Versailles, lacked a unified political outlook.[16] Statistical studies of the social background of French legislators in the nineteenth century make clear that nobles were heavily overrepresented given their percentage in the population.

Despite inconsistencies in the definition of who was noble, particularly in the exclusion of some of those who claimed titles, one study revealed that nobles were persistently overrepresented given their proportion of the electoral body, let alone of the nation, from 1800 to 1834.[17] In the Chamber of Deputies between 1837 and 1839, 35 percent of the representatives were nobles—or in numerical terms, there were 74 *noblesse,* 55 *titrés* from the First Empire, 19 from the Restoration and July Monarchy, and 12 with a particle.[18] An analysis of the Chamber of Deputies elected between 6 August 1846 and the February Revolution, 1848, again showed that more than a third of the deputies were noble. This meant that under the July Monarchy the numbers of noble deputies tended to increase steadily between 1831 and 1848.[19] Less systematic evidence is available for the Second Empire, but the senators and members of the Corps législatif included large numbers of nobles. Paradoxically, this impressive overrepresentation never became effective political power for the simple reason that noble deputies shared no common program. Tocqueville, himself involved in politics, observed that the social unity perceived by commoners and outsiders did not constitute an ideological or practical political cohesion.[20]

A recent study has reminded us of the growing power of the bureaucracy as it seconded the policies of successive regimes.[21] This has awakened interest in the family backgrounds of the staffs of such powerful bodies as the Council of State, the prefectoral corps, the different ministries, and the departmental administrations.[22] Not surprisingly, men from the lower classes were conspicuous rarities in the higher levels of the bureaucracy. Peasants and artisans rarely commanded the means to educate their sons to requisite standards, nor did they connect with the web of patronage that could place their offspring on the ladders leading to the Council of State, the diplomatic service, or even the administrative staff of the prefectures. However, nobles with wealth and education similar to that of the prosperous middle classes, who provided the majority of such officials, were not unusual in the ministries. The great aristocrats, of course, considered ill-paid posts too far removed from the exercise of power to be a *dérogeance* of their belief in their natural place at the pinnacle of society. For Alfred de Musset's Bonapartist father it was respectable enough to be an official in a ministry, since the family was not well-off or prominent; however, it was unthinkable to a La Rochefoucauld, Crillon, Raigecourt, Choiseul-Praslin, or Harcourt. Thus, under the Empire the central bureaucracy at the Foreign Ministry included less than one in ten nobles or individuals with particled names, but these groups made up more than 20 percent of the consular corps, and more than half of the ambassadors were nobles. Until the July Monarchy there was practically no movement between the three groups.[23]

In the higher reaches of the bureaucracy the rich *noblesse* might make an appearance from time to time. This was especially true immediately after the Revolution, as in the case of comte Séraphin de La Tour-du-Pin, who had served in the artillery, cavalry, and infantry before 1789. Subsequent to his return to France after emigration to the United States from 1792 to 1800, under the Consulate and the Empire, he took posts as prefect of Brussels and Amiens before being named one of the French plenipotentiaries at the Congress of Vienna. He followed Louis XVIII to Ghent in 1815, and in August of that year he was named to preside over the Somme electoral college. Two days later he was named a peer. A little later his good fortune continued with his nomination as minister plenipotentiary to Holland, and in 1820 he was named ambassador to Turin. At the news of the Revolution of 1830 he gave up his post, and after 1832 he lived abroad intermittently until his death in 1837. La Tour du Pin's service in the Napoleonic prefectoral corps was vital to his transition into the political class of the Restoration over and above his earlier record as a young soldier, courtier, and then émigré with strong connections, since his wife had been one of Marie-Antoinette's ladies-in-waiting.[24]

Later in the century the prefectoral corps did not always serve as such a useful stepping stone. Vicomte Aldebert Pineton de Chambrun was the youngest and one of the wealthiest of the prefects appointed by Louis-Napoleon before the December coup of 1852 which established the Second Empire. Although of a distinguished lineage, he had realized the limitations of remaining confined to the Legitimist camp. Perhaps the fact that his father-in-law was an industrialist (director general of Baccarat Crystal) was itself a clue to his iconoclastic attitudes towards public service. However, his career did not prosper once Bonaparte became Napoleon III, and he angrily resigned in 1854, turning his energies to the crystal factory. The two other men who with Chambrun made up the richest trio of appointees under the prince-president also had names with a noble ring: Paul de la Hante (in fact Delahante) and baron Dubois de Romand; like Chambrun they had left the service by 1856.[25]

These noble participants in the bureaucracy do not seem to have had a qualitatively different attitude towards government service from that of their commoner colleagues. Those nobles who had accepted state service in the hundreds under the stable conditions of First Consul Bonaparte were in no position to impose a new viewpoint on the administration that gave them a salary. Indeed, comte d'Herbouville, who remained in France during the Revolution and was named prefect at Antwerp in 1800 and at Lyon in 1806, seemed to have more concern with changing the outlook of his social equals. In 1814–15 he was urging on the royalists the need for a uniform training in administration, in which nobles were to shine. Herbouville felt that only if nobles were properly trained could they staff a modern state, and this involved jettisoning the idea bequeathed by history that only a military career was a suitable ambition. One might add that Herbouville here was describing his own career: he had risen to the rank of *maréchal de camp* before 1789, but after lying low during the Revolution he had begun a new career in state service which was to continue under the Restoration, when he was made a peer and director of the postal service from 1815 to 1816. He was thus in a position to know a lot about the views heard at the mess as well as at the ministries.[26] The force of tradition molded bureaucrats regardless of their personal antecedents.

The way in which the bureaucracy and state service could ingest nobles was exemplified by the six brothers of the well-established Caffarelli family of petty *noblesse*. Of two ecclesiastics one took the oath to the Civil Constitution, while the other emigrated to Spain, and of four military men one died fighting in the Napoleonic assault on Acre, another was an émigré shot at Quiberon, a third a Napoleonic state councillor and maritime prefect of Brest, and the fourth a general. After the Concordat the émigré ecclesiastic was made bishop of Saint-Brieuc, while his *constitutionnel* brother became prefect of the Ardèche, then of the Calvados, and finally of the Aube, which he left in 1814 at the time of the allied invasion to retire to the village of his birth, Falga, in the Lauraguais. There he resumed wearing his habit, was named an honorary canon of Albi cathedral, and became a member of the departmental

general council until his death in 1826. His nephew was an assistant at
the Council of State in the 1830s, prefect of the Ille-et-Vilaire in 1849,
and deputy for the same department from 1852 to 1869. If nothing else,
the Caffarellis show emphatically noble adaptability to the course of
events.[27]

Paid noble officials were not, of course, easily compared with those
who accepted positions such as that of mayor without salary. The satisfactions they derived were entirely different from the psychological ones
of deference to a man assumed to have credit with the prefect and
ultimately with Paris. There may also have been the calculation that
local standing would prove useful later. One Nivernais family, the Bour-
goings, might be cited among hundreds to show that development.
Under the Directory, Adolphe de Bourgoing was a member of the *jury
d'instruction,* a justice of the peace, a member of the Nevers town
council, inspector of the *droits réunis* (taxes levied on items of general
consumption) in 1799, a dragoons captain in 1805, as well as *receveur
principal des droits réunis* at Auxerre and president of the agricultural
society. In 1853 Adolphe-Pierre became a prefect. This was a not uncommon mixture of paid and unpaid positions. One historian suggested
that nobles accepted state service in order to amass the cash necessary
to set up a *majorat;* however, my own investigation of the origins and
wealth of the men who set up *majorats sur demande* does not support
this.[28] Certain bureaucratic positions were always held to be particularly suited to nobles. The Protestant commoner Guizot believed that
only aristocrats made proper ambassadors for major posts. However,
noble demography set limits on the number of candidates for such
positions.

In the judicial system *parlementaire* nobles no longer had the primacy enjoyed by proud families of *robins* under the Old Regime. The
higher ranks of the judiciary had been largely hereditary and were in
the hands of nobles by 1789; the impetus behind the legal reforms of
1789–94 came from the lower levels of the system. With the collapse of
the old judicial structure early in the Revolution, notaries, *avocats*, and
procureurs were suddenly presented with the opportunity to find new
jobs. This time they did not make the error of supporting their noble
superiors, as they had at the time of the Maupeou reforms. Once seated,
the new judiciary felt comfortable in its new eminence. There was no
question after 1800 of recalling former magistrates by right. Instead,
they had to find a place in a functioning judiciary staffed by men with
many grudges against the *parlementaire* haughtiness of the past. *Parlementaires* and their sons put their hopes in support by the emperor, who
wanted them back to give a little more tone to the administration of
justice.[29] One hundred and fifty former *parlementaires* were reseated

following the reorganization introduced by the law of 20 April 1811. This was 10–20 percent of the higher judiciary but no more than 10 percent of those who had been judges in 1789. If the legal system is seen as a support of the status quo and a source of power, nobles had suffered a grievous reverse.

Alan Spitzer has said that only under the First Empire and the Restoration was the nineteenth-century French political class not dominated by lawyers. If the Chamber of Deputies of 1824 was the elected French parliamentary assembly with the highest proportion of nobles during the century, in the three years to 1827 men of law came to wield increasing power in national politics. Nevertheless, after 1830, because of their assumed Legitimist sympathies, noble candidates for appointment to the bench were discriminated against and declined as a proportion of the judges. Under the Second Empire that trend was reversed—that is, an increasing number of the post-Revolutionary *titrés* now sat on the bench. Nobles who entered the legal system usually remained for their entire career despite changes in government. One example among many is baron Tholet from Montpellier, an émigré during the Revolution who returned to France to study law and took a post in 1809 as president of the tribunal of the small town of Lodève, in the Massif. By 1811 he was an assistant to the regional appeal court prosecutor, and in 1812 he himself became prosecutor at Carcassonne. In 1816 he was made a judge of the Pau Appeal Court, and in 1822 he was appointed first president of the appeal court in the larger town of Limoges. At this stage in his steady ascent through the professional hierarchy of the judiciary, Louis XVIII bestowed upon him another baronal title. He ran as a moderate candidate at Tulle in the Corrèze but returned in 1837 to the judiciary, advancing to the place of councillor at the Paris Cour de cassation by 1849. Under Napoleon III he returned to the city where he had first seen the light of day, Montpellier, and sat there as the chief presiding judge in the appeal court. He died in 1856.[30] Baron Tholet was particularly successful under different regimes, but significant numbers of nobles with robe family traditions flourished in the career.

In Pau at mid-century four out of twenty judges descended from *parlementaire* families, but they were individuals of great local prestige: Dombidau de Crouseilles, nephew of the bishop of Quimper; Bedouch, who was mayor of his commune; Courrèges d'Agnos; and the son of the last first president of the Parliament of Pau, Charitte. The staffs of appeal courts such as those in Nancy, Dijon, Rennes, and Rouen still included the names of local noble dynasties that had found their roots in the former *parlements* in those cities.[31] At least one noble completely departed from a sword family tradition: the impoverished Saint-Gresse from the Gers, who also spurned the intense Legitimist sympathies of his father when he studied law and became a known republican, although he managed to exercise as a barrister throughout the Second Empire and received his reward under the Third Republic when he became the first president at the Toulouse court.[32]

Law was certainly good training and sometimes an acceptable career for nobles to follow if they were obliged to earn their bread. Did noble judges administer the law differently than their commoner colleagues? One might guess at a discretionary sympathy for an aggrieved noble physically threatened by a dishonest *métayer,* or extra severe treatment for a drunkard who bellowed anti-noble slogans; however, there seem to be no grounds for supposing that this went beyond the individual variations revealed by the sentencing patterns of judges at all times. Nobles were too conscious of the eyes of the public upon them to have encouraged the suspicion that they judged in a way flagrantly partial to their minority.

Present in the national assemblies, bureaucracy, and judiciary, in the nineteenth century nobles were never able to count on the predominance or even connivance of their fellows. The area of French life where they might hope to make their influence most felt was in the countryside.[33] Napoleon sought to harness the advisory councils in each department—the general council and those of the arrondissements—to the prosperous local worthies and nobles who enjoyed social prestige. Their views could be voiced in the departmental general councils by the grandest of noble landlords and in the arrondissement councils by the slightly less well-off. Suggestions and laments over the state of the roads, taxes, the price of imported grain, education, beggars, and other topics that attracted local interest were passed on to the prefect.

The main purpose of this system was to serve as a safety valve and a listening post, but it also provided a mini-stage for many ambitions.[34] To be on the general council was a sign of *considération,* like taking part in a secular ritual to reassure and comfort the inhabitants of one's department, even though in fact it had scant connection to national decision making. Prestige explained the draw for nobles to serve on these councils, where from 1800 to 1870 they were always massively overrepresented in terms of their number in the population at large although not in terms of their presence among the great landowners. They often served from one regime to the next.

In the case of the Choiseul-Praslin, Raigecourt, and Villèle families, we find that all sat during the century. In 1842 no member of the Legitimist Villèle family sat besides baron de Malaret and the 10 percent of the Haute-Garonne councillors who were nobles. In Seine-et-Marne, however, the duc de Choiseul-Praslin, comte Greffulhe, and comte de Ségur were among the 20 percent of the titled council members, while in nearby Nièvre marquis de Raigecourt and baron Dupin were among the 16 percent with titles. In 1862 there were even more titles on the Seine-et-Marne general council (24 percent) but no Choiseul-Praslin; in Nièvre there were again more titles (32 percent) but no Raigecourt; and in Haute-Garonne, no Villèle but a constant 10 percent of nobles.[35]

Among those who served on the general councils are numerous examples of nobles who adjusted to changing times. Paul de Chazot as a young man was an officer of the royal guard of Charles x, resigning his commission in 1830. Subsequently he became mayor of Eperrais (Orne) before joining the departmental general council in 1852. He was elected to the Corps législatif in 1858 and again in 1863, but the chronicler of the departmental council lauded him for his local efforts: "He will be remembered as a member of the general council, as president of the agricultural committee and the society for [horse] races at Mortagne, and the secretary of the advisory committee for agriculture."[36] Small wonder that similar nobles were vociferous in the debate about decentralization.[37] Too much should not be made of this, however. Just as the speeches made to the agricultural societies often expressed wishful thinking for a seigneurial past, so these tirades praising localism, far from a genuine exercise of power, were an indirect discourse on family distinction.

Noble power was closest to the lives of at least some Frenchmen on the bottom rung of civic life: in the communes, the basic administrative unit, which had replaced the parish after 1789. Even before 1789, however, nobles never fully controlled local affairs in their parishes, whether rural or urban. One study of Rheims at the end of the Old Regime showed a sizable group of nobles on the municipal council, but they were politically polarized, with commoner officials against the clergy and its privileges. In Troyes, by contrast, there were few nobles. In both cases nobles were part of a plurality of local powers, without any clear control of distinct policies. They shared a community of economic interests with wealthy commoners.[38] Elsewhere similarities of the sort showed that there was no specific "noble" approach to municipal politics. In rural parishes the former seigneur, however, probably enjoyed the closest thing to a vestige of the Old Regime in the deference he was accorded.

The Napoleonic use of lists of those with sufficient wealth, respectability, and political docility to be candidates for official positions provides us with some insights into the relative prestige of such individuals. The complicated electoral procedures presented to the Corps législatif by Roederer on 10 February 1801 made provision for the election of municipal, arrondissement, and departmental notables but were not easy to put into practice. Complaints arose on all sides, such as from those people at Bordeaux whose names began with the letter L, who had been completely left off the list by oversight. Those lists have bequeathed French archives a remarkable documentation from which it is possible to examine the national elite in its largest sense. Even to figure on the lists of notables was in a sense power, or the first step towards it, since from the lists were chosen the officials. Chaptal described the lists on 23 ventôse XIII as an amalgam drawn from all who might serve the Empire: "The motherland at this time interrogates all men of good will: the government asks of them magistrates worthy of associating themselves to its efforts." Another circular, of 18 July 1809, called the lists "the moral catalog of the nation, the history of every individual, a fright to the wicked and a hope for the meritorious . . . a rich source of information for the government."[39]

The numbers of nobles present on the lists is not entirely clear, since there was an injunction on imperial officials to use only those titles granted by the emperor after 1808. To an extent this was rectified under the column dealing with the status of the individual before 1789, but a number of *noblesse* were listed only by family name and without particles. What quantitative studies have been done of the survival of the nobility in the "political class" of the Empire are thus certainly minimal statements. Napoleon's implementation of the suggestion by Sieyès to replace the Revolutionary principle of election by the technocratic one of co-option of the competent—those who enjoyed "considération," as the texts endlessly put it—marked a revival of a quasi-seigneurial and paternalistic view of local government. From the lists of national notability came the names of candidates for posts such as those of mayor, municipal councillor, juryman, and so on. Mayors were chosen by Paris, although councillors were elected during most of the period 1800–1870. From the lists we can trace the chain of family appearances in local office, not necessarily continuous but repeated, which was typical of many of the 37,000 communes that existed under the Second Empire. Particularly in the first decades of the century, officials often referred to family relationships when addressing the public and liked to cast the mayor of a commune *in loco parentis*. The Bagnères subprefect (Hautes-Pyrénées) addressed local mayors on the subject in May 1813: "Nearest to those administered, a mayor is the public official who can most effectively cause authority to be loved and respected: he is a father in the middle of his family."[40] Regardless of whether Napoleon thought of notables as civilian corporals, or perhaps as adults by contrast with a childish people, this system gave nobles a commodious niche in the new institutions.

There are relatively few studies of nineteenth-century French local elites, although the works of Agulhon, Chaline, Tudesq, and Vigier have provided a variety of methodological insights. Nobles were present in the local elites of French regions in varying degrees, as would be only natural in view of the uneven distribution of them throughout France. Perhaps the most promising material is to be found in municipal histories, particularly those of the major provincial capitals, which provided a sufficiently complex universe of roles and aspirations for the tensions between rival components of the elite to become manifested in elections, membership of different societies, religious rituals or the lack of them, and so forth. One study wisely remarked that "it is necessary to place oneself on a relative plane in order to understand the characteristics and the level of the group that passes locally for an elite."[41]

Noble participation in municipal government during the changing conditions of the nineteenth century was not constant. However, it always far exceeded the place of the nobles in the national population at large, even during the purges carried out by the July Monarchy and the Second Republic. The posts often came to them when they were quite young. Leclerc de Fleurigny at age twenty-four with a revenue of six thousand francs lived in his château and was made mayor of the commune of his name in 1809, and he held the post for decades. Joseph de Villèle was made mayor of the commune in which he lived under Napoleon. The mayoralty was the first rung towards other responsibilities: member of the local consultative councils, deputy, and even peer or senator for the most successful.

Figure 4 reveals the fluctuations of the participation of nobles in two rather different departments, the Aude and the Sarthe. Both witnessed a steep drop from 1830 to 1834, but then the rising trend returned. The Aude had fewer resident nobles than the Sarthe, although they were still disproportionately represented among the mayors, particularly in the years before 1830. One of them was marquis d'Hautpoul, who returned unexpectedly to his château at Saint-Papoul in the winter of 1829 and was promptly named mayor; in his memoirs he spoke of services rendered to his fellow citizens in restoring order to the communal budget.[42] The Sarthe generally had wealthier nobles than did the Aude. Between 1810 and 1872 the proportion of nobles among the department's mayors never dipped below 20 percent, and it sometimes surpassed 50 percent and more.[43]

The Restoration rapidly increased the numbers of mayors of the largest cities who were from the *noblesse*. The number of prominent individuals ready to take these posts probably increased. In 1816 the royal almanac listed marquis de Montgrand as mayor of Marseille, Joseph de Villèle in Toulouse, vicomte de Fourges in Bordeaux, marquis d'Ax-Daxat in Montpellier, marquis de Valogne in Nîmes, and vicomte de la Peyrade in Sète, to sample only the major southern cities. In the

FIGURE 4. Percentages of Nobles Serving as Mayors in the Sarthe and Aude Departments, 1810–1872

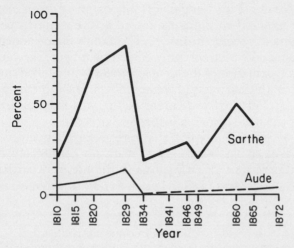

Source: Data from M. Grosbois, "Les Nobles sarthois au xixe siècle, 1805–1872" (Le Mans, [1973?], Typescript), table 3; and *AD* Aude, 2M 329, 336, 337–38, 346.

same period nobles sat more frequently on municipal councils: sixteen out of twenty-seven in Toulouse in 1824.[44] However, the more onerous jobs in the municipalities—those of deputy, secretary general, section chief, and so forth—were less frequently held by nobles.

The noble perception of the value of office depended on how far the office could influence higher-level administrative choices and decisions. Particularly during the Restoration, mayors filtered the traditional patronage system involved in local appointments.[45] On the Mediterranean littoral and in the Midi this was especially evident. A typical viewpoint was expressed by the elder Villèle in a note to his son, the mayor of Toulouse, on 12 October 1815: "It is a good thing to be mayor of Toulouse. Certainly one gets from it a great *considération,* which usually is useful. On the other hand, you know the responsibilities—I participate a little in both. I receive ten compliments that otherwise would not have been offered to me, and ten hats are raised that would not have been raised. Also I have many requests."[46]

Prestige could be expressed in a more tangible way in civic ceremonial, as at the funeral of a former émigré who had returned in 1797 to Monistrol (Haute-Loire), where his family château was located, to serve for many years as the mayor. His funeral procession in 1824 was described in the municipal registers with great precision: "All the corporations, colleges, communities, the gendarmerie brigade, the municipal council, the hospital board, that of Charity, the secular clergy, the National Guard, with flag unfurled and decorated with crepe, four cavaliers of the Royal Order of the Legion of Honor carrying the corners of the mortuary shroud, and an immense crowd of the common people [*peuple*] accompanied by four drums."[47] The family name remained well-known when his son, a former army officer, member of the general council, and a representative of the people in 1848, was killed during the June fighting on the rue Saint Antoine in Paris. His funeral, also at Monistrol and also celebrated with great pomp, was followed by the renaming of the principal square as la place Charbonnel.

For much of the period 1800–1870 the bureaucracy actively sought out nobles to take positions of prominence in the countryside. The administrators' attitude towards such posts in the hands of noblemen was put clearly by the prefect of the Hautes-Pyrénées when he wrote that

> the misfortune of the times has placed, in some communes,
> nonresident mayors or mayors who are not landowners there. In this
> way communes were condemned to the humiliation of not having a
> single distinguished [*honnête*] person in its bosom. The mayor who
> arrived yesterday, without contact to the old families of the region
> [*pays*], will find only cold hearts, ill-disposed and soon excessively
> soured by the presumption or certainty that the magistrate inposed
> on them more as an overseer than as the father of all maintains
> himself in the graces of the higher authorities by ties that are
> favorable to nobody.[48]

This desire for a mayor with political "weight" and *clientèle* ties was fundamental in a nation organized around the concept of notability. Despite the use by historians of political labels—Legitimist, liberal, Orleanist, conservative, Bonapartist, and so forth—in the operations of the mayoralties ideology was inconsequential. What was evident was that service in municipal government provided prestige and social authority.

This return to an essentially local, quasi-seigneurial view of power had borne its first fruits with the submission of France during the Empire and continued to do so until the end of the constitutional monarchies. A primarily peasant society remained passively obedient to the national government in the villages and small towns. The Revolution—particularly the anti-noble legislation and the holocaust of executions, both emphasized in constantly repeated martyrologies—convinced many noble families that the fundamental defense of their interests was to be found in rural complicities. They were known best in the countryside; in the urban anonymity, despite the immediate obligations of servants and purveyors, nobles were less sure of their ground. Was it not true that nonresident families who lost intimate local contacts, such as the aristocratic Saulx-Tavanes, so rarely seen in Burgundy, were those who suffered most from the Revolution? Too distant an estrangement from rural obligations in the pursuit of more profitable but riskier court advantages made any noble vulnerable. Indeed, one can loosely equate the despoliated nobles with those most distanced from their home communities. After the Revolution nobles personally well known in local society kept their preeminence in it.

The nature of such attachments, however, depended on many things. Apart from individual characteristics, such as a particularly blatant extortionism in leases or exceptional arrogance, there were regional considerations and differences in rank. A prefect reporting from the Haute-Garonne in December 1815 contrasted the noble outlook of southwestern France with that of western France: "In this department the royalists and especially the nobles show none of those pretensions capable of affrighting the common people [peuple] as [I encountered] in the Charente department, which I have administered, or others adjacent."[49]

If country attitudes changed slowly from 1800 to 1870, they were certainly not immobile. While many nobles expected deference by right from the peasantry, the latter came to realize that control over land and other resources was one measure of power, and influence in political and bureaucratic decisions quite another. While peasants were not averse to obsequiousness at this time, they naturally wanted to know its rewards. In the changing political circumstances of nineteenth-century France this was the calculation not easily made. When after the Hundred Days the duc de Vicence retired from a political and military career that had begun in 1788 and had raised him to the position of Napoleon's *grand écuyer,* he was clearly out of the restored Bourbons' good books. In the spring of 1816 the former intimate of Napoleon was under surveillance at the family's Caulaincourt château. The First Military Division commander noted his local popularity and considered him dangerous because of the influence his great wealth gave him over the peasantry.[50] This was the kind of situation where a peasant weighed immediate advantages from a good relationship with a wealthy landowner, in this case of lands that had been a *marquisat* in the Caulaincourt family since August 1715, against more distant benefits that might be forthcoming from government or bureaucracy. Of course, immediate advantage was generally preferred to the distant and abstract. Peasants at the bottom levels of rural society almost never enjoyed direct contact with the estate owner in person any more than with members of the departmental bureaucracy. The distinction between noble and bureaucrat was often blurred when nobles served as mayors, subprefects, or local councillors. Such office holding kept alive a nostalgia for Old Regime feudal and seigneurial responsibilities towards tenants, particularly on the lips of the *noblesse*. What they liked to think of as noblesse oblige was now a variant of nineteenth-century patronage systems, too partial and manipulative for one section of society to control in all its ramifications even in the remoter countryside.

An isolated southwestern department like the Hautes-Pyrénées illustrated what was involved in the local manipulation of power during the Restoration. Bertrand Barère de Vieusac, a former member of the committee of public safety, was simply one of an extensive patronage clan that included a Napoleonic *titré* and sought honorific and local posts over a span of more than sixty years. A later generation saw a similar network emanating from the Goulard family, who also claimed to be nobles. In the Cher, closer and more responsive to the political and economic rhythms of Paris, a similar network sprang from the Vogué family. As contemporaries observed, the Cher was spared the Reign of Terror's worst rigors thanks to a moderation often ascribed to the "innately" placid Berrichon temperament. It was equally comprehensible as the result of local nobles' refusal to become involved in counterrevolutionary politics. Their property was thus not confiscated, nor was their social place undermined. By the 1840s the most powerful noble family network was that of the marquis de Vogüé, a well-known farmer, often elected to *comices agricoles* during the Second Empire and holding substantial investments in the wood-fired ironworks of the area. Noting Vogüé's free-trade sympathies, his moderation in opposition, and his local prestige, the prefect made some shrewd remarks about the marquis's election by acclamation as president of the Bourges agricultural society:

> Mr. de Vogüé is a practiced agriculturalist, prizewinner of all
> regional competitions, member of the Central Agricultural Society in
> such a fashion that I am certain, to the exclusion of political
> preoccupations, it was the very special position of Mr. de Vogüé that
> inspired the choice made of his person in the circumstances. . . . as
> a private individual and agriculturalist. [Public] opinion of Mr. de
> Vogüé is so placed that the administration remains powerless in any
> efforts that it would undertake to hamper the expression of public
> sympathy in his favor. I shall add that it would be dangerous and
> clumsy to carry out such a defiance of opinion.[51]

Like so many other contemporaries, the Cher prefect sensed that proclaimed "orthodox" Legitimist attitudes were symbolic statements of social identity, to be divorced from their apparent political meaning.

Legitimism had always been charged with ritual meanings. This was increasingly true after 1830. Subscriptions to Legitimist newspapers like the *Journal des Modes,* the *Gazette de France,* and other provincial emulators; contributions to fund raising for monuments or for gifts to the exiled Bourbon family; and participation in local banquets and religious services to mark the pretender's birthday or the anniversary of Louis XVI's execution were gestures of complicity and an occasion for sociability without true hardship or real risk. Comte d'Adhémar correctly saw that "Legitimist opinions are a conviction—better than that, a religion." Royalist newspapers spoke of the "pilgrimage" in December 1843 of nine hundred faithful supporters to Henri V's Belgrave Square home in London.[52] Not everybody could sustain the reverential tone. The young duchesse d'Uzès, Legitimist both by birth and by marriage, described a visit to the pretender at Frohsdorff in 1867 with refreshing candor: "Monseigneur, of medium height, dissimulating badly his limp but with a royal majesty, Madame, big, ugly to the point of making one believe that ugliness had been invented for her, but trying to be amiable. . . . She was deaf and heard none of my words. The comte de Chambord took up the interview and helped her to reply. The conversation was banal, and I have retained no memory of it."[53] The point of such visits was, of course, to carry out a social ritual proper to the nobility.

The more legitimism took on ritual forms associated with Catholic piety, however, the easier it became to obey the injunction to "render unto Caesar. . . ." Those occasions were often pleasurable. Let the press report from the Camargue of a picnic to celebrate the 1846 wedding of the pretender suffice as an example. Local nobles figured prominently: marquise de Pontères, *née* Castellane, MM. de Barthélemy, de Surian, de Sabran, de Roux, de Trets, and de Campou, baron de Flotte, vicomte de Sairas, as well as a chorus of "good people," including those standbys of *provençal* traditionalism, the *patrons pêcheurs.*[54] Symbolic legitimism could thus be international, Parisian, or strictly local and provided opportunities to reaffirm social distances in secular and religious settings. These activities did not preclude nobles' sharing the advantages enjoyed by wealthy commoners, but they gave those satisfactions a special noble stamp.

All this is to say that sorting nobles into neat political sets overlooks symbolic politics, as well as the divisions within families. Individuals were sometimes at loggerheads on specific matters of public policy while sharing a common pride in rank. Thus liberal nobles felt a bemused affection for the ostentatiously orthodox Legitimists, who, while avoiding high-risk politics, exemplified in its purest state the belief in noble separateness and superiority. As an old lady the comtesse d'Armaillé recalled with pride that her husband had rejected an indirect approach to discover whether he was interested in a post of chamberlain or écuyer to Napoleon III without consulting her, so unthinkable was such activity within the family notion of honor. Her own family (Ségur) had been on good terms with successive governments, but she saw nothing inconsistent in this:

> Our politics were close to religion. In getting close to the new regime we would have believed that we were disobeying our dearest and most respected traditions. Comte de Chambord was our king, our prince. His portrait (before which at eighty-one years of age I now write these lines) was suspended in M. d'Armaillé's room like a pious picture. We did not reason about it, we felt ourselves honored to love him and to remain faithful to him. In this feeling there was no bitterness, no hatred against those who did not share it. I love to recognize it and to consider this kind of elevation as the effect of a sincere and true faith. No exaltation mixed with it. We found in it, on the contrary, a calm and a profound independence.[55]

Behind the internal squabbles, snubs, recriminations, and slander between "old" and "new" families over their merits and genealogy there was always a tacit recognition that all of them cared for the same things. All *titrés* at one level rejoiced in the existence of the most rigidly orthodox *noblesse,* who affected to despise them, since the *noblesse* preserved the rejection of democracy, egalitarianism, and individualism by a raw affirmation of racial and moral superiority over commoners.

The semipolitical activity in which this became explicit was participation in local charity, especially in the countryside. This could be seen as a neofeudal concern for retainers, in the event rural beggars. Of course, nobles had been prominent in eighteenth-century philanthropic efforts: the great aristocrat François-Alexandre-Frédéric de la Rochefoucauld-Liancourt had presided over the Assemblée Législative's Comité de mendicité and after his return to Napoleonic France from emigration he had continued to search for work for paupers and abandoned children in the Oise. Under the Restoration his politics still had been those of a liberal.[56] More representative of conservatives was his cousin and fellow peer of France, duc Michel de la Rochefoucauld Doudeauville, celebrated for his defense of noble and clerical privileges as much as for his generosity to the Montmirail hospital and for service on the boards of directors of Paris hospitals during the Restoration.[57]

Noble charity typically began at the country home, which is to say at the château, which provided the main source of relief to the poor peasants and beggars. The Gouville château (Eure) was said to succor an average of 200 needy weekly and as many as 1,600 in a week during a famine in 1817.[58] Joseph de Villèle's father wanted to go into the very homes of the poor to ensure that help went to those who were truly in need and so that wholesome pressure could be exerted to make the able-bodied work in the fields: "every capable beggar put to work in the fields is a conquest for the countryside where he uses his arms."[59] The Leveneur family felt responsibility for the poor of Carrouges canton (Orne), where their smithy was located. During the penurious summer of 1812 the château was used for rice distribution and coordination of food and money collections; in the winter of 1847, another time of acute rural distress, comte Leveneur permitted needy parishioners to gather fuel for their fires from his woods.[60]

A more wholehearted commitment is illustrated by Adolphe de Bourgoing, liberal before 1830 but Legitimist afterwards, who threw his energies into the management of his 170-hectare estate at Mouron-sur-Yonne (Nièvre). He bombarded the ministry with petitions and memoranda on the need to honor agriculture, to stimulate positive rivalry between farmers, and to encourage economic innovation. He bore witness for noble solicitude for the dire conditions of the rural as well as the urban poor. Parisian and provincial emulators of the charitable Armand de Melun, as members of charitable associations, contributors to journals like the *Annales de charité*, speakers on poor relief at the Chamber of Deputies and local councils, and writers of books and pamphlets, revealed the hopes for noble involvement. An 1840 memoir of Bourgoing captured those hopes for an interdependency of noble and peasant: "How many wounds would have closed and healed, how many illnesses assuaged, how many miseries diminished for the poor inhabitants of the countryside, if those who possessed the big properties had stayed put in them for a few months only?"[61]

Under Napoleon III, Bourgoing joined the prefectoral corps that included another noble reformer, Le Rat de Magnitot, who struggled with some success against the ravages of poverty in Bourgoing's native department of the Nièvre from 1853 to 1863.[62] In his 1863 pamphlet Robert Tancrède de Hauteville insisted on the need for nobles to exercise charity so as to demonstrate to the rural masses a genuine concern for their well-being: "The great difficulty is to vanquish this disdain and this ingratitude and not to become weary of going before the common people [*peuple*] who come with such difficulty to you, who only welcome your kindnesses most of the time with a doubting gratitude and a suspicious coldness." He insisted that charity be given directly, "without passing through strange hands, so that he who receives may be thankful to he who gives."[63] At the same time, this quotation implies less subservience from the peasantry than was earlier the case.

These charitable campaigns by nobles can be seen as having other ends than the self-evident one. One noble pamphleteer in the 1860s thought that charity could help one enter into contact with a better type of person:

> Associate yourself with all the charitable works [*bonnes oeuvres*], you will get to know all the great names from whom charity flows as from a spring. . . . Keep a good table in Paris and in your fine country château, you shall receive all those whom your charitable works shall have introduced you to. . . . Be the providence of your village, of your canton and your arrondissement; let it be that you are found always disposed to help with your purse for a bridge, a road, church repairs, agricultural associations.[64]

While this advice can be taken as somewhat ironic, its message was not. The indefatigable Armand de Melun encountered in the salons of charitable Catholic noblewomen a network of acquaintances to whose attention he commended the needy of Paris. That gave him an eminent place in the *bonne compagnie*.[65] Gobineau satirized such modish inspiration of volunteer work, to which he certainly donated neither time nor funds, in his novel *Les Pléiades*. Although the Lady Bountiful motif became part and parcel of the noble identity, it encouraged highly deserving efforts to alleviate human misery at a time when the state had not taken up its responsibilities in that regard. If the eighteenth century was the time of philanthropists discussing the extinction of beggary, the ninteenth was the heyday of voluntary efforts by the Catholic nobles to help the poverty-stricken.

Throughout this chapter I have stressed that nobles at large, and particularly aristocrats, ultimately rallied to every regime. During the Restoration the fewest doubts were encountered, since only Napoleonic *titrés* could have any reason to boycott a regime that could present itself as the Old Regime in new clothes. For their part the Bourbons were more solicitous of the Napoleonic nobility than the popular stereotype recognizes. Moreover, under each successive regime in France from 1800 to 1870, with the possible exception of the Second Republic, nobles were overrepresented, given their proportion in the French population, in all political assemblies and many bureaucratic and official posts. Similarly, nobles profited by neoseigneurial and patronage politics in the countryside. This potential strength relative to their numbers forced upon the more reflective *noblesse* a realization that this place in the sun resulted not from the nation's homage to their intrinsic excellence but from their landed wealth, political allies, adaptability, and continuing monopoly of the forms of social distinction.

The highest aristocracy had grasped those facts of life centuries past in the ongoing wars of family cliques struggling for royal approval at court. They were, especially through their women, the first to make overtures to the rulers of France thrown up by Revolution. Daughters could be extremely useful in this regard, as the aristocratic Léontine de Noailles demonstrated. She went to school under the instruction of one of Marie-Antoinette's ladies-in-waiting in the company of the first consul's sisters. At age seventeen she married her cousin Alfred (which kept her dowry within the cadet branch); shortly thereafter he fell in Russia. Meanwhile, a brother continued the family "insurance" as an émigré diplomat for the exiled Louis XVIII. This served the Noailles well during the Restoration, when he was a deputy for the Corrèze. After 1830 Léontine's entry into court circles was maintained thanks to her relatives, the Mouchy, well-known partisans of the Orléans family. The proclamation of the Second Republic in 1848 meant that the elite connections which had been good under four reigns now needed serious attention, and once her son-in-law was elected for the Oise, Léontine came to Paris from her château in order to open an elegant salon to serve as a clearing house for political information. Her life typifies aristocratic attention to the family network of interests quite independent of symbolic Legitimist sympathies, with which she was, inevitably, credited in the privately printed eulogistic 1855 biography of her, produced with mock eighteenth-century typeface.[66] Her burden was taken on by other members of the Noailles family who continued to flourish at Napoleon III's court. The ability to come to the top of the nexus of wealth, power, and social prominence was the essence of an aristocrat.

Lesser nobles had to content themselves with thinner wine, since they lacked the wealth and metropolitan contacts that would permit a redressment of their family situation. In the case of an impecunious young member of the *noblesse* who became a career soldier, Laveaucoupet, political flexibility was necessary despite the Legitimism that he was described as having: "He was a Legitimist by family tradition: without making any show of it, he could not understand how a well-born man could be of any other persuasion." He continued his career begun under the Bourbons as an officer of Louis-Philippe and as a general for Napoleon III.[67] Tens of thousands of others made similar adjustments to reality while nodding approvingly as their womenfolk declaimed about the historic purity of their devotion to the elder line.

It becomes apparent to the student of nineteenth-century noble politics that although Parisian and provincial families, aristocrats, *noblesse*, and titrés, followed different trajectories in their careers, all traveled in the direction of the goals set by their family membership. No family better exemplified stylish opportunism than the remarkable Choiseuls, fortified by an ancestry traceable to 1060. At any given time the bold strokes of the Choiseul political maneuvers might repel, at least in causal gossip, some more fastidious contemporaries in the faubourg

Saint-Germain, but with their lineage, their contacts, their style and great wealth, the Choiseul-Praslins retained an unquestioned place at the pinnacle of good society.[68]

The aristocracy tolerated the full range of loyalties within their own ranks, and individual animosities were never permitted to rend the social fabric. Only family ruin definitely expelled them from the glittering circle of those who, in Paris and the country, mediated the blend of distinction and power. The observant Austrian fop comte Apponyi commented on the realignments and continuities of Parisian high society after 1830, as it became apparent that Louis-Philippe had truly come to power. Writing of the opportunism of the Montmorency, he noted that they "do not disapprove of the behavior of the Bauffremont [who affected Carlist disdain for the Orleanist court], finding it prudent that the family members should be represented in all of the day's opinions, in order to have somebody, whatever happened, who might protect them and facilitate their return into the good graces of power once consolidated."[69]

In many provincial centers the *noblesse* and local *titrés* came to the same conclusion. The *noblesse* had entered the general councils of the departments on a massive scale under Napoleon I when he told them to do so, and in time increasing numbers made their appearance in the prefects' salons, especially if the prefects were of their own background. They served as mayors or on committees for the encouragement of agriculture and poor relief. Gradually they became used to meeting the *titrés* as equals. The Legitimist rhetoric that sprang to many lips served as decoration to the job of tradition carriers and was gracefully acknowledged, if not acted upon, by all who claimed to be nobles.

At this point, after the discussion of land and wealth in earlier chapters, it is germane to ask how economics and politics impinged on the existence of nineteenth-century nobles. In an article published in 1971, I suggested that noble influence declined not as a result of the Revolution but because of a failure to adjust to new economic forms while keeping capital in land.[70] Ralph Gibson demurred by observing that nobles in fact played a disproportionately large part in big business—he might have added that nobles were almost always investors and not entrepreneurs or managers.[71]

Even more cogently, Gibson denied that economic innovation—or stagnation for that matter—had much to do with the exercise of political power, since the outlook of backward and rural France was typical of republicans and the notables who supported Napoleon III as much as of royalists of Legitimist or Orleanist stripe. Instead, Gibson argued, there was a political evolution in which nobles were again designated as

national enemies—as they had been during the Revolution—in a di-
atribe fed particularly by republicans, who were *increasingly* able to
turn popular animosity against nobles, especially during the Third Republic. This is a striking argument which goes against the common
assumption that it was the French Revolution that set the high-water
mark of dislike of noble pretensions in a France where all were equal
before the law. Instead, an obsessive and widespread hostility to nobles
was manufactured at the same time that they dwindled in number.

The author of *Jacquou le Croquant*, Eugène Le Roy (1836–1907), the
son of an estate manager for the comte de Damas, described in his novel
published in 1899 the depredations of the odious, and recently ennobled, seigneurial Nansac family. The setting was his native Dordogne
under the Restoration, which allowed for precise and detailed descriptions of rural life combined with a time, more than eighty years earlier,
sufficiently remote for purposes of historical distortion.[72] (Many other,
less well written pieces of literature can be advanced to show how
nobles provided an object for loathing to large sectors of the French
public under the Third Republic, like Jews from the 1880s to 1945 or
North African and other immigrant workers after the Second World
War).

Gibson suggested that the hatred of nobles was manipulated by usu-
rers, who were not nobles but "men who started off humbly." These
individuals had every interest in elaborating a rhetoric that blinded the
peasantry, who borrowed money (that is, those peasants who were in a
position to do so), from their worst enemy, the usurer. They ranted
about noble hopes to restore the tithe, *corvée*, and a host of other feudal
obligations, not to overlook that favorite of the lubricious imagination of
indignant republicans, the *droit de jambage*, the alleged feudal right to
deflower the virgin wife of the newly wed tenant. Gibson concluded his
discussion, which he limited to descendants of the *noblesse*, by observing that "there is no economic necessity about it; the nobles simply lost
the battle for the hearts and minds of Frenchmen."[73]

This is a stimulating thesis, although one is hard-put to imagine
nineteenth-century nobles battling for anybody's hearts and minds save
those of their own families. The argument founders on the implication
that nobles were ever capable of collective political action. Nobles would
have to admit that their shared identity was itself bound up with recriminations and dissension, and this necessarily precluded any rallying against the enemy. Moreover, as argued throughout this study, it is
highly artificial to insist on some absolute difference between nobles
with titles before 1791 and those who gained or added to theirs later.
Indeed, when the Association d'Entr'aide de la Noblesse Française was
set up in the 1930s, it included, as had Article 71 of the Charter, the

post-Revolutionary creations.[74] What needs to be understood is not only nobles' economic behavior or their politics seen in isolation but how they kept themselves apart from the mass of the nation, took in new recruits, rejected egalitarianism, and maintained considerable social authority. To do so we must turn our attention to their religious outlook.

6

Nobles and Religion

Before 1789, nobles counted the French church as their choicest fiefdom. They had total control of the episcopacy, predominated among the fat livings of the cathedral canonries, and held the top posts in many opulent regular orders. Noblewomen frequently headed the wealthiest and most prestigious nunneries of the contemplative communities. Already in the decades before the Revolution, however, the rate of noble vocations declined more steeply than that of commoners'. In the rural parishes which served the bulk of the population a noble curé was rarely found, and if perchance he was, he usually came of a family in straightened circumstances. The peasant saw the seigneur in the front row of the parish church, but he almost never saw a noble at the altar, save on those rare occasions when the bishop, served by an entourage of attentive chaplains, made a visitation. The dissensions brought about among those who accepted or rejected the Civil Constitution of the Clergy, the jolting effects of the sale of urban and rural property belonging to the Church, and the emergence of secular alternatives in matters ranging from education to the calendar were all lamented with especial feeling by nobles. In some eyes the 1801 Concordat appeared a major step towards restoring Catholicism to an eminent place in France, but to ecclesiastical nobles it was of slight consolation. It is true that half of the new bishops had been born noble, as had many of the vicars general, but the total number of dioceses had fallen from 139 to 50. Only with the Bourbons' return in 1814 could nobles hope to recoup past advantages as a more confident Church leadership undertook a vigorous recruitment policy to rejuvenate an aging clergy and to proselytize parts of France where Christianity had been forgotten—if indeed it had ever been introduced. For nobles with any sense of recent history a nagging question was whether the Church would ever return to aristocratic direction. Much ground had been lost.

Can we generalize about noble attitudes toward religion after the Revolution? Here we confront the eternal questions of typicality. Were there marked differences in behavior between men and women, young and old? Do Chateaubriand's effusions in the post-Concordat best seller *The Genius of Christianity* represent the provincial *noblesse*, or are they more a testimony to his shrewd sense of a good topic for the right time? What of Saint-Simon's insistence on civil burial in 1825, the same year as the appearance of comte de Montlosier's impassioned attack upon the Jesuits? Was not the most virulently anticlerical of Blanqui's associates the baron Antoine de Ponnat? Were Napoleon's *titrés* less pious than the *noblesse*? Were *noblesse* reticent towards that growing nineteenth-century ultramontanism that culminated in the exaggerated deference accorded to Pius IX? These social questions are made more complex by the bewildering galaxy of theological tendencies of the time, Gallican and ultramontane, although we should recall that only a minority of the laity, almost exclusively male, interested themselves in doctrinal niceties.

The reasons why particular regions of France contrasted markedly with each other in the level of religious practice have exercised several generations of scholars. That is especially true of those places in the country like western France, where during the Revolution the nature of the popular religion affected politics. It was equally true of Gard, where hatred of Protestants was lively during the Restoration and the July Monarchy. Urbanization or land tenures do not provide any completely satisfactory key to local politics and beliefs, and historians place more and more emphasis on events that led families to political or doctrinal polarizations. This leads us to ask whether nobles reflected the religious behavior of the area where they lived or whether they set the tone of such conduct. Only a comparison of the religious traditions of noble families from different parts of the country would make possible tentative conclusions. However, as pointed out below in chapter 7, nobles were more likely to marry partners from distant birthplaces and more dispersed properties than were most other monied French people.

There is little evidence to throw into doubt the noble consensus on the great worth of respect, obedience, hierarchy, and sacrifice as taught by the Church. These virtues were as self-evidently desirable in a submissive spouse as in a servant or a tenant farmer. Common assumptions underlay innumerable conversations, letters, and sermons and were usually justified by a simplistic contrast between eighteenth-century wickedness and the chance to reform it in the nineteenth century. The father of the future prime minister Joseph de Villèle wrote to his deputy son in October 1815, at the height of the White Terror in the southwest:

This immorality, which cannot be destroyed save by religious
principles that the anarchists, sons and successors of the eighteenth-century philosophes, have busied themselves to destroy by
degrees to lead us into the deplorable state where we are and from
which we shall only escape when we shall truly return towards God
and the religion that we honor, the worthy priests: nothing can
better save us than He who brought punishment upon us for having
neglected him, and for having strayed from the sentiments and
probity that the Creator placed in the bottom of our hearts and from
which we have distanced ourselves.[1]

The self-conscious paternal pronouncement to a son who had taken on
national responsibilities rings rather forced. However, most nobles, and,
we may add, particularly their mothers, wives, and daughters, thought
along similar lines about the need for Catholic practice to expunge the
recent past.

Nobles were not, of course, exclusively Catholic. Lucien des Mes-
nards, a Protestant Legitimist, was imprisoned in connection with the
duchesse de Berry adventure in 1832; most of his erstwhile fellows
disapproved of his evangelical sympathies.[2] The Paris consistory counted the marquis de Jaucourt among its members. Protestant titles were
found among the major Parisian bankers—baron Turckheim, for example.[3] Jews figured among the Second Empire *titrés;* baron Rothschild
and others intermarried their converted daughters with titled gentiles.[4]
Indeed, the tension between the religious and social links among nobles
merits much more investigation.

Certain professions attractive to nobles weakened the religious commitment. That would seem to be true of the army. A former prefect of
provincial *noblesse* was scandalized by the misconduct of military officers attending mass at Bourges: even the general thought it good form
to chat constantly during the service.[5] That officers did not always
conduct themselves like prize seminarians enhanced the merit of more
reverent members of the armed services. Lieutenant General Par-
touneaux wanted an entire regiment to attend the 1819 mission in
Toulouse, and in October 1820 a procession of priests at the end of a
retreat was headed and closed by detachments of cavalry.[6] General
Aurelle de Paladines gave a mark of his deference to religious sensibilities when he ended, in 1867, the long-established custom of play-
ing a musical *retraite* next to Metz Cathedral in order that the martial
din would no longer disturb religious services.[7]

At the fourteenth degree of the old military family from the Bas
Limousin which had produced a flock of noteworthy senior officers over
the centuries, Anatole de Ségur was a prolific author on the theme of

religious instruction for the troops. Between 1856 and 1879 there were nine editions of his uplifting biography of the twenty-nine-year-old marquis de Villeneuve, testimony to the interest in the exemplary death of a Zouaves sergeant killed at Sebastapol: "[Villeneuve-Trans], which he has just again illustrated by dying, was already in the time of Saint Louis one of the greatest and most venerated names of France."[8] There were even more editions of Ségur's *La Caserne et le presbytère*, a collection of stories in the same spirit, and his book of military hymns. The listings of his publications runs to over eight pages in the general catalog of the Bibliothèque Nationale, attesting to his proselytizing efforts over and above those required as a prefect and a state councillor.[9]

Nobles themselves believed that family tradition best preserved religious purity. In individual cases this seemed dubious: the devout Albert de Mun counted Helvétius among his forebears, while Paul de Magallon d'Argens was a grandson of the marquis d'Argens, who had been a friend and chamberlain of Frederick the Great and author of the *Lettres juives, chinoises et cabalistiques* which were full of malicious, irreligious asides. Such strong contrasts are untypical; it is the persistence of loyalty to religion in a family that is more likely to impress. In Toulouse we find the same family names in protests before the Revolution (*Réclamations de l'église de Toulouse* [1788]), during the agitation against the Civil Constitution of the Clergy, among the members of confraternities and congregations established after the Concordat, and in protests against anticlericalism in the 1860s.

Family piety can scarcely be guessed from nineteenth-century political affilitations. Among the Toulouse noble conspicuously devout families were those who had rallied to Napoleon (Malaret, Cambon), ultraroyalists and Carlist supporters (Aspe, Dubourg, Malafosse, Saint-Félix), and supporters of the Orleanists (Aldéguier). There were no absolute linkages between Catholicism and right-wing politics despite such striking exceptions as the Gard department, with its polarization against the Protestant minority.[10] Were not the blues and the whites of Brittany both Catholic in practice but with different politics?[11] Many families displayed lukewarm devotion, contenting themselves with decent respect for form while avoiding any suspicion of excessive enthusiasm. For nobles as for the lower classes, religious practice and devotional exercises were a type of sociability. In towns like Nancy, Nantes, or Aix the *noblesse* had been little touched by the unbelief or deism of the tiny coteries of the intellectual critics of Catholicism.[12] The assertion that counterrevolution wrought a wholesale change of heart on the part of impious nobles is open to question, even though the theme was insistently repeated by royalist propaganda. Only the court nobility made an ostentatious return to manners which had never ceased to be current among their country cousins.

Respect for Catholicism did not necessarily mean respect for priests. Often the curé was the only spokesman with any moral authority on behalf of the peasantry, from which he frequently sprang. Out of the distant medieval past came conflicts between priest and seigneur over matters of tithes, precedence, and obedience, and in changing form those tensions remained widespread into the nineteenth century. In a rural setting the curé and the chatelain were sometimes two rival authorities. Many nobles continued to view the curé as someone whose status was between that of a head gardener and that of a notary. In the 1830s the immensely aristocratic bishop La Tour d'Auvergne left a château dinner party so that he might join his clergy, who had been convoked to the nearby rectory.[13] He at least wished to underline that his birth did not come before his episcopal unity with his lowlier-born clergy.

For their part, secular priests complained bitterly that they dropped in public estimation because of their subordination to bishops laid down by the Organic Articles. The situation might change for the better, two of them wrote poignantly, if only their independence were respected: "In seeing it honored and respected a crowd of candidates would come forward; it would be possible to recruit them among the highest classes and to distribute positions according to the nature of talents and the importance of merit."[14] One study of the northern diocese of Arras claims that after the 1848–51 agricultural crisis clerics were more respected by noble landowners than earlier in the century, mainly because the latter now looked for clerical aid in dealing with less docile peasants.[15] Nineteenth-century nobles, particularly women, came to realize that their attitude was wanting towards their most effective intermediary with the population. One aspect of the "feminization" of French Catholicism was a heightened respect for the clergy from laywomen, and nuns, who sought their approval and guidance.

The drawing together of noble and clergy in the nineteenth century was not a mere product of right-wing politics, waxing and waning in the light of the government's clericalism. It varied according to family and locality. Needless to say, officials usually saw this closeness in a political light. According to the Valence prefect in 1861, "The village curés search out the Legitimists, and these priests, who almost all belong to poor families, are proud to eat at the table of the château."[16] The conflicts that emerged were individual ruptures of a tacit alliance. A dispute over the refusal to ring church bells in honor of the Mayenne prefect, Napoléon-Charles Legendre de Luçay, a château guest of the

Hautefeuille family, led to a scene between the marquise and two priests over Napoleon III's Italian policy. With her *dame de compagnie* the marquise shouted and gesticulated "with violence" that the priests had come to "confuse these poor peasants," and when the clergy returned to the priest-house, they were again menaced, this time by the marquis, who furiously (and anachronistically) described the bishop as an "intruder" (recalling the Revolution), as well as an "animal": "You are all from the gutter [*canailles*], especially you, curé of Javron. If I didn't have more self-esteem, I would punch your face."[17] This left something to be desired as noble respect for religion.

Nor was politics the only bone of contention, as an altercation between curé Chopard and the former seigneurial family of Rochegude (Drôme) shows. Between the arrival of the curé at Rochegude in 1828 and 1841 the relations between priest and noble were excellent, but then there was a row over extending church buildings that adjoined property belonging to the Rochegude family. The curé wished to demolish a connecting archway between the château and the church, an archway deriving not from now-abolished seigneurial privilege, as the pugnacious curé claimed, but from a property transaction "enacted in 1728 between the marquis de Rochegude's father and the commune, an act by which the marquis kept this right in return for a donation to the commune of a property known as the Guard House, which had, I believe, actually been used to enlarge the church."[18] The same curé had sued the son-in-law of the marquis, the comte de Guilhermier, for setting a river dam that affected fishing and the water flow. Other priests in France waged similar struggles against local chatelains who tried to maintain outdated seigneurial claims.

Perhaps occasional friction between curés and nobles is more understandable if we look at the striking absence of noble priests among the parish clergy. This continued the pre-Revolutionary situation, although assiduity of practice still varied by region, as did the number of vocations. Nobles were more numerous among postulants to the clergy in Brittany, the west, and Lorraine than in Paris or the Midi.[19] Just as under the Old Regime, the nineteenth-century secular clergy recruited primarily among urban artisans and shopkeepers and the well-to-do peasantry. Until the 1830s the careers of these lower-class postulants unfolded differently from those of the few well-born men who studied with them in the seminaries. Students from homes with more social graces and a higher level of general culture were favored for bishoprics and canonical stalls. In general, however, the rich nobles and bourgeois of the nineteenth century had a similar response to the lower clergy: as one historian phrased it, they refused the Church their children. In

1821 de Frayssinous regretted that the priesthood was given over "to the vulgar classes."[20]

The evidence from a variety of diocesan studies points in one direction. In Montpellier diocese between 1846 and 1870, of 341 priests whose origins are known 80 percent were of modest background, while the local nobility and wealthy middle classes combined provided only 13 priests, or 3.8 percent of the total.[21] Among the aristocracy as among wealthy commercial, manufacturing, and professional circles in Marseilles vocations in the mid-nineteenth century were "exceptional."[22] In the Sarthe, where the social origins are known, among more than 1,500 ordinations during more than a century (1800–1905) only 2 nobles were found, and that in a region where the local nobles were said to be generally very attached to Catholicism and the Church.[23] At Nantes, of 53 students attending the grand seminary in 1811 only 6 were of bourgeois or higher background; the remainder were from the families of small farmers.[24] These findings apparently confirm the idea that nobles in the priesthood scarcely exceeded, if at all, the proportion of nobles in the French population: perhaps half of 1 percent.

This sparse noble recruitment was regretted in many an eloquent sermon after 1800. In 1851 the son-in-law of Hercé, bishop of Nantes, deplored the absence of the "hautes classes" from the priesthood and was ingenuous enough, in the conservative atmosphere following the events of 1848, to suggest that an understandable repugnance of high society for an excessive egalitarianism ("a too great leveling") was reason enough to reserve for them the most desirable posts as deans and archpriests to stimulate vocations. Abbé Collet made a tart rejoinder to those notions in a pamphlet in which he claimed that virtue and piety were more needful to priests than polished table manners.[25] In devout circles where the role of the French church was taken for granted as a bulwark against the philosophes' insidious poison noble leadership seemed proper. It implied a return to the pre-Revolutionary days.

Why nobles so markedly kept away from secular clerical life but entered into the regular orders is not self-evident. Was there a dislike for a lifetime of contact with the lower classes? Was the poor pay of the curés (despite improvements over the pre-Revolutionary salaries brought about by nineteenth-century governments) a special disincentive? Individual noble careers reveal some possible changes in a lifetime. De Charbonnel, of a sword family from a highly pious part of France, the Velay, showed a desire to become a priest early in life. He trained at Saint Sulpice, subsequently taught in various seminaries, and then was named bishop of Toronto although completely innocent of pastoral experience. After serving in Canada from 1851 to 1861, he returned to France and became a Franciscan, a rule that allegedly attracted him because of its simplicity, although Charbonnel constantly showed great pride in his family's nobility.[26] Henri de Bonnechose, of Norman *noblesse* with a Protestant mother, studied law and was appointed a public prosecutor before his ordination by monseigneur de Rohan in 1833, whereupon he taught in seminaries and also in the college in Rome for French Seminarians renowned for the ultramontane outlook of its teaching staff, Saint Louis of the French. At age forty-eight he began his episcopal career, serving successively at Carcassonne, Evreux, and Rouen.[27] Although we do not yet have all the information needed for an accurate comparison, it seems clear that among male nobles there was a lower rate of entries into religion during the nineteenth century than during the eighteenth. The proportion of nobles fell even more than their demographic decline among the rising annual totals of ordinations (averaging 1300–1750) between 1850 and 1868.[28] We are confronted with the paradox of a more churchy nobility but fewer nobles in the Church.

In the hierarchy's upper reaches the percentage of nobles always remained higher than among the clergy at large (see table 9). In 1828 they were numerous among the 468 vicars general, the 864 titular canons, the 1,788 honorary canons, and the 439 chaplains and 1,044 priests who taught in seminaries—all as enumerated in the *Almanach du clergé de France*. Despite the rally of the Restoration years, however, the proportion of noble bishops fell steadily. The fairly young men named bishops under the Restoration threw a long shadow, but once that generation began to die off, they were not replaced. They reflected the ecclesiastical policies of the successive regimes in France. The First Empire advanced bishops of Old Regime noble families who were sufficiently docile to Bonaparte. The Restoration markedly appointed nobles (seventy-five of ninety-six new bishops) especially during its first five years: the gratified new incumbents were now styled monseigneur instead of monsieur as in the Old Regime. The July Monarchy displayed the opposing tendency, as when the successful candidate for bishop of Langres could be praised for, among other sterling qualities, "the merit of having come up by his own efforts [*s'être fait seul*]. His birth is very obscure."[29] The Second Empire was concerned above all to find compliant candidates.[30]

Bishops overlapped regimes. An example is the former émigré monseigneur de Cosnac, who had taken part in Charles x's coronation and who became archbishop of Sens in April 1830, a few months before the July Revolution. Passionately devoted to the Bourbons, he encouraged to good effect his clergy in hostility to the Orleanist regime, particularly in the Avallonais. The age of the clergy was important. In 1828 the

TABLE 9. Nobles as a Percentage of the French Episcopacy, 1804–1870

Year	Total Number of Bishops	Noble Bishops	
		Number	Percentage of Total
1804	46	23	50
1817	51	30	58
1847	76	26	34
1870	76	9	12

Source: Pius Bonifacius Gams, *Series episcoporum ecclesiae catholicae* (Regensburg, 1857; reprint, Graz, 1963).

eldest of the cardinals and archbishops of France was Clermont-Tonerre of Toulouse, 80, and the eldest bishop was Sébastiani della Porta at Ajaccio, 83. The youngest cardinal was the prince de Croy, grand almoner of France at age 55; the youngest archbishop was Quelen, of Paris, 50; and the youngest bishop was Bonald, at Puy, 41.

Even more influential than age was the length of time a particular bishop remained on his episcopal seat. The average incumbency was twelve to thirteen years, but how misleading this can be is revealed by the case of the Moulins diocese. Named by the royal ordonnance of 8 August 1817, the first bishop, Antoine de Pons, of ancient Auvergnat nobility, had served in Moulins as a vicar general since 1804 and as titular canon since 1814. Only in 1823 did the episcopal nomination receive canonical institution. Born in 1759, he managed to outlive both the Bourbons and the July Monarchy, dying in 1849. Staunchly Legitimist, de Pons was as conspicuously lacking in zeal for the July Monarchy as in personal humility: in 1843 an irate relative attacked him in an anonymous pamphlet disputing his right to use a heraldic coat of arms. His successor was appointed in the 1849 conservative reaction. Pierre-Simon-Louis-Marie de Dreux-Brézé, born in 1811 and third son of Louis xvi's master of ceremonies, showed the mark of his clerical education in Rome, where he became a convinced ultramontanist. He spent his early career as a canon of Notre Dame in Paris, but in 1840 he became deeply involved in one of the mutual aid societies, which Legitimists encouraged warmly (that of Saint Francis Xavier), as well as in work for the Oeuvre de Saint-Jean, dedicated to the moral welfare of young apprentices in the capital. Dreux-Brézé was the youngest prelate in 1850, when he took possession of his see. Everything in his outlook and manner proclaimed him to be a grand seigneur: he enforced the full splendor of the Roman rite, on occasion entered into disputes with the civil authority, and was one of the three bishops who swept aside the prohibition of the diffusion of Quanta Cura and the Syllabus of Errors which he promulgated with particular solemnity in his cathedral in 1865. He vehemently upheld papal infallibility. Such strong views inevitably produced growing opposition among part of his clergy, but he maintained his ultramontane and conservative sympathies intact until his death in 1893, by which time he was the oldest of French bishops.[31]

The disproportionate presence of noble bishops compared with their presence in the clergy at large and even more so with their part in the French population meant that they exercised greater influence in the post-Revolutionary Church than in any other major institution. To what extent noble bishops helped other nobles in appointments to positions of influence is difficult to know. Very likely it was unconscious, or at least rationalized into fulsome praise of the piety or excellent upbringing of each individual. The fiery and ascetic *provençal* bishop of Marseilles, Eugène de Mazenod, was solicitous of the foundress of the Sisters of Saint-Joseph of the Apparition, the noble Mme de Vialar, and gave particular encouragement to the hospital of the Brothers of Saint John of God, established in Marseilles by the noble Paul de Magallon, a personal friend of the Mazenod family in Aix-en-Provence.[32]

The undoubted fervor in religion of all concerned made the help offered to fellow nobles more agreeable. Bishop Mazenod, in fact, irritated his secular clergy more by his obvious partiality to the Oblate Fathers of Mary Immaculate, an order founded by him, than by his background in the robe nobility of Provence. Only by investigating each diocese with a noble bishop could one begin to know exactly how much aid was accorded to other nobles, and the range of personalities involved would make generalizations difficult. Suffice it to say that there is no evidence of a noble bishop *opposed* to his ilk in the Church. On the other hand, the steady fall in the numbers of noble bishops presumably brought about new ways in dioceses now led by men of less exalted origins.

Nowhere was the noble contribution to the nineteenth-century religious revival more pronounced than in the female regular orders. Noble girls surged into religious orders, as exemplified by the five daughters among ten children of an impoverished Breton family of Saint-Pol-de-Léon one of whom became superior general of the Nantes Religieuses de la Retraite.[33] Between 1851 and 1861 the number of nuns more than doubled—from 34,200 to 89,200—and the sharp increase continued unabated over the following decade.[34] Particular orders such as the Rennes Augustines or the Nantes Ursulines, attracted noble postulants especially. Whether the rise in the numbers of nobles

resulted from pinched family economies is not easy to say, although this
was widely believed at the time.

Noble women were particularly drawn to the more emotional and
ritualized faith of the nineteenth century. This sometimes lay between
secular and cloistered life. Mme de MacCarthy was attracted to the
religious traditions of the Franco-Irish family into which she married at
Toulouse. She became when still young a leading light among the local
society ladies who made donations of nursing and of money to an association involved with dressing the sores of poor women. In due course
she adopted a female relative who later became a nun. After the death of
her husband, Mme de MacCarthy spent her last years in a community.[35] This kind of religiosity was in no sense limited to nobles, as a study
of the middle-class women in the Lille region during the nineteenth
century has clearly demonstrated. It is worth emphasizing, however,
how that charitable behavior was to a significant extent a mimicry of
nobles.[36]

The eighteenth century had been marked by the establishment of
charitable and educational orders of nuns, but noblewomen preferred
the cloistered orders. After the upheavals of the Revolution this tendency diminished. The government and prefects particularly encouraged
the return of the hospital orders. During Napoleon's visit to Bordeaux in
1808, imperial largesse was granted to a charitable foundation working
with penitent prostitutes (filles repenties) housed in the former convent
of the Annonciades which was headed by Marie-Thérèse-Charlotte de
La Mourous, of one of the city's noble families.[37] There was a new
welcome for nuns such as the Cordelières, Benedictines, Visitandines,
and Ursulines, engaged in socially useful work.[38] Noblewomen were
now more prominent: Mlle Négrier de la Ferrière founded a hospital for
poor incurables at Le Mans in 1815 which survived for nine years.
Nobles also served in teaching orders, such as the Ladies of the Sacred
Heart, whose mission was the education of middle-class and noble
girls.[39] Noblewomen were still well represented in contemplative orders
such as the Bénédictines du Saint-Sacrément, established by Mother de
Cossé-Brissac.[40]

A number of remarkable noblewomen entered religion after marriage, such as Mme Bonnault d'Houet, whose husband died less than a
year after their 1804 wedding. In 1817 she took a vow of chastity and
henceforth devoted herself to the establishment of free schools for
young girls by a society of the Fidèles Compagnes de Jésus, which
received papal approval in 1837. Mme Bonnault d'Houet had a pronounced taste for bodily mortification, a devotion to virgin martyrs, and
a regret to have ever known conjugal life.[41] Baronne de Chatillon, born
at Autun in 1819, was brought up in a profoundly religious atmosphere

until her marriage at age twenty-two with Rambert de Chatillon, a Savoyard senator. They were childless, noted for piety and good works. After twenty years her husband died, and the baronne entered the Franciscan Third Order and established the Chambéry Providence.[42] Hélène de Raigecourt became a hospital nun after the death of her husband delivered her from an unhappy married life. Among the 103 biographies of nuns examined in a study of the theme of physical mortification and the exaltation of the soul during the nineteenth century, at least 10 percent concerned sisters born nobles.[43]

Noble laywomen were affected by the new sympathies of the upsurge of belief in the miraculous which was a feature of the nineteenth century. The Marian cult reached new heights with the appearance of the Virgin in 1846 at La Salette and the apparition seen by Bernadette Soubirous in 1856 at the Massabielle grotto. Monseigneur Philibert de Bruillard, bishop of Grenoble, was extremely cautious about the La Salette apparitions, but in response to the numerous pilgrims he permitted Mass to be said. Some of his clergy appealed against him to the metropolitan, Archbishop Bonald of Lyons, before addressing the pope.[44] Not all noble ladies cared for the new enthusiasms: Mme de Ventavon of Grenoble supported a debunking noble priest who said that the La Salette shepherd boys were hoodwinked by a dotty local spinster, Mlle de la Merlière, who dressed up for the purpose.[45] By and large, however, noblewomen followed the marked trend of the century towards a more emotional religion. Both at home and at school noble girls were encouraged to respect religion and to feel intensely on the subject, as Mme d'Armaillé recalled.[46]

Nowhere was this more evident than in the education of children. Clerical tutors were sometimes employed by families of sufficient wealth, but nobles actually preferred to send their sons to clerical-run schools. Religious colleges run by Jesuits and Dominicans prolonged the ascendancy that they had enjoyed in the education of nobles under the Old Regime and that continued into the twentieth century. Catholic education was intimately bound up with the teaching orders with many noble pupils which transmitted the deportment and beliefs suitable to young nobles, as well as gave access to the network of friendship and acquaintance among their peers that would be useful later in their careers or perhaps marriages. Lamartine met at school at Belley his lifelong friend Virieu, of one of the oldest families of nobility in Dauphiné, and sought his advice throughout his life despite a growing contrast in their politics.[47] Many less illustrious nobles owed to school friendships contacts with their peers who were not related to them.

With the technical improvement in printing during the first half of the nineteenth century, ever more books could be cheaply printed to carry the moral and religious injunctions proper to young nobles. The work of Mme S. de Renneville, although not directed exclusively at her peers, was permeated with this morality. A case in point is her *Galerie des jeunes vièrges, ou modèle des vertus qui assurent le bonheur des femmes*. Mme de Rémusat wrote on women's education. Noble matrons were numerous among writers of children's books: Mmes de Tastu, de Witt, and de Genlis and, of course, the immortal Russian, comtesse Sophie de Ségur. Their works dissimulated class distinctions behind a pink haze of religiosity, but ultimately they were totally opposed to egalitarianism.

Between 1801 and 1814 more than fifty new male congregations appeared or were developed despite Napoleon's disapproval of regulars, and this increase accelerated during the Restoration. Like noblewomen, noblemen were more drawn to closed orders. The Trappists appealed to the émigré Le Clerc de la Roussière of the Maine: he had stayed with French Trappists at Darfeld in Westphalia. Upon his return to France in 1807, he bought a former priory for a Cistercian foundation, and in 1815 a new community (five fathers, ten brothers) began life in common. One Trappist who wrote devotional works, such as the *Aspirations aux sacrées plaies de N.S. Jésus-Christ,* emphasizing religious exaltation, was a former chamberlain of the Austrian emperor, General de Géramb.[48]

Mendicants and teaching orders dedicated to the poor had less social cachet than the others. The Jesuits, by contrast, had always drawn upon an aristocratic clientele for their colleges. Like the Dominicans, they attracted noble vocations. One of the most famous society preachers of the 1830s and 1840s was a Gascon noble Jesuit, Lacroix de Ravignon. Numerous new congregations continued to be set up, and the middle years of the nineteenth century saw a massive increase in the numbers of monks—tenfold from the three thousand of the 1840s. A former imperial general staff captain, Paul de Magallon, was elected superior in 1819 of the Saint John of the Cross hospital by companions mostly of modest background with a weaker general culture and less knowledgeable about administration and society than the nobleman. His family connections proved useful in collecting from the local aristocracy and again in 1852, when he established at Marseilles an Association d'âmes d'élite parmi les Catholiques de la Haute-Société Marseillaise.[49]

If we turn from nobles within the Church to their lay attitudes, the education of the lower classes was of great importance. Almost all accepted that clerical teachers were best suited to instill respect, moral uprightness, and deference to betters. In newspaper articles, books, and sermons the contrast was tirelessly drawn between the "good," pious

Old Regime peasants and the Revolutionary officials, usually portrayed as urban men-of-law, schoolteachers, grasping speculators, and occasionally renegades and ungrateful overseers, from whose malice the peasants saved their (always benevolent) former seigneurs during the Revolutionary holocaust. Education for the masses should be primarily catechetical, emphasizing continuity in an unchanging rural order. This viewpoint had some validity in a country still composed predominantly of peasants, but it was alien to the squalid new suburbs of the rapidly growing cities of France which attracted migrants.

Nobles put their faith in the Ignorantins (Brothers of the Christian Doctrine) and others especially concerned with lower-class education who would reinforce deference and submission to the status quo. They were deeply grieved by damaging scandals like that of Brother Léotade, found guilty in 1847 of attempted rape and murder of a fourteen-year-old girl in Toulouse, or that of Brother Alexandre, convicted in 1869 of *attentats à la pudeur* on young boys at Beauvais. There were many obsessional sexual innuendos or overt claims of clandestine sexual activity in mid-century anticlerical writings. Conversely, nobles and supporters of Catholic education emphasized that it was a purer form of instruction than that in the state schools.

A measure of the importance attached to the schools' social mission to the lower classes were the legacies in wills, donations, and fund-raising efforts on their behalf. When the Sisters of Providence were established at Arras to train teaching nuns for work in country schools, many local nobles gave one hundred to six hundred francs (at a time when a laborer's hire was 1F 50 per day), and the comte de Bryas donated two thousand francs.[50] Only a few liberal nobles supported the Lancastrian system, as it was called in reference to its English origin, where older children taught the younger what they had learned.[51] The duc de Lévis vigorously attacked Belgian exponents of this mutual instruction system on the grounds of intrinsic inequalities between individual and racial abilities. Women, he felt, could only be encouraged in reprehensible disobedience and desire for social change by such instruction.[52]

Noble laywomen were at the forefront of a variety of Catholic agencies of edification and instruction. This was less true before the Revolution. A variety of studies made clear a decline in Old Regime male devotional associations in the decades before 1789, but it is unclear whether the same was true of females. Apparently such lay bodies revived during the nineteenth century. Often involved with particular institutions, such as orphanages or prisons, women in particular were concerned with collecting dowries for poor girls, training in skills such as lace making, and saving girls from prostitution. Men were associated with similar activities. The Toulouse prefect in 1809 was startled during a mission at the ostentatious religiosity of noble participants whom he had never thought to be devout, while the city's traditional confraternities underwent a jump in noble membership.[53] The confraternity at Laval (Mayenne) was presided over by nobles throughout the 1850s and the 1860s and was involved in works of charity.[54] The records of the Moulins Engilbert (Nièvre) Association de Bienfaisance et de Charité in the late 1860s showed that nobles, both men and women, consistently gave more money than the local curé or the commoner members.[55]

Noble interest in charity was both theoretical and practical. The interest of writers on poor relief and participants in programs of public assistance was, more or less consciously, social control. Nevertheless, it would be a serious injustice to belittle any desire to alleviate suffering. The efforts of Louis-Auguste Guays des Touches, son of a Restoration magistrate, may stand as representative of this aspiration at its best. This bachelor possessed a townhouse on Laval's place de Gast and a château in the commune of Bignon, where he became mayor in 1855. From 1848, at the age of twenty, he filled many of his days with good works. He was a member of the Saint Vincent de Paul conference, organized the leisure of young workers and apprentices, and set up lotteries for the benefit of the poor. He collected money and oversaw the construction of a new parish church at Bignon (1859–62) and went on pilgrimages to Rome, to Saint Julien du Mans, and to the newly reestablished Solesmes abbey. His most important activity was the 1855 foundation at Laval of an organization to help poor children in prayer and play, and in 1874 he left his estate to the diocesan grand seminary, doubtless with the intent of supporting young priests' education.[56] One could multiply instances of nobles who preached by example, although rarely with such complete abnegation as Guays des Touches. The Hagerue family of the Pas-de-Calais conveyed their fervent regard for the newly proclaimed dogma of the Immaculate Conception by giving sixty-eight indigents dinner on silver plate with due attention to etiquette. A daughter of the family served the table, seconded in her efforts by the Enfants de Marie.[57]

In the history of nineteenth-century Church-state relations nobles had an increasing propensity to support the clericals. The more fervently they did so, the less were they marked off sharply from the other faithful. In one sense ultramontanism increasingly outweighed legitimism, as Michel Denis and Stéphane Rials have pointed out, despite the dual loyalties of most nobles and many priests. After 1830 Rome became ever more important than the Austrian court of the pretender, but the shift was already going on before. For this reason it is vain to look for a precise collective "noble" outlook on the policies followed by successive governments towards the Catholic church. There was no particular "noble" consensus on how to respond to Napoleon's imprisonment of Pius VII from 1809 to 1814, or the 1817 Concordat, or the 1825 Sacrilege Law, or the anticlericalism of the 1830s, or the anxieties generated by the collapse of papal temporal power in Italy in the 1850s other than to say that in the majority nobles followed the mainstream of Catholic opinion in France. When Charles, comte de Montalembert, denounced the cooperation of the Church with the state in his celebrated polemical book *Les intérêts catholiques au XIXe siècle* (1852), he wrote above all as a son of the Church rather than as a noble.

It is perhaps possible, however, to see a particular noble style in the way nobles supported the clerical cause. The reconstruction of the Laval diocese (curiously enough first established as a juring diocese in 1790) was largely the result of a campaign by local nobles. At the death in 1854 of the Le Mans bishop (monseigneur Bouvier), the new diocese was authorized by Napoleon III, crowning the efforts of a local devout noble, Guillaume d'Ozouville, who persuaded Mme de Vaufleury of Laval to donate the property that served as an episcopal palace in order to obviate the general council's fear that the new establishment would be a burden on local taxes.[58] Ozouville was the author of a pamphlet calling for the return of the upper classes to the clergy, as mentioned above. There was fiscal support from local nobles as though to compensate for the paucity of vocations. In a similar way at Rennes in December 1843, when none of the local authorities attended the benediction of the cathedral bells in an official capacity, the Legitimist nobles turned out in droves. Legitimist nobles enthusiastically seconded the devotion to the Sacred Heart when it was made a festival of the Church Universal by Pius IX in 1856 and often recalled that the counterrevolutionary Vendéens had used it for their symbol.[59]

In general the linkage of religious ritual with political anniversaries was promoted. A report from Aix in 1860 noted: "Today, 21 January, at 11 A.M. was celebrated in the Church of St. Jean de Malte a commemorative Mass for the death of Louis XVI; the nave was draped in black. In the numerous and contemplative congregation which took part one numbered few common people [*gens du peuple*], but on the other hand one saw joined together many ladies belonging to the *classe aristocratique*."[60] At Toulouse in 1863 a performance of Emile Augier's anticlerical play *Le fils de Giboyer* provided a pretext for young nobles to provoke a stylish uproar against the notion that clericals were "vicious hypocrites, the Legitimists laggardly dunces, the gentlemen insolent and haughty, the rich bourgeois compliant ninnies."[61] As at the Aix memorial Mass, the common people were conspicuously absent from this Legitimist demonstration, revealing the steep loss of interest in royalism by the lower classes.[62]

What was noble was the ostentatious derring-do: a commoner supporter of clerical concerns would not kick a police commissioner or threaten duels in the manner of the marquis Buisson de Bounazel. The papal Zouaves provided a new galaxy of ultramontane heroes. Even more than the colonial adventures, which provided stirring prospects to Lamoricière to display feudal values of superiority over inferiors, the decision to defend the Holy Father fitted into a nineteenth-century catalog of knightly values. The highly conservative prefect Joseph-Antoine Ferlay, who was a native of the Drôme department which he administered, saw the extravagance in 1861:

> The clergy and a little Legitimist coterie has made a great fuss about the departure for Rome of a young man called d'Arblatier; this youth has been an N.C.O. in a cavalry regiment. (He left it because his officers thought he was incapable of being an officer.) His father served bravely during the First Empire; but then he fell into an excess of devotion, and he is considered as an intense Legitimist to the point that he did not wish to swear the oath as a municipal councillor of his commune.[63]

This "excess of devotion" advanced among nineteenth-century nobles. Of the sixty from Mayenne of the two thousand French Zouaves, most were nobles.[64] Among them was Georges d'Héliand, whose ancestors had been military and whose grandparents were imprisoned under the Revolution. He left for Rome at age eighteen and arrived at the Terni camp on 27 August. Within a month he was shot dead in battle at Castelfiardo. Upon receiving the news his widowed mother wrote, "I ought to thank God, who let my Georges taste a happiness that I could not give him. . . . Happier than many mothers, I have been able to enjoy for an instant the good conduct of my Georges."[65] On the same day six nobles and two commoners had been killed on the battlefield.[66]

The first seven decades of the nineteenth century provided a contrast to the legends of irreverent aristocrats at Versailles, legends derived from Parisian models instead of country squireens. Now, from the 1801 Concordat and on through the century, regular attendance at Mass, education in clerical establishments, and a decorous observance by womenfolk in particular of the moral dictates of the Church were more typical. This was part of the larger shift of pious practice which contemporaries saw when they looked at congregations: "In Paris, one hardly meets anybody in the churches save elegant men belonging to the enlightened classes," wrote one 1837 author, who seems not to have noticed the women present.[67]

Throughout the 1830s and 1840s there was an implicit ambivalence, not often recognized, between the primacy to nobles of Legitimist doctrine, itself marked with "miraculous" elements such as the birth of the pretender after his father's assassination, and a Catholicism particularly congenial to feminine ideas of the family and of the support provided by its womenfolk as the "invisible sustainers" of all that made nobles in their own eyes superior to the mass of the population. It made little difference whether the national government was conspicuously sympathetic to Catholicism, as were the ultra ministries of the Restoration, or hostile, as during the alarming days of 1848. The Revolution had detached practice from being part of the support of the state itself, and this turned many towards a family piety where the celebration of the feast days of Saints and dynastic birthdays provided a self-absorbing and inward-looking religious ritualism. Perhaps only the hostility aroused by the French position on the temporal sovereignty of the Holy See for a time reversed the dichotomy that increasingly characterized the century. Under the reign of Napoleon III the Catholic nobility could reflect that for the first time since the Wars of Religion their blood had flowed for the faith at Castelfiardo. The difference between the 1870 nobles and those of a century earlier was not so much their observance or their doctrinal views as it was the conspicuous affirmation of ritual and orthodoxy which an earlier generation would have found clumsy.

Catholicism of the sort praised by nobles set itself against the triumphant forces of the century. Latter-day seigneur and parish priest both advocated a solicitous paternalism which many in society disputed, as did a number of clerical intellectuals. Whole sections of the urban lower classes became indifferent to the faith, while nobles made ostentatious practice an obligation for their families. Nobles tacitly agreed on an ideal concept of religious behavior which, if it did not describe their conduct, at least served to propose to their peers how they ought to behave. The noble biographer of the young Hélion de Villeneuve-Trans described him as having begun to slip into Parisian temptations when he heard the news of his father's fatal illness and was recalled home to more pious conduct:

> After having received one last time in the presence of his family the
> sacraments of the Church with a great calm, the marquis de
> Villeneuve-Trans spoke to his son of the life that he should lead and
> of the honor of his name which he left to him pure and unstained;
> he urged him to have always in his mind the memory of his
> ancestors, great by faith and by their chivalrous devotion to France,
> to always carry in a worthy way a name illustrated by so many
> generations; then he gently went to slumber in the arms of his dear
> son and in the peace of the Lord.[68]

The biographer assured readers that this deathbed homily returned the young man to more virtuous paths. His message was that the noble family was a shield against urban vices.

This insight was especially directed at females. Noblewomen played a more important role than at any time since the seventeenth century as an intermediary between state and the poor. They tried to provide occasional employment for "their" destitute, as well as support for the needy. In towns women were active in fund raising, from a duchesse de Rohan in Paris, who shamed the deputy from Bergerac Maine de Biran into increasing his charitable donation, to the ladies in diocesan societies who took up collections at the cathedral doors. We have no in-depth study of women's charity in France from the eighteenth century to the twentieth, but there seems little doubt that noblewomen were increasingly at the forefront of efforts undertaken. At a time when noblemen were a shrinking minority in Church leadership and the number of their vocations fell more than their group declined as a proportion of the national population, noblewomen were ever more important to the social activities of the Church.

7

The Noble Family

THE SITUATION IN THE LAW

Legislation between 1790 and 1794 lessened the authority of French husbands over wives, established divorce, and gave children equal inheritance rights. Marriage was henceforth a secular engagement that required ratification by public officials. By those measures the Revolution weakened legal constraints inside families and by doing so struck at an essential root of the nobility. Now equal with commoners before the law, nobles felt even more keenly than them how innovations undermined the ways in which the family head could control his dependents. Female family members had exercised a great deal of initiative in protecting property belonging to French noble émigrés by invoking dotal rights and those of children. Those women had a more independent outlook, as well as a clear title to more assets in their marriage. Nobles had always put the utmost emphasis on preventing individual whims, grievances, or natural rights from upsetting their family's destiny, and the disruptions and innovations of the Revolution were bitterly regretted.

After 1800, hard-pressed patriarchs welcomed Napoleon's return to sterner practice, particularly with the 1804 Civil Code, which reaffirmed the senior males' domination of the French family. The family council convoked to deal with disputes had to be composed of six or more males evenly divided to represent the interests of spouses or children in a variety of situations (Articles 405–19, 755, 758, 767). Divorce was made more difficult to accomplish. Like other property owners, nobles generally applauded limiting wifely rights against husbands or those of children against their progenitors. The Chambre introuvable (1815–16), an assembly in which the collective outlook of the petty *noblesse* was enunciated more clearly than at any time since the calling of the second estate to Versailles in 1789, took another step along the

road to reasserting masculine authority by abolishing divorce completely. Despite these retreats from the Revolutionary enactments, the
support accorded in law to the family head was much reduced from that
bestowed by the Old Regime.[1]

Nowhere was that more evident than in inheritance laws. Essentially
the Civil Code upheld the equal inheritance rights of children and in so
doing reasserted the death of the system of primogeniture, the *droit
d'aînesse,* which gave the first-born male advantage over his siblings.
No longer could nobles by their wills ensure the survival of unified
family property in the hands of the senior male heir. Renunciation of a
child's rights could only be achieved by voluntary obedience to family
spirit. In publications directed to the nobles it became commonplace to
lament the pernicious new laws on inheritance. Although they are hard
to appraise, we can at least be sure that these legal novelties did not slow
the economic decline of the poorer noble families.

NOBLE ATTITUDES TOWARDS THE FAMILY

Many nobles regretted the Old Regime educational system, and they
hoped that henceforth the kindred could sustain an outlook that previously teachers and the very organization of society itself had transmitted to the young. Bonald frequently invoked the necessary triangle of
paternal power, maternal authority, and juvenile subjugation: "The
child, subject to the action and will of the father and of the mother, has
only one duty: to listen and to obey."[2] However, when writing on domestic education, Bonald expressed fears of the corruption resulting from
disorder in the paternalist hierarchy if servile and feminine influences
on the child predominated. "Domestic education," he wrote,

> is dangerous because children learn or divine from it all that they
> should be ignorant of; because it puts a child in the midst of women
> and servants; that if he learns there how to greet people graciously
> he acquires the habit of trivial thinking; if he is taught how to eat
> correctly he is molded to unjustified vanity, to pointless curiosity, to
> be temperamental, to slander, to give a lot of interest to little things,
> and to pontificate gravely on inconsequentialities.[3]

Bonald was self-evidently speaking of well-to-do, patriarchal lineages in
a rural setting complete with servants. During the nineteenth century
that breed remained the yardstick for Catholic writers on the family
such as baron de Gérando or baron de Watteville.

The divergence of the condition of the urban and industrial workers
from this peasant-noble idyll gave reforming writers on the social question and poverty the confidence to recommend drastic interference in
the lives of the city poor. Economic individualism, promiscuity, and

geographical mobility were the scourges of society; the submission to paternal ideology, purity of morals, and love of place were their rural antidote.[4] Comte de Falloux observed of the agricultural profession that "no order . . . is less damaging to the primordial and patriarchal character of the family, grouped behind its chief and meeting every evening around the same hearth. What a difference from the worker and the small artisan, who, in most towns, have hardly room for the domestic hearth."[5]

Bonald's myriad imitators believed that early noble training should form character before intellect. Instinct and reflex would preserve the child from temptation and sin more easily than would reason. In his customary pious way vicomte de Melun expressed it: "God has attached so much power to family influence that the child cannot completely escape it, even in passing through the wasting fire of the *collège*."[6] Running through these generalized remarks about the effect of upbringing by kin there was praise but also warning. The mother, representing sensibility and emotion, could not only convey paternal values but also corrupt them by indulgent femininity.

The transmission of family lore and the training of small children in desirable conduct almost invariably were left to women, but the education of noble youths was clearly male work. Vicomtesse de Gontaut was raised to the position of a duchesse in 1826 in recognition of her labors as governess of the duc de Bordeaux. The seven-year-old henceforth studied under male instructors, with the baron de Damas de Cormaillon as his *gouverneur,* or principal tutor.[7] This distinction between the first six years of life and later was, in practical education, the contrast dear to Bonald between sentiment and reason: women molded instinct, while men trained intellect. The handful of aristocratic ladies who wrote on education themselves subscribed to this instinct/reason dichotomy. Mme de Rémusat's *Essai sur l'éducation des femmes* was published in 1824 by the same publisher who had produced Mme Campan's *De l'éducation*. Rémusat stressed the importance for women of private and family virtues over public and civic ones: "One must thus regard the status of citizen as the prime purpose of man's social existence. Woman's destiny is in turn included in those two titles no less noble, wife and mother of a citizen. . . . Supportive friends of the project of a husband, we cannot act suitably [*convenablement*] save at his order, and our submission, result of duty and sentiment, contents the heart as much as it does the conscience."[8]

Women charged with instilling in young children the basic we/they taxonomies of noble attitudes only rarely theorized about their pedagogical aims. That task was more likely to be found in a highly stylized way in the Catholic press during the Restoration—and this was generally the work of male writers who were often unmarried celibates. Raymond Deniel produced a useful analysis and guide to recurrent themes in his study of images of the family. The female vision of how noble families developed is a great deal more difficult to find. Two accounts by elderly noblewomen of literary bent are especially informative about interpersonal dynamics within the noble family and merit more extended treatment elsewhere. Mme d'Armaillé was a fairly prolific authoress of a variety of feminine noble biographies and came from a highly cultivated and aristocratic family, the Ségurs. She wrote memoirs describing her childhood and her early married life with the comte. Mme de Castelbajac, *née* Villeneuve, lived in a more constricted and provincial milieu of small nobles in southwestern France. She had encountered Chateaubriand as a girl, and this inspired her to produce in old age an evocation of her family life at the start of the nineteenth century. Both women placed the focus of their memoirs on relationships within the family rather than upon the interminable *politologie* which is usually the matter of the recollections of men who have been involved in public affairs. Of the two the account by Mme de Castelbajac is perhaps the more unusual, since there are other women witnesses to family life among the Parisian aristocracy but fewer sustained descriptions of that of provincial nobles.

Childrearing among nineteenth-century nobles was less sentimental than among bourgeois; at least noblemen frequently made this claim. Tocqueville contrasted the affectionate *douceur* of the American democratic family with the formalism of the French aristocratic family, about whose members he remarked, "Their hearts are rarely on good terms."[9] M. de Ségur's daughter recalled of her father in the 1830s: "He only kissed us on special occasions. He did not like caresses."[10] The comtesse de Bradi recommended in her 1842 etiquette guide that in a good family the familiar *tu* form of address should never be used. She added that "kissing and other caresses" are demonstrations of affection "disapproved of by *la bonne compagnie*" and that kisses on the cheeks between girls and a single *baise-main* ("hand kiss") from boys are "the only evident marks of tenderness that it is proper to show each other in the family."[11] Nobles did not like the drift towards the child-centered family which many authors claim began in the mid-eighteenth century. In 1851 comte Lezay-Marnésia praised his Old Regime upbringing in a Jura château ("nothing on either side which resembled tenderness"), comparing it with the "idolatry" shown for children in his old age by (presumably) bourgeois parents.[12] Comte de Rességuier, born during the Restoration, recounted how his mother went off to Paris three days after his birth, leaving him with a country wet nurse. Eighteen months later he was turned over to a blacksmith and then to a veterinarian's family for care. Half a century later Rességuier felt a need to justify this indifference: "This way of bringing up children must seem barbarous to mothers who in our day like so much to play at dolls and trinkets with theirs, and yet there was good in it."[13] There is, of course, scattered evidence for the opposing view. The baron de Damas's daughter remembered her father bestowing a morning and evening kiss and making the sign of the cross on her forehead, as well as the southwestern lady praised in the family for affection expressed by breast-feeding all nine of her offspring, although her husband's straightened finances might suggest that this was motivated as much by thrift as by maternal sentiment.[14]

Perhaps it is artificial to distinguish between the emotional bonds between parents and children and the educational intent of upbringing, but to do so makes plainer how nobles differed from commoners of similar wealth. The nobles wished their children to place family matters before those of sentiment or sexuality. Private custom was more important than public law. There are few adequate sources to inform on the matter: the doctors, ethnographers, and local historians who provided E. L. Shorter with information on different levels of sentiment in France between 1750 and 1900 were less observant about contemporary nobles who stood above them in the social scale. We turn to journalism, noble memoirs, and, most promising of all, correspondence or papers written without any thought of subsequent publication.

The problem with such testimonies to the feelings between parents and child, between husband and wife, and between siblings is that they are usually autobiographical, in a setting where family history was to be exemplary. The improving memoirs of the nineteenth-century nobles were intended to instruct and improve posterity rather than to tell the truth. Comte Lezay-Marnésia spoke of his wife in terms that were perhaps accurate but encourage suspicion that the felicity of his marriage to a girl from a financier family, Marie-Antoinette-Clémentine de Laage de Bellefaye, was slightly overstated: "It is now forty-three years that we have been married, and during this long time there was never a single instant of deviating from the perfect accomplishment of all her obligations—religious, social, domestic, charitable—and from her tender care for her husband and children: not one instant that did not make me honor her more and more and cherish her."[15] A multitude of similar texts make plain the noble convention that any suggestion of marital dissatisfactions should be glossed over in the formal discourse of the memoirs.

Yet there is no shortage of evidence about the absence of family spirit. We find it in an 1827 correspondence between the siblings of a general who presided over the *noblesse* of the Alençon baillage in 1789, served in the army throughout the Revolution, and subsequently became mayor of his seigneurial village. One brother wrote to the eldest from Alençon asking for a display of the "frankness and confidence that is owed between family members when they want to live on good terms" and expressing surprise that there had been no consultation on the apportionment that was about to take place upon the death of his wife. The other replied that he regretted "the forms and precautions indicated or prescribed by law, which unfortunately take away in family matters on all the mutual occasions that might be found to bend oneself to the particular desire of one's relatives and to seek to give them pleasure. . . . it is my children, not me, who are your coheritors in the rights of their mother."[16]

Of course, it is less common to encounter family squabbles than more elevated sentiments. However, a case of such animosity was found in the reminiscences of comte Horace de Viel-Castel, a malicious writer of the early 1860s Parisian smart set. He described being sent away by his son and daughter from the deathbed of his estranged wife, ("my wife, with whom I had passed days of peace and more numerous days of storm") so that they might have an opportunity to go through her papers in order to extract the relevant ones, as well as have the apartment lease made over to the young woman. Foiled in his hopes to control his wife's papers, Viel-Castel wrote: "Edouard and Cécile are behaving towards me in a way I can no longer tolerate, they have failed in all their duty, they have lacked heart . . . I shall not see them any more, I cannot be in the presence of children who have slighted me and who have treated me as they have treated me."[17]

In general, the saccharine prevailed in the written and perhaps in the oral accounts of the lineage, as expressed in the prudish atmosphere of the nineteenth century, an age in which correct sentiments were still valued highly. Once nobles desisted from anxious scrutiny of the Civil Code or reading of the loftier flights of Catholic social thought, it remained plain that practical training in noble manners, gesture, symbols, and bearing was primarily a family matter. *Titrés* for their part sought to emulate the indefinable distinction of bearing and manners, the *je ne sais quoi* that distinguished the *noblesse* and the aristocracy from social inferiors. This was necessary if they were to pass into the *bonne compagnie* just as they needed wealth to enter the Parisian *haute société*. Nineteenth-century nobles and particularly aristocrats found their last redoubt of social power in control of the criteria of elegant behavior. No sooner had an erstwhile M. Jourdain carefully learned the current forms of good manners than his patient mimicry was derided. It was in this sense that Marx scornfully said of the nobility of his time that they had become the dancing masters of Europe. Nevertheless, the ability to set the tripwires that marked social boundaries was one that inspired healthy respect and fear in the social climbers—that is, the newly successful—in France.

Family memories among the *noblesse* of the first years of the nineteenth century were marked most vividly by the Revolutionary years, when the second estate's former members found themselves singled out for hatred and suspicion. Recent misfortunes were blended with traditional exaltation of the lineage. Louis de Carné's mother put herself to some trouble to immerse her son in this frame of mind, teaching him to read in a folio-sized history of Brittany produced by Benedictines and pressing a treat upon him each time he came across the name of an ancestor in the text. She made him memorize his genealogy. Noble victims of the Terror provided the habitual topic of evening conversation.[18] In a similar fashion, Horace de Viel-Castel, in his early childhood at Versailles between 1803 and 1804, met elderly survivors of the old court, "escaped from the slaughterers of '93 and who filled the conversation of their last years with the story of monstrous things that they had seen." A fellow resident in their rented house, the marquis de Valfons, described how he had watched the massacre of the Orléans prisoners from his window and frightened the children to tears with his stories of the dauphin delivered into the hands of the infamous Simon.[19] Adèle d'Astorg, the young comtesse de Choiseul d'Aillecourt, who died in 1818 at a Pyrenean spa, liked to describe her childhood under the Revolution as "the sadness of a spring without smiles."[20] Another example of this obsession with the Revolution was that of the daughter of major de Marguerye, only eight years old when her father was guillotined in 1794. Fears of the Revolution haunted her, poisoned her marriage, and drove her to mental breakdown; it lay at the root of the publications whose titles speak for themselves: *Souffrances* (1834), *Fleurs de tristesse* (1857), and *Malheur et sensibilité* (1859).[21]

Sometimes the legendary faithful servant might be the purveyor of the family oral history, as in the case of a forty-year veteran with the Rességuier family:

> We were still near those dreadful times; the air that one breathed was full of exile, war, or emigration. Everything about this great social upheaval which had shaken everything, where prison, pillage, violence, proscriptions, drowning, and the guillotine had dispersed or decimated families and wiped out fortunes, was constantly on the lips of those who had survived. The children, always drawn towards what moves their emotions, in spite of the fright they felt, were the first to ask for these stories. . . . Dupuy [the servant] was for me the historian of our ruin and of the misfortunes of our family.[22]

These appalling narratives were not entirely without remedy, since the Rességuiers were quite prosperous thanks to their grandmother, who saved from confiscation the bulk of her *parlementaire* family's property. What mattered was the elaboration of legends of struggle, heroism, and virtue of which nobles were the fulcrum. They were often retouched to edify the young. Long after her father's death, Gobineau's daughter was surprised—and disappointed—to learn that the family patrimony had not been confiscated by the Jacobins as she had always been told but had passed into other hands because of bankrupcy.[23] As in so many other noble households, family "oral history" was not intended to be an accurate chronicle. Rather it was to strengthen that historical consciousness of family considered by the marquis de Bailly in 1826 to be more important than titles, positions, or wealth: "The work of time is necessary to constitute an aristocracy."[24] A *provençal* noble journalist repeated the same point under the Second Empire when he said that the solidarity that tied the generations must never be denied and that men should not be isolated from those who had gone before them and those who would follow.[25] Even more than the written *texts* of noble history it was the family *legends* that produced the pride of origin and the sense of stigma and apartness from the mass of the nation. Indeed, nobles anchored their historical perceptions on family events as much as on the public and political developments that affected them.

Nobles figuratively at least believed themselves to be descendants of an elite bonded by shared family values. Of course, nineteenth-century nobles married with the same legal aims as did the notables: to give legitimate status to future children, to place women under a husband's legal tutelage, and to transfer money by dowries from generation to generation. However, these arrangements were subordinated to their social identity which placed them outside society at large. Nobles could only sustain nobility with their own kind.

OFFSPRING

Hopes for the continuing prosperity and fame of a bloodline were all dependent on the presence of children. Did nineteenth-century nobles have more children in each marriage than commoners? The first official publication to give precise information on the size and composition of French families appeared in 1906.[26] One study showed that the frequency of marriages differed quite widely from department to department and that from the nineteenth century to the 1950s the trend was one of increasing numbers of marriages but fewer births per couple.[27] Moreover, departments with the largest numbers of unmarried also had the highest fecundity per couple. To my knowledge, however, no nineteenth-century demographer attempted to find out whether nobles had more children than other categories of the population. This has been attempted by some twentieth-century historians.[28] A sample from vicomte Révérend reveals that *noblesse* had, on average, increasingly more children than commoners taking titles over the same time period, but we must bear in mind that these were *noblesse* sufficiently successful and wealthy to obtain new titles. Yet we know from chapter 1 that the absolute numbers of noble families and the proportion of individuals as a segment of the national population were falling. Obviously it will be necessary to return to the questions of age at marriage, the number of offspring who never married, and the number of married couples who did not produce a son or were infertile.

Evidence from more than a thousand individuals granted titles between 1815 and 1830 and listed by Révérend, as well as those who received a *majorat sur demande* in the same period, shows that those born noble who married had more children than those born commoners.[29] Mme de Ségur, *née* Rostopchine, authoress of the famous *Sophie* stories, for many years produced a child annually: "She lost some, and three sons and four girls remained."[30] If she is set aside as scarcely typical because of her Russian birth, the feature to be more strongly emphasized among nobles is that pointed to by Houdaille in his excellent study of the descendants of the *grands dignitaires* of the First Empire (incidentally a study of how nobles were joined by new recruits over time). What seems to be crucial is the trend among noble families who had from zero to three children (increasing in numbers), those with three to five (falling), and those with six and above (increasing).[31] The families with more babies were in the best position to multiply kinship marriages and thus to receive property transferred in dowries. This should be added to Zeldin's observation about ducs in the nineteenth and twentieth centuries: "Thus in 1858 half of French dukes had one or two children; in 1878 two thirds of them had reduced their families to this size but by 1898 they had already reverted to larger families and only 48 percent had one or two children, while in 1938 only 40 percent had that number. In 1938 people with noble titles in general had significantly more children than those without them."[32]

Those nobles with the largest families were best able to keep systematic linkages running back to the collateral lines, linkages which attached them to wealth and new recruits. For those purposes marriages had to be with nobles, as we see clearly in one distinguished old southern family. The Villeneuve-Bargemont family is best known for a writer on political economy (Jean-Paul-Alban) and for its strong representation in the prefectoral administration under Napoleon and the Restoration, especially Christophe at Marseille from 1815 to 1829, who willed that his heart should be buried in that city. There was also a strong military tradition, with men at the battles of Montebello and Trafalgar, another lost in the retreat from Moscow, and another present at the siege of Algiers in 1830. Thanks to a highly detailed genealogy, we can trace their demographic contribution and marriage strategies over the first half of the nineteenth century.[33]

At the eighteenth degree a marriage between nobles at Aix-en-Provence in 1770 (Villeneuve-Bargemont/Bausset-Roquefort) produced fourteen children—nine males, of whom six married, all to nobles either once or twice. These married sons begot a total of fifteen girls and six boys. Five females were born to the 1770 marriage, of whom three married: child number 4 to a half-noble (on the groom's maternal side) and child number 13 to a commoner doctor. If she had issue, this is not recorded in the family genealogy, presumably because it was of no interest. It is true that she had waited until the age of thirty-six to marry. The last girl, number 14, married before her older sister but died without issue, bequeathing her property to a great-nephew. We see that the males of this ancient family remained strictly within the noble marital reserve, but as a counterpart of this endogamy, they were quite open to accommodation with post-Revolutionary regimes, with men fighting for Republic, Empire, the Bourbons, and, in due course, the Second Empire, when the only son of number 9 died, at the siege of Sebastapol in 1855. The women, by conspicuous contrast, did not obey the caveat: two out of the three who married did so with commoners.

It is possible to ask how close was the social proximity of nobles and commoners in the nineteenth century on the basis of the choice of noble or non-noble godparents. Abbé Berthet recorded the decline of the numbers of noble godparents to common children from the sixteenth century to 1789 in the village of Château-Gontier (Jura), but it remains to be investigated whether that shrinkage continued in the nineteenth century at an even faster rate than the demographic decline mentioned above.[34] Although we lack systematic studies, it appears that nobles were no more likely to admit commoners to their baptisms from 1800 to 1870 than under the Old Regime.

THE AVERAGE AGE AT MARRIAGE

The age at which weddings took place is obviously important to any discussion of the number of children born to couples, but it is not easy to ascertain in a socially selective way. One celebrated study of Genevan patrician families, who at first sight might seem quite similar to the nobles in France, showed a steady fall in the age at first marriage of both men and women during the period 1700–1850: from 30.5 and 24.2 years, respectively, at the start of the period to 28.2 and 21.3 at the end.[35] However, a family of the nearby Lorraine *noblesse* with fifty marriages over the same years as the Genevan families showed no consistency or steady trend: the men averaged 27, and the women 21.1, at the start of the period, while at the end males averaged 29, and the women 20.6.[36] A study of the pre-Revolutionary peerage showed that from 1650 to 1789 both men and women were marrying younger, but despite the longer period of fertility for each couple, there was a steadily smaller average completed family size.[37] Descendants of the *grands dignitaires* of the First Empire, the archtype of the *titrés* of the nineteenth century, consistently married older than Frenchmen at large (from 29.5 years to 29.8), while their wives gradually came closer to them in years, from 20.7 to 22.2. What typifies the *titrés*, however, is the wider difference in age than among French couples in general.[38] Tudesq, writing of the wealthy *grands notables,* who included nobles and commoners, concluded that in family matters the average notable married between the ages of 25 and 35 and had two or three children.[39]

Individuals, of course, do not fit into these majestic trends: of the five Villeneuve-Bargemont men whose first marriage took place between 1801 and 1824, the youngest was aged twenty-nine and the oldest thirty-eight, while the only daughter who married a noble was aged seventeen. An older sister, number 13 in the lineage as mentioned above, had waited until age thirty-six to marry a commoner doctor. Another example was a prince and duc de Bauffremont aged thirty when he married a twenty-seven-year-old Neapolitan in 1822; in 1849 his eldest son, at twenty-six, married the seventeen-year-old daughter of a banker. His second son, a general, waited until age thirty-four to marry the twenty-two-year-old comtesse de Caraman-Chimay. Let us cite an example of one of the impecunious younger sons, who could only marry when the family fortunes looked up. The fifty-year-old bachelor brother of the post-Concordat bishop of Limoges had returned to France after a career in the Spanish service, a classic occupation for the cadets of southwestern families. He accompanied his episcopal relative to the newly found financial security of the Limoges diocesis. One bit of good fortune in the family brought another to the retired army officer, as he wrote in a letter to yet another brother:

> On the morrow of Easter Day I hope to receive from my brother the nuptial benediction. It will be with Mlle Suzanne de Cardaillac, whom I saw for the first time yesterday in the evening. This demoiselle is thirty-five years old and of a valuable character. She ought to have been a sister of charity; her parents, under the pretext of health, were opposed to carrying out this plan; she has kept all the religious feelings that this vocation had given to her. You see, my dear friend, that this marriage, which is not the result of passion,

suits me well [*remplit mes vues*]. . . . The demoiselle has nothing, I
have very little; as a result we must go along very carefully.[40]

The couple had a daughter despite the relatively advanced age of the
mother. For individuals, such differences, just as much as those of
sickness, second marriages, and so forth, had a great deal to do with the
number of children in the family. They remind us that in matters of
marriage and childbearing aggregate statistics reveal only abstract
mathematical truths.

FAILURE TO PRODUCE MALE HEIRS; INFERTILITY; ILLEGITIMACY

The most energetic pursuit of status by a family could ultimately founder on the accidents of reproduction. Here again the particular example
tells more than the statistical generalization. The Pastorets exemplified
the upwardly mobile legal profession of the eighteenth century, moving
from Marseille to northern France in the person of Claude-Emmanuel-
Joseph-Pierre, who became a judge in the Paris Cour des aides before
1789 and a Seine deputy at the Conseil des Cinq-Cents under the
Directory, taking his first title (chevalier) within months of the establishment of Napoleonic titles, and in 1810 became a comte. Meanwhile
he had become a senator, which led in due course to a peerage (June
1814) which letters patent of 20 December 1817 made into a hereditary
marquis-peer. A little historical veneer was added to this avid collecting
of distinctions by letters patent of 11 September 1818 which recognized
the family's descent from a family with *noblesse* since 1298, the motto
"Bonus semper et fidelis," and the war cry "France! France!" (Révérend
sourly observed that the Pastorets were "an old family in the Marseille
bourgeoisie" but had never proved nobility in Provence before 1789.)

Beyond the normal satisfaction at such a collection of distinctions,
Pierre Pastoret was presumably thinking of his sons, Amédée-David
(1791–1857) and Maurice (1798–1817). The former married the
daughter of a robe noble colleague among the *maître des requêtes* in
1815 and soon thereafter became a *commissaire du roi près la Commission du sceau*, which permitted him to ensure that all was in order with
the documentation naming his father-in-law, A. S. Alexandre de Neu-
fermeil (1756–1839), comte in 1819. Amédée-David expired a senator
of the Second Empire, but his only son, born in 1819, died young. His
only daughter married the marquis de Plessis Bellière, a cavalry officer.
Maurice, the younger brother, died in 1817. Despite assiduous practice
of the attitudes recommended by Sam Rayburn's dictum "To get along,
go along," the name Pastoret disappeared from the nobility in the century in which it emerged.[41]

An even wealthier member of the legal profession was the marquis E. J. F. C. d'Aligre (1770–1847), perhaps the richest noble in all France at mid-century. If he had the partial satisfaction of having his name added by law to that of his grandson on the female side (marquis de Pomereu [1813–89], he also lacked a son to carry on his lineage.[42] Pomereu had no male descendent.

Childless weddings were not uncommon: of 1,082 Restoration ennoblements who were married 172, or 17.6 percent of those born common and 13.8 percent of those born noble, produced no children. Sometimes whole lineages seemed to be touched by celibacy and sterility, as in the case of the military family of the Le Lièvre de la Grange, at the twelfth degree in the nineteenth century. An Old Regime noble who became a baron and comte of Napoleon and a hereditary marquis under the Restoration had two sons and three daughters. However, one daughter never married, and neither sons nor daughters had children. In a poorer family of country *noblesse* not able to take new honors, baron F. J. E. R. Blay de Gaix married at age twenty-two a nineteen-year-old bride from a family in his neighborhood in December 1800: they were blessed with a son two years later, followed by four daughters before the mother's death in 1820. The son died a bachelor of fifty-four, and the eldest daughter stayed a spinster, but the three younger sisters contracted marriages in the local nobility. The name of the family in that branch became extinct.[43]

The desire for a male heir to carry a name—combined with the wish to retain family wealth—seems a likely explanation of the marriage at age fifty-two of M. d'Albon to his brother's eldest daughter. The senior d'Albon had married a commoner in 1830 without issue, the second d'Albon had two daughters, and at that stage uncle and niece embraced their responsibilities for perpetuating their family name. They had two sons.

Another solution for nobles without a male heir was adoption or the legalized transfer of their name to some other man. Unlike the feudal practice of Japanese Samurai adoptions, according to which the male simply changed his own surname to that of his bride's family, in France it was attached by particle to the family name of the ingested male, who might in due course prefer the new name to the old. Among those who set up a *majorat sur demande* during the Restoration it was specified that the title might pass in the case of no heredity to grandsons, nephews (the most frequent with nine out of the eighteen specifications), sons-in-law, brother-in-law, husband of a niece, or an adopted son from the first marriage of a twice-wedded wife. Among many examples found in Révérend are Semonville, whose name passed to his grandson by his only daughter (1825); and the comte de Goubert, whose title was given to S. M. O. Bernard in 1846 and then was confirmed as reverting to a nephew in 1864, letters patent in 1866, with the title Forestier de Goubert. Twenty years after his death in 1843 the bachelor Fleurigny's name was legally taken on by his grandnephew and universal inheritor, Raigecourt. Régnault Saint-Jean d'Angély's comtal title was passed to the husband of his adopted daughter in 1870, although it was not confirmed because of the fall of the Second Empire. These examples suffice to illustrate the range of possible ways to keep alive a family name, but they were never numerous enough to reverse the steady demographic decline discussed in chapter 1.

We have seen how nobles ranging from the newest and brashest recruits such as the Pastorets to ancient knightly families such as the Le Lièvre de la Granges stumbled over the same obstacle as that identified among the pre-Revolutionary nobility of Forez, where half the ennobled families disappeared within each century more because of a lack of male posterity than because of poverty.[44] Possibly what eighteenth-century moralists called the "dread secrets"—birth control practices—so notorious among the court nobility of that century were less used in a devoutly Catholic century. As yet we do not have a detailed study of disruptions in the post-Revolutionary noble family to match investigations of the breakdown of marital life in common under the Old Regime.[45] Nobles chastened and affected by the religious revival possibly did not forget in their bedrooms the earnest strictures of the interminable sermons of the early nineteenth century. At a less explicit level there may have been among the women of those age cohorts fertile between 1800 and 1825, as well as their husbands, a desire for larger families, a need felt to extend and multiply the family links menaced and destroyed by the Revolution. Demure prudery makes it difficult for us to know how often couples discussed matters so vital to their lives. Only a dim echo of intimate conversations can be found, carefully filtered into generalizations, in articles in the Catholic press.

Genealogies record the majestic grandeur of family trees for unborn posterity; they rarely record wind-blown fallens. Bachelor uncles and adolescent boys were assumed, although not expected, to find sexual satisfaction with women servants, whose dependent situation made them easy prey. Alphonse de Lamartine fathered his first illegitimate child by a servant girl at sixteen, while still at school, and his second a little later by the wife of a noble friend, who remained unaware of the infant's real paternity.[46] If unmarried servants were impregnated, they might, if lucky, be supported, or they might be sent packing. One recent study, however, claimed a decline in master-servant sexual contact during the nineteenth century as a result of the new family prudery and unity among the middle class and suggests that this was compensated by widespread recourse to prostitutes.[47] Perhaps the same could be said for nobles.

Married women also might engage in affairs but were not permitted the same license across class barriers, despite vaudeville pleasantries about handsome young footmen, for fear that the servant might forget his station. Once married, on the other hand, nobles made acceptable lovers. This was commonly thought to be the situation before the Revolution, but in the nineteenth century there was more hypocrisy about such matters. The historian is left to wonder about the significance of scraps of information about bastards.

One prominent ultraroyalist publicist fathered an illegitimate daughter at age sixty-two and in his will made his two legal daughters each responsible for half of the annual payment of 6,000F, to be paid in quarterly installments. He died in 1829, and by 1861 his illegitimate daughter, married to a Haute-Vienne landowner since 1842, had received some 192,000F in payments. Invoking the Civil Code in selling off their testamentary obligation, the comtesse de Choiseul and the marquise de Crillon together paid 121,500F to be invested in 3 percent government bonds inalienable in their half-sister's name as part of her dowry secured in her marriage contract by the *régime dotal*. Herbouville's daughter had thus been exceptionally well provided for by her father.[48]

What motivated the generosity of this sizable legacy by a noble lady of Paris in 1838, some twenty-three years after the presence of many Englishmen in the capital?

> I leave to John Piper, a young Englishman whom I have brought up and who is in my service since his childhood, 30,000F. . . . I wish, for his advantage, if however his intention was to remain in France, that the amount of this legacy might be used by him to buy a furnished hotel business in one of the good quarters of Paris: a speculation that he may be able by order and good conduct to render profitable. . . . By means of my present legacy I recommend to John, in the interest which I have in him, to give up henceforth being a servant.[49]

There was no need to speculate about the reasons for the generosity of comte de Moussy to Mlle Maria Blampois, to whom he left his entire fortune: "I had from Mademoiselle Maria Blampois a male child born 25 January 1850. presented him at the town hall of la Chapelle and recognized [my legal responsibility for the child]. He carries the names of Charles-Alfred-Gustave de Moussy de la Contour . . . done in Paris in perfect sanity 3 February 1850."[50] Such a "recognized" child had the right to one-third of the portion of any legitimate offspring, but those who had not been legally acknowledged had no rights to their parents' estate.

We cannot easily know if nobles fathered—or mothered—a disproportionate number of illegitimate children in comparison with the general population.[51] Discretion could usually be purchased. A pregnant maid could be married to a gardener for a consideration at best, or simply shown the door at worst. A child reclaimed in due course from a discreet country wet nurse could be brought up as a servant. Bastards had a more furtive place among nineteenth-century nobles than at earlier times. Only a psychologist could correctly explain the motivations of the comte and general, father of the successful journalist Emile de Girardin, who permitted his adulterine son by a Parisian judge's wife to eat lunch in the gardener's cottage but not under the paternal roof. Only the most exceptional among the illegitimate, such as Morny or Flora Tristan, are remembered as being of noble descent.

KIN AND THE ECONOMICS OF MARRIAGE

Post-Revolutionary nobles generally subscribed to the view that love or passion that overcame common sense was bad. The same could be said for insistent libido in general. Persistent homosexuality or a desire to marry one's social inferior, just as much as extravagance or excessive religiosity leading to unwanted celibacy on the part of those who had to transmit the family name and wealth, threatened family stability. Weddings were generally arranged. Not only the dowry but also the number, influence, and wealth of the spouse's relatives were prime considerations in any decision on future unions. When J. V. A. de Broglie, a future senator of the Second Empire and member of the Académie française, was engaged in 1845 to Mlle de Gallard de Brassac de Béarn, he scarcely knew her: "This union had not been at first, following French usage, anything other than an affair of convenience discussed between friends and relatives, because I was not known to Mademoiselle de Béarn and I had never myself met her, and I even had some difficulty in obtaining permission for us to see each other two or three times in the houses of mutual friends before becoming engaged to each other."[52] The notaries of the respective families, however, were certainly on more familiar terms.

All nobles viewed marriage as crucial to their status. Each child was a potential link in a chain of contracts, obligations, and understandings between families. The apparently excessive sentiment of baron Favard de Langlade in his 1811 legal manual did not appear in the least overstated to nobles or, indeed, to socially ambitious commoners: "The marriage contract is the most important act of all those that affect civil society; it is not of a purely private interest restricted to those who have contracted it; the whole social order is interested in it; it is on the faith of the conventions there stipulated that families join themselves together and form new ones; and families are the richness of the State, the source of public prosperity."[53] A bride's dowry was normally the largest infusion of wealth into the groom's fortune until he finally entered into his inheritance from both parents.

As the banns were announced for each wedding, the gossips buzzed with speculation about the economic strength not only of the two parties but also of collateral relatives from whom funds might be received in due course. Small wonder that an encyclopedic knowledge of eligible nubile partners and the wealth of their relatives was of paramount interest to older family members. Mme d'Armaillé recalled the preliminaries of her 1851 marriage: "The informations on M. d'Armaillé were so good, and coincided so completely with those that my parents had gathered from other sides, that they decided to give me in marriage. There was an exchange of notes on our fortune, *according to the custom* [my emphasis]."[54]

Land and cash were the most important components of dowries, as is illustrated by the 1810 marriage contract between an aristocratic second lieutenant of cavalry, Balbès de Crillon, the son of an Old Regime lieutenant general of the French army, and the daughter of the Rhône prefect and former *maréchal de camp,* Herbouville. Both families were strikingly wealthy, had good pre-Revolutionary standing, and served the Empire. The groom was promised 400,000F provided equally by his mother and father, and in earnest of this he was given a large Seine-et-Marne estate. (Incidentally, the contract noted that this land belonged to the Crillons as a result of Mme Nolasque de Couvay's will, dated 1756, just as Herbouville noted of the dotal property they provided that it was a legacy to the bride's father, "who owns it from his ancestors." Both were using the marriage contract to emphasize that this was not new— particularly not *biens nationaux*—property.) The Herbouvilles provided to their daughter 300,000F, with the promise of paying 5 percent annual interest at six-month intervals until the principal was fully paid off. They mortgaged an estate near Dieppe in the Seine-Inférieure. These excellent terms made endogamy congenial to the young couple.[55]

ENDOGAMY AND MARITAL STRATEGIES

With the directness of a soldier, Napoleon I briefly attempted to oversee the arrangement of marriages to encourage the fusion of the pre-1789 *noblesse* and the notables who had emerged from the Revolutionary and imperial interlude. He ordered prefects to draw up in each department a list of the nubile rich girls over fourteen years of age with whom

matches might be encouraged. This bizarre document has survived in a
number of archives at least as much for its curiosity as for anything else.
At Le Mans (Sarthe), for example, the list of heiresses, together with the
exchange of correspondence following the initial request for information from the general police, that branch of police particularly responsible for public security, health and morals, individual safety, industry,
highways, mines, and so forth, have been preserved. An 1810 letter
from Paris complained that recent marriages "of public interest" had
taken place without information or estimates of the wealth involved
being sent to Paris:

> These pieces of information are all the more necessary to me, since
> you must know that the majority of the former families are opposed
> to our institutions and only seek to form alliances with each other,
> because they are determined to give life and more brilliance to titles
> that the government does not recognize and that today are not
> anything other than the recompense of those who have dis-
> tinguished themselves in combat or rendered numerous services in
> the civil career.
>   These combinations have still for their aim, on the part of these
> families, to perpetuate among their descendants the spirit of
> opposition that animates them against the present dynasty. . . . I rely
> upon you, Sir, to exercise the greatest care to inform me in time of
> these marriages so that you may receive my orders before their
> conclusion, if I think it necessary to address any to you.[56]

The Sarthe prefect, understandably wishing to avoid the invidious role
of busybody in such matters, protested that neither were the local nobles of "so high an extraction as to fix attention" nor were they subversive. In February 1811 the Vaucluse prefect also was being chided for
his failure to produce this information.[57] In the troubled conditions of
the Empire's last years this odd policy lapsed.

Noble endogamy was more absolute among provincial *noblesse* (as
has been demonstrated in Normandy) than among those resident in the
capital.[58] This may well reflect the greater attraction of Paris for the
ambitious and successful. Did sons marry commoner women more
often than the reverse? The July 1821 marriage of Auguste-Esprit de
Osmont, son of a former *trésorier de France,* chevalier de Saint Louis,
and a landowner member of the Legion of Honor, with the daughter of a
Nîmes landowner, Buguet (27,000F cash and more than 400,000F property in due course) was not exceptional. The groom's witnesses were
titled, but while the bride's side included a banker and two wholesale
merchants, close relatives, she also produced a peer, a lieutenant general, and a gentleman of the bedchamber.[59] In the Villeneuve-Bargemont
family at the same period all males married nobles in first and second

marriages, but two out of the three women who married did so with commoners.

Particularly from 1835 to 1840 marriages between nobles and commoner Parisian families of equally substantial wealth became more frequent.[60] This, of course, did not mean that nobles became more bourgeois but rather the reverse. The children of a noble father and commoner mother almost always married nobles. The provinces were more resistant to exogamy, if we can judge from one impression of the Vaucluse under Louis-Philippe that claimed that marriages were always among nobles between "gens à particule," such as the marriages of the daughter of marquis de Forbin des Issarts with comte d'Averton, Dulaurens d'Oiselay with Scholastique de Crillon-Mahon giving a daughter who married Athénosy, and so forth.[61]

While we lack a series of regional studies to examine the question on a comparative level, it does seem that under the Second Empire disapproval of marriages between nobles and commoners weakened considerably. Nobles realized that suitable female recruits could be made over into noble ladies. The existence of other elites made some family links with the rich and powerful desirable, and many nobles seemed to accept this. The imperial nobility were among the most active. Louis-Napoléon Suchet, duc d'Albuféra, married in 1844 the daughter of a Prussian businessman and incidentally became a brother-in-law to a Choiseul-Praslin; the vicomte de Chambrun wedded the daughter of the deputy owner of the Baccarat glass factory. The ironmaster Benoist d'Azy (whose particle in the surname was approved in the 1840s) saw his son Augustin married in 1859 to the granddaughter of comte Daru of the First Empire (1809) and a peer de France (1819), and the daughter of a hereditary peer who sat from 1833. One of her aunts had married into the Baconnière de Salverte family of the Legitimist *noblesse* of Fougères. In 1865 Antonin-Juste-Léon-Marie de Noailles, duc de Mouchy et de Poix, married Anna, princess Murat, daughter of a senator. These randomly noted unions show that when stakes were high, with linkages to the powerful, traditional political loyalties were extremely malleable.[62]

The marriage of the Schickler girls—rich, foreign, and commoners—to French aristocrats reminds us of the international dimensions of the noble marriage market. Some French noble girls married foreign nobles, especially Belgians and Italians, but also further afield. It is not yet clear whether the balance was the same as the national trend in the twentieth century, when Frenchwomen consistently married more foreigners than did Frenchmen: in 1948 Frenchwomen married 36 foreigners per thousand, while Frenchmen married 25 foreigners per thousand.[63] However, the links between French nobles and their Brit-

ish, Belgian, Polish, Russian, Austrian, Italian, and German counterparts, while fascinating, cannot be explored here. Exogamy, whether
with wealthy Frenchwomen, foreign partners, or others, can only be
weighed correctly when following the marriage patterns of those children born to the union. Habitually commoner women were "ingested"
into the *noblesse* in the sense that their children married nobles. The
children of *titrés* were somewhat less likely to marry nobles.

Liquidity available to young couples was generally scant if the parents
were still alive, since noble family fortunes were habitually held in real
estate. Marriage contracts only spelled out mutual obligations of the
spouses and enumerated claims on future inheritances. In one sense
the contract changed the credit-worthiness of two individuals and was a
crucial step in each generation's financial progress. At least since Martial's epigrams on the topic, writers have pointed out that a balance
between the social levels of the marriage partners is an excellent thing.
Nineteenth-century noble weddings generally took place between families of roughly comparable wealth. A nonpracticing *provençal* doctor,
Antoine de Courtois, made the same point in 1812 when he longed for
sufficiently large estates to permit him to set up a hereditary title for his
sons: "honorable marriages are the alliance of two respectable [*honnêt-
es*] families of equal fortune who in future will make only one."[64] The
need for parity of fortunes—marriage "without disparagement" in the
medieval English phrase—to maintain levels of propriety and dignity
was keenly felt by nobles. Each wedding concerned their collective
reputation as well as the happiness of the newly wed. When Mlle de
Mun married comte de Biron in Paris in 1828, "all the relatives put
themselves to a great deal of trouble; all that was Gontaut and Gontaut-
Biron and even the Mun gave evening parties without end."[65]

An improper marriage which lowered a family's social tone was collec-
tively disapproved. When marquis de Boissy, a peer of France, married
one of Byron's alleged former Italian mistresses twenty years after the
poet's death, it was considered a regrettable eccentricity. Her first entry
into the chancellor's fashionable salon was marked by an abrupt silence
as all eyes in the company turned to the door. "The poor woman seemed
at first a bit excluded."[66] Doubtless humiliated by her reception, Mme
de Boissy was nevertheless received. This serves to remind us that the
nobles shunned newcomers more frequently in novels than in reality.

Nineteenth-century nobles consolidated their situation by careful
management of the patrimony. The courts of Louis xvIII, Charles x, and
Louis-Philippe were in no sense threadbare, even if they did not compare in magnificence to pre-Revolutionary Versailles. However, with
fewer state pensions, aristocrats spent less of their money on conspicuous consumption, particularly now that mere extravagance could be

emulated on an equal footing by rich commoners. Even more caution was displayed by the provincial nobles. No longer able to count on the profits from venal offices or feudal dues, they had to concentrate on the product of their estates. A Mayenne noble described the importance of land for the local gentry when he said of the acceptable dowry, "It ought to be in real estate, for we have little taste for landed or industrial speculations."[67]

More than ever, wealth was to be amassed by parsimonious management of estates or detailed leases for rents. The noble wife dragged the heavy burden of maintaining a seemly noble establishment, managing household expenses so that demands on family hospitality could be met in a decent way, and ensuring that children were raised correctly. What has been called the economy of makeshifts among the eighteenth-century poor was, with adjustments in scale, appropriate to the middling range of nobles, struggling to maintain appearances with an annual income of less than 5,000F. Lamartine's mother noted the difficulty of keeping the family purse at the start of the century: "One doesn't think enough when one marries that it is also a vow of poverty, since one puts her fortune in the hands of her husband, and that one can only dispose of what he allows us to spend."[68] The Burgundian estate at Milly provided a mere 2,000–3,000F in annual revenue, the threshold of poverty for those who wished to maintain a noble look of things, and Mme Lamartine was obliged to impose rigid restraints on spending.

Noblewomen in fact were often burdened down with financial responsibilities. In the absence of husbands, they often took over estate management, as in the case of the wife of Président d'Aiguesvives, the newly elected deputy from Toulouse, given in 1816 power of attorney so that she could "generally carry out the full management and administration of his goods and properties that [M. d'Aiguesvives] would himself do in person. . . . and he promises to accept all that shall be done by the lady with the procuration."[69] Joseph de Villèle left estate management in his wife's hands during his long absences in Paris during the 1820s, and he sought her advice on business affairs.

Thanks to their witnesses and terms, marriage contracts provided a range of information about professional and geographical aspects of marriage patterns and tell us about family status. They are less informative about money. They can be found in full in notarial records or in abbreviated form in departmental archives in the registers of the *Enregistrement des actes civils publics* or those of the *Table alphabétique des contrats de mariage*. One extensive search of the former showed that only 1.3 percent of marriage contracts concerned nobles. It is quicker to locate nobles, such as the 1829 judge of the Chartres *tribunal de première instance,* described as écuyer, in the alphabetical listings of marriage contracts.[70] In full or abbreviated form, contracts rarely lend themselves to establishing what was the wealth of the "average" noble couple. This is not merely because prospective claims on family resources varied for reasons as simple as those of the number of girls to be married compared with the number of boys or because of the age and health of the parents at the time of the marriage. It is because the sum of those considerations makes it difficult to find like to compare with like.

If those distinctions are brushed aside in the name of the law of large numbers, a new and forbidding obstacle appears. Numerous contracts never specified the monetary value of property but only the inheritance rights to it. Among a group with extensive family ties as indebted to each other as the nineteenth-century nobility, the contracts were often a Byzantine maze of fractions of estates, farms, or fields and partial claims to payments for loans or shares themselves payable at the death of a third party. Indebtedness stretched over years and could predate the Revolution. The 1763 marriage of Le Bascle d'Argenteuil and Mlle Duban de la Feuillée noted the donation of a piece of land in return for taking on a commitment to pay a rent worth 40,000 livres. By February 1800, when the widow died at Soissons, this rent was worth 39,506F 17, or an annual revenue of 1410F 92, which was to be paid to nine individuals from four families. One claimant owned half of the *rente*: Anne-Joachim-François de Melun, of a *noblesse* family, baron of the Empire in 1811, *auditeur* to the Council of State, and later a member of the guards of Louis XVIII and mayor of Brumetz (Aisne). The remaining quarter belonged to the widow de Nicolay and seven further individuals each possessing 3.5 percent. M. d'Argenteuil and Mme de Maillé promised to pay three-fifths and two-fifths, respectively, of the annual interest in those proportions on 1 January and 1 July. In 1838 the comte de Melun received for complete repayment of his annual *rente* the sum of 14,109F, but the other amounts were presumably still being paid. This seventy-five-year-old obligation in a noble wedding contract from the Old Regime had thus been passed on through nine and perhaps more sets of inheritances.[71]

Such examples could be multiplied, but to little purpose. The extent of those family financial networks defies any hope of reducing the linkages to a diagram or all-embracing generalization save to say that noble financial arrangements were of stupifying complexity and were mainly secured by land and real estate in the hands of relatives. The social life of elderly nobles was largely taken up with collecting information about the future prospects of families, the debt burdens present and foreseeable, and the number of wealthy old bachelors in the collateral lines. Signature of a marriage contract was fraught with unenvisaged contingencies, the worst being too long-lived relatives and the best, windfall inheritances.

Besides promises of future inheritances of land, many contracts also provided for cash payments. With an annual revenue of 3,000–10,000F, the lesser of which was the threshold of poverty for the modestly secure *noblesse*, one could rarely expect large cash dowries, despite particularly dazzling hopes for future prospects. Even the most ferocious economies would not permit the accumulation of large capital sums. The middling prosperous nobility—those whose mid-century annual revenue was 10,000–30,000F—would expect more in cash, as in the case of Mogniat de l'Ecluse's daughter, given on the occasion of her wedding (vendémiaire XIV) 20,000F in silver coins and a house in Lyon worth 130,000F. Interest on this dotal property was to be paid by her husband to her parents.

This arrangement was quite common. A minor only child such as Angélique-Charlotte Celier de Bouville, with a château and estate in Auteuil bringing in an annual return of 135,000F, was a very good catch for M. d'Argent, écuyer, squadron leader in the cavalry, and quartermaster of the royal lodgings, who later in life was to be deputy for the Eure-et-Loire in 1852.[72] The aristocratic 1808 wedding of Rohan-Chabot (who later in life as a widower would take his vows and enter the episcopacy) with the minor Mlle Serent brought on the groom's side 200,000F, secured on the Moisson forest near Mantes (Seine-et-Oise). His aunt, the widow of M. de la Rochefoucauld, now living on the rue Saint Honoré, made a gift to her nephew which she noted was a proof of her tenderness on the occasion of such a desirable marriage—in the event, 200,000F of her estate, secured on a property near Issoire (Puy-de-Dôme). On the bride's side came another 200,000F, from property near Château-Chinon (Nièvre), and also a house of which the ownership if not the enjoyment was given to her by M. Giraud with the statement that it would yield a revenue of 8,000F payable from the day of his death. A list of eighteen mirrors in the house was attached to the contract.[73] As the century progressed, weddings of similar aristocrats would involve ever larger dowries.

Only rarely were the amounts of Paris noble dowries matched in the provinces. In a small town like Tarbes in the Hautes-Pyrénées in 1832 the future wife of the wealthiest landowner in the department, marquis de Palaminy, brought 36,000F.[74] In Toulouse, the nearby regional capital, the cash (*mobilier*) brought by noble girls to marriages increased by 64 percent between 1816–19 and 1862–65—from 64,000F to 95,000F. Over the same period the cash brought by men increased by a lesser amount, 44 percent, from an average of 15,000F to an average of 35,000F.[75] Generally the period 1800–1870 saw a steady rise in the amounts of dowries: *mobilier* under 10,000F accounted for 72 percent of the 1810 declarations but only 36 percent of those in the 1860s; conversely, 6 percent exceeded 100,000F in the earlier period but rose to 38 percent in the latter. There was, however, a falter in the steady rise in the amounts of money reported in dowries during the 1840s with the political upheaval and, what was even more important, the agricultural crisis. Contemporaries perceived a connection between the profitability of farming and the family well-being; the subprefect in the Toulousain, for example, lamented the rising "voluntary sterility" caused by increased difficulties in procuring dowry payments.[76] The rise in dowry amounts resumed in the years of the Second Empire.

The above discussion makes plain that the wealth levels of the *noblesse, titrés,* and aristocrats at marriage varied widely. A later study might plot the trajectories of networks of families in a series of dowries and *partages* to discover the clusters of wealthy nobles, those of middling fortune, and those who were, relatively speaking, the penurious. Certainly the regional contrast is plain over time. The Crillon-Herbouville marriage in Paris in 1810 involved 700,000F in estates located in northern France.[77] The 1865 Ducos de Saint Barthélemy de Gélas–de Joly marriage in Toulouse involved 100,000F in cash from the bride on the condition that as soon as possible the money would be used to acquire buildings free of mortgages or investing in government or banking bonds, in shares on the French railways, or in municipal bonds on the large French cities, evidently an enumeration of secure investments. The groom's contribution was an annual revenue of 4,000F secured on half of an estate near Nérac in the Lot-et-Garonne worth perhaps 100,000F.[78] Fifty years separated the contracts in one of which the southern families provided less than a third of the dowry amounts listed in the other by prestigious Parisian families during the First Empire.

The nineteenth-century dotal arrangement considered the norm by the Civil Code, *communauté*, meant an equal sharing of profit or losses from the management of the joint fortunes, including the dowry. The other favored form was the *régime dotal,* which entrusted management of dotal funds and property to the husband but specified that neither directly nor indirectly could the dotal property be disposed of by either partner; at death that property had to be passed on to the heirs. A variant form was the *séparation des biens*, which went further in ensuring the independence of the wife's property against her husband's depredations. The 1802 marriage before the implementation of the Civil Code between Destutt de Tracy's daughter and the son of the marquis de Lafayette specified that there would not be a *communauté de biens* between them but the husband would be authorized to manage and

TABLE 10. Contract Types in 374 Noble Marriages, 1801–1870

| Decades | Regimes | | |
	Dotal	Communauté	Mixed
1801–10	19%	81%	—
(N = 16)			
1811–20	40	50	10%
(N = 10)			
1821–30	22	78	—
(N = 9)			
1831–40	33	45	22
(N = 60)			
1841–50	28	35	35
(N = 39)			
1851–60	41	26	33
(N = 104)			
1861–70	57	26	17
(N = 130)			

administer the present and future property of his wife to be. One of their daughters married a commoner official from the Cour des comptes, another a nobleman who was a *conseiller d'état*, and a third a noble who was a *représentant du peuple*—all three marriages rejected the *communauté de biens*.[79] An examination of several hundred noble marriage contracts over the first half of the nineteenth century showed an increasing preference for *régime dotal* contracts over those of *communauté* (see table 10).[80]

This was the opposite of the national trend. By the 1860s more than two-thirds of nobles chose forms of the *régime dotal* (including *dotal et acquêts* and *séparation des biens*), although earlier this trend had not been so predominant. Of 106 marriage contracts known for the *majorats sur demande* (1814–30), 66 percent were *communauté*, 19.8 percent *séparation des biens*, and 14.2 percent *régime dotal*.[81] The nobles' growing preference in the nineteenth century for the *régime dotal* is clearly a significant marker in distancing them from the way in which the mass of French commoners organized their weddings. This remained true into the twentieth century. A 1903 study surveyed informants from different parts of France on preference for the *régime dotal* by the rich and the noble. Bordeaux made the salient comments: "It is among the *noblesse* that one encounters it the most often to ensure the conservation of a family estate. . . . it is adopted in other circumstances when there might be grounds to suspect that the husband, by hazardous speculation or through habits of exaggerated luxury, might put the dowry of his spouse in peril."[82]

In saying that nobles in particular liked a form of contract that placed the wife in a subordinate position to that of her husband but also protected her independence, it is worth remembering that local fashions came into the matter. In Normandy the Old Regime custom actually prohibited *communauté*. The traditional financial independence of the woman was summed up in the adage "Dot de femme ne peut périr," and this found an echo in practice as late as 1898, when the Seine-Inférieure still attained 29.19 percent of *régime dotal* marriage contracts, at a time when the national average for the form was down to 12.27 percent.[83] Under modern legislation regional traditions in the matter survived, since almost all former arrangements could be recreated by availing oneself of loopholes and permitted exceptions under the Civil Code.

The main reason for the noble preference for the *régime dotal* was the wish to keep money and property in the hands of those who had received them from their own family, to which in due course it would revert through inheritance if there were no children. The *communauté* could be damaging to the wife's interests, as the family council acting for a deranged Breton noble widow in 1819 recognized when it recommended that in view of the bad state of the succession, it would be better for the widow to renounce in law the *communauté* that had existed between her and her husband, a sea captain.[84] The *régime dotal* was a significant drag on the speculative instincts of the noble husband and also hindered the conversion of family property into more liquid forms which might prove profitable but which could even more easily be lost. The *régime dotal* thus not only was a bond of subservience but also gave independence to women. Both movables (*mobilier*) and real estate (*imobilier*) were of higher average value in dotal contracts than *communauté* save at the top levels of over 150,000F.

NOBLES AND DEATH

During the nineteenth century nobles paid respects to the dead more emphatically than before the Revolution, and this reflected the rising religiosity described in chapter 6. This was particularly true after midcentury. However, the publication of Chateaubriand's *Génie du Christianisme* in 1802 can serve as a symbolic marker of this nineteenth-century insistence on death and salvation in a way almost reminiscent of the fervid seventeenth-century Catholicism, although occurring in a vastly different intellectual climate of rationalism and positivism. To make a good death—which is to say a pious and proper one—was a central preoccupation of elderly nobles. The elements of this were constant: the condition in which life ended, ideally with a priest to administer the sacraments and with grieving relations in attendance to testify to its meaning to the family; the proclamation of the death by announcements (*faire-part,* printed on cards or heavy bond paper sheets with a statement of the time and place of the funeral) and printed obituaries in suitable publications read by nobles and notables alike; the funeral itself, with public procession, Mass, and burial; family echoes in the form of the tomb and inscriptions, and memorial Masses to be said subsequently.

Since the work of Philippe Ariès and Michel Vovelle, historians have examined these and other aspects of the French way of death, but it can fairly be said that the nineteenth and twentieth centuries have been less studied than the fifteenth to the eighteenth. Moreover, the emphasis has fallen on defining what was typical in regional rituals of death rather than the contrasts by social categories. Albeit in a preliminary and cautious way, some tentative suggestions can be gleaned from a group of ninety noble wills drawn up between 1800 and 1870, as well as from newspapers, books of costume, and correspondence. In particular we can see how the element of family pride, or what nobles preferred to call family spirit, gave a special cachet to noble death rituals. The most direct echo of this was to be found in their wills.

For more than a century French scholars have analyzed wills as a key to the legal systems of the past and as a window into *mentalités,* but there are no large-scale studies of noble wills in the nineteenth century.[85] Noble wills governed the money flow between generations; in fact, they are the historical pendant to marriage contracts. Both, however, suffer frequently from imprecision. Just as the actual cash value of many dowries was not given, neither was the worth of many legacies. That is why *enregistrement* probate records, which imposed a tax on the values of estates, are more useful to the social historian investigating whether nobles became wealthier or poorer over time. On the other hand, wills provided an immediate witness to concerns quite other than those of the tax collector. Exhortations to children, the symbolism of some bequests, the religious views of the deceased, and evidence of family feuds and alliances, all may be found in wills. This was particularly true of the *testament mystique,* sealed and secret and consigned to the care of the notary until death, or the *testament olographe,* written entirely in the handwriting of the testator, then signed and dated. The other type of will, the *testament public,* was drawn up by the notary and witnessed.[86] The latter was more impersonal in language and detail but even so provides much information on the economics of many noble families.

The most evident feature of noble nineteenth-century wills is their frequent anachronism. A variety of studies have confirmed that the use of Catholic religious terminology declined markedly in commoner wills made since the mid-eighteenth century in France. After the Revolution nobles reverted to earlier forms, although it can be noted that even during the Enlightenment they were more resistant than commoners to the rise of secularism. Noblemen were less likely than noblewomen to make provision for Masses or to give detailed instructions about their tombstone, and so forth, but there was still a general religiosity present.[87]

More than a third of the male wills and a half of the female wills contained explicit invocations, such as that of Mme Choiseul d'Esguilly in her testament (1810), repeated word-for-word by her daughter in 1837: "I commend my soul to God and beg him to show mercy upon the intercession of the Blessed Virgin, of Saint Joseph, and of my patron saints."[88] Vicomte de Bruges, a *provençal* living in Paris who died in November 1820, headed his will with "In the Name of the Holy Trinity: So Be It" and began with the following statement: "I leave my soul to God, praying him to receive it in the bosom of his mercy, wishing to be buried in the most modest way possible, and in a cemetery of the Roman and Apostolic Catholic Church; wishing that my children may be maintained in the exercise of my religion, and begging my dear wife to demand from them the carrying out of all that it lays down."[89]

There was a general proliferation of rituals surrounding noble funerals. One ingenious study of almost four hundred death announcements primarily from noble families of southeastern France noted the steady increase in the number of lines of print enumerating the relatives of the deceased, which grew from an average of almost six prior to 1850, rose to over sixteen from 1860 to 1870, and reached more than forty-two by 1910–20.[90] The conclusion drawn was that thanks to a national postal service, it was possible to make apparent long-distance stylized affirmations of the family possession of its dead, or at the least a reminder of the network of relatives. It was quite different from the handbills of the eighteenth century inviting the public to attend the funeral to aid the departed soul with their prayers. The growing stress on the private networks of families is a central argument to this study.

Ostentation in those rituals was at odds with the actual texts of wills, which frequently requested a simple funeral. Mme de Choiseul-Praslin, *née* O'Brien Thomond, in her 1808 will said, "I ask to be buried in the most simple way possible, and without these invitations that are scattered about in recent times and are neither received nor sent by sentiment."[91] Of course, there may have been a tacit understanding that executors would, on social grounds, disregard what the defunct wanted on religious ones, just as medieval kings pardoned in their wills prisoners and enemies although well aware that their successors would not implement their pious intentions. The duc de Choiseul-Praslin seemed to make this point in his will of 25 August 1835:

> I ask that this multitude of announcements [*billets de part*] not be sent out to strangers or the indifferent: the regrets of my friends, if I have the happiness to inspire such, are the only retinue that I wish to see accompany my mortal remains. I want my funeral to be without ceremoniousness or ostentation, and as I have always seen that despite such a recommendation in fact magnificent catafalques are always put up, and in order to prevent that, I want my funeral expenses not to exceed twelve hundred francs, not including those of transportation.[92]

At the same time that the number of those named on the "multitude of announcements" was increasing (quintupling from the 1820s to the 1890s) there was also a steady increase in the number of those of whom the public was informed they died "furnished with the sacraments."[93] There was now a conscious anachronism, reaching back to the piety before that collapse of religious references that has been discerned in the middle decades of the preceding century.

THE FUNERAL CEREMONIES

Requests in wills about the type of ceremony ranged from asking for a fifth-class funeral to limiting the sums of money to be spent, to specifying the number of paupers who were to follow the bier in the procession, and to other details of the occasion. Over two-thirds of bachelors and married women gave instructions about their funerals and graves, but only one in four married men did so. In general, spinsters were less likely than married women to be given an elaborate funeral. Spinsters were more likely than married women to die intestate, as the low frequency of their wills in notarial archives illustrates. Mlle Bolle de la Salle was an exception on both counts, noting in July 1838 that "I want to be placed in a walnut coffin screwed down. I want twenty of the most unfortunate paupers in the arrondissement where I shall die to follow my convoy, each to be given three francs and a candle, and four carriages in mourning to follow my convoy and bring back the twenty poor paupers." She left money for the elevation of a single sarcophagus of antique form over her own grave, and that of her woman friend, at Père la Chaise cemetery, and she asked a vicomtesse to ask her husband and father to follow her funeral possession. Since women did not participate in the procession (they only started to do so in the 1880s), male mourners were needed to give the occasion its due gravity.[94] Spinsters were less likely than married women to express fulsome "family" sentiments in their extant wills, as though their lives had failed their purpose without child or husband.

Instructions about the location of one's tomb were common. Mme de Choiseul-Praslin specified in 1808 that her body was to be buried with her husband's (at Praslin) but her heart was to be interred "in the special little garden at Auteuil" with the body of her second son, who had died in that house. There was a distinction between the body which belonged to the family and the affections of a mother.[95] In 1826 Mme de Bohm, *née* Girardin, decided that "I do not wish to be put in a lead coffin nor in a sepulchral vault nor in any massive, closed, stone structure; some shrubs that do not need annual cultivation shall be planted in the enclosure where I shall lie."[96] Mme. de Choiseul-Sérent wished to be buried at Picpus, with its memories of the victims of the Terror, and her will, made in 1840, rang with Catholic piety—was not her widowed son-in-law cardinal Rohan-Chabot?

> In the name of the Father, of the Son, and of the Holy Spirit, My God, I commend myself to your mercy, the intercession of the Blessed Virgin, Saint Joseph, and my patron saints, I thank you for having made me a Christian, for having given me a father, a mother, a sister, a husband, a daughter, and a son-in-law that I have so justly cherished: you have given them to me, you have taken them away, may your indulgence reunite us in the heavenly home [*demeure du ciel*]. I wish to be taken to Picpus, where are deposited the remains of those who were dear to me. I want to be buried without ceremony, only at the door of the church, in the most simple drapery, no drapery in the interior of the church, nor coat-of-arms—what is called a fifth-class burial. . . . I want if twelve priests are able to take part in my burial that each receive twenty-five francs. If that is possible, I hope that one hundred Masses may be said for the repose of my soul in the month of death and that each one is paid three francs.[97]

There seems to be evidence that elaborate tombs were erected more frequently towards the end of the nineteenth century than at the beginning, a trend not confined to French nobles, as can be confirmed from the burial grounds of Victorian English Canada. Vovelle is provocatively excessive when he speaks of these ornate tombs as a barricade against death, but certainly the cult of the dead took on a rotund vehemence in the nineteenth century. For nobles the distinction was made between those who could be interred in the noblest ground of all, that of their château chapel, and those who lay in a public place. Joseph de Villèle was buried in the consecrated ground of the chapel beside the Mourvilles-Basses château which was built and dedicated in the decade before his death. The Choiseul-Praslins were buried in or around their chapel at Vaux-Praslin, but after the sale of the estate in 1875 the remains were moved to the Maincy parish church. Comte de Maillé, who died in 1839, wished to be buried in the Montmartre cemetary in a plot purchased for perpetuity: "It is to be surrounded with an iron grill. On my tomb shall be placed a simple marble stone on which shall be written in gold letters: the Cte de Maillé Latour Landry, g.h.d'h. de Monsieur [*gentilhomme d'honneur de Monsieur*—later Charles x] born the 24 June 1771 died the. . . ."98 Mme de Briey (1857) also specified the inscription she wanted on her tomb, one emphasizing that she was doubly a comtesse: "Maximilienne, Ctesse de Coudenhove, née Ctesse de Briey l'an 1780–décedée à lâge de _____ passant, priez pour elle."99 The text of these inscriptions was evidently intended to remind members of the family of elements of the personal biography that they should keep constantly in mind.

MASSES FOR THE REPOSE OF THE SOUL

The importance of memorial Masses as an indicator of religiosity has not passed unnoticed by historians. In the nineteenth century nobles had both the wealth and the inclination to make such provision more often than any other sector of the French population. Mme Choiseul d'Esguilly, a wealthy widow, specified in 1810 what arrangements were to be made on her behalf:

> During the week of my death fifty Low Masses will be said in the Church of St. Thomas d'Aquin, my parish, for which three francs will be paid for each. Forty days after my death twenty-four Low Masses shall be said in the said church, of which the honoraria shall be paid at six francs each: four candles will be lit on each of the altars where these masses shall be said. This shall be done on free days, so they will be said in black [priestly robes]. These honoraria for the Masses shall be given to the curé of the said parish, and he shall be charged to do them [four donations to the poor]. I want every Sunday during the year of my death to have a *de profundis* sung at the end of the High Mass for the repose of my soul, in the parishes of St. Parize and of Montigny (Niévre), and the curés of the said parishes are to be paid an honorarium of 150F for the year, quarterly. It shall also be paid to the churchwardens of each of the said parishes six francs every three months during the said year.100

Mme Geneviève-Françoise de Machault d'Arnouville showed a typical concern for intercessionary Masses after her death (which took place in September 1869). She bequeathed six hundred francs of perpetual annuity to the local curé at Arnouville to say Mass each Sunday, and upon days of obligation when invited to do so, at the château chapel for the repose of her soul, that of the parish's benefactors, and for her husband and son.[101] Among the wills examined there is a slight progression towards more numerous Masses, particularly in those years of the religious revival associated with Lourdes and the polarization of Catholic opinion in the 1860s, but the small numbers incite caution.

BEQUESTS TO THE POOR

Charitable bequests to the poor were more likely from married women, especially widows, and bachelors than from married men or spinsters. In general these bequests were to the paupers of specified places, self-evidently underlining the idea of "feudal" charity, or at least to the parish of which the deceased was a distinguished member. Such donations were often intertwined with provisions for the saying of Masses, as in the will of Mme Choiseul d'Esguilly above. The widowed duchesse de Choiseul-Praslin established six small incomes ranging from 1,500F to 3,000F which she insisted were to provide not a cash distribution to the indigent but bread, wood, and other necessities for the poor born in the communes or living there for at least ten years. She added that she had already set up *rentes* in several communes where her husband had held properties and where she wanted his name to be always blessed and that she hoped to augment these *rentes* during her own lifetime, since "I believe that it is more meritorious to impose upon oneself some privations and to give during one's life what one can, rather than to charge one's beneficiaries with it."[102]

SERVANTS

Nobles were fairly sensitive to rewarding servants of long standing. Bachelors were more responsive to the surrogate family relationship with long-term servants who cared for them in age, while married men and women were only half as likely to make provisions for employees in their wills. There was a limit to the loyalties enunciated in the theory. The researcher soon encounters a less fulsome devotion on the part of some legatees who had to carry out the injunctions. One Leveneur wrote to another member of that wealthy family of the Orne in December 1827 to exhort him to respect their father's wishes about generosity to the servants, who were to be paid a year's wages. These could be calculated as pay during the current year, which had begun the previous July, and so "it is only seven months of which we make them a present." He added that since their father left no debts and could have burdened them with still heavier obligations, they should respect his wishes. Clearly there had been a discussion about reneging on that obligation.[103] Similar fears may explain the precision with which Mme de Girardin in 1864 made payments of her bequest to servants a condition of her legacy of mortgages to a young niece. If the mortgages were sold, sufficient funds to carry on payments to the servants were to be invested by the notary in the Lyon railway.[104]

Similar bequests would be most onerous in the aristocratic houses in Paris. A large and wealthy household had a hierarchy of servants. Baron de Canouville (whose will is reproduced in appendix 3) made a handsome bequest to his *maître d'hôtel*. In larger Paris houses there were other male servants, such as valets, grooms, gardeners, and porters, as well as housemaids and so forth. In a provincial city such as Nancy, where local nobles were less wealthy, they rarely had more than two servants, and these were almost always women, serving and cleaning in the rented apartments close to the cours Léopold, where the nobles passed the winter months, and then traveling with them to country properties during the summer months.[105]

Comte Maillé Latour Landry's 1839 will asked friends to visit and care for his grave, left a legacy to the Bons Secours sisters, and bequeathed his valet a *rente viagère* of 800F.[106] Vicomte de Bruges provided an annual pension of 300F for "Louis my negro for his faithful services" and admonished his wife and children to continue to look after him "even if he was no longer of any use for anything."[107] Davessens de Moncal, a Toulouse landowner, left a cook an annual pension of 924F, presumably for his culinary efforts.[108] Pons de Fumel in 1832, quoted below, was concerned for his employees and asked his son to look after his former nursemaid, who had been with the family for twenty-nine years, by giving her an annual revenue of 300F and the furnishing of a room. He went on to enumerate among other donations to the faithful servant three teaspoons and a silver goblet.[109] A noble bachelor living in Sens, M. de Fleurigny, in his will made between 1839 and 1843 was tight-fisted in his legacies, giving a single *rente perpetuelle* to his maidservant (250F per annum) and leaving to his other servants in one case an overcoat and in another clothes at the executor's discretion. His will thus reveals the absolute minimum that the stingiest noble not dead to posthumous shame could leave to servants: subsistence to those closest to him ("to old Gérard the job he is doing") and some personal effects.[110]

FAMILY SPIRIT

While explicit Catholic invocations and requests for Masses were part of the will, so were repeated injunctions to family members not to squabble over the bequests. In some ways this was an "invocation" of the *lares et penates,* the collectivity of the family and unity. The former officer Pons de Fumel married the daughter of a former *conseiller* in the Parlement of Bordeaux, Dusault, and observed in his will of 3 May 1832 that "being of an advanced age, and having to undertake a voyage at the time when a murderous illness ravages France [cholera], it is the duty of a good Christian and the father of a family to make a will, for what little he has, in order to be sure in his last moments of the future tranquillity in his family."[111]

Other wills showed the desire to avoid dispute as well as to uphold formal religiosity in family documents where bourgeois rarely used it. E. G. J. de Pérusse Descars Ctesse de Bréon douairière, as she signed her 1852 will, was concerned that her son would take care of his sister in recompense for her care and affection, remembering that because she was unmarried she had never had a trousseau—that is to say, she had never been a drag on the family purse and had not required a dowry— and a little later she asked her son not to take what might be owing to him on the share of his sister, "my daughter, who has always shared the constraints and privations that I have had to impose on myself since the bad state of our affairs."[112]

MEMENTOS AND FAMILY LEGACIES

Bequests often revealed a desire to celebrate the family history. Joseph de Villèle had highly systematic social and political beliefs. He began his will with an invocation of divine *misericordia* and left to his wife during her lifetime and then to his son Henri family portraits, papers, titles, decorations, engravings, medallions, and other items that had come into his possession through his parents, from Louis XVIII and Charles X, and from foreign rulers. The order of provenance is carefully given:

> Not certainly that I want to make of them an object of vanity in my
> family, but the same motivation that makes me transmit after me the
> documents that I have been able to gather on our origin, the same
> motivation that causes me to wish to be buried at Mourvilles, brings
> me to desire the conservation among the heirs of my name of
> everything that can inspire in them family spirit and attachment to
> the place where [the family] has been established for a long time as
> an element of happiness, of wisdom, and of good conduct for those
> who shall come after me.

His son was enjoined again to look after his sisters throughout his life, "especially if they should have the misfortune to lose us before being married or if they should survive their husbands."[113] The will ended with another religious invocation. The Villèle will reiterated family ideology just as much as it made arrangements to bequeath property. For her part the duchesse de Maillé (whose marriage contract is reproduced in appendix 2) went into elaborate detail in her 1850 will on the subject of her manuscripts, which she requested Salvandy to edit and publish in a select edition of ten copies. She assured posterity that her motive was not literary vanity, but "it is sweet for me to be sure that I shall never cease to exist through my thought for my family and my friends."[114]

FAMILY SPIRIT IN PRACTICE

Points raised here about family life can be seen with more clarity if we examine a particular *noblesse* family. The *berrichon* Aiguirande family had been titled for sixteen generations at the start of the nineteenth century, descending from medieval, chevalresque origins.[115] The oldest brother, Armand, a dragoon captain before the Revolution, in 1799 at age thirty-nine married a first cousin, from whom he had no issue. He was wealthy, with a sizable estate. The second oldest brother was thirty-seven in 1800, having joined the Cistercians in 1785 before leaving them in 1792 as a result of the dissolution. Then he returned to the family château at Levroux (Indre), where he lived until his death on 29 August 1843. Charles, the youngest of the three, was thirty-five in 1800.

Unlike his eldest brother, who had an estate, and the other, who enjoyed the security of ecclesiastical life, before the Revolution Charles was required to show the initiative of cadets. When the Revolution began, he showed no hostility; instead he continued to serve in the army until 1793. He returned briefly to the Republican armies in 1795 and then went on to take up a position in the Parisian legion of the general police. In one sense such divergencies might prove politically useful to a family. The Aiguirandes, for example, could invoke both Revolutionary and royalist sympathies as required, although as will become apparent, there was no love lost between the eldest and the youngest brothers on that score.[116] Early in the century Charles returned to the Cher, but without a noble bride. Instead he lived with the daughter of a local day laborer born at Levroux. Doubtless the house he bought in the year XIII was to facilitate this liaison. Two daughters were born to the couple before their civil marriage when the mother was thirty-eight. Only in 1826, within a year of Charles's death, did the religious marriage take place. Even in a province like the Berry, notorious for its tepid piety, such blatant disregard for moral conventions by a member of a distinguished family was scandalous. Charles's heir, Alexandre-Charles-François, was the third child.

The elderly abbé Aiguirande, who had lived with Charles for some time despite this unedifying situation, sent a note from Levroux to the oldest brother inviting him to attend the funeral. The abbé noted that only Armand, the head of the family and the oldest, was suitable to take legal responsibility for three minor children. He could not assume such a charge himself because of gout. The annotation made on the back of the death notice, obviously returned to the abbé, is a dry statement that Article 433 of the Civil Code permits a person over sixty-five years of age to refuse that responsibility and points out that he, Armand, is sixty-seven:

I refuse to be the guardian of the children of late monsieur, your
brother. I believe, however, that I have to observe that the man who
wanted to make an attempt on my life, who was constantly my
cruelest enemy, was never able to wish that I replace him in his
family and that this would be to go against his intentions. . . .
Nobody better than you can more agreeably for the family take on
the title of *tuteur* and *curateur* [legal designations of responsibility].
I am distant from all this and could only displease, and perhaps I
would upset the common peace. I cannot forget that this marriage
was made with the intention of driving me to despair. That aim has
been completely successful, and it would be impossible for me to
overcome the wounds that have been inflicted on me. They still
bleed and would poison whatever vestiges of sentiment remain to
me. Farewell my brother. Look after yourself well.

The bitter antipathies between the brothers shown by this letter need no
emphasis. Despite this outburst, Armand in fact accepted his blood
responsibilities and accepted the guardianship of his brother's children.

Armand, head of the family, was a careful manager. He sold his
Villedieu estate on 20 July 1792 and by acts of 10–11 May 1793 he
acquired the Romsac château which had been confiscated by the nation. He paid 369,300F and also paid off various *rentes*. This display of
patriotic investment did not save him from several months' imprisonment in Chateauroux in the autumn of 1793, but upon his release he
returned to activites in local administration that he had first begun in
1789. The mayor of Saint Phalier commune near Levroux in the year IX,
he was among the richest landowners of the department under the
Restoration, paying 7,555F 76 in *cens*. (At his death in 1831 he left five
rentes viagères of 600F to servants which were to revert to the estate in
due course.) In time this wealth devolved on the son of Charles
d'Aiguirande, born on 13 May 1815, who, together with his sisters, had
gone to live at Romsac with Uncle Armand upon their father's death. In
1832 the younger sister married M. de Piègu. On 10 April 1839 Alexandre-Charles married the widow de Preaulx, daughter of one of Marie-
Antoinette's pages. Their child was born prematurely and died. Alexandre-Charles himself died at Romsac in May 1841. After an interval of
ten years, his widow married a former French cavalry officer, according
to the Anglican rite and in London, but he was killed just three years
later in a hunting accident. Alexandre-Charles's widow returned to
Romsac, where she lived until her own death in 1878. A cadet branch of
the family survived until 1866 in the Pas-de-Calais, but only daughters
were born, and the family name died out. Nobody could control the sex
of the unborn nor calculate in advance an adult's marriage chances;
even less could one know the hour of his own end. However, if the

Aiguirandes display anything, it is behavior sharply at variance with what was preached by the *bien pensant* press. Irreligion, purchase of *biens nationaux, mésalliance,* bastards, and family squabbling were all found in this wealthy old knightly family.

Precisely the same tensions could be found in many thousands of other noble households, but as in the case of the Aiguirandes, these are best studied in public archives, where there is more likelihood of encountering unedulcorated historial records. The permutations in every family's conduct could bewilder. The number of daughters to dower, the inheritance in near or distant view, the profitability of estates and their location, the political favors enjoyed—all modified the family hopes and fears. The noble lineage's fate depended on far more than simply the prescriptions of the Civil Code.

There is little doubt that the post-Revolutionary *noblesse* became more parsimonious. Ascetic self-control had always been respected as an aristocratic virtue, almost as much as its equally rare opposite, truly majestic extravagance. Democratic pleasures are those accessible to all: wide-throated, full-bellied enjoyments dreamed of by those who had known penury. If the rich commoner was "fat" in the indicators of social life, the noble was "thin" without being obliged to be. The *nouveau riche* was derided by nobles as a glutton in an overdecorated home. Comtesse de Bradi wrote a chapter in her 1842 etiquette book on the need to avoid any appearance of gourmandism when invited to dinner. She exhorted her readers not to indulge in effusive praises of rich dishes.[117] Modesty and economy, genteel penny-pinching, now became a distinctive cachet. Thriftiness that increased the family patrimony was excellent. One Toulouse noble's 1846 eulogy proclaimed, "In the buildings that he put up one would look in vain for any appearance of a luxury which he never liked. He limited himself to the point that each of them displayed all the decorum desirable."[118]

Tocqueville's aside that "the respect paid to wealth in England is enough to make one despair" is a commentary on the same theme.[119] So too is the description given by Mme d'Armaillé in her evocative recollection of aristocratic family life in the 1850s:

> Family assemblies under the same roof remained as a kind of privilege, and it is a fact that patriarchal traditions and the most respectable virtues remained there and were perpetuated. I shall add that intelligence, conversation, politeness gained from this, instead of losing as some like to think. The vast mansions of the faubourg Saint-Germain lent themselves, moreover, to these kinds of family phalansteries. Far from being embarrassed by the lack of fortune, by the need to live economically, to dress modestly, to be content with old servants with country manners, of using antique carriages and of

observing the abstinences and religious and charitable practices of
the past, the heads of family and the mistresses of the houses
showed in all this a very justified pride and thus succeeded in again
displaying some dignity. It was in that manner that it was known
how to live in the houses of Gontaut, de la Rochefoucauld, de
Périgord, etc., the families of Montesquiou, de Biencourt,
d'Orglandès, de Vogué, Champagne, many others, and finally ourselves, although the habits of my parents were less severe and less
austere than those of the houses of the faubourg Saint-Germain and
of those who remained purely Legitimists.[120]

If simplicity and thriftiness were virtues respected by all nobles, the
century saw a widening gap between those who successfully increased
their wealth (and whose names later appeared in *Le Figaro* as the gratin
so assiduously studied by Marcel Proust) and the provincial *noblesse*
fearful of Parisian life, which revealed their wallets' limitations. Few
daughters of the middling Gascon or Breton gentry could aspire to take
part in the spectacle in the Bois breathlessly recorded by Peat North in
1866:

> Princess de Bauffremont on a dark bay mare, the Duchess of
> Fitzjames and her two sons, Baroness Lejeune, Countess de
> Baulaincourt, Baroness de Pierre and Baroness Saint Dider may be
> seen almost every morning enjoying a canter in the shady alleys of
> the Bois, riding better than any women in France, capitally mounted,
> and dressed as ladies ought to dress on horseback. *Du reste,* each
> and all I have mentioned ride to hounds, and manage their hunters
> as well and as gracefully as they do their park hacks, as anyone who
> hunted last season the Touraine and Anjou country can testify.[121]

The continuing trajectory of these great aristocratic fortunes towards
the end of the nineteenth century was recalled by Elisabeth Clermont-
Tonnerre, born a Gramont, who described with her incomparable
sprightliness a style of life enjoyed from the Second Empire to the *Belle
Epoque* in terms that illustrate a number of our themes:

> Saint-Assise was a nice Louis XVI château on a terrace rising out of
> the Seine, surrounded by woods full of game. I often used to go
> there on a visit to my grandfather Beauvau. He lived there in
> patriarchal fashion with his second wife, Adèle de Gontaut (who had
> twenty-one brothers and sisters: Joseph, afterwards member for the
> Basses-Pyrénées. Paul, Bernard, Edmond, Gaston and Xavier, who
> went through Saint-Cyr, Geneviève, the canoness, Madame de
> Gaigneron, Madame de Liedekerke, the Comtesse Armand, Madame
> d'Hurst, etc. . . .); his daughters, Jeanne de Mun and Loulou de
> Blacas; his sons-in-law; and his sister Béatrix, who had married
> Comte Horace de Choiseul. The Choiseuls occupied a villa by the

waterside at Seine-Port and spent their days at Sainte-Assise.

I must say that extreme bonhomie and a pleasant spirit of indulgence prevailed. A state of placidity such as that has disappeared from our social life. There were no "parties," as they are called, at Sainte-Assise, but always between twenty and thirty people staying there and living together after a fashion impossible nowadays. . . .

Though a rich man he (Beauvau) indulged the usual French niggardliness. At his table he served piquette, the thin wine sent him in casks from his vineyards of La Sarthe. He possessed sumptuous tapestries and furniture, but never had anything repaired. The second floor rooms were paved, and I used to build castles with the loose tiles. No need to remark that there was no water laid on in the house. Every morning a footman used to carry up two buckets of cold water and a kettle of hot water which smelt of smoke.

Yet my grandfather passed, and rightly passed, for one of the largest landed proprietors of his time. He had biens, to use that obsolete expression, in the départements of Seine-et-Marne and La Sarthe, in Nivernais, that Royal Dutch of landed estates, and lastly goodness knows how many farms in Multien. He used to make tours through his domains and good farmer and wise administrator as he was knew how to manage them. A lot in the avenue Montaigne awaited but his pleasure to be transformed into a mansion, but he preferred to look at it as it was from the windows of an inexpensive flat he inhabited just opposite. In his youth he had owned racehorses; then he was appointed conseiller général for La Sarthe and held that post for some time.

Saint-Assise was his favourite home. In autumn he used to organize great battues of partridge and rabbits, much sought after, but he did not preserve pheasants. Thanks to his thrift he was able to increase his fortune, and to this day a dozen families, my own among them, live on the Beauvau money.[122]

The description shows well the place of family and château among the wealthiest aristocrats. By the 1870s the minor gentry had grasped what Choiseul saw in 1800. Political and ideological loyalties were henceforth secondary to the ongoing interests of the noble family. A whole code of conduct that protected the family predominated among French nobles; at the same time, they realized that they could never again aspire to rule the nation.

During the century since Louis xvi's accession the noble family became more and more inward-looking, particularly among the aristocracy, which despite their bishops, ambassadors, and general councillors, had less of a handle on the highest state positions than before the Revolution. One constant, however, was that girls were given little or no say in the choice of their partners. Certainly the very young marriages of aristocrats of both sexes before the Revolution did not take place afterwards, but most girls were married before they were twenty. Their husbands were more likely to be older, and by a wider margin than in the total French population. The women who had played such an important part in protecting the interests of noble families during the Revolution were followed by generations whose stress was again on paternalism. This also meant, paradoxically, that the old women were most likely to survive from each generation, and thanks to the provisions of the *régime dotal*, they often possessed great means. French noblewomen did not, however, use their advantages in education, wealth, and privilege to question the primacy of the family realm in their lives.

What set nobles apart from commoners under democracy was their different use and understanding of kinship bonds. Their family links were not so much different in kind as they were an extra extension of the feelings of family solidarity normal in France at that time. These emphasized economic support and production and, it need hardly be said, were quite different from twentieth-century European ideas of love and affection.[123] Noble kinship had the same base but also included the custody of ancestral prestige, either real or fictive, which had to be passed on. It may be objected that concern for family reputation and renown was not restricted to nobles, as can be inferred from the pride of political and business dynasties both past and present; however, one could not continue to be noble outside of the kinship network. The bourgeois politician and businessman were not so limited. Both gloried in essentially individual accomplishments in the nineteenth century, and if the commoner placed himself at the behest of his relations, he was not obliged to do so. On the other hand, the noble under the conditions of Frenchmen equal before the law who jettisoned the family gradually ceased to exist as a noble. The bourgeois pursued the road that led to the affective marital link at the heart of the modern family. Nobles accepted and indeed rejoiced in those obligations of kinship that meant a real limit on individualism.

Conclusion

> As members of the same body, there is a consequence: all nobles
> carry a certain responsibility for the conduct of each other, as
> happens in a family; the fault of an individual alone does not render
> them all guilty, but all are obliged to make a certain reparation.
>   —Grimouard de Saint-Laurent, *Questions sur la noblesse*

Noble family conventions derived from a preindustrial, prebourgeois
past which was opposite—and at least to that extent opposed—to the
new urban, egalitarian society, with its promise of plenty and democracy, that was emerging slowly and unevenly in nineteenth-century
Europe.[1] The 1789 Revolution accentuated in the short run the economic and agricultural backwardness of France compared with England, but simultaneously it broadcast throughout the world liberal,
Jacobin, socialist, and *dirigiste* ideologies. As everybody knows, France
was a political exemplar, not to say a nightmare, to her neighbors at that
time. Recent French history became as familiar to European intellectuals as the classical past which they were obliged to study in their
secondary schools.

Nobles were leading contenders in that narrative, but they lacked
unity, and they did not obey the same political strategies. In the main
the *noblesse* had been opportunist under Napoleon, with a significant
number rallying to some form of state service, usually on the local level.
Even under the Restoration a handful of the old *noblesse* retained loyalty
to the Bonapartist cause, such as the marquis de Las Cases and
Montholon, both of whom accompanied Napoleon to Saint Helena. The
imperial nobility, of military origin, took an understandable pride in
their origin, exemplified by Junot's motto to the effect that *he* was the
ancestor, not his forebears. In due course other nobles became keen
partisans of the Orleanists. Too much ink has flowed in describing the
different currents of opinion among the nobles without emphasizing

216

the social values held in common which transcended the search for advantage in political affiliations. In this book I have attempted to portray something of the social landscape of nobles in France. Their economic strategy, their relationship to power, the extent of their influence, and above all, the importance to them of family ties were fundamental to that reality.

For their part those men and women would have been impatient with so bald a claim. In their eyes nobility was based on personal distinction and ancestral tradition; quite literally this refinement was inexplicable to those who did not partake of the *je ne sais quoi.* Nothing damaged their intricate psychological constructs more than crude factual examination of the conventions that marked them as patricians. Madame de La Tour du Pin was content in her memoirs to tell posterity that Napoleon I immediately recognized in the simplicity and good cut of her outfit the style, taste, and deportment of an aristocrat of the old court; to her it would be otiose to explain why too many expensive diamonds or elaborate dress were a mistake. She and her husband had retained the wealth, the contacts with their ilk, and the confidence in their innate abilities to gain for him highly responsible posts under Bonaparte and the Bourbons. Aristocrats and petty *noblesse* believed that nobles had an instinctive habit of authority. Nobles felt it unseemly to enquire too closely into those matters. To describe their wealth, contacts, professions, and so forth makes for a less awesome and more untidy subject than an examination of noble dreams of inborn superiority.

If nobles thought they were the polished summit of good society, they knew they were no longer the rulers of France. No misconception about nobles has been more sedulously cultivated in republican textbooks than the claim that nobles had learned nothing and forgotten nothing since 1789. In fact, nobles very quickly learned the distinction between public and private realms of power and social influence when the *noblesse* became a victimized minority during the Revolution.[2] By 1800, nobles could see that they were far from being the public superiors of the notables; on the contrary, they were dependent upon them if the new France was to prove remotely to their taste. What they hoped to preserve in the private sphere was a way of life and its attendant comforting mythologies.

However, like their tormentors during the Revolution, those "anciennes factions révolutionnaires" of whom Talleyrand observed to Louis XVIII in 1815 that they were now tied to the monarchical system by titles and property, nobles found that their kinfolk's interests compelled cooperation with, and a transfer of their values to, the new rulers of France.[3] Not surprisingly, nobles could hardly trumpet this truth about—indeed, perhaps they could not themselves see it—since the ambiguity between their public and private stances was at the heart of their mystique of *distinction*. If they said that they were on an even footing with notables, they were diminished as nobles, but if they exulted in superiority, they risked antagonizing those whose tacit acceptance was essential.

Nobles wanted to retain the complicity with relations that lay behind hierarchical views of society proper to a preindustrial and prebourgeois world. On the occasion of an 1829 marriage one noble of petty territorial *noblesse* from the Midi wrote to another who was disheartened by Parisian politics and of the same mind: "If there is still for us any happiness, it must not be sought anywhere save in domestic joys, and I know you well enough to know that you have always been very aware of it, even when the highest interests absorbed your entire attention and filled your every moment."[4] Vicomte de Bonald was here putting into words to comte de Villèle the idea of the noble family shut in upon itself and its ancestral virtues as the source of their identity and worth.

Even if nobles had wished to oppose the post-Revolutionary society, they lacked any satisfactory political organization. The last nationwide assembly of the *noblesse* had been held at Versailles in May 1789, and to recall it conjured up memories of injurious animosities, repeated calumnies, wrangling, and envy. There would not again be a national association of nobles until the *Journal officiel* of 22 November 1932 announced the establishment of the Association d'entr'aide de la noblesse française. Between those two dates the nobility had no recognized forum or national leadership. Indeed, the provincial *noblesse* had outdone themselves in vituperating the Chamber of Peers of the constitutional monarchies as being in the hands of aristocrats and *titrés* and as being unrepresentative of the antique *noblesse* of the kingdom, although no other body was better placed to defend their interests. Despite the overrepresentation of nobles in the upper chamber, under the Second Empire its membership was also derided as venal and timeserving, so that the Senate also could not serve as a rallying point for the concatenation of the titled.

With declining numbers, nobles never controlled any national government in their collective interest save perhaps briefly during the Villèle ministry. That is not to say that they were absent from the exercise of political power; the most cursory survey of nineteenth-century political history leaves no doubt that titled politicians appeared in authority at all levels of government, bureaucracy, and administration. The success of that adjustment was still evident in the 1970s, when a study of the post–World War II French ruling class found that if nobles constituted no more than 0.3 percent of the active population, they constituted up to 9 percent of the elite, with, moreover, a marked presence in the limited and inaccessible posts with the most power.[5] The practice of success, as much as anything else, was the hallmark of nobles.

The central fact about the nobility between 1800 and 1870 was its fall in numbers. None of the rulers of the century gave out new titles fast enough to reverse the trend. The cost of the entailments required by Napoleon on the property of individuals who wished to pass on a hereditary title to their eldest son was restricting and applicable only to wealthy individuals. In 1834 the duc de Bassano pointed out that under the First Empire new creations had averaged thirty-six each year but had fallen under the Restoration to an average of seventeen annually, and since 1830 there had been only two.[6]

If the state failed to make enough new titles to offset the extinction of the older ones, social practice might do so, particularly the commercial genealogies: "It is with the aim of preventing the usurpation of Noble Titles that this book is published annually which indicates the true Nobles, and appearing annually is destined to follow up the *Etrennes à la noblesse* and the *Etat de la noblesse* published by La Chenaye-Desbois."[7] That 1848 almanac gave the address where proofs of nobility were to be sent by those who wished to appear in the next issue: the editor's address was place de la Bourse, Paris. A listing in one of the various genealogies constituted a legitimation of sorts when the central government was indifferent to policing such claims, but that facility did not end the demographic hemorrhage.

A few among the *noblesse* called for recruits, such as one who signed himself "a village mayor" as he made the argument in 1861 that individuals who before the Revolution had been mere écuyers or chevaliers, both obsolete titles in contemporary usage, should henceforth be called barons and vicomtes: "Alas, one knows with what speed noble families are dying out. . . . Look around us, examine among our relatives and friends, how many noble families are on the point of extinction: the number is truly horrifying. How many have we seen disappear in the last half-century!"[8] However, neither the creation of new titles, genealogical laxities, nor greater permissiveness among nobles about the use of titles could reverse the steady shrinkage of their group.

The idea that nobles constituted "a graceful ornament to the civil order," as Burke had put it, became widely acceptable to the wealthiest commoners. Rancor against nobles had flared up at different times in the French past, but deference and admiration for their way of life and bearing was much more normal. Echoes of the Revolutionary campaign against the *noblesse* were found in the anti-noble books and articles of the Restoration liberal press; however, the balance was definitely shifting. In the early nineteenth century noble idylls of aristocratic flavor gained enormously in literary esteem. The dandy was one form of this, the epitome of the romantics for studied artificiality and rarified sensibilities derived from wealth, leisure, and upbringing.[9] Authors like Stendhal, Barbey d'Aurevilly, Balzac, Sandeau, and Cousin gave an aesthetic evocation of nobles in their novels and biographies. So too did innumerable serial novels, inexpensive lithographs, fashion plates, vaudevilles, perfume labels, and restaurant menus.[10] The vehement republican attack on noble pretension under the Second and Third republics was fueled by frustration that in the formal works of artists and writers the cultural ambiance of the middle classes did not offer a compelling alternative to noble attitudes. There always existed a simultaneous "dark" literature about nobles which reached a peak with the 1890s novel *Jacquou le Croquant,* but even in that text there are sympathetic characters drawn from the old *noblesse* as well as from the hateful recent recruits to nobility.

Nobles themselves had little to do with shifting attitudes towards them. They were beneficiaries of the general distaste for egalitarianism in a nation where the bourgeois usually emphasized his distance from peasants and workers. Throughout French society the clear limits on the Revolutionary message of liberty and fraternity were found in the persistent search for hierarchy and formalism. This was self-evident enough in the Napoleonic prefectures, where lists of provincial notables were compiled: the "influence" and "consideration" of each individual was noted. Under all regimes to 1870 there was a recognition of the Old Regime idea of natural deference and respect for hierarchy in society. Distinguished families were more important than individuals in maintaining the fabric of society. Napoleon wanted his young officials to display the kind of tone and bearing suitable to those placed in authority when he admitted junior members of the Council of State to the imperial court: "The intention of His Majesty is that the *auditeurs* should be admitted to the Court so that on the one hand they become accustomed to their work but on the other they will acquire the urbanity, the bon ton, and worldy assurance that are necessary in the posts to which they may be named."[11] The author who recalled this text pointed out how wealth and bearing of officials constantly concerned recruiters to the bureaucracy's higher echelons throughout nineteenth-century France.[12]

The ambitions of all noble families were cruelly dependent on wealth which permitted them to maintain a way of life. While modern historians have tried to know when, and in what circumstances, nobles were "financially outgunned by industrialists or financiers," as one recent essay put it, we must appreciate that their prestige and standing rested on more than a substantial income.[13] Like the bulk of big fortunes in early nineteenth-century France, noble wealth was based on landownership. As agriculturalists, nobles were not perceptibly different from untitled neighbors on the land, unless in that they were less likely to be resident. As Cobban noted, they were part of the dominant class of landed proprietors, always united against those with little or no property, although I have argued in this book that the shared sense of noble identity went far beyond the unity of "the wealth and values of landowners."[14]

There were differences between the bigger, more efficient estates of northwestern France and the smaller, more arid and less fertile farms often found in the south. Living below the Loire generally meant that even a frugal noble lifestyle took too much out of annual profits to permit the reinvestment in agriculture at a sufficiently high level to match the advances of productivity in the more fertile parts of France. Nobles in agricultural societies or on the advisory panels of model farms obscure the fact that the 1846–48 crisis and the big structural changes in French agriculture resulting from improved transports and new markets, as well as better crop varieties, tended towards the consolidation of the larger, profitable estates that underpinned the wealthy aristocratic families of the *Belle Epoque*.

Nobles have too often been seen as holding unchanging political and economic attitudes. That was as true in the period 1800–1870 as it was in the twentieth century. Considered in the mass, nobles were opportunists in their political conduct, despite the grandiose rhetoric of their symbolic universe of excellence. Young Gobineau quickly saw that fatuity of "the dear party," as he ironically dubbed the ineffectual Legitimists of the 1840s. Indeed, a modern study of the Chamber of Deputies in 1837–39 revealed that the Legitimist representatives were more likely to be silent and inactive in parliamentary work than almost any other political group.[15] After 1830 shrewd prefects realized what their predecessors had come to appreciate during the days of the emperor Napoleon. Legitimist ceremonials of the "orthodox" *noblesse,* from anniversary Masses for the death of Louis xvi, pilgrimages to Belgrave Square in London to salute the pretender to the throne, or gestures or disdain for the Orleanist dynasty, could be characterized as self-satisfying politics, a pleasure indulged without any risk of social consequences.

As the Second Empire replaced the July Monarchy and the years passed, the gap between this family mythology and the real place in French society of those who called themselves noble became increasingly obvious. The public debate of the 1820s over the supposed menace posed to the political order by nobles had generated real heat, but by the 1860s it was derisory to believe that a lackluster clientele of tenants, grateful beggars, valets, housemaids, and deferential shopkeepers constituted an effective power base. When, as a result of war and political upheaval, electoral politics offered an apparent chance to govern in the 1870s, the nobles involved deliberately, if not knowingly, sabotaged the encounter with reality.[16]

Ultimately the study of nineteenth-century nobles and their tangled pursuit of wealth, politics, and career points us towards a particular ideology of the family. Nobles simply willed their collective difference from the bourgeoisie, and that was as important as the numbers of children born or the incidence of unmarried relatives, in which they indeed differed from the notables. They also preserved discipline and formalism. Above all, they inculcated in their progeny the importance of visualizing their world as a network of families rather than of individuals. Egalitarianism and individual accomplishment could never outweigh a society based on distinguished families that preserved the values of the past. As Hauteville wrote in 1863, "It is said that there is nothing left to it [the nobility] save its memories: that is enough, and we have no need to ask anything else. With this last appanage it will play a more honorable role than when it had the preponderant voice in the council of kings and rendered justice to its vassals."[17]

The 1789 Revolution had denied the nobles' legal right to preeminence in civil society. Recent history was retold with increasing obsession by a generation that knew the decade of the 1790s only at second hand. Christian imagery, with its emphasis on sacrifice and victimization leading to an assurance of salvation, was congenial in the extreme. (This lachrymose and self-indulgent view of themselves as victims at a time when nobles were the wealthiest per capita group in nineteenth-century France induced irritated responses from egalitarian journalists.) This blend of history, religiosity, and genealogy became highly stylized and swollen with rhetorical embellishments and itself merits study by semioticians. Comtesse de Champagné described her dead husband in this kind of language: "With a sometimes severe look, M. de Champagné had a perfect heart, good, lenient to all the faults of others, very loved by his farmers and the poor, to whom he gave a lot."[18] Prisoners as much as inventors of their mythologies, nobles recited what they found psychologically satisfying. Paradoxically, the inability to fit the ideal and the real permitted them to retain prestige as they kept their position as the richest large category of French society before 1870. The proclaimed differences from others, the industrious vituperation of the bourgeoisie, the denial of egalitarianism, and the veneration of minority refinements were strongest among nobles.

Regardless of the recognition accorded or denied by the larger society, the use of titles underlined the nobles' otherness from fellow Frenchmen. It would be rash indeed to see love of hierarchy and rank as particularly Gallic when it was equally prominent in other European states, but the "formal" French retained as the touchstone of judgments on sociability, politics, and taste the values of their nobles. Indeed, in the closing decades of the twentieth century the continuing popular fascination with the imagery of noble family life and loyalties seems to be on the increase in a world of broken marriages and isolated individuals who live outside the constraints of any sort of tradition. A good example was Jean d'Ormesson's 1974 novel about a fictional lineage whose château, Plessiz-les-Vaudreuil, was demolished to make way for the Charles de Gaulle Airport.[19] A television serial based on the story was *un tube,* a huge popular success.

In this book I have shown something of the transition of nobles from a feared minority to the guardians of an idealized way of life which took place between 1800 and 1870. Nobles had confronted the nineteenth century stripped of legal privileges and with a variety of unfortunate fellows actually despoiled, but their keenest weapon to ensure collective survival remained unblunted: the determination to resist absorption into the mass of the nation by maintaining a family ethic of stigma and otherness. Recent studies of the diverse forms of social power in nineteenth-century France have taken us far beyond the traditional realms of male politicians and warriors who decided the national destiny. Local elites have been scrutinized, although not enough, along with businessmen and other professionals, priests, intellectuals, and the burgeoning information industry as democratic systems of voting waxed. There is a growing scholarly concern for the past of women and of racial, sexual, and cultural minorities whose tentative sense of worth and history was denigrated or denied in other times. Nobles after 1800 evoked an earlier supremacy, but they also had to strike a modus vivendi with their real or imagined enemies.

The combination of the wealth of the richest large social category in France from 1800 to 1870 with their uncontested ownership of the taxonomies of excellence and status for the rich delivered into their hands a remarkable authority. It is a power not to be shrugged off too lightly.[20] Many historians have dismissed nineteenth-century nobles as no more than social fossils, a declining world of "society" lightweights with anachronistic pretensions troubled by inextricable jealousies, no more than a quaint residue of the Old Regime. A. J. P. Taylor wrote of one enumeration of prominent French nobles at the end of the nineteenth century that they were "not men of political stature. They sound rather like an array of rich cream cakes."[21]

However, to trivialize and dismiss nobles is to overlook a fundamental ingredient of nineteenth-century culture. Nobles in France won a victory over the egalitarian message of the French Revolution when their conceptions of behavior captured the hearts of the most influential part of the national elite. The failure of their opponents to formulate a plausible new symbolism of power—or, if preferred, the ability of nobles to make accommodations sufficient to retain a distinct sphere of social authority without being forced into the bourgeoisie—was a triumph for all nobles in the long century that only died in World War I. French nineteenth-century nobles had kept the covenant with their forerunners, if not always their forefathers, when they maintained a world safe for their kind.

Appendix 1

THE TAX LOAD OF FRENCH DEPARTMENTS, 1831

Department	Rank	Net Land Revenue
Seine	1	1,573F
Loiret	2	1,769
Eure-et-Loir	3	1,769
Seine-et-Marne	4	1,769
Marne	5	1,769
Seine-et-Oise	6	1,769
Vienne (Haute-)	7	1,769
Loir-et-Cher	8	1,769
Mayenne	9	1,769
Aube	10	1,769
Sarthe	11	1,769
Cantal	12	1,769
Lot	13	1,769
Ardennes	14	1,769
Aveyron	15	1,769
Corrèze	16	1,769
Seine-Inférieure	17	1,868
Calvados	18	1,868
Herault	19	1,868
Eure	20	1,868
Tarn	21	1,868
Indre-et-Loire	22	1,868
Sèvres (Deux-)	23	1,868
Somme	24	1,868
Oise	25	1,868
Maine-et-Loire	26	1,868
Nièvre	27	1,868
Charente-Inférieure	28	1,868
Orne	29	1,868

Department	Rank	Net Land Revenue
Aisne	30	1,868
Manche	31	1,868
Puy-de-Dôme	32	1,868
Meuse	33	1,868
Creuse	34	1,868
Aude	35	1,966
Tarn-et-Garonne	36	1,966
Lort-et-Garonne	37	1,966
Garonne (Haute-)	38	1,966
Vienne	39	1,966
Saône-et-Loire	40	1,966
Vendeé	41	1,966
Allier	42	1,966
Charente	43	1,966
Gers	44	1,966
Indre	45	1,966
Cher	46	1,966
Lozère	47	1,966
Yonne	48	1,966
Marne (Haute-)	49	1,966
Landes	50	1,966
Loire	51	1,966
Moselle	52	1,966
Côte-d'Or	53	1,982
Dordogne	54	1,988
Isère	55	1,994
Morbihan	56	1,997
Rhône	57	1,999
Ille-et-Vilaine	58	2,001
Loire (Haute-)	59	2,054
Alpes (Hautes-)	60	2,054
Pyrénées-Orientales	61	2,064
Drôme	62	2,092
Meurthe	63	2,104
Finistère	64	2,121
Nord	65	2,129
Pas-de-Calais	66	2,135
Doubs	67	2,227
Côtes-du-Nord	68	2,249
Jura	69	2,281
Gard	70	2,284
Loire-Inférieure	71	2,338
Alpes (Basses-)	72	2,369
Vosges	73	2,391

Department	Rank	Net Land Revenue
Rhin (Haut-)	74	2,438
Saône (Haute-)	75	2,442
Ain	76	2,583
Rhin (Bas-)	77	2,585
Gironde	78	2,715
Pyrénées (Hautes-)	79	2,747
Ardèche	80	2,933
Vaucluse	81	2,998
Corse	82	3,047
Bouches-du-Rhône	83	3,049
Var	84	3,085
Ariège	85	3,260
Pyrénées (Basses-)	86	3,478

Source: AN F1cII53.

Note: Departments are ranked according to the net landed revenue necessary to pay 300F in land tax (contribution foncière).

Appendix 2

THE MARRIAGE CONTRACT BETWEEN CHARLES-FRANÇOIS-ARMAND DE MAILLÉ DE LA TOUR LANDRY AND BLANCHE-JOSÉPHINE LE BASCLE D'ARGENTEUIL, 1809

Charles-François-Armand de Maillé de la Tour Landry (1770–1834), duc de Maillé at the eighteenth degree of the seigneur of the Entrammes branch of a family of chevaleresque *noblesse* of Touraine dating from the eleventh century, had been first gentleman of the bedchamber of the youngest brother of Louis XVI, the comte d'Artois, from 1784. He became a *maréchal de camp* and peer of France in 1814 and subsequently governor of the Compiègne fort. His first marriage (1784), with Mlle de Fitzjames, had yielded a daughter, who became by marriage the duchesse de Castries, and a son, who died young; his second marriage, with Blanche-Joséphine Le Bascle d'Argenteuil, daughter of lieutenant general marquis Le Bascle d'Argenteuil and of Marie-Joséphine-Caroline Barjot de Roncé, produced two sons, Jacquelin-Armand-Charles (1815–74) and Armand-Urbain-Louis (1816–1903) (See A. Ledru et al., *La Maison de Maillé,* 3 vols. [Paris, 1905], 1:419–20).

2 Juillet 1809
Mariage entre Mr. de Maillé et Melle D'Argenteuil.
PARDEVANT Me Denis Trutat et Me Préau son collègue Notaires impériaux à
  Paris soussignés,
Furent Présents
Monsieur Charles François Armand de Maillé La Tour Landry, domicilié à
  Lormois, Canton de Longjumeau, Département de Seine et Oise, de
  présent à Paris au Pavillon de Belle Chasse rue St. Dominique faubourg St.
  Germain veuf avec deux enfants de Dame henriette Victoire de Fitzjames,
  Stipulant pour lui et en son nom.
Et Madame Madelaine Angélique Charlotte de Bréhant Ve de M. Charles
  René de Maillé La Tour Landry demeurant susd. château de Lormois
  présentement à Paris Pavillon de Belle Chasse rue St. Dominique stipulant
  aussi en son nom à cause de la garantie qu'elle va contracter pour Charles
  François Armand de Maillé son fils. Tous deux. . . . D'une Part.

Source: MC LVIII 644.

228

Et Mademoiselle Blanche Josephine Le Bascle d'Argenteuil majeure, fille de déffunts Jean Louis marie Le Bascle d'Argenteuil et de Marie Josephine Caroline Barjot de Roncé son épouse décédée sa veuve. Demeurant mond. D^{elle} à Paris rue du Bac No. 88. 10eme arrondissement stipulant pour elle et en son nom D'Autre Part.

Lesquels dans la vue du mariage proposé entre mond. Sr Charles François Armand de Maillé La Tour Landry et mad. D^{elle} Blanche Josephine Le Bascle D'Argenteuil, et dont la proclamation sera faite incessament dans les formes voulues par la loi.

En ont fait et arrêté les conditions civiles ainsi qu'il suit:

En présence de leurs Parents et amis ci-après nommés savoir:

Du Côté du futur époux, De M. Charles Jean de Maillé La Tour Landry son frère, De Mme de Soran sa cousine.

Et du Coté de la future épouse de M. hyppolite Louis rené Charles Le Bascle d'Argenteuil, frère, de M. Charles Joseph Fortuné d'Herbouville préfet du Départment du Rhône Commandant de la légion d'honneur, à Mad^e Marie Louis Victoire Le Bascle d'Argenteuil son Epouse, oncle et tante, de M^{elles} Cousines, de M. henri Louis françois Philippe Le Bascle d'Argenteuil oncle paternel, de Made de Vibraye douairière grande tante de M. Charles françois Hurarde de Vibraye de mad^e Marie françoise Adelaide le Vicomte de Blangy son Epouse grand oncle et grande tante, de M. Erard Louis Guy de Chastenay Lanty et de mad^e son Epouse, cousins, de M. henry Louis de Chastenay Lanty Cousin et de mad^e son Epouse, Cousins, de M. henry Louis de Chastenay Lanty Cousin, et M^{de} Victorine de Chastenay Lanty Cousine, de M. Maximilien Louis Gaspard de Menou et de Mad^e Marie auguste frédéric hurault de Vibraye son Epouse Cousin et Cousine, de M. Louis Marie Estourmel, general de division, membre du Corps législatif et de la Légion d'honneur, et de Mad^e Philiberte renee Galard de Béarn son Epouse oncle et tante à la mode de Bretagne, de M. Adelaide Louis Reimbold d'Estourmel et de M. Joseph d'Estourmel cousins, de M. Anatole de Vibraye et de mad^e Camille de la Luzerne son Epoux cousins, de made de Dampierre de Brisay ami et de M. Guillaume de Vernon ami.

Article 1er.

Les futurs époux entendent se marier sous le régime de la communauté, conformément aux dispositions du Code Napoléon, et sauf les modifications ci-après. En conséquence ils seront communs en biens meubles et conquêts immeubles, mais ils ne seront pas tenus des dettes ni hypothèques l'un de l'autre, antérieures au mariage; s'il y en a elles seront acquittées par celui des deux qui les aura contractées et sur ses biens.

Art. 2.

Mr de Maillé apporte en mariage et se constitue en dot les biens qui suivent.

1º La nue Propriété des Terres de Lormois Launay S^t michel et dépendances, sises prés Monthery arondissement de Corbeil Départment de Seine et Oise, qui lui ont été données par Mad^e de Bréhant par son Contrat de mariage avec henriette Victoire de Fitzjames passé devant Picquait

Notaire à Paris le vingt Juin mil sept cent quatre vingt quatre, insinué à
Paris le Treize novembre de la même année et à Montlhéry la [left blank]
Les d. terres d'un produit annuel de vingt six mille francs franc
d'impositions.

2° La nue propriété du mobilier qui garnit le château de Lormois Observant
le future époux que Mad^e de Maillé sa mère a l'usufruit et jouissance sa
vie durant des d. terres et du mobilier de Lormois en vertu des dispositions
testamentaires de Mad^e de Bréhant.

3° Soixante cinq hectares (ou environ Cent trente arpents) ancienne mesure
de bois situés sur le territoire de St Michel et provenant de la Terre du
Plessis, les quels il a acquis des representants de Mme de la Rivière
héritière de M^{de} d'Eselignac d'un produit annuel de Deux mille francs
nets.

4° Et un troupeau de pure race Espagnole composé de trois cents bêtes qu'il
a établi sur la Terre de Lormois, de l'agrément de Mad^e sa mère, et de
valeur de Cinquante mille francs en principal.

Art. 3.

Melle d'Argenteuil se constitue en dot

1° Tous les biens qui lui sont échus par le partage des successions de ses
Pere et mère et de M. Eugène d'Argenteuil: son cousin, passé devant M^e
Trutat notaire à Paris le Dix Sept Décembre mil huit cent huit enregistré
consistant
Dans les Terres de la Jumelière et de Chaudefonds [-sur-Layon] sises 4eme
et 1er arrondissement de Maine et Loire.
Dans cent quatre vingt treize hectares environ de bois dits de Cravant
[-les-Coteaux] dépendant cidevant de la Terre de Roncé Departement
d'Indre et Loire.
Dans la ferme de la Loulière et ses dépendances sises Commune d'Avon
[-les-Roches]
La Terre de Vannaire sise arrondissement de Chatillon Sur Seine [arr.
Montbard, Côte d'Or].
Une maison située à Paris rue St. Sebastien N° 44, et dans differents fonds
placés à hambourg en commun avec M. son frère, et dont la moitié a elle
appartenant est de valeur de quatre vingt mille francs environ.

2° Quinze cent trente neuf francs de rente perpetuelle sur l'Etat cinq pour
cent consolidés.

3° Seize Cent Soixante dix francs de rente viagère aussi sur l'état, tiers
consolidé.

4° Une somme principale de quinze mille francs placée à son profit sur
particuliers et produisant intérêts.

5° Le sixième à elle appartenant comme héritière en partie de Mme de haie
dans un créance de Deux cent quatre vingt un mille quatre cent trente
neuf francs sur le gouvernement et dont les intérêts se touchent annuellement sur les coupes des bois dè Vibraye [arr. Montbard, Sarthe].

6° La moitié qui lui appartient indivisement avec son frère dans trois cent
soixante quinze hectares environ de bois situés à frolois et voisins

Département de la Côte d'or, et dans trente cinq hectares aussi de bois au Canton de Surrigne finage d'abstrué même Départment.

7° Sa part dans d'autres Domaines situés dans le Départment de Maine et Loire pour lesquelles la future épouse est en réclamation, et dans lesquels elle doit être réintegrée.

8° Sa moitié dans une rente perpetuelle de Cent quatre vingt dix neuf livres sur les héritiers Cambault suivant un titre nouvel passé devant Me Jean de St Gilles Notaire à Paris le dix sept Thermidor an dix et dans la nue propriété de Terres situées à Roncay commune de Pansou Départment d'Indre et Loire dont M. Ragueneau a la jouissance.

9° La somme de Trente mille francs tant en deniers comptans qu'en meubles, effets et bijoux à son usage et revenus échus déduction faite de toutes charges.

10° La moitié d'une créance de Trente mille francs sur M. de Dampierre dont la recouvrement est incertain.

Sur tous lesquels biens il est du environ cinquante mille francs en capitaux et neuf cent quarante francs cinquante centimes de rentes viagères et pensions pour la moitié remise à la charge de lad. Demoiselle.

De tous lesquels biens elle a donné connaissance au futur époux qui consent de demeurer chargé par le seul fait de mariage seulement des deniers comptans et effets mobiliers ci dessus fixés à la se de trente mille francs.

Art. 4.

De tous les biens ci dessus désignés il entrera de part et d'autre en Communauté jusqu'a concurrence de Vingt mille francs. Le surplus des d. biens ensemble tous ceux qui échoiront à chacun des futurs pendant le mariage tant en meubles qu'immeubles par succession, donation, legs ou autrement lui seront et demeureront Propres.

La future épouse touchera annuellement sur ses simples quittances et sans avoir besoin d'autorisation la somme de six mille francs sur les revenus de tels de ses biens quelle voudra désigner, et ce pour servir à son entretien personnel et au payment des Gages et dépenses de ses femmes de Chambre.

Art. 5.

Le survivant des futurs époux prendra à titre de préciput et avant partage sur les biens de la communauté tels d'iceux qu'il voudra choisir, jusqu'à concurrence de la somme de vingt mille francs, suivant la prisée de l'inventaire, ou la somme en deniers comptans à son choix. Il reprendra en outre les habits et effets à son usage et un carosse attelé de deux chevaux aussi à son choix.

Art. 6.

Le futur époux fait donation à la future épouse survivante pour lui tenir lieu de douaire, d'une rente viagère de six mille francs sans retenue. Cette rente viagère sera réductible à celle de quatre mille francs, dans le cas seulement ou la future épouse devenue veuve avec enfants passerait à de

secondes noces, de la quelle rente seule jouira sur les revenus des biens de
son mari prédécedé.

La future épouse aura en outre pour son habitation le Chateau de Lormais
dans le cas ou la jouissance en seroit libre en la personne du futur époux,
ou tel autre Chateau dont son mari décéderait propriétaire, et qu'elle
désignerait à moins qu'elle ne preférat une somme annuelle de Deux mille
francs aussi sans retenue, dont aud. cas le futur lui fait donation pour lui
tenir lieu de la.d. habitation.

Art. 7.

Mad^e Madeleine Angelique Charlotte de Bréhant Ve de M. Charles René de
Maillé et mère du futur époux garantit le payement de lad. rente viagère de
six Mille francs, dans le cas ou les biens du mari prédécedé (les reprises
dotales de la Veuve prélevées) ne suffiraient pas pour acquitter tant qu'elle
aura cours lad. rente de six mille francs, ou seulement jusqu'à concurrence de ce que les d. biens ne pourroient pas fournir.

Art. 8.

Le futur époux survivant aura et prélevera sur la succession de son épouse la
somme de quarante mille francs une fois payée pour l'indemniser des frais
de noces, de la quelle somme la future épouse lui fait donation.

Art. 9.

Le futur époux sera tenu de faire emploi au profit de son épouse, des deniers
qui proviendroient des aliénations de biens à elle propres, que des circon-
stances imprévues forceroient à vendre, lequel emploi se fera dans l'année
de la vente en biens fonds avec les déclarations nécessaires de l'origine des
deniers pour en assurer l'effet.

Le remploi des propres du mari, aliénés, se fera aussi à son profit, et dans le
cas ou lors du partage de communauté lesd. remplois n'auroient pas été
antérieurement éffectués il en sera dû indemnité à celui des futurs qui
aura droit de l'exercer.

Art. 10.

Arrivant la dissolution de la Communauté il sera loisible à la future épouse et
aux enfans qui pourront naître du mariage de reprendre en y renonçant
tous les biens par elle apportés en mariage, et en outre tous ceux qui
seront échus pendant le mariage tant en meubles qu'immeubles par
succession, donation, legs ou autrement et si c'est elle qui exerce cette
faculté elle reprendra en outre son Préciput et augmentation de préciput cy
dessus stipulés, le tout franc et quitte des dettes de la Communauté quand
bien même elle s'y serait obligée ou y auroit été condamnée, dont aud. cas
elle sera garantie et indemnisée sur les biens de son mari.

Il sera pris pour la future épouse toutes inscriptions nécessiares sur lad.
Terre de Lormois.

Pour l'execution des Presentes les Parties font élection de domicile en leurs demeures susdites aux quels lieux nonobstant, Promettant, obligeant, Renonçant.

Dont Acte,

Fait et passé à Paris en la Demeure de Mr. et Mᵐᵉ d'Herbouville oncle et tante de la future sise rue du bac Nᵒ 88.

L'An Mil huit cent neuf le Deux Juillet et ont toutes lesd. parties signé avec leurs Parens et amis ci dessus nommés et les dits notaires après lecture faite.

Signatures follow

Appendix 3

THE WILL OF ALEXANDRE-CHARLES-MARIE-ERNEST DE CANOUVILLE, 1861

A nineteenth-century *titré* from the old Norman *noblesse*, Alexandre-Charles-Marie-Ernest de Canouville, baron of the Empire (letters patent 22 October 1810), awarded an entailment in Hanover (15 August 1809), *maréchal des logis du palais* of the emperor Napoleon, officer of the Legion of Honor, state councilor, and landowner was born in Paris on 22 February 1784 and died in Paris, unmarried, 8 September 1863. At the time of his death he was living on the rue Miromesnil, close to the Elysée Palace. His brother, Armand-Jules-Elisabeth (b. 19 May 1783), became baron of the Empire on the same day and also remained a bachelor. They were sons of Antoine-Alexandre-Marie-François de Canouville (1763–1834), baron of the Empire (letters patent 2 July 1813), deputy at the Corps législatif (1810–15), peer (11 October 1832), who on 25 February 1783 married Amable-Louise-Félicité de Saint Chamans. Marie d'Armaillé, *née* Ségur, recalled A. C. M. E. de Canouville from her childhood in the 1830s "dans un entresol Louis xv tout doré, tout brillant de glaces; plus tard rue Royale, il arrangeait des parties à Séraphin; il nous racontait mille histoires, nous chantait des romances de sa jeunesse" (*Quand on savait vivre heureux (1830–1860: Souvenirs de jeunesse* [Paris, 1934], 18).

Ceci Est Mon Testament

J'institue pour mon légataire universel en pleine propriété mon filleul Louis-Ernest-Mathieu de la Redorte[1] fils du comte Mathieu de la Redorte[2] ancien ambassadeur et ancien pair de France à la charge par lui d'executer les legs particuliers ci-après.

Je lègue au vicomte Mathieu de la Redorte[3] frère du précédent les bois qui m'appartiennent dans les communes de Vignacourt et de Bethencourt [-sur-Mer] arrondissement d'Amiens département de la Somme. Je lègue les bois que je possède dans les communes de Tréloup et de Ronchères arrondissement de Château-Thierry département de l'Aisne à ma cousine la marquise

Source MC LVII 856.

de la Rochedragon née Macdonald,[4] à ma cousine la comtesse Augustine de Montaigu, à mon cousin le comte Gustave de Sparre[5] et à Madame la vicomtesse Cornudet née [Valentine] Mathieu de la Redorte.[6]

Je lègue de plus à la vicomtesse Cornudet la montre garnie de diamants qui vient de ma mère et la somme de vingt cinq mille francs.

Je lègue à mon ami le duc d'Albuféra toute mon argenterie ainsi que mes chevaux, voiture et équipage.[7]

Je lègue à Auray mon maître d'hotel la somme de vingt quatre mille francs. Je lui donne en outre ma garderobe en habits et en linge, ainsi que les montres et bijoux à mon usage.

Je donne une année de gages payés intégralement à chacun des domestiques qui seront à mon service au jour de mon décès.

Je lègue mille francs aux pauvres de la commune de Vignacourt (Somme). Je lègue mille francs aux pauvres des communes de Treloup [-sur-Marne] et de Ronchères, Aisne. Je lègue mille francs aux pauvres de mon arrondissement à Paris.

Je demande à être enterré auprès de mes parens au cimitière de l'Est.

J'annule par le présent tout autre testament, codacilles et autres dispositions testamentaires. J'entends que tous mes legs de sommes d'argent et objets mobiliers soient nets de droits. J'institue comme mes executeurs testamentaires Messieurs Jules Fourchy ancien notaire et Emile Fourchy mon notaire actuel. Je leur lègue la somme de dix mille francs en souvenir d'amitié. Ecrit de ma main à Paris le sept décembre mil huit cent soixante et un. Le Cte de Canouville, Alexandre Charles Marie Ernest.

1. Louis-Ernest, vicomte de la Redorte, officier supérieur, Legion of Honor; born in Paris on 25 October 1841. On 24 November 1891 he married Stephanie-Marie Abeille, widow of comte de Gouy d'Arsay, without posterity.

2. Joseph-Charles-Maurice-Mathieu de la Redorte, comte, deputy of the Aude (1834–40, 1849, 1871), peer of France (20 July 1841), ambassador of France, Legion of Honor; born in Paris on 20 March 1804, died in Paris on 20 January 1886. On 11 October 1830 he married Louise-Honorine Suchet d'Albuféra (who died in Paris on 23 October 1885), daughter of the Marshal and duc de l'Empire. Louis-Ernest was their second child; their third was Valentine.

3. Louis-Maurice-Mathieu de la Redorte, the elder brother of Louis-Ernest, born in Paris on 7 January 1832, here called vicomte according to the decrescendo of titles prior to the death of his father. In October 1893 he married Charlotte-Emilie Bouchez, widow of General Caillier; there was no issue.

4. Alexandrine-Anne-Sidonie MacDonald (b. 1803), daughter of Jacques-Etienne-Joseph-Alexandre MacDonald, duc de Tarente (1765–1840), and his second wife, Félicité-Françoise de Montholon (d. 1804). In 1824 she married Anselme-François-Marie-Henry, marquis de Rochedragon, *general de brigade* (d. 8 August 1851).

5. Louis-Ernest-Gustave de Sparre, comte, officer of cavalry; born on 23 March 1802, died in Paris on 6 July 1866. He married Louise-Marie-Hippolyte-Gabrielle de Gramont-Caderousse (d. 21 January 1844) without posterity. In 1847 he married Louise Chapelain de Sereville de Crenay (who died in Vaucluse on 15 March 1897), adopted daughter of M. de Poilvillain, marquis de Crenay, *maréchal de camp,* and daughter of baron Charles-Dominique-Marie Chapelain de Sereville and Louise-Françoise de Bracquemont; they had three sons and two daughters.

6. Born on 23 November 1834, died in Paris on 3 February 1889. On 25 January 1854 she married Joseph-Alfred, comte Cornudet des Chomettes.

7. Louis-Napoléon Suchet, duc d'Albuféra, peer of France by hereditary claim; born in Paris on 23 May 1813, died in Paris on 22 July 1877. On 11 June 1844 he married Eleonore-Isabelle-Malvina Schickler (who died in Paris on 15 May 1877); they had a son and two daughters.

Note on Sources

Historical sources for studying a group as variegated as nineteenth-century French nobles are almost innumerable. A list of all books, magazines, journals, pictures, poems, and manuscript collections dealing with them in some way would constitute a text far longer than this study, as Gaston Saffroy's *Bibliographie généalogique, heraldique et nobiliaire de la France* (3 vols. [Paris, 1968–70]) makes plain. Other sources at least touch upon the place of nobles or nobility in France. The present note points out some types of materials consulted in writing this book that could be used to extend its findings.

The most valuable single reference work for nineteenth-century titles is the massive compilation by vicomte Albert de Révérend of grants of titles and ennoblements by governments. Republished (1974) by the Librairie Honoré Champion in Paris, the collection unfortunately lacks a general index which would facilitate consultation and cross references in all six volumes. In his 1894 volumes on the First Empire, Révérend complained of poor cooperation from the descendants of the *titrés* to whom he had mailed questionnaires. He also lamented the difficulty of getting access to bureaucratic archives. He provides fuller notices for the *titrés* of the Restoration and sometimes corrects earlier entries, as in the case of that dealing with Reiset. For the mid-century nobility closer in time to his milieu he was more exacting about family composition and professions. He omitted July Monarchy peers named after the abolition of heredity in 1830, since the Chamber of Peers "ne représentait que des éléments auxquels la noblesse n'était plus attachée," leaving Orleanist creations like Victor Cousin beyond the pale.

Equally fundamental are the various regional genealogies, such as the incomplete work of Jules Vilain, *La France moderne; grand dictionnaire généalogique, historique et biographique, Haute-Garonne et Ariège,* 3 vols. (Montpellier, 1911–13), 3, pts. 1 and 2. Some of these reference works were reprinted in the 1970s. Apart from the percentage of errors inevitable in any compilation, there are different levels of accuracy or bias. Nevertheless, genealogies, particularly those produced by nobles, provide a valuable census "from within" concerning a time when the French state took no official cognizance of the numbers of the former *noblesse*. For this book, where nobility is considered as volitional, commercial "vanity" genealogies are especially useful.

At the Archives Nationales de France are found the records of entailments (*majorats*) and later grants of titles, 1815–35. These entailments were registered by letters patent. The official body that registered honorific titles underwent a variety of changes from the First Empire to the Second. It was called, successively,

1 March 1808	Conseil du sceau des titres
15 July 1814	Commission du sceau des titres
1815 (Hundred Days)	Conseil du sceau des titres
1815	Commission du sceau (suppressed 31 October 1830)
1830	Conseil d'administration auprès du garde des sceaux (suppressed 1835)
8 January 1859	Conseil du sceau des titres (suppressed 1872)

The composition of the commissions is given by Nicolas Batjin. Initially, three senators, two *conseillers d'état*, one *procureur général*, and a *secrétaire général* met on Mondays and Thursdays under the direction of the *archichancelier*, Cambacérès. During the Restoration more legal skill was required. The Second Empire had three senators, two members of the Cour de cassation, two *conseillers d'état*, three *maîtres des requêtes*, one *commissaire imperial*, and one *secrétaire*, with a justice minister presiding. The decree of 10 January 1872 suppressed the commission and transferred attributions to an administrative council of the Ministry of Justice. *Registres du sceau* are classified at the Archives Nationales under BB12, BB29, and *in extenso* in the series BB30 965–1120.

> On y trouve un ensemble de dossiers, i.e., constitutions de majorats, pour la période 1808–30 et des pièces relatives à des anoblissements, des changements de noms, des concessions de titres . . . le tout formant un complément des articles cotés BB30625 à 724 dans la première partie de la sous-série. (From the *note préliminaire* of the *inventaire* at the Archives Nationales)

The documentation brought together for *majorats* between 1808 and 1835 is summarized in three registers, with the cote BB29782–84, containing the requests for the setting up of a *majorat* with the titles marquis, comte, vicomte, and baron. BB29785 deals with requests to set up the title chevalier. From this documentation it is possible to see who the aspirants for noble status were. Similar information is to be found in a summary form in the registers of the *Direction des affaires civiles et du sceau relatifs aux titres: Collations, confirmations, transmissions: 1808–1870*, available on microfilm at the Archives Nationales in the series 149 mi 1–38, as listed in the 1968 *Etat des microfilmes* (repertoire available at the Service Photographique of the Archives Nationales, 87, rue Vieille du Temple, Paris). Cartons AB xix 2644–83, deposited at the

Archives Nationales in 1929, deal mainly with the period 1860–90. AB xix 2684 is a table. Much information is available in nineteenth-century *papiers privés* classified with the cotes AB xix 2644–84. These documents are listed in a manuscript repertoire kept at the Salle des Inventaires of the Archives Nationales which includes a name index, a summary description of each dossier in the cartons, and its dates. Letters patent of the First Empire are found in the series CC.

Besides these documents concerned with the establishment of titles in nineteenth-century France, administrative documents dealing with the departments (F1cIII), as well as records of other branches of government service and police, offer a wide range of information. The departments with the top quintile of the number of noble voters in the electorate (i.e., 240–300) in the 1830s were Calvados, Haute-Garonne, Hérault, Ille-et-Vilaine, Loire-Inférieure, Loiret, Maine-et-Loire, Pas-de-Calais, Orne, Seine, Seine-Inférieure, Seine-et-Oise, and Somme.

French nobles are listed on electoral rolls. The first series of these, of great interest, are the lists of notables of the year XII, recently analyzed by Guy Chaussinand-Nogaret, Louis Bergeron, and Robert Forster, which are being published in part for each department with additional biographical information. Although titles of pre-Revolutionary nobles not decorated by the Empire were deliberately omitted, the lists of *notabilité* do show the survival of important families in the departments.

Found in departmental archives, electoral lists of the constitutional monarchies doubtless derived from the *notabilité* lists and those of the six hundred highest taxed in each department. The electoral lists reached a high standard of accuracy by the 1820s. Thomas Beck has assembled a data bank from electoral rolls of the 1840s primarily, as he details in "A Data Bank: France, 1800–1847." *Social Science History* 4, no. 3 (Summer 1980): 347–56, and he very generously furnished me with a list of his statistics, by department, further broken down under other headings. I have supplemented this overview with samples of earlier lists. Many departments have incomplete series, and others lack them altogether. In the course of my research I have found departments like the Basses-Pyrénées, Ariège, Sarthe, or Yonne, where only fragmentary or random remnants of the lists can be found, while others, such as Maine-et-Loire and Haute-Garonne, have remarkably full collections. Supplementary or replacement information can be gleaned from jury lists (compiled from the same matrices), the municipal electoral lists of the July Monarchy, and local almanacs.

The financial information given on these lists is the reason for much of their historical importance. At the same time, many individuals clearly declared only enough taxes paid necessary to justify the right to vote or to stand as deputy. Another limitation on the use of the lists was the unequal rates of the *foncière,* the tax on the land, paid in different departments. These inequities were the subject of polemics under the Restoration. Unweighted statistics do not accurately reflect the same amount of revenue everywhere in France (see appendix 1). Another aspect of these lists that limits their value in providing a view of the wealth of the elite was their restriction to voting males of the legal age categories. Noblewomen generally outlived their husbands and often had dotal proper-

ty in their own name. Grosbois found in his study of *mutation par décès* entries
of nobles in the Sarthe department between 1825 and 1834 deaths of six noblewomen whose fortunes totaled 1,710,500F. Three of them, according to the
cadastral matrices of their communes, had landholdings of 2,335 hectares or 28
métairies and 2 mills. Such wealth often was not represented on the electoral
lists.

The registers of *mutations par décès* provide a better overview of society's
wealth, since throughout the nineteenth century each individual death was the
occasion, within six months of decease, of an entry in the *enregistrement* registers. The problems of dealing with an immense volume of documentation that
has been preserved in very large measure are obvious. They have been discussed in detail by Adeline Daumard in two recent studies. Despite problems,
they yield knowledge of local nobles, as in the remarkable *maîtrise* by M.
Grosbois on the Sarthe.

The study of noble landholding can be seen in a summary way either in the
amount of land tax paid on electoral rolls or, if all the necessary *renvois* are
followed up, in the *mutations par décès*. Only extensive exploitation of cadastral
records corroborated by estate records, when they exist, gives a more precise
picture. That involves the use of the *tables d'acquéreurs* and the *tables des
locations des baux*. Needless to say, this would require large-scale *travail en
équipe* to be feasible.

Insights into noble marriage patterns and family relations can be gleaned
from the *tables des contrats de marriage,* which may also lead on to the full text
of the contract in a notarial étude. From the study of addresses, the use of titles
in witnesses' signatures (which was customary in the nineteenth century), the
residences, and other information about kinship and acquaintances is informative about noble weddings.

MINUTIER CENTRAL DES NOTAIRES DE PARIS

The Minutier Central, located in the Archives Nationales, is an inexhaustible
source for French history of the nineteenth century of which some random use
was made. I used intensively the records from 1800–1870 of one notarial office's
archives, that of the two Trutats, father and son, who were succeeded in the
same étude by the two Fourchy, father and son. This fashionable office was
located on the left bank of the Seine on the quai Malaquais, no. 5. I examined
one hundred liasses as follows: LVIII 597(ᵇis), 636–52, 731, 739, 750–60, 765–
83, 801–24, 842–64, 880–87.

Notes

INTRODUCTION

1. A. B. C. Cobban, *The Social Interpretation of the French Revolution* (Cambridge, 1964); C. Lucas, "Nobles, Bourgeois and the Origins of the French Revolution," *Past and Present*, no. 60 (August 1973): 84–126; F. Furet, *Interpreting the French Revolution* (Cambridge, 1981).

2. Patrice Higonnet, *Class, Ideology, and the Rights of Nobles during the French Revolution* (Oxford, 1981), provides an overview of the topic.

3. G. De Vos, "Ethnic Pluralism: Conflict and Accommodation," in *Ethnic Identity: Cultural Continuities and Change*, ed. G. De Vos and L. Romanucci-Ross (Palo Alto, 1975), 9. There are inadequate general definitions of a minority that insist on its disadvantages, as in the claim that the numerical position of a minority excludes it from taking an effective part in politics (see H. van Amersfoort, *Immigration and the Formation of Minority Groups: The Dutch Experience, 1945–1975* [Cambridge, 1982], 29–30).

4. Arno J. Mayer, *The Persistence of the Old Regime: Europe to the Great War* (New York, 1981), 5.

5. *Annuaire de la noblesse de France, 1871* (Paris, 1872), 349; A. Mahul, *Cartulaire et archives des communes de l'ancien diocèse et de l'arrondissement administratif de Carcassonne*, 8 vols. (Paris, 1857–82), 2: 291–92. A more famous long-lived noble of the time was Etienne-Denis Pasquier, active in the Parlement of Paris before 1789, baron and then duc of the First Empire, Restoration peer, hereditary duc under the July Monarchy, who died in 1862 at the age of 95.

6. Jean Bouvier, "Histoire sociale et histoire économique," in *Colloque d'histoire sociale, Saint-Cloud, 15–16 mai 1965* (Paris, 1967), 250.

7. Antoine Bachelin-Deflorenne, *Etât présent de la noblesse française, contenant le dictionnaire de la noblesse contemporaine . . . 1866* (Paris, 1866), cols. 763–64.

8. Gaston Saffroy, *Bibliographie généalogique, héraldique et nobiliaire de la France*, 3 vols. (Paris, 1968–70).

9. Perhaps a quotation from the late vicomte de Marsay (1874–1941) best illustrates some of these possibilities:

   Beaucoup de ces gens dont les ascendants n'auraient pas même pu prendre part aux Assemblées de la Noblesse en 1789 (et qui par conséquent ne possèdent pas la plus petite des références qui puisse fournir une famille avant la Révolution), s'érigent cependant de nos jours en juges de noblesse

. . . il ne suffit pas de s'affubler d'un nom harmonieux et d'un titre retentis-sant pour avoir une seule des traditions de la classe à laquelle on s'est, regulièrement ou non, agrégé. Cependant il est juste que ceux qui se sont introduits volontairement dans une famille en adoptent les idées. Or, des idées d'autrefois, ces personnes ont tout à apprendre. Nous pensons donc acquérir des droits en leur enseignant quelques unes des notions les plus indispens-ables au métier de gentilhomme dont elles font profession. (Jacques de Marsay, *De l'âge des privilèges au temps des vanités . . . : Essai sur l'origine et la valeur des prétensions nobiliaires,* 2d ed. [Paris, 1946], xxviii.)
Note that Marsay calls the nobility "une famille." A general survey of the meaning and manipulation of genealogical forms in culture is given by Judith N. Sklar, "Subversive Genealogies," in *Myth, Symbol, and Culture,* ed. C. Geertz (New York, 1974), 129–54.

10. André-Jean Tudesq, "Les Survivances de l'ancien régime: La Noblesse dans la société française de la première moitié du XIXe siècle," in *Colloque d'histoire sociale, Saint-Cloud, 24–25 mai 1967* [Paris, 1973], 200–203.

11. Many writers have noticed the linguistic contamination between descriptions of qual-ity or excellence and the vocabulary of nobles. This is particularly striking in the food business—Roquefort being a product of "L'aristocratie des artisans," for example (see François de Negroni, *La France noble* [Paris, 1974]). A more theoretical discussion of the manipulation of the symbols of class and social distance is found in Pierre Bour-dieu, *La Distinction: Critique sociale du jugement* (Paris, 1979).

12. Ezra Suleiman, *Elites in French Society: The Politics of Survival* (Princeton, 1978), rightly stressed that an appreciation of adaptability is more relevant than that of origin to studies of elites. "There is no doubt that studying the social composition of a group is far easier than trying to gauge its coherence, its policies, and its strengths for survival" (p. 10).

1. THE NUMBER OF NOBLES

1. There are numerous definitions of *nobility.* Guy Guerin, *Législation et jurisprudence nobiliaires* (Lille, 1961), 26, defines it as the quality of having the right to pass the title of écuyer to younger sons.

2. As in the sixteenth-century jingle of Gabriel Meurier's *Thrésor de sentences dorées et argentées* (1617): "Faveurs, femmes et deniers / Font de vachers chevaliers."

3. Marc Bloch et al., "Enquête: Les Noblesses. Sur le passé de la noblesse française: Quelques Jalons de recherches," *Annales d'histoire économique et sociale* 8, nos. 39–40 (1936): 238–55, 366–78.

4. Peter Laslett, "Social Promotion, Social Descent and Demography" (Paper delivered at the Social History Society [U.K.] meeting, Lancaster University, 3 January 1976).

5. R. Dauvergne, "Le Problème du nombre des nobles en France au XVIIIe siècle," in *Sur la population française au XVIIIe et au XIXe siècles* (Paris, 1973), 181–92.

6. Guy Chaussinand-Nogaret, *The French Nobility in the Eighteenth Century: From Feudalism to Enlightenment,* trans. William Doyle (Cambridge, 1985), 30; Thomas D. Beck, "The French Revolution and the Nobility: A Reconsideration," *Journal of Social History* 15, no. 2 (Winter 1981), 224–26.

7. Jean Meyer, "Un Problème mal posé: La Noblesse pauvre," *Revue d'histoire moderne et contemporaine* 78 (1971): 161–88; Chaussinand-Nogaret, *French Nobility,* 28, adds that of those living families some had several branches by 1789.

8. Francis W. Blagdon, *Paris as it was, and as it is; or a Sketch of the French Capital, illustrative of the effects of the Revolution,* 2 vols. (London, 1803), 2:339–40. After the 1808 establishment of Napoleonic titles this continued. In 1811 the Sarthe prefect

noted of an ex-officer and an Old Regime regiment that "souvent on lui donne dans la société son ancien titre de marquis auquel il répond avec complaisance" (*AD* Sarthe, M 79).

9. Ernest d'Hauterive, *La Police secrète du premier empire,* 5 vols. (Paris, 1908–64), 3:145.

10. In a convenient summary by Philippe Du Puy de Clinchamps, himself claiming descent from an Old Regime knightly lineage, the comparison is drawn between what he calls variously "la qualité réelle," "une noblesse réelle," and "une noblesse sacrée," on the one hand, and inferior, modern titles of an "apparence noble" (*La Noblesse,* Collection "Que Sais-Je?" no. 830 [Paris, 1959], esp. 73–97). The same sentiments pervade his earlier work, *L'Ancienne Noblesse française en 1954* (Paris, 1955). The traditional *ressentiment* of the pre-1789 petty *noblesse* against *titrés* and court aristocracy is thus echoed in the twentieth century.

11. See further on this F. Waquet, *Les Fêtes royales sous la Restauration* (Paris, 1981), 120–21.

12. Alain Guillemin, "Patrimoine foncier et pouvoir nobiliaire: La Noblesse de la Manche sous la Monarchie de Juillet," *Etudes rurales,* nos. 63–64 (1976): 117.

13. Guy Chaussinand-Nogaret, Louis Bergeron, Robert Forster, "Les Notables du Grand Empire en 1810," *Annales, économies, sociétés, civilisations* 25, no. 5 (September–October 1971): 1052–75.

14. Emile Campardon, *Liste des membres de la noblesse impériale* (Paris, 1889), gives 3,263; Jean Tulard, *Napoléon et la noblesse d'Empire suivi de la liste complète des membres de la noblesse impériale* (Paris, 1979), 93, gives a slightly lower figure.

15. Pierre Durye says that 22.5 percent of title holders held pre-1789 titles, excluding those whose Napoleonic title was for military service, many of whom were nobles (19.5 percent). The remaining 58 percent of Napoleonic titles were bourgeois (see "Les Chevaliers dans la noblesse impériale," *Revue d'histoire moderne et contemporaine* 17[1970]: 671–79).

16. *AN* BB²⁹783.

17. A. Palluel, *Dictionnaire de l'empereur* (Paris, 1969), 809.

18. *AN* BB³⁰1115.

19. *AN* BB²⁹782. Following the family custom of seeking titles under successive regimes, his son became a hereditary comte by letters patent of 29 November 1842.

20. Petition of 15 January 1813 in Eugène d'Hautefeuille's dossier, Ministère de la Guerre, as cited in Alfred Marquiset, *Ballanche et Mme d'Hautefeuille* (Paris, 1912), 6.

21. *AN* BB³⁰1015.

22. Edmond Pierson, *Etudes de la noblesse d'Empire créée par Napoléon Ier* (Orléans, 1910), 13–14.

23. *AN* F¹ᶜIII (Garonne, Haute-), 9; *compte rendu* 26 June 1812.

24. Phillip Mansel, *Louis* XVIII (London, 1981), 199.

25. Administration of title grants was under the charge of the Conseil du sceau, established in 1808. The Bourbons modified this into a commission, established on 15 July 1814, headed by the chancellor and comprising three state councillors, three masters of requests, three other officials, and six *référendaires* (increased to twelve in December 1816 because of the volume of work).

26. Augustin-Jean-Marie Schonen, *De la noblesse française selon la Charte* (Paris, 1817), 43.

27. Mansel, *Louis* XVIII, 260.

28. A. L. de Laigue, *Les Familles françaises considérées sous le rapport de leurs prérogatives honorifiques héréditaires* (Paris, 1818), 89–115, gives the relevant texts.

29. P. Biston, *De la fausse noblesse en France* (Paris, 1861), 35.

30. A. V. Arnault et al., *Biographie nouvelle des contemporains,* vol. 19 (Paris, 1825), 407–15.

31. Letter of J. B. J. C. Bernard, 9 February 1821, quoted in Josette Gadeau, "Les Magistrats de la Cour Royale de Poitiers sous la Restauration, 1815–1830" (Thesis, advanced studies in history, University of Poitiers, 1972), 24. Bernard (1756–1832) was the son of a Grenoble merchant, and his son (1794–1863) was also a judge at Poitiers.

32. His quarter of his deceased parents' estate, worth in total 3,830,433F, was fixed in the 1821 division at 957,608F and included the château of Verderonne (Oise) (*AN* BB³⁰966).

33. A. L. Imbert de Saint Armand, *La Cour de Charles x* (Paris, 1892), 114–15.

34. *AD* Yonne, 2M¹37, *Liste electorale du collège . . . 1820,* J 482/4: "Brevets divers en faveur d'Auguste-Michel-Félicité de Souvre." See the article on the château and lands of the family at Ancy-le-Franc in the *Annuaire statistique du departement de l'Yonne* (Auxerre, 1838), 229–32.

35. J. B. A. d'Aldéguier, *Histoire de Toulouse,* 4 vols. (Toulouse, 1834–35), 4:650.

36. J. A. Lallier, *De la propriété des noms et des titres* (Paris, 1890), 159.

37. E. F. de Beaumont-Vassy, *Les Salons de Paris et la société parisienne sous Louis-Philippe Ier* (Paris, 1866), 4–5.

38. *Archives parlementaires de 1787 a 1860,* 2d ser., 72 (Paris, 1889): 320 (session of 7 December 1831).

39. Chambre de Députés, *Discours de M. Eusèbe de Salverte . . . extrait du Moniteur du 5 octobre 1831* (Paris, 1831), 17.

40. Domna C. Stanton, *The Aristocrat as Art: A study of the Honnête Homme and the Dandy in Seventeenth- and Nineteenth-century French Literature* (New York, 1980), 92; Michael G. Lerner, *Maupassant* (London, 1975), 18; Jean Boissel, *Gobineau* (Paris, 1981), 38–39.

41. Marie d'Armaillé, *Quand on savait vivre heureux (1830–1860): Souvenirs de jeunesse* (Paris, 1934), 95. However, she recalled that by 1852 the violent antipathies of the July Monarchy had already passed (ibid., 156).

42. Antoine Bachelin-Deflorenne, *Etat présent de la noblesse française, contenant le dictionnaire de la noblesse contemporaine . . . 1866* (Paris, 1866), ix.

43. A. L. P. J. G. de Belboeuf, *De la noblesse française en 1861 par un maire de village* (Paris, 1861), 14.

44. *AD* Nièvre, 37J99, Victor to abbé de Naisey at Avalon, Yonne, 26 September 1817 (of the genealogist): "Je voulais lui parler et point lui écrire; il m'a demandé du temps poour mettre de l'exactitude dans ses Recherches et m'a promis répondre d'une manière ou de l'autre sous peu, je n'ai rien stipulé pour son travail, ce sera a reglé lorsqu'il sera terminé."

45. A. A. de Grolée-Virville, *Les d'Hozier* (Paris, 1978), 103.

46. The 1817 prospectus is in *BN* Lb⁴¹2271.

47. Grolée-Virville, *Les d'Hozier,* 103–4.

48. *Revue historique de la noblesse.* 2 (1842): 2.

49. H. J. G. de Milleville, *Prospectus . . . l'armorial de la noblesse de France en 1844* (Paris, 1844). See also idem, *Armorial historique de la noblesse française et étrangère, recueilli et rédigé par un comité* (Paris, 1845), *BN* 4°Lm¹69.

50. F. de Croy-Chanel, *Petite semonce au Sieur Laîné . . .* (Paris, [1836]), 30. P. Louis Lainé was the author of *Dictionnaire véridique des origines des maisons nobles ou anoblies du royaume de France,* 3 vols. (Paris, 1818–19), and other works, such as *Archives généalogiques,* 11 vols. (Paris, 1828–50).

51. Printed statement in the form of a letter dated 25 August 1850, signed J. [François-Jules] Lainé, refuting the allegations of Borel d' Hauterive about the *Dictionnaire*

véridique des maisons nobles (Paris, n.d.), *BN* Lm^{3}483. See also [André Borel d'Hauterive,] *Notice sur Hauterive en Dauphiné . . . Réponse au généalogiste Lainé* (Paris, 1848), *BN* Lm^{3}482.

52. *Almanach de la noblesse du royaume de France, année 1848* (Paris, 1848), xix.

53. Alphonse Brémond, *Histoire du nobiliaire toulousain* (Montpellier, 1868), *BN* Lm^{2}140 (bis).

54. This may partly explain the increasing percentage of noble deputies who sat in the Chamber of Deputies during the July Monarchy (See Patrice Higonnet, "Class, Corruption and Politics in the French Chamber of Deputies, 1846–48," *French Historical Studies* 5[1968]: 204–24).

55. Alphonse Henri d'Hautpoul, *Mémoires du général marquis Alphonse d'Hautpoul, pair de France, 1789–1865* (Paris, 1906), 305.

56. *MC* LVIII 801, 22 December 1849.

57. F. Germain, *Du rétablissement légal de la noblesse . . . par le rédacteur en chef du Bulletin de Paris* (Paris, 1857), 47–48. He counted among 160 members of the Senate 9 princes, 9 ducs, 17 marquis, 37 comtes, 2 vicomtes, 17 barons, and 15 "particules nobiliaires." Among the 256 members of the Corps législatif he espied 1 prince, 3 ducs, 13 marquis, 32 comtes, 8 vicomtes, 29 barons, and 38 "particules nobiliaires."

58. Charles Tourtoulon, *De la noblesse dans ses rapports avec nos moeurs et nos institutions* (Paris, 1857), 9–10: "Étrange inconséquence! Elle n'est soumise à aucun contrôle, elle n'est régie par aucune loi, et nous offre le spectacle, inouï chez une nation policée, d'une distinction honorifique mise à la disposition du premier venu."

59. P. de Semainville, *Code de la noblesse française, ou précis de la législation sur les titres, la manière d'acquérir et de perdre la noblesse, les armoiries, les livrées, la particule, etc. avec des notes* (Paris, 1858), vii–viii.

60. V. A. D. Dalloz, *Jurisprudence générale du royaume. Répertoire méthodique et alphabétique de législation, de doctrine et de jurisprudence en matière de droit civil, commercial, criminel, administratif, de droit des gens et de droit public,* 2d ed., 44 vols. (Paris, 1846–73), 34, pt. 2:172–73. The Senate commission was headed by Hautpoul, Segur d'Aguesseau, and Grivel de la Grange, with Delangle as *rapporteur.* The project was adopted on 18 May 1858.

61. A comparison of the status antecedents of individuals given new titles under the Second Empire (a sample of over half the Second Empire titles as given by Révérend, letters *A* to *K*) with those of individuals who received a *majorat sur demande* in the period 1814–30 (*AN* BB^{29}783–84) shows that if 46.2 percent received their first title under the Bourbons, only 16.7 percent received their first title from Napoleon III.

	Majorats sur demande		Second Empire	
	Number	*%*	*Number*	*%*
Old Regime	107	38.2	70	25.4
Old Regime & imperial	33	11.8	—	—
Imperial	9	3.2	90	32.6
Restoration	129	46.2	43	15.6
July Monarchy	—	—	12	4.3
Napoleon III	—	—	46	16.7
Papal/foreign	1	0.3	4	1.4
First Empire & Restoration	—	—	2	0.7
Total	279	100.00	267	100.00

62. Biston, *De la fausse noblesse*, 80.
63. *Receuil Dalloz*, no. 12 (1858): 47. See also Roger Barbier de Felcourt, *Des titres de noblesse et des noms dits nobiliaires* (Paris, 1867), 166.
64. Noble families sometimes found themselves in similar situations, as in the case of the du Gouyon family, authorized by the Nantes Tribunal on 24 January 1817 to take the form *de Goyon* as their "véritable nom de la famille" (*AN* BB[29] 784).
65. Edmond About, "Causerie," *Opinion nationale*, 31 March 1866. See the reply made by E. Renaudin in *Revue nobiliaire*, n.s., 2 (1877): 233–34.
66. *AD* Eure-et-Loire, "Tableaux alphabétique des contrats de mariage, Bureau de Chartres" (1829), A. P. H. Roissard de Mainville.
67. C. de Chergé, *Lettres d'un paysan gentilhomme sur la loi du 28 mai 1858 et le décrêt du 9 janvier 1850 relatifs aux noms et titres nobiliaires* (Poitiers, 1860), 37.
68. Marie-Léopold-René Barbier, *avocat*, born at Alençon, according to Vicomte A. Royer de Saint-Micaud, *Y a-t-il une noblesse française?* (Paris, 1899), 20. However, Barbier is not cited in the tables of the *Journal officiel* under "Etat civil (1891–96)." The name of the vicomte does not figure in the 1848 *Dictionnaire de la noblesse* nor in the much less severe Bachelin-Deflorenne, *Etat présent . . . 1866*. His book was a success.
69. Ibid., 27, 29.
70. Bloch et al., "Enquête," 249.
71. A. Gain, *La Restauration et les biens des émigrés: La Législation concernant les biens nationaux de seconde origine et son application dans l'est de la France, 1814–1832*, 2 vols. (Nancy, 1928).
72. Henri de Woelmont, *Notices généalogiques* (Paris, 1923). A French noble contemporary claimed that "verbalement" Woelmont admitted his mistakes: "Quant aux 5200 noms environ ayant un principe de noblesse française qu'il avait retenu, il reconnaissait volontiers qu'on pourrait les ramener à 3000 ou 3500" (M. Pradel de Lamase, "L'Idée de noblesse en France depuis la Révolution," *Mercure de France* 294 [1939]: 324 n. 7).
73. Jacques de Marsay, *De l'âge des privilèges au temps des vanités. . . : Essai sur l'origine et la valeur des prétensions nobiliaires*, 2d ed. (Paris, 1946).
74. Guérin, *Législation et jurisprudence*.
75. Jacques Houdaille, "Les Descendants des grands dignitaires du premier Empire au XIXe siècle," *Population* 29, no. 1 (January–February 1974): 272–73.
76. Charles Rey, *De la noblesse et de la législation nobiliaire en France depuis la Révolution* (Paris, 1902), 103.
77. Royer de Saint-Micaud, *Y a-t-il une noblesse française?*
78. Bachelin-Deflorenne, *Etat présent . . . 1866*.
79. John E. C. Bodley, *France* (London, 1898), 175, echoed contemporary French opinion when he wrote that "the so-called noble class has increased enormously in proportion to the population," but he gave no precise figures. Like Royer de Saint-Micaud, he appeared to believe that the Third Republic was a primrose time for false titles: "The exponents of sterile aristocratic pretension are an expanding multitude, not suffering from stagnation of the blood which has destroyed many a genuine aristocracy" (ibid.). Legal discussions of the rights of descendants of lapsed *majorats*, of the decrescendo of titles for nineteenth-century creations, and of the proprietary rights to a title were addressed by a variety of law theses at the end of the nineteenth century, e.g., Lallier, Tournade, and Rey. Since the end of the Second Empire the French head of state has never bestowed noble titles, simply titles of merit.

2. NOBLE LANDHOLDERS

1. Jean Meyer, *Noblesse et pouvoirs dans l'Europe d'ancien régime* (Paris, 1973).
2. Jean Meyer, *La Noblesse bretonne*, 2 vols. (Paris, 1966), vol. 1.

3. Theoretically "an index of concentration" of nobles could be drawn up by multiplying the population of each canton (or arrondissement) by the number of nobles known to be resident there and then multiplying that by the area of the canton. Displayed on a cantonal map of France, the variations would provide a factor analysis. However, this method lacks merit until more complete information is available about the location and particularly the size of noble families in each canton at any given time.

4. S. Icard, "Les Provençaux titrés et anoblis au XIXe siècle," *Mémoires de l'institut de l'histoire de Provence* 4 (1927): 181–202. The population distribution in percentages was as follows: Bouches-du-Rhône, 37 percent; Var, 33 percent; Hautes-Alpes, 13.4 percent; Basses-Alpes, 16.1 percent.

5. See Thomas D. Beck, "The French Revolution and the Nobility: A Reconsideration," *Journal of Social History* 15, no. 2 (Winter 1981): 225.

6. Jacob-Frédéric Lullin de Chateauvieux, *Voyages agronomiques en France,* 2 vols. (Paris, 1843), vol. 1, map. He added: "Cette division est destinée à grouper dans les mêmes masses les portions du Royaume dont le climat, la nature géoponique, celle des productions ainsi que le système de l'agriculture ont assez d'homogénéité pour que l'on puisse les envisager sous le même point de vue et traiter en commun des améliorations rurales dont la culture de chacune de ces régions peut être susceptible, sans qu'il soit possible pourtant de les considérer d'une manière absolue." See also ibid., vol. 2, bk. 6, chap. 1; and A. de Caumont, *Des cartes agronomiques* (Paris, 1847), *BN* GE FF8745.

7. D. Bergman, "L'Etat présent de l'agriculture française," *Annales de géographie* 63 (1952): 339–57.

8. A. Correch, *La Cour d'appel de Pau: Ses origines, son histoire, son personnel* (Tarbes, 1920).

9. Pierre Guillaume, *La Population de Bordeaux au XIXe siècle* (Paris, 1972), 18.

10. A. B. N. Peat, *Gossip from Paris during the Second Empire* (London, 1903), 121, 116.

11. Gabriel Desert, "Structures sociales dans les villes bas-normandes au XIXe siècle," in *Conjoncture économique, structures sociales: Hommage à Ernest Labrousse* (The Hague, 1974), 492.

12. Philippe-Régis-Denis de Keredern, comte de Trobriand, *Les Gentilshommes de l'ouest* (Paris, 1841).

13. The enquiry during the 1820s into the financial situation of elderly and impecunious chevaliers de Saint Louis, records from which are to be found in some departmental archives, would, if systematically collated, provide a national survey of the residences of the former military *noblesse.*

14. G. Frêche, *Toulouse et la région Midi-Pyrénées au siècle des lumières vers 1670–1789* (Paris, 1974), 373–76.

15. Paul Bois, *Les Paysans de l'ouest* (Paris, 1960), 338–39.

16. A. Daumard et al., *Les Fortunes françaises au XIXe siècle* (Paris, 1973).

17. M. Grosbois, "Les Nobles sarthois au XIXe siècle, 1805–1872" (Le Mans, [1973?], Typescript).

18. Anne de Rochechouart-Mortemart, duchesse d'Uzès, *Souvenirs* (Paris, 1939), 30.

19. Ibid., 31.

20. Léontine de Castelbajac, *née* Villeneuve, *Mémoires de l'Occitanienne, souvenirs de famille et de jeunesse,* preface by P. B. Gheusi (Paris, 1927), 127.

21. C. E. d'Harcourt, *Réflexions sur l'état agricole et commercial des provinces centrales de la France* (Paris, 1822). He was a deputy for Seine-et-Marne from 1822 to 1827. Gabriel d'Harcourt was on the general council from 1820 to 1830 and was a liberal deputy from Provins from 1827 to 1831.

22. A. L. Imbert de Saint Amand, *La Cour de Charles* x (Paris, 1892), 46.

23. Tancrède de Hauteville, *De la mission des hautes classes dans la société moderne* (Paris, 1863), 25.

24. B. Révoil, "Revue et chronique: 1841," in *Revue historique de la noblesse publiée sous la direction de M. André Borel d'Hauterive, archiviste paléographe,* vol. I (Paris, 1841), 384. A similar observation in a somewhat different terminology was made by a sociologist of the French ruling class in the 1970s: "Or, on peut dire que le lieu d'habitation n'est pas un faible indice de l'intégration de la classe dirigeante: il est même l'un des indicateurs les plus saisissants de l'homogénéité de l'image sociale de l'élite. Le mode d'habitat est en fait l'une des composantes essentielles de l'habitus des catégories dirigeantes, un signe de reconnaissance, un indice d'appartenance à la classe dirigeante" (Pierre Birnbaum et al., *La Classe dirigeante française* [Paris, 1978], 152–53).

25. Thomas D. Beck, from his data collection of electoral lists of the 1830s and 1840s which he described in "A Data Bank: France, 1800–1847," *Social Science History* 4, no. 3 (Summer 1980): 347–536, furnished me with the following information concerning the average tax paid by nobles in the 1830s and 1840s:

Electors' Residences	Northern France	Southern France
Large cities (+40,000)	1,269F (N = 1,481)	1,082F (N = 578)
Mid-sized cities (20,000–40,000)	1,218F (N = 636)	1,049F (N = 1,049)
Small cities (10,000–20,000)	1,305F (N = 1,051)	1,055F (N = 1,605)
Towns (5,000–10,000)	1,500F (N = 1,619)	984F (N = 1,884)
Rural areas (under 5,000)	1,414F (N = 1,001)	1,001F (N = 1,707)
Averages	1,359F (N = 5,788)	1,023F (N = 6,823)

26. *AN* BB[29]783–84. Details of estates that follow are drawn from those registers.

27. Phillip Mansel, *Louis* XVIII (London, 1981), 208. In official usage by notaries, etc., it was still, of course, called *palais*.

28. According to data amassed for 424 of the 459 electoral arrondissements of France in the 1830s–1840s, the average "contribution personnelle et mobilière" was: commoners, 38F; individuals with particle names, 62F; and individuals with titles, 104F (Beck, "The French Revolution and the Nobility," 222).

29. Thomas D. Beck, "Occupation, Taxes, and a Distinct Nobility under Louis-Philippe," *European Studies Review* 13 (1983): 417.

30. Alain Guillemin, "La Noblesse de la Manche sous la Monarchie de Juillet," *Etudes rurales,* nos. 63–64 (1976): 129.

31. Marie d'Armaillé, *Quand on savait vivre heureux (1830–1860): Souvenirs de jeunesse* (Paris, 1934), 38–43.

32. E. Bougeâtre, "Etat des châteaux et domaines considérables," in *La Vie rurale dans le Mantois et le Vexin au XIXe siècle* (Paris, 1971), 220–22.

33. *AD* Haute-Garonne, WQ 5752.

34. *MC* LVIII 753, "Château de Villiers . . . 17 septembre 1836 et jours suivants." This building was the most valuable part of the succession of this chevalier de Saint Louis and former cavalry officer. He also had a four-story house in Paris on rue Choiseul and another small house near his Villiers estate. The Selve had served in the Rouen and Paris *parlements* in the sixteenth century and had been seigneurs of Villiers since at least the third member of the lineage, who in 1534 had married the daughter of a *conseiller* in the Chambre des comptes (Francois Alexandre Aubert de La

Chenaye-Desbois and Badier, *Dictionnaire de la noblesse, contenant les généalogies, l'histoire et la chronologie des familles nobles de France* . . . . 19 vols., 3d ed. [Paris, 1863–77], 18:502–11).

35. Corélie de Gaix, *Une Amie inconnue d'Eugénie de Guérin: Correspondance et oeuvres* (Paris, 1912), 4.

36. *AN* BB²⁹783.

37. Michel Denis, *Les Royalistes de la Mayenne et le monde moderne (XIXe–XXe siècles)*, Publications de l'Université de Haute-Bretagne, no. 6 (Paris, 1977), 346.

38. Armaillé, *Quand on savait vivre heureux*, 64. The château needed huge expenditures, and the duchesse wished to preserve her personal fortune for use in dowries for her children.

39. Denis, *Les Royalistes*, 353–55.

40. *Le Tout-Pyrénéen; guide annuaire, mondain et commercial de la région pyrénéenne* (Paris, 1905).

41. G. Fayolle, *La Vie quotidienne en Périgord au temps de Jacquou le Croquant* (Paris, 1977), 174–75.

42. *Almanach historique, typographique et statistique du département de Seine-et-Marne . . . 1864* (1864; reprint, Dammarie-les-Lys, 1984), 141–42.

43. Jean des Cars, *Haussmann* (Paris, 1978), 318.

44. *Description d'une propriété de revenu et d'agrément* (Pau, 1854), 19.

45. Antoine Bachelin-Deflorenne, *Etat présent de la noblesse française, contenant le dictionnaire de la noblesse contemporaine . . . 1866* (Paris, 1866).

46. *AN* BB²⁹783. See also A. P. Cardevac d'Havrincourt, *Notice sur le domaine d'Havrincourt* [Arras arrondissement, Pas-de-Calais] (Paris, 1867), 9, 28.

47. *AN* BB²⁹784. See also Maillé Latour Landry: "Il destine au majorat des biens qui sont dans sa famille depuis plusieurs siècles" (*AN* BB²⁹783).

48. *AN* BB²⁹782.

49. *AN* BB²⁹783.

50. Amédée d'Andigné, *Armand de Melun: Un Apôtre de la charité, 1807–1877* (Paris, 1961), 96.

51. Fernand de Rességuier, *Récits de grand-père* (Toulouse, 1901), 77.

52. Mary Boddington, *Sketches in the Pyrenees with Some Remarks on Languedoc*, vol. 2 (London, 1837), 228.

53. Marc Girouard, *Life in the English Country House* (New Haven, 1978).

54. See the chapters by Maurice Agulhon in G. Duby and A. Wallon, eds., *Histoire de la France rurale*, Collection l'univers historique, 4 vols. (Paris, 1976), vol. 3, *L'Apogée et crise de la civilisation paysanne, 1789–1914*, ed. Etienne Juilliard.

55. H. D. Clout, *French Agriculture on the Eve of the Railway Age* (London, 1980).

56. Sherman Kent, *Electoral Procedure under Louis-Philippe* (New Haven, 1937), esp. chap. 2, pp. 19–58.

57. Ibid., 32. On the origins of the *foncière* see Marcel Moye, *Précis élémentaire de législation financière à l'usage des étudiants des facultés de droit*, 4th ed. (Paris, 1912).

58. Clout, *French Agriculture*, 219, fig. 12.2, "Value of Output: F/ha."

59. Robert Forster, "Obstacles to Agricultural Growth in Eighteenth-Century France," *American Historical Review* 75, no. 6 (October 1970): 1606–7.

60. A. Hugues, *Le Département de Seine-et-Marne . . . conseil général* (Melun, 1895), 121–22.

61. Henri Martin, *La Vente des biens nationaux . . . district de Toulouse* (Toulouse, 1916), xi.

62. P. Clémendot, *Le Département de la Meurthe à l'époque du Directoire* (N.p., 1966), 182.

63. Michel Denis, *Les Royalistes de la Mayenne,* 2 vols. (Thesis, Lille III, 1976), 1:268–72.

64. René Descadeillas, *Rennes et ses derniers seigneurs, 1730–1820,* Bibliothèque méridionale, 2d ser., 39 (Toulouse, 1964), 148–50.

65. Joseph-Daniel Guigniaut, "Notice historique sur la vie et les travaux de M. le Cte. Alexandre de Laborde," *Mémoires de l'Académie des inscriptions et belles-lettres* 23, pt. 1 (1868): 275–318.

66. Mansel, *Louis* XVIII, 57.

67. A. Gain, *La Restauration et les biens des émigrés: La Législation concernant les biens nationaux de seconde origine et son application dans l'est de la France, 1814–1832,* 2 vols. (Nancy, 1929), 2:454–76.

68. Louis Bergeron, "Profits et risques dans les affaires parisiennes à l'époque du directoire et du consulat," *Annales historiques de la Révolution française* 185 (July–September 1966): 264, 367, 376.

69. Denis, *Les Royalistes* (Thesis), 1:277.

70. Charles Girault, *La Noblesse èmigrée et ses pertes foncières dans la Sarthe* (Laval, 1957).

71. Bois, *Les Paysans,* 338–39.

72. Philippe Bossis, "Recherches sur la propriété nobiliaire en pays vendéen avant et après la Révolution," *Bulletin de la Société d'Emulation de la Vendée,* 1973, 123–47.

73. Denis, *Les Royalistes* (thesis), 1:266.

74. Jean-Bernard Charrier, "La Propriété foncière en Nivernais à l'époque du Ier cadastre," *Etudes sur la Bourgogne* (Dijon, 1978), 78–85.

75. David Higgs, "Politics and Landownership among the French Nobility after the Revolution," *European Studies Review* 1, no. 2 (April 1971): 110.

76. France, Ministère de l'agriculture, du commerce et des travaux publics, *Statistique de la France . . . Agriculture: Résultats généraux de l'enquête décennale de 1862 . . .* (Strasbourg, 1868). These figures were compiled from taxes paid by each commune; thus, several properties within a single commune constituted a single return, and an individual with the same amount of property located in two communes would report twice, and so on.

77. Thomas D. Beck, "A Research Note on the Nobility" (unpublished ms.); Adeline Daumard, vol. 3, pt. 1, pp. 640–48, of *Histoire économique et sociale de la France,* edited by Fernand Braudel and Ernest Labrousse, 4 vols. (Paris, 1970–80).

78. D. M. G. Sutherland kindly supplied these illustrations from his researches into the *matrices cadastrales* of Charnay and Sénozan, Saône-et-Loire.

79. *MC* LVIII 640, "Vente de la terre de Gineste, 27 août 1808."

80. *MC* LVIII 805.

81. *MC* LVIII 803, 15–18 May 1850, *vente.*

82. Frêche, *Toulouse et la région Midi-Pyrénées* 373–76.

83. *MC* LVIII 760, 2 July 1839; see also the 1851 *partage* of the Girardin family in *MC* LVIII 802.

84. Clout, *French Agriculture,* 3–18.

85. Hauteville, *De la Mission des hautes classes,* 22.

86. Speech of J. B. S. de Gaye, vicomte de Martignac, 3 January 1825, as quoted by Léonce de Lavergne in *Economie rurale de la France depuis 1789,* 3d ed. (Paris, 1866), 26. This is a résumé of the speech that was later reprinted in full in *Archives parlementaires de 1787 à 1860,* 2d ser., 43 (Paris, 1879): 594–604.

87. Léonce de Lavergne, *Economie rurale de la France depuis 1789,* was first published

in Paris in 1860. The second edition was published in 1863, the third in 1866, and the fourth in 1877.

88. *AN* AF IV (1076) contains a list drawn up in 1803–4 of the twelve adult males paying the highest land tax in each department. The duc de Choiseul-Praslin is listed as paying 30,000F in Seine-et-Marne and 27,000F in the Sarthe. This document yielded a map of the departments with the most nobles among the twelve highest-taxed residents, slightly flawed by leaving a blank in the shape of the Tarn-et-Garonne department, which was not in fact formed until 1808 (see Louis Bergeron, *L'Episode napoléonien: Aspects intérieurs, 1799–1815* [Paris, 1972], 140). The same documentation was used by A. M. Boursier and A. Soboul in "La Grande Propriété foncière à l'époque napoléonienne," *Annales historiques de la Révolution française* 53, no. 245 (July–September 1981): 405–18.

89. Georges Dupeux, *Aspects de l'histoire sociale et politique du Loir-et-Cher, 1848–1914,* preface by Ernest Labrousse (Paris, 1962), 144.

90. A. F. P. de Falloux, "Dix ans d'agriculture," in *Etudes et souvenirs* (Paris, 1885), 161–210. He protested against the agricultural enquiry of 1866.

91. Harcourt, *Réflexions,* 37.

92. Georges De Chambray, *De l'agriculture et de l'industrie dans la province de Nivernais* (Paris, 1834), 35. He wrote exclusively in terms of profitability and made no mention of noble farmers as such.

93. Lavergne, *Economie,* 318.

94. In this paragraph and the next I follow R. Laurent very closely (see *Histoire économique et sociale de la France,* vol. 3, pts. 2 and 3, pp. 663–712).

95. F. Faillon, *Annuaire du département de la Haute-Garonne pour l'an 1807* (Toulouse, 1807), 58.

96. C. L. Lesur, *La France et les français en 1817: Tableau moral et politique* (Paris, 1817), 474; Lullin de Chateauvieux, *Voyages,* 1:57; Kent, *Electoral Procedure,* 34.

97. N. Bergasse, *Essai sur la propriété* (Paris, 1821): "De ce que la campagne est le lieu des souvenirs, il résulterait donc qu'elle est essentiellement le lieu des moeurs" (p. 51).

98. Havrincourt, *Notice,* 6.

99. Jean Vidalenc, *Le Peuple des campagnes* (Paris, 1972); Adeline Daumard et al., *Les Fortunes françaises au XIXe siécle* (Paris, 1973).

100. E. G. Ambroise de Courte, cited in Denis, *Les Royalistes* (Thesis), 1:280–83.

101. *AD* Yonne, VIII M²5.

102. Ibid., letter of 12 March 1819.

103. France, Ministère de l'intérieur, Conseil d'agriculture, *Liste des membres-correspondans* (Paris, 1821).

104. *Bulletin de la société centrale d'agriculture et industrie du départment de la Nièvre* 1 (1839):27–33.

105. Lullin de Chateauvieux, *Voyages,* 2:79.

106. Harcourt, *Réflexions,* 13.

107. F. Galeron, *Statistique de l'arrondissement de Falaise,* 3 vols. (Falaise, 1826–29), 3:127.

108. Havrincourt, *Notice,* 9.

109. Ibid., 28.

110. Forster, "Obstacles to Agricultural Growth," 1610.

111. T. J. A. Le Goff, *Vannes and Its Region* (Oxford, 1981), 151–75.

112. C. J. A. Mathieu de Dombasle, *Annales agricoles de Roville,* 2d ed. (Paris, 1829), 319–20.

113. A. Jardin and André-Jean Tudesq, *La France des notables (1815–1848)*, vol. 1 *La Vie de la nation* (Paris, 1972), 29.
114. Michel Lagrée, *Mentalités, religion et histoire en Haute-Bretagne au XIXe siècle: Le diocèse de Rennes, 1815–1848* (Paris, 1977), 105.
115. A. d'Angeville, *Essai sur la statistique de la population française* (Bourg, 1836; reprint, with an introduction by E. Le Roy Ladurie, Paris, 1969), vi–xxvi.
116. Dupeux, *Aspects*, 145.
117. Havrincourt, *Notice*, 196.
118. R. Moulinas, "Le Pays légal dans le Vaucluse: Sa composition et son rôle dans la vie politique de 1830 à 1848," (Thesis, Advanced studies in History, Université d'Aix-en-Provence, 1965), 35–36.
119. G. A. de Puybusque, *Généalogie de la famille de Puybusque* (Toulouse, 1912). "Premier rameau: Dit de Caraman," 282–88, deals with François-Maurice-Achille de Puybusque (1813–98).
120. Ibid.
121. Descadeillas, *Rennes et ses derniers seigneurs*.
122. Arthur Young gave a laborer's average daily wage in 1789 as 19 sols (*Travels in France during the years 1787, 1788, and 1789*, ed. Constantia Maxwell [Cambridge, 1950], 314); Lavergne gave it in 1860 as 1F50 (*Economie*, 60).
123. Lavergne, *Economie*, 276, 354.
124. Henri Sée, *Esquisse d'une histoire du régime agraire en Europe du XVIIIe au XIXe siècles* (Paris, 1921), 231.
125. Henri Fourastié, "L'Enquête de 1856 sur la désertion des campagnes," *Bulletin de la société des sciences historiques et naturelles de l'Yonne* 97 (1957–58): 271–73.
126. Lavergne, *Economie*, 48–49. A. Gain, in *La Restauration*, contested the picture of large estates breaking into smaller units and claimed that they increased, so that there were more than fifty thousand of them at the end of the Second Empire.
127. See George W. Grantham, "Scale and Organisation in French Farming, 1840–1880," in *European Peasants and Their Markets*, ed. E. L. Jones and W. N. Parker (London, 1975).
128. *AD* Yonne, 3E 83–592.
129. P. Simoni, "Agricultural Change and Landlord-Tenant Relations in Nineteenth-Century France: The Canton of Apt (Vaucluse)," *Journal of Social History* 13, no. 1 (1979): 127–29.
130. For the percentages of the French population classified as urban dwellers between 1846 and 1886 see André Armengaud, "Le Rôle de la démographie," in *Histoire économique et sociale de la France*, vol. 3, *L'Avènement de l'ere industrielle (1789–années 1880)*, pt. 1 (Paris, 1976), 230.
131. Harold Perkin, using data from 1880 to 1959, showed the median worth of large landowners' estates stadily increasing. Although data from years before 1880 were not available, this steady enrichment of large landowners may have been widespread in nineteenth-century Europe ("The Recruitment of Elites in British Society since 1800," *Journal of Social History* 12, no. 2 [Winter 1978]: 222–34).

3. THREE FAMILY PROFILES, 1800–1870

1. Robert Forster, *The House of Saulx-Tavanes, Versailles and Burgundy, 1700–1830* (Baltimore, 1971); idem, *Merchants, Landlords, Magistrates: The Depont Family in Eighteenth-Century France* Baltimore, 1980.
2. Information on the house of Choiseul-Praslin in the nineteenth century appears in the two best books about the fearful 1847 scandal over the murder of the duchesse de

Choiseul-Praslin, *née* Sébastiani, by her husband: M. Rousselet, *L'Affaire du duc de Praslin et la magistrature: Thèse complémentaire* (Paris, 1937); and S. Loomis, *A Crime of Passion* (New York, 1967). J. T. Mesmay, *Horace Sébastiani* (Paris, 1948), examined the career of the duchesse's father. The murder's shadow caused an understandable reticence in other family members during the remainder of the nineteenth century. The papers relating to the investigation by the Chamber of Peers are contained in *AN* CC 808–12. Additional scraps of information about subsequent generations of the family and reproductions of portraits are in M. Lucas, *Contribution à l'histoire de Maincy: Vieilles familles* . . . [Dammarie-les-Lys, 1980], 126–80.

3. See above chap. 2, n. 88. In the 1830s the banker Perier paid the largest tax in the country, 56,503F, but the duc de Choiseul-Praslin was still in the top ten, together with five other nobles (see Thomas D. Beck, "Occupation, Taxes, and a Distinct Nobility under Louis-Philippe," *European Studies Review* 13 [1983]: 412).

4. *MC* LVIII 638.

5. M. Michaud, *Biographie universelle*, 2d ed., vol. 34 (Paris, [1861]), 289.

6. *MC* LVIII 648.

7. *MC* LVIII 645.

8. *MC* LVIII 635.

9. *MC* LVIII 597(bis).

10. *MC* LVIII 648.

11. *MC* LVIII 647.

12. *MC* LVIII 636.

13. *AD* Nièvre, M 117.

14. *MC* LVIII 726.

15. *MC* LVIII 773.

16. *MC* LVIII 756.

17. *MC* LVIII 753.

18. *MC* LVIII 751.

19. *MC* LVIII 863.

20. *A MM. les électeurs de la Ire circonscription de Seine-et-Marne* (*10 mai 1869*), cited in Lucas, *Contribution*, 166.

21. *MC* LVIII 760, *communauté* contract.

22. *MC* LVIII 854.

23. *MC* LVIII 856.

24. *MC* LVIII 639.

25. *MC* LVIII 781.

26. *MC* LVIII 861.

27. *MC* LVIII 849.

28. There is no detailed study of the Raigecourts despite their ancient prominence in Lorraine. A posthumous note by a daughter appeared at the end of the nineteenth century: Marie-Lucie de Goyon, *née* de Raigecourt, *Quelques pages sur l'ancienne Lorraine et la maison de Raigecourt* (Mesnil-sur-l'Estrée, 1893), *BN* 8°Lk²4027. According to the introduction, she wrote this memoir when she was nineteen, thus c. 1880. The post-Revolutionary fortunes of the Raigecourts can be traced in part in the minutes of their Paris notaries, whose chambers (étude) have the number LVIII in *MC* and passed from two members of the Trutat family to two members of the Fourchy family during the nineteenth century, but the inventory notes many documents not left in the archives of the étude ("en blanc").

29. Guy Chaussinand-Nogaret, *The French nobility in the eighteenth Century: From Feudalism to Enlightenment*, trans. William Doyle (Cambridge, 1985), 54.

30. A. V. Arnault et al., *Biographie nouvelle des contemporains*, vol. 17 (Paris, 1824), 216.

31. Anne-Bernard-Antoine Raigecourt de Gournay, *Correspondance avec le marquis et marquise de Bombelles pendant l'émigration, 1790–1800* (Paris, 1892), 273, *BN* 8° L⁴563(1).

32. Gain, *La Restauration et les biens des émigrés: La Législation concernant les biens nationaux de seconde origine et son application dans l'est de la France, 1814–1832*, 2 vols. (Nancy, 1928), 2:331.

33. C. Pfeister, *Histoire de Nancy*, 3 vols. (Paris, 1902–9), 1:272.

34. Ibid., 654–55.

35. *MC* LVIII 642, *communauté* contract.

36. *MC* LVIII 657.

37. *MC* LVIII 731.

38. *MC* LVIII 808.

39. *MC* LVIII 731.

40. *MC* CXI 513.

41. Ibid.; André de Leusse, *Souvenirs de la famille: Notice historique et généalogique sur la famille de Leusse* (Lyon, 1848), *BN* 8°Lm³989; Robert de Leusse de Syon, *Histoire généalogique de la famille de Leusse: Souvenir de famille* (Vienne, 1924), *BN* 4°Lm³1869A.

42. *MC* LVIII 822.

43. In 1838 the Fleurigny château was described as "d'une construction ancienne et très soignée, environn. de fossés remplis d'eaux, avec ponts levis, tours, etc. Il y a une chapelle remarquable par un beau vitrail peint par Jean Cousin, natif de Jouy près Sens. La famille de Fleurigny qui possède cette terre a fourni un chancelier de France sous Charles VI" ("Notice sur les châteaux anciens et modernes . . . arrondissement de Sens," *AD* Yonne, 74 T2). It was by no means the grandest château in the department. That at Ancy-le-Franc paid almost ten times more doors-and-windows tax.

44. Gaston Saffroy lists a thirteen-page eighteenth-century genealogy of the Le Clerc de Fleurigny family in the municipal library of Auxerre (*Bibliographie généalogique, heraldique et nobiliaire de la France*, 3 vols. [Paris, 1968–70]).

45. Charles Porée, *Département de l'Yonne: documents relatifs à la vente des biens nationaux dans le district de Sens*, vol. 1 (Auxerre, 1912), 312–13.

46. *AD* Yonne, 111 M¹10.

47. Henri Forestier, *L'Yonne au XIXe siècle. lre. partie (1800–1830)*, vol. 1 (Auxerre, 1959), 88.

48. J. Leviste, "Le Testament du marquis de Fleurigny en 1839," *Société archéologique de Sens: Bulletin de liaison*, 3d ser., no. 17 (1973): 29–30.

49. *AD* Yonne, VIII M¹12.

50. *AD* Yonne, 40B 97.

51. *MC* LVIII 822.

52. "Du choix de Poussery comme ferme-modèle," *Annales de Poussery* 6 (1846): 230–33.

53. *MC* LVIII 822.

54. Philippe Picot de Lapeyrouse, *The agriculture of a district in the south of France. Tr. from the French . . . To which are added, notes, by a recent traveller in France* (London, 1819); Louis Théron de Montaugé, *L'Agriculture et les classes rurales dans le pays toulousain depuis le milieu du XVIIIe siècle* (Paris, 1869).

55. There is no adequate family monograph dealing with the Villèles in their local setting. Their genealogy is given in Jules Vilain, *La France moderne; grand dictionnaire généalogique, historique et biographique, Haute-Garonne et Ariège*, 3 vols. (Montpellier, 1911–13) 3:147–59. Louis-François, father of the minister, was a prolific writer on agricultural topics. Comte de Neuville, *Notice historique sur M. le comte*

de Villèle (Paris, 1855), included the Lespinasse de Saune "Notice nécrologique" read in the Haute-Garonne agricultural society on 25 June 1854. Edulcorated memoirs and extracts from correspondence were published at the end of the nineteenth century. The most recent biography is J. Fourcassié, *Villèle* (Paris, 1954), but it made little use of the technical papers on national finance in the family archive. Fourcassié is strong on family matters. The local political power base of Villèle is discussed in David Higgs, *Ultraroyalism in Toulouse* (Baltimore, 1973). An inventory of the family papers was in preparation (1985) by staff of the departmental archives of the Haute-Garonne.

56. *AD* Haute-Garonne, WQ 10440, table, 1853–58, canton Caraman.

57. F. Faillon, *Annuaire du départment de la Haute-Garonne pour l'an 1807* (Toulouse, 1807), 64.

58. *AD* Haute-Garonne, 3E 1274. The Villèles had owned property in this area for centuries.

59. *AN* F^{7}7602. Villèle lived at 76 rue Pharaon.

60. Ibid., 17 thermidor VII (4 August 1799), request for information; 1 complèmentaire VII (17 September 1799): Villèle "ne cesse de s'occuper d'observations agricoles; il répand autour de lui l'instruction; ses voisins profitent de ses vues, de ses essais et de ses succès. Rien n'est étranger à ses travaux . . . il semble qu'un homme uniquement occupé des progrès de l'agriculture ne peut être en même temps un conspirateur."

61. *AN* F^{1c}III (Garonne, Haute-) 5. In fact, another man, son of a *conseiller* at the Parlement of Toulouse, was put forward on a list of candidates for cantonal president. Nor was Villèle's name on the arrondissement list. This may have been because the prefecture thought him either a royalist or troublesome—or likely both. After the year VII insurrection he published three pamphlets attacking tax collectors at Bazième and those who held sequestered crops of the year VII from Caragoudes and nearby (Villèle Family Archives, Mourvilles-Basses, Haute-Garonne).

62. *AD* Haute-Garonne, J 608.

63. *Journal des propriétaires ruraux du Midi* 13, no. 9 (September 1817): 326–32.

64. Ibid.

65. *AD* Haute-Garonne, 3E 1769, marriage contract, 15 February 1772.

66. *AD* Haute-Garonne, 3E 1274, sale, 23 May 1777.

67. *AD* Haute-Garonne, 3E 21456, sale, 9 October 1807.

68. Fourcassié, *Villèle*, 429–30.

69. N. Belcastel, "Notices nécrologiques sur le comte Henri de Villèle," *Journal des propriétaires ruraux du Midi*, 4th ser., 11 (June 1883): 277–88.

70. Alain Guillemin, "Rente, famille, innovation: Contribution à la sociologie du grand domaine noble au XIXe siècle," *Annales, economies, sociétés, civilisations* 40, no. 1 (January–February 1985): 54–70; Henry Higgs, *The Physiocrats* (Cambridge, 1897).

4. NOBLE WEALTH

1. R. McGraw, *France, 1815–1914: The Bourgeois Century* (London, 1983).

2. There is an overview of French nobles in business in the nineteenth century in a chapter with the inappropriate title "La Noblesse et le tiers" by E. Beau de Loménie in *Le Monde des affaires en France de 1830 à nos jours*, ed. J. Boudet (Paris, 1952), 549–65.

3. A. d'Angeville, *Essai sur la statistique de la population française* (Bourg, 1836; reprint, with an introduction by E. Le Roy Ladurie, Paris, 1969), 359; see map 4, "Industrie."

4. Adeline Daumard, "L'Evolution des structures sociales en France à l'époque de l'in-dustrialisation, 1815–1914" (Paper presented at the Colloque international des sciences humaines sur l'industrialisation en Europe au XIXe siècle, Lyons, 1970), published in *L'Industrialisation en Europe au XIXe siècle* (Paris, 1972), 324. In the discussion that followed Daumard's presentation, it was Daumard's ideas on the pauperization of the bottom levels of French society, rather than her remarks on the elite, that excited comment (Ibid. 328–34).

5. Louis Bergeron, *Banquiers, négociants et manufacturiers parisiens du Directoire à l'Empire* (Paris, 1978), 21.

6. AN F^{1c}III (Indre), 2. Lists were pruned of *ci-devants* either because they were too penurious or because they were of uncertain politics. The 1809 lists for Civray arrondissement (Vienne) showed of 109 names 44 crossed out, of whom 11 were *noblesse*. Of the 16 *ci-devants* only 5 figured among the 65 names put forward for the *statistique des notables* (AD Vienne, M^{105}). Put another way, the original list showed 14.7 percent of local notables to be noble, but after scrutiny, this figure diminished to 7.7 percent, almost half. The distribution of wealth on those lists arranged by each arrondissement in France has been shown on a map and in histograms by Louis Bergeron and Guy Chaussinand-Nogaret in *Les Masses de granit: Cent mille notables du premier empire* (Paris, 1979), 56–57, 68–122.

7. Guy Chaussinand-Nogaret, Louis Bergeron, and Robert Forster, "Les Notables du Grand Empire en 1810," *Annales, économies, sociétés, civilisations* 25, no. 5 (September–October 1971): 1061: "La vieille aristocratie terrienne laisse une place en blanc dans nos collèges electoraux, et ni la guillotine, ni l'emigration, ni certains appauvrissements ne peuvent suffire à l'expliquer."

8. Bergeron and Chaussinand-Nogaret, *Les Masses de granit*, 49–52.

9. AN F^{1c}II 53, documentation of the 1831 report by Allard. See also appendix 1, below.

10. The electoral lists are not everywhere complete, and there is no central collation of them. See on the subject Sherman Kent, *The Election of 1827 in France* (Cambridge, Mass., 1975), esp. 209–16. Lists were consulted from the 1820s in the following departmental archives: Calvados M 333; Drôme 6 M 22; Indre M 144; Loire-Inférieure 3 M 9; Maine-et-Loire 6 M 18; Sarthe M 61/3; Tarn IIM^{3}3; Vienne 3 M 36; Yonne IIM^{1}37. See also Thomas D. Beck, "Occupation, Taxes, and a Distinct Nobility under Louis-Philippe," *European Studies Review* 13 (1983): 405–13, for a convincing demonstration of the noble aversion to commerce and industry, although capitalist activities in the strict sense of the profits produced by the financial manipulation of capital did not pay a tax shown on the printed electoral lists.

11. Guy Richard, *Noblesse d'affaires au XVIIIe siècle* (Paris, 1974). On the same problem in neighboring Spain see W. J. Callahan, *Honor, Commerce, and Industry in Eighteenth-Century Spain* (Boston, 1972).

12. Guy Chaussinand-Nogaret, *The French Nobility in the Eighteenth Century: From Feudalism to Enlightenment*, trans. William Doyle (Cambridge, 1985), 86, 90.

13. AN BB^{29}784.

14. *Bulletin de la Commission Historique et Archéologique de la Mayenne* 18 (1902): 379–80, as cited in Michel Denis, *Les Royalistes de la Mayenne*, 2 vols. (Thesis, Lille III, 1976), 2:631.

15. Jean Lacouture, *Le Mouvement royaliste dans le sud-ouest (1797–1800)* (Hosségor, 1932), 7.

16. Bergeron, *Banquiers*.

17. W. H. Adams, *A Proust Souvenir* (New York, 1984), 74.

18. G. Antonetti, *Une Maison de banque au XVIIIe siècle: Greffulhe Montz et Cie, 1789–93* (Paris, 1963); *An* BB^{29}782. From 1820 comte Greffulhe was noted in official circles

for the highly advanced agricultural equipment on the estate of his Bois-Boudran château at Fontenailles, Seine-et-Marne (F. A. Denis, *Histoire de l'agriculture dans le département de Seine-et-Marne* [Meaux, 1880], 361–62).

19. Bergeron, *Banquiers,* 319; Guy Richard, "La noblesse d'affaires en France de 1750 à 1850. *"Revue internationale d'histoire de la banque* 13 (1976): 1–58.

20. René Mantel, "La Rochefoucauld-Liancourt: Un Novateur français dans la pratique agricole du XVIIIe siècle," in Albert Rigaudière, *Etudes d'histoire économique rurale au XVIIIe siècle, par Albert Rigaudière, Evelyne Zylberman et René Mantel,* preface by Robert Besnier (Paris, 1965), 158–59; J. D. de la Rochefoucauld, C. Wolkow, and G. Ikni, *Le Duc de la Rochefoucauld-Liancourt, 1747–1827* (Paris, 1980).

21. *Annuaire statistique du départment de l'Yonne* (Auxerre, 1838), 231.

22. Alphonse Henri d'Hautpoul, *Mémoires du général marquis Alphonse d'Hautpoul, pair de France, 1789–1865* (Paris, 1906), 165.

23. Denis, *Les Royalistes* (Thesis), 1:645.

24. Adeline Daumard regretted this lacuna in the collection of essays she edited entitled *Les Fortunes françaises au XIXe siècle* (Paris, 1973). Family *partages* and notarial documents sometimes permit a fuller and more complete knowledge of family wealth.

25. A. V. Arnault et al., *Biographie nouvelle des contemporains,* vol. 1 (Paris, 1820), 112.

26. E. Sylberman, "Auget de Montyon, partisan de l'agriculture nouvelle," in Rigaudière et al., *Etudes,* 151–206. F. Labour, *M. de Montyon d'après des documents inédits* (Paris, 1880), 240–41, reproduces his will. See also Louis Guimbaud, *Un Grand Bourgeois au XVIIIe siècle: Auget de Montyon (1733–1820)* (Paris, 1909), esp. 271–99.

27. *AN* BB^{29}784.

28. *MC* LVIII 814, 28 February 1853.

29. *MC* LVIII 811, 9 June 1852.

30. *AD* Haute-Garonne, WQ 5621, 27 July 1854.

31. Georges Dupeux, *Aspects de l'histoire sociale et politique du Loir-et-Cher, 1848–1914,* preface by Ernest Labrousse (Paris, 1962), 143.

32. David Higgs, "Social Mobility and Hereditary Titles in France, 1814–1830: The Majorats-sur-Demande," *Histoire Sociale/Social History* 14, no. 27 (May 1981): 42–43.

33. *AD* Loire Atlantique, 3 M 9. His trading company imported colonial products and engaged in the slave trade. This was extremely profitable. At his death in 1833 he left 540,000F in business interests, with real estate worth 50,000 in the Loire-Inférieure but much more in Morbihan (see R. Kerviler, *Un Centenaire: Le Procès des 132 Nantais avec une relation inédite de leur voyage à Paris* (Vannes, 1894), 221–22; and the notice in Louis Bergeron and Guy Chaussinand-Nogaret, *Grands notables du Premier Empire,* vol. 8 [Paris, 1982], 189–90).

34. Guy Richard, "Du moulin banal au tissage mécanique: La Noblesse dans l'industrie textile en Haute-Normandie dans la première moitié du XIXe siècle," *Revue d'histoire économique et sociale* 46 (1968): 305–38, 506–49.

35. Comte Tanneguy de Leveneur, owner of the Carrouges furnace and forge (Orne), in an undated estimate of total annual revenues probably compiled in the 1830s gave 66 percent from farmlands, 16.4 percent from mills, 9.4 percent from woodlands, and only 8 percent from his metallurgical activities (*AD* Orne, J 16).

36. H. Enjalbert et al., *Histoire de Rodez* (Toulouse, 1983), 280.

37. André Armengaud, *Les Populations de l'est aquitain au début de l'époque contemporaine: Recherches sur une région moins développé vers 1845–vers 1871* (Paris, 1961), 121–26.

38. M. P. A. Butet, *Statistique du Cher* (N.p., 1829), 98–99.

39. Louis Gallicher, *Le Cher agricole et industriel* (Bourges, 1870), 315–33.

40. Denis, *Les Royalistes* (Thesis), 1:394.

41. G. J. H. E. de Marcieu, *Deux lieutenants généraux des armées du roy commandant en Dauphiné au XVIIIe siècle*, 3 vols. (Grenoble, 1928), 2:42–43; AD Isère, 16 J 116.

42. R. Sédillot, *La Maison de Wendel de 1704 à nos jours* (Paris, 1958); Bertrand Gille, *La Sidérurgie française au XIXe siècle: Recherches historiques* (Geneva, 1968), esp. chap. 2; Peter Fritsch, *Les Wendel: Rois de l'acier français* (Paris, 1976).

43. Bertrand Gille, *Recherches sur la formation de la grande entreprise capitaliste, 1815–1848* (Paris, 1959), 25.

44. AN F¹ᶜIII (Drôme) 8.

45. L. J. Gras, *Histoire économique générale des mines de la Loire* (Saint Etienne, 1922), 227–34.

46. AN BB²⁹784, no. 95.

47. Reed G. Geiger, *The Anzin Coal Company, 1800–1833: Big Business in the Early Stages of the French Industrial Revolution* (Newark, 1974), 32–33, 320.

48. Gille, *Recherches*, 104.

49. Rolande Trempé, *Les Mineurs de Carmaux, 1848–1914* 2 vols. (Paris, 1971), 1:xx.

50. MC LVIII 771, agreements of 31 August 1841 and 29 April 1842.

51. AN F¹ᶜIII (Tarn), 3.

52. Joan W. Scott, *The Glassworkers of Carmaux: French Craftsmen and Political Action in a Nineteenth-Century City* (Cambridge, Mass., 1974), 7, 9, 16, 74.

53. Translated in M. Blanchard, "The Railway Policy of the Second Empire," in *Essays in European Economic History, 1789–1914*, F. Crouzet, W. H. Chaloner, and W. M. Stern (London, 1969), 102.

54. A. de Clermont-Tonnerre, *Chemin de fer d'intérêt local de Beauvais à Amiens par Crèvecoeur: Note sur l'état d'avancement des études entreprises pour l'établissement de cette ligne* (Beauvais, 1866). Numerous pamphlets of this sort were published in the 1850s and 1860s.

55. MC LVIII 852, 3 September 1869.

56. P. J. Richard, *Histoire des institutions d'assurance en France* (Paris, 1956), 34.

57. Ibid., 38, 44.

58. André-Jean Tudesq, "Les Survivances de l'ancien régime: La Noblesse dans la société française de la première moitié du XIXe siècle," in *Colloque d'histoire sociale, Saint-Cloud, 24–25 mai 1967* (Paris, 1973), 211.

59. See the *BN* catalog. Courcy also wrote novels of noble interest: *L'Honneur* (1857), *Un nom* (1860), and *Château à vendre* (1882).

60. Philippe Levillain, "Un Chevau-léger de 1871 à 1875: Joseph de la Bouillerie," *Revue historique* 257, no. 1 (January–March 1977): 82–83 n. 1.

61. MC VII 800, 29 August 1849.

62. See the reproduction of a page of the *Revue des notabilitiés de l'industrie* in 1847 in Bordet, *Le Monde des affaires*, 552.

63. Pierre Guiral, *La Vie quotidienne en France à l'âge d'or du capitalisme, 1852–1879* (Paris, 1976), 13.

64. Richard, *Histoire*, 70.

65. A. Fayet, *Biographie de M. de Genoude* (Paris, 1846), 80–81.

66. William Serman, *Les Origines des officiers français, 1848–1870* (Paris, 1979), 1. Only 8 percent of officers serving between 1848 and 1870 came from the *noblesse*.

67. Jean des Cars, *Haussmann* (Paris, 1978), passim.

68. Paul Charbon, "Un Inspecteur général du télégraphe sous le Second Empire [Ferdinand de Dürckheim]," *Revue des postes télécommunications France* 30, no. 2 (1975): 41–48.

69. Yves Durand, *Les Financiers au XVIIIe siècle* (Paris, 1976), 36.
70. Robert R. Locke, "A Method for Identifying French Corporate Businessmen (the Second Empire)," *French Historical Studies* 10, no. 2 (1977): 261–92.
71. For this period see J. B. H. R. Capefigue, *Histoire des grandes opérations financières: Banques, bourses, emprunts, compagnies industrielles,* 4 vols. (Paris, 1855–60).
72. Pierre Birnbaum et al., *La Classe dirigeante française* (Paris, 1978), 152. See also the section entitled "La Présence de la noblesse au sein des classes dirigeantes," 153–56.
73. *Le Nouvel Observateur* 1020 (25–31 May 1984): 39–42, describing M. Jacques de Larosière de Champfeu, a graduate of the Ecole nationale d'administration and official of the Ministry of Finance, who joined the International Monetary Fund in 1978.
74. A. C. L. Victor de Broglie, *Souvenirs, 1785–1870,* 2d ed., 4 vols. (Paris, 1886), 2:94.
75. Charles Albert de Moré de Pontgibaud, *Mémoires . . . (1758–1837) . . .* (Paris, 1898), 200 and passim. He returned to France in 1804 and lived for almost a quarter of a century at the Place des Vosges. See also Alain Guillemin, "Aristocrates, proprietaires et diplômés: La Lutte pour le pouvoir local dans le département de la Manche, 1830–1875," *Actes de la recherche en sciences sociales* (Paris) 42 (1982): 51–53.
76. Session of 10 July 1821 in protest of "lettres de relief" given to a noble, Chavin, who sought to erase the "dérogeance" of his father's business activities. Ironically, all of Chavin's children married commoners.
77. G. de Bertier de Sauvigny, "Un Grand Capitaine d'industrie au début du XIXe siècle: Guillaume Ternaux, 1763–1833," *Revue d'histoire moderne et contemporaine,* 2 (1981): 335.
78. L. M. Lomüller, *Guillaume Ternaux (1763–1833): Créateur de la première intégration industrielle française* (Paris, 1978).
79. T. Zeldin, *France, 1848–1945,* 2 vols. (Oxford, 1973–77), 1:17, 405.
80. Beau de Loménie, "La Noblesse," 555.

5. NOBLES AND POLITICS

1. Joseph Barnave, *Introduction to the French Revolution and Other Writings,* ed. E. Chill (New York, 1971). It is worth noting that according to the information gathered in Beck's 1981 data bank, eight coastal departments (Pas-de-Calais, Somme, Seine-Inférieure, Calvados, Ille-et-Vilaine, Loire-Inférieure, Gironde, and Hérault) but only six interior ones were among the departments with the most noble electors in the 1840s.
2. As cited in Robert L. Koepke, "The Loi des patentes of 1844," *French Historical Studies* 11, no. 3 (Spring 1980): 418.
3. Albert Maurin, *Histoire de la chute des Bourbons: Grandeur et décadence de la bourgeoisie,* 6 vols. (Paris, 1849–52).
4. Phillip Mansel, *Louis XVIII* (London, 1981), 205.
5. L. Passy, *Marquis de Blosseville* (Evreux, 1898), 373–74.
6. René Rémond, *La Droite en France,* 2d ed., (Paris, 1974), 6. See esp. Stéphane Rials, *Le Légitimisme,* Collection "Que Sais-Je?" no. 2107 (Paris, 1983).
7. Jules Rais, *La Représentation des aristocraties dans les Chambres Hautes en France, 1789–1815* (Paris, 1900), 142–45.
8. E. F. A. d'Arnaud Vitrolles, *Mémoires,* vol. 2 (Paris, 1951), 280.
9. H. Remsen Whitehouse, *The Life of Lamartine,* vol. 1 (Boston, 1918), 135.
10. C. M. d'Irumberry, comte de Salaberry, *Souvenirs politiques . . . sur la Restauration, 1821–1830,* vol. 1 (Paris, 1910), 68.
11. Félix Ponteil, *Les Institutions de la France de 1814 à 1870* (Paris, 1966), 355–64. See

also Raoul Warren, *Les Pairs de France au dix-neuvième siècle*, Les Chaiers Nobles, nos. 20 and 21 (Paris, 1959).

12. Antoine Bachelin-Deflorenne, *Etat présent de la noblesse française, contenant le dictionnaire de la noblesse contemporaine . . . 1866* (Paris, 1866).

13. A. V. Clerc, *Nos députés à l'Assemblée Nationale: Leur biographie et leurs votes* (Paris, 1872), 23.

14. Ibid., 145.

15. For example, Cantalauze, Villèle, Chalvet de Rochemonteix, Dubourg, Dupin de Saint André, Palarin, Escouloubre, Raynal de Saint Michel, and others were ultras; Hargenvilliers, Tauriac, Escouloubre fils, Rémusat, and Suze were constitutionals; and Picot de Lapeyrouse, Malaret, Cambon, Aiguesvives, and Castellane were liberals. See David Higgs, *Ultraroyalism in Toulouse* (Baltimore, 1973).

16. M. Lartigue, "Les Elections à la chambre des députés et l'esprit public en Corréze sous la seconde Restauration" (Thesis, Université des Sciences Sociales de Toulouse, 1974), 141–42.

17. Thomas D. Beck, *French Legislators, 1800–1834* (Berkeley, 1974), 135–36. However, Beck is mistaken in his belief that 1830 saw the noble deputy "reduced to a position that was much closer to his share of the population."

18. Louis Girard et al., *La Chambre des députés en 1837–1839*, Travaux du centre de recherches sur l'histoire du XIXe siècle, fasc. 3 (paris, 1976), 19.

19. P. L. R. Higonnet and T. B. Higonnet, "Class, Corruption, and Politics in the French Chamber of Deputies, 1846–1848," *French Historical Studies* 2 (Fall 1967): 206–7. This article questions the calculations of J. Becarud, "La Noblesse dans les Chambres, 1815–1848," *Revue d'histoire politique et constitutionnelle*, n.s. 11 (July–September 1948): 220.

20. Alexis de Tocqueville, *Souvenirs,* ed. Luc Monnier (Paris, 1942), 202.

21. Clive H. Church, *Revolution and Red Tape* (Oxford, 1980).

22. On diplomats see E. A. Whitcomb, *Napoleon's Diplomatic Service* (Durham, N. C., 1979); Henry Contamine, *Diplomatie et diplomates sous la Restauration (1814–1830)* (Paris, 1970); and *Les Affaires étrangères et le corps diplomatique français* (Paris, 1984), vol. 1, *De l'ancien régime au second empire.* On prefects see E. A. Whitcomb, "Napoleon's Prefects," *American Historical Review* 79, no. 4 (1974): 1089–1118; Nicholas Richardson, *The French Prefectoral Corps, 1814–1830* (Cambridge, 1966); Tom Forstenzer, *French Provincial Police and the Fall of the Second Republic* (Princeton, 1981); B. Le Clère and V. Wright, *Les Préfets du second empire,* Cahier de la fondation nationale des sciences politiques, no. 187 (Paris, 1973), 178–84; and France, Archives Nationales, *Les Préfets du 11 ventôse an VIII au 4 septembre 1870: Répertoires nominatif et territorial* (Paris, 1981). On the Council of State see V. Wright, *Le Conseil d'état sous le second empire,* Travaux et recherches de science politique, no. 19 (Paris, 1972). On *fonctionnaires* see C. Charle, *Les Hauts Fonctionnaires en France au XIXe siècle* (Paris, 1980); Francis de Baecque et al., *Les Directeurs de ministère en France (XIXe–XXe siècles): Communications présentées au colloque organisé le 27 avril 1974 par l'Institut français des sciences administratives et la IVe section de l'Ecole pratique des hautes études* (Geneva and Paris, 1976); and P. F. Pinaud, *Les Trésoriers-payeurs généraux au XIXe siècle: Répertoires nominatif et territorial* (Paris, 1983). And on the military see William Serman, *Les Origines des officiers français, 1848–1870* (Paris, 1979).

23. *Les Affaires étrangères.*

24. Henriette-Lucie de La Tour du Pin Gouvernet, *née* Dillon, *Journal d'une femme de cinquante ans,* 16th ed., vol. 1 (Paris, 1914), v–xvii and passim.

25. Forstenzer, *French Provincial Police*, 90–91.
26. Guy Thuillier, "Un Projet d'école d'administration en 1815: Le Comte d'Herbouville," in *Bureaucratie et bureaucrates en France au XIXe siècle*, ed. Guy Thuillier (Paris, 1980), 471–78. Herbouville was the author of a novel, *L'Émigré* (Paris, [1802], and a variety of reports on technical subjects, as well as articles in *Le Conservateur*.
27. Clément Tournier, *Un Saint Vincent de Paul Toulousain: Le Chanoine Maurice Garrigou, fondateur de l'Institut de Notre-Dame de la Compassion, 1766–1852* (Toulouse, 1945), 246–48; France, Archives Nationales, *Les Préfets*, 73.
28. G. de Bertier de Sauvigny, *La Restauration*, 2d ed. (Paris, 1963), 247. See also David Higgs, "Social Mobility and Hereditary Titles in France, 1814–1830: The Majorats-sur-Demande," *Histoire Sociale/Social History* 14, no. 27 (May 1981): 29–47.
29. AN BB⁶11–13, "Rapports adressés à l'empereur sur les anciens parlementaires."
30. Lartigue, "Les Elections," 116–17.
31. A. Maulion, *Le Tribunal d'appel et la cour de Rennes: Personnel, an VIII–1904* (Rennes, 1904); A. Correch, *La Cour d'appel de Pau: Ses origines, son histoire, son personnel* (Tarbes, 1920).
32. [Polydore-Jean-Etienne] Fabruegettes, "Eloge de M. Charles de Saint-Gresse," *Mémoires: Académie des Sciences, Inscriptions et Belles Lettres de Toulouse* (Toulouse, 1891), 463–90.
33. André-Jean Tudesq, *Les Grands Notables en France*, vol. 1 (Paris, 1964), 130–84.
34. Higgs, *Ultraroyalism*, 109–21.
35. *Almanach royal* (Paris, 1842); *Almanach impérial* (Paris, 1862).
36. Louis Duval, *Les Présidents du conseil général de l'Orne* (Alençon, 1905), 65.
37. Compare discussions in the Chamber of Deputies (26 December 1816–8 January 1817) (*Archives parlementaries de 1787 à 1860*, 2d ser.) with those in the 1870 Commission on Decentralization: B. Basdevant-Gaudement, *La Commission de décentralisation de 1870*, Travaux et recherches en droit, Université de Paris, série sciences historiques, no. 5 (Paris, 1973).
38. L. Hunt, *Revolution and Urban Politics in Provincial France: Troye and Reims, 1786–1790* (Stanford, 1978).
39. Irene Collins, *Napoléon and his Parliaments, 1800–1815* (London, 1979), 47–55.
40. AN F¹ᵇII (Pyrénées, Hautes-) 4.
41. Christophe Charle et al., *Prosopographie des élites françaises, XVI–XXe siècles: Guide de Recherche* (Paris, 1980), 48.
42. Alphonse Henri d'Hautpoul, *Mémoires du général marquis Alphonse d'Hautpoul pair de France, 1789–1865* (Paris, 1906), 168.
43. M. Grosbois, "Les Nobles Sarthois au XIXe siècle" (Le Mans, [1973?], Typescript), table 3: 1810, 20 percent; 1815, 42 percent; 1820, 70 percent; 1829, 82 percent; 1834, 20 percent; 1841, 25 percent; 1846, 30 percent; 1849, 20 percent; 1860, 50 percent; 1865, 40 percent; 1872, 45 percent.
44. *Annuaire de la Haute-Garonne* (Toulouse, 1824), 116–17.
45. This noble patronage was extremely common during the Restoration. Thus, comte de Kerespertz, a cavalry colonel and former émigré and subprefect of Fougères arrondissement (Ille-et-Vilaine), wrote to the prefect on 1 February 1816 to denounce the storekeeper of the town arsenal. He said that the town arsenal, "ayant toujours montré un grande dévouement contre le parti royal," should be replaced by a good royalist and merchant "dont les services remontent jusqu'au M. du Boisguy à qui il fit dans le tems [of the Chouans] plusieurs livraisons de poudre" (*AD* Ille-et-Vilaine, 5M 18).
46. Private archives of the Villèle family, Mourvilles-Basses (Haute-Garonne).

47. Candide de Nant, *Vie de Monseigneur de Charbonnel: Évêque de Toronto* (Gembloux, 1931), 29–30.

48. J. F. Faure-Soulet, *Les Premiers Préfets des Hautes Pyrénées* (Paris, 1965), 57.

49. *AN* F⁷9691. Villeneuve to Minister of Interior, 12 December 1815.

50. Marquis A. A. L. de Caulaincourt, duc de Vicence, *Mémoires*, vol. 3 (Paris, 1946), 209.

51. *AN* F¹ᶜIII (Cher) 9, Prefect to Minister of the Interior, 6 December 1865.

52. Quoted in André-Jean Tudesq, "L'Influence du romantisme sur le légitimisme sous la Monarchie de Juillet," in *Romantisme et politique, 1815–1851: Colloque de l'école normale supérieure de Saint Cloud, 1966* (Paris, 1969), 27–29.

53. Anne de Rochechouart-Mortemart, duchesse d'Uzès, *Souvenirs de la duchesse d'Uzès . . . préface de son petit-fils le comte de Cossé-Brissac* (Paris, [1939]), 24–25.

54. *AD* Bouches du Rhône, M⁶944.

55. Marie d'Armaillé, *Quand on savait vivre heureux (1830–1860): Souvenirs de jeunesse* (Paris, 1934), 165.

56. A. Forrest, *The French Revolution and the Poor* (Oxford, 1978).

57. A. V. Arnault et al., *Biographie nouvelle des contemporains*, vol. 18 (Paris, 1825), 111–18.

58. Jean Vidalenc, *Le Département de l'Eure sous la monarchie constitutionnelle, 1814–1848* (Paris, 1952), 443.

59. L. F. J. de Villèle, "De la suppression de la mendicité par des secours à domicile," *Journal des propriétaires ruraux du Midi* 14 (1818): 372–80.

60. *AD* Orne, J 17 (Carrouges), letters of 4 June 1812 and 7 December 1847.

61. Adolphe de Bourgoing, *Mémoire en faveur des travailleurs et indigents de la classe agricole des communes rurales de France présenté aux Chambres . . .* (1844), reprinted *in extenso* in A. Thuillier, *Economie et société nivernaises au début du XIXe siècle* (Paris, 1974), 201.

62. Le Clère and Wright, *Les préfets*, 80.

63. Robert Tancrède de Hauteville, *De la mission des hautes classes dans la société moderne* (Paris, 1863), 21.

64. A. L. P. J. G. de Belbeuf, *De la noblesse française en 1861 par un maire de village* (Paris, 1861).

65. Amédée d'Andigné, *Armand de Melun: Un apôtre de la charité, 1807–1877* (Paris, 1961).

66. S. Noailles-Standish, *Notice sur Madame la vicomtesse de Noailles* (Paris, 1855).

67. C. H. R. Latour du Pin Chambly de la Charce, *Feuillets de la vie militaire sous le second empire, 1855–70* (Paris, n.d.), 38.

68. Elisabeth de Clermont-Tonnerre [de Grammont], *Pomp and Circumstance*, trans. Brian W. Downs (New York, 1929), 79–92: "He infected me with his contempt for the idle rich, and to my uncle Choiseul I also owe my republican ideas. When I was a child my aunt gave me a little necklace of blue, white and red pearls. 'But that's the tricolour; I don't want to wear a Republican necklace!' The Choiseuls looked at me with such contemptuous irony that it struck me and gave me pause" (p. 88).

69. R. Apponyi, *Vingt-cinq ans à Paris (1826–1850): Journal du comte Rodolphe Apponyi, attaché de l'ambassade d'Autriche-Hongrie à Paris*, 2d ed., vol. 1 (Paris, 1913), 401.

70. David Higgs, "Politics and Landownership among the French Nobility after the Revolution," *European Studies Review* 1, no. 2 (April 1971).

71. Ralph Gibson, "The French Nobility in the Nineteenth Century—Particularly in the Dordogne," in *Elites in France: Origins, Reproduction, and Power*, ed. J. Howorth and P. G. Cerny (London, 1981), 5–45.

72. Eugène Le Roy, *Jacquou le Croquant, présenté par Emmanuel Le Roy Ladurie* (Paris, 1978).

73. Gibson, "The French Nobility."
74. Baron Barclay de Latour in collaboration with Joseph Schermack, *Paradoxe de la noblesse française* (Paris, [1967], 112–13. This is an eccentric, almost crackpot book, but it makes some interesting points.

6. NOBLES AND RELIGION

1. Louis-François de Villèle to Joseph de Villèle, 12 October 1815, Villèle Family Archives, Mourvilles-Basses (Haute-Garonne).
2. S. Mours, *Le Protestantisme en France*, 3 vols. (Paris, 1959–72), 3:261.
3. André-Jean Tudesq, *Les Grands Notables en France (1840–1849)*, vol. 1 (Paris, 1964), 443 ff.
4. Bernard Blumenkranz, *Histoire des juifs en France* (Paris, 1972).
5. Pons-Louis-François de Villeneuve-Villeneuve, *De l'agonie de la France*, 2d ed., vol. 1 (Paris, 1839), 87–88.
6. Pierre Genevray, *L'Administration et la vie ecclésiastique dans le grand diocèse de Toulouse (Ariège, Haute-Garonne, arrondissement de Castelsarrasin), pendant les dernières années de l'Empire et sous la Restauration* (Toulouse, 1941).
7. Henry Contamine, *Metz et la Moselle de 1814 à 1870. . . : Étude de la vie et de l'administration d'un département au XIXe siècle . . .* , vol. 1 (Nancy, 1932), 58.
8. Anatole-Henri-Philippe de Ségur, *Vie de Hélion-Charles-Alban marquis de Villeneuve-Trans, mort sergent de Zouaves* (Paris, 1856), 6.
9. Anatole-Henri-Philippe de Ségur was the son of the celebrated Sophie de Rostopchine, authoress of the *Malheurs de Sophie*, and a grandson of the grandmaster of ceremonies of Napoleon I and a peer of France (M. L. Audiberti, *Sophie de Ségur née Rostopchine* [Paris, 1980]).
10. Brian Fitzpatrick, *Catholic Royalism in the Department of the Gard, 1814–1852* (Cambridge, 1983).
11. Michel Lagrée, *Mentalités, religion et histoire en Haute-Bretagne au XIXe siècle: Le Diocèse de Rennes, 1815–1848* (Paris, 1977), 79–80, 162–63.
12. For more information see Olwen Hufton, "The French Church," in *Church and Society in Catholic Europe of the Eighteenth Century*, ed. W. J. Callahan and David Higgs (Cambridge, 1979), 13–33.
13. Y.-M. Hilaire, *Une Chrétienneté au XIXe siècle? La Vie religieuse des populations du diocèse d'Arras, 1840–1914*, 2 vols. (Villeneuve d'Asq, 1977), 2:561.
14. C. Allignol et A. Allignol, *De l'état actuel du clergé en France et en particulier des curés ruraux appelés desservans* (Paris 1839), 348.
15. Hilaire, *Une Chrétienneté*, 1:305.
16. AN F1cIII (Drôme) 12, report, 31 March 1861.
17. Abbé Vincent to Bishop Bouvier, 5 June 1851, quoted in Michel Denis, *Les Royalistes de la Mayenne*, 2 vols. (Thesis, Lille III, 1976), 1:681.
18. AN F1cIII (Drôme) 12, Prefect of Drôme to Bishop of Valence, 9 August 1866.
19. The geography and social origins of nineteenth-century vocations are complex and can be compared with the equally intractable problem of the response to the Civil Constitution of the Clergy (see F. Lebrun, ed., *Histoire des catholiques en France du XVe siècle à nos jours* [Toulouse, 1980], 305–14; Christiane Marcilhacy, *Le Diocèse d'Orléans au milieu du dix-neuvième siècle: Les Hommes et leurs mentalités*, Histoire et sociologie de l'église, vol. 5 [Paris, 1964]; Marius Faugéras, *Le Diocèse de Nantes sous la monarchie censitaire, 1813–1848*, 2 vols. [Fontenay-le-Comte, 1964]; and Claude Langlois, *Le Diocèse de Vannes au XIXe siècle, 1800–1830* [Paris, 1974]).
20. Quoted in Raymond Deniel, *Une Image de la famille et de la société sous la Restauration (1815–1830): Etude de la presse catholique* (Paris, 1965), 141.
21. G. Cholvy, *Géographie religieuse de l'Hérault contemporain* (Paris, 1968), 264.

22. Jean Leflon, *Eugène de Mazenod, Bishop of Marseilles, Founder of the Oblates of Mary Immaculate, 1782–1861*, vol. 4 (New York, 1970), 13.

23. Pierre Foucault, "L'Origine socio-professionnelle du clergé sarthois durant la période concordataire (1801–1905)," in *Mentalités religieuses dans la France de l'ouest aux XIXe–XXe siècles: Etudes d'histoire sérielle*, Cahiers des Annales de Normandie, no. 8 (Caen, 1976), 155.

24. Faugéras, *Le Diocèse de Nantes*, 2:1–25.

25. Guillaume d'Ozouville, *De la rentrée des hautes classes de la société dans le sacerdoce* (Laval, 1851), 12; Abbé Collet, *Pourquoi les hautes classes n'entrent pas dans le sacerdoce* (Laval, 1852), 14. There was a renewed call for elite recruitment at the dawn of the twentieth century (Cholvy, *Géographie religieuse*, 266).

26. Candide de Nant, *Vie de Monseigneur de Charbonnel, évêque de Toronto* (Gembloux, 1931).

27. Louis Besson, *Vie du cardinal de Bonnechose, archévêque de Rouen*, 2 vols. (Paris, 1887).

28. Gabriel Desert, *La France de Napoleon III* (Paris, 1970), 126–27.

29. Hilaire, *Une Chretienneté*, 1:258.

30. G. de Bertier de Sauvigny, *La Restauration*, 2d ed. (Paris, 1963), 305–6; P. Féret, *Histoire diplomatique de la France et le Saint-Siège*, vol. 2 (Paris, 1911), 142–43; Tudesq, *Les Grands Notables*, 436–40; J. Gadille, *La Pensée et l'action politique des évêques français au début de la Troisième République, 1870–83*, vol. 1 (Paris, 1967), 27.

31. The information in this paragraph is drawn from G. Rougeron, *Le Personnel épiscopal bourbonnais, 1789–1969* (Moulins, 1970), 23–31.

32. Leflon, *Eugène de Mazenod*, 60–63.

33. Arthur Du Bois de la Villerabel, *A Mère de Kertanguy, 1796–1870* (Paris, 1925), 44.

34. Desert, *La France*, 126–27. Expressed another way, in 1790 nuns constituted about one-third of the clerical community, in 1830, 40 percent, and by 1878, 58 percent (Lebrun, *Histoire*, 324).

35. Clément Tournier, *Un Saint Vincent de Paul Toulousain, le chanoine Maurice Garrigou, fondateur de l'Institut de Notre-Dame de la Compassion, 1766–1852* (Toulouse, 1945), 182–94.

36. Bonnie Smith, *Les Bourgeoises of the Nord* (Princeton, 1980).

37. C. Parra, *Une Sainte Bordelaise: Marie-Thérèse-Charlotte de Lamourous, fondatrice de la Miséricorde, 1754–1836* (Bordeaux, 1924), 15–20.

38. G. M. Oury, "L'Oeuvre de la réconstruction: Eglise concordataire et petite église (1801–1830)," in *Histoire religieuse du Maine* (N.p., 1978), 216.

39. G. Bernoville, *Une Fondation sous la Terreur: René Bérault et Anne de la Girouardière, fondateurs de l'Institut du Sacré Coeur de Marie* (Paris, 1954).

40. M. J. Couturier, *Madame de Cossé-Brissac* (Paris, 1914).

41. *Histoire abrégée de Mme de Bengy, vicomtesse d'Houet* (Paris, 1895), 42.

42. Henri Monachon, *La Baronne de Chatillon* (Chambéry, 1890).

43. Odile Arnold, *Le Corps et l'âme: La Vie des religieuses au XIXe siècle* (Paris, 1984).

44. Thomas A. Kselman, *Miracles and Prophecies in Nineteenth-Century France* (New Brunswick, N.J., 1983), 150–52, 154–55, 175–79.

45. Pierre Guiral, *La Vie quotidienne en France à l'âge d'or du capitalisme, 1852–1879* (Paris, 1976), 232.

46. Marie d' Armaillé, *Quand on savait vivre heureux (1830–1860): Souvenirs de jeunesse* (Paris, 1934), 58. She described the preparations in 1842 leading to her first communion in the Paris Roule parish: "Le Chant des vêpres, les cantiques, les exhortations, tout me ravissait pendant cette belle semaine. . . . Mon père et ma soeur

assistèrent à tous les offices dans une petite tribune. On tenait à émotionner les enfants à cette époque. Nous pleurions beaucoup. Je ne sais se cette méthode était bonne ou mauvaise, mais j'ai conservé un souvenir très vif et très doux de ces cérémonies." As uplifting reading in the same year she was given the 1837 biography by abbé A. J. M. Harmon of cardinal de Cheverus, the noble first Catholic bishop of Boston.

47. W. Fortescue, *Alphonse de Lamartine: A Political Biography* [London, 1983).

48. Oury, L'Oeuvre, 217, 221.

49. Jean Caradec Cousson, *Un Promoteur de la renaissance hospitalière et religieuse au XIXe siècle: Paul de Magallon d'Argens, capitaine de la Grande Armée (1784–1859)* (Lyon, 1959), 66, 263.

50. Hilaire, *Une Chrétiennete,* 2:559.

51. The mutualist system was supported by some liberal nobles, such as Jean-Louis-Joseph de Lespinasse, chevalier de Saint Louis, whose 1831 will designated 150,000F to be used to set up two schools for free mutual teaching, one for boys and another for girls (Germaine Bourgade, "L'Enseignement féminin à Toulouse à la fin du Second Empire: L'Ecole mutuelle de filles," *Annales du Midi* 124, no. 87 [October–December 1975]: 488).

52. Eugène Boutmy, *Considérations sur les résultats importants qu'obtient en Belgique le nouveau mode d'éducation inventé par M. Jacotot . . . et d'une lettre de M. le duc de Lévis sur la doctrine de l'égalité intellectuelle, avec la réponse de M. Jacotot* (Paris, 1829).

53. Genevray, *L'Administration.*

54. Denis, *Les Royalistes* (Thesis), 1:702.

55. *AD* Nièvre, 1 J 70.

56. Denis, *Les Royalistes* (Thesis), 1:700–701.

57. Hilaire, *Une Chretiénneté,* 2:559.

58. Pierre Foucault, "Aspects de la vie chrétienne de 1830 aux lois de séparation," in Histoire religieuse du Maine (N.p., 1978), 227.

59. Lagrée, *Mentalités,* 455.

60. *AD* Bouches du Rhône, M⁶944.

61. *Compte-rendu de débats judiciaires à l'occasion de la représentation du "Fils de Giboyer" à Toulouse* (Toulouse, 1863), 99–103.

62. Ron Aminzade, *Class, Politics, and Early Industrial Capitalism: A Study of Mid-Nineteenth-Century Toulouse, France* (Albany, 1981), 55.

63. *AN* F¹ᶜIII (Drôme), 12, 31 March 1861.

64. Denis *Les Royalistes* (Thesis); Oscar de Poli, *Les Soldats du Pape (1860–1867)* (Paris, 1868).

65. Michael Denis, *Les Royalistes de la Mayenne et le monde moderne (XIXe–XXe siècles)*, Publications de l'Université de Haute Bretagne, no. 6 (Paris, 1977). 404.

66. Charles de Noüe and Gaston de Villèle, *Les Français Zouaves pontificaux, 5 mai 1860–20 septembre 1870* (Saint Brieuc, 1903), 39.

67. Amedée Duquesnel, *Du travail intellectuel en France depuis 1815 jusqu'à 1837*, 2d. ed., vol. 1 (Paris, 1839), 113.

68. Ségur, *Vie,* 56.

7. THE NOBLE FAMILY

1. James F. Traer, *Marriage and the Family in Eighteenth-Century France* (Ithaca, 1980).

2. L. A. de Bonald, *Démonstration philosophique du principe constitutif de la société* (Paris, 1830), 105.

3. L. A. de Bonald, *Théorie du pouvoir . . . suivi de théorie de l'éducation sociale,* C. Capitan (Paris, 1966), 243.

4. For a fuller discussion of a subordination of the sexes and age groups within the nineteenth-century French family see Isaac Joseph, Philippe Fritsch, and Alain Battegay, "Disciplines à domicile: L'Edification de la famille," *Recherches,* no. 28 (November 1977).

5. As cited in H. Baudrillart, *Gentilshommes ruraux de la France* (Paris, [1893]), 339.

6. Amédée d'Andigné, *Armund de Melun: Un Apôtre de la charité, 1807–1877* (Paris, 1961), 31.

7. Marie-Louise-Joséphine de Gontaut-Biron, *Mémoires de Madame la Duchesse de Gontaut-Biron . . . 1773–1836* (Paris, 1891).

8. Elisabeth de Rémusat, *Essai sur l'éducation des femmes* (Paris, 1824), 87, 95.

9. Alexis de Tocqueville, *De la démocratie en Amérique,* vol. 2 (Paris, 1942), 204. Pierre Manent, *Tocqueville et la nature de la démocratie* (Paris, 1981), chap. 7 has an interesting analysis of the Tocquevillian contrast of convention and nature as it emerges in democratic and aristocratic manners.

10. Marie d'Armaillé, *Quand on savait vivre heureux (1830–1860): Souvenirs de jeunesse* (Paris, 1934), 14.

11. [A. P. Caylus de Ceylan, comtesse de Bradi,] *Du savoir-vivre en France au dix neuvième siècle,* 2d éd. (Strasbourg, 1841), 157–58.

12. A. C. M. Lezay-Marnésia, *Mes souvenirs* (Paris, 1851), 8.

13. Fernand de Rességuier, *Récits de grand-père* (Toulouse, 1901), 15.

14. A. H. M. de Damas, *Mémoires du baron de Damas (1785–1862) publiés par son petit-fils,* vol. 2 (Paris, 1923), 284; G. A. de Puybusque, *Généalogie de la famille de Puybusque* (Toulouse, 1912), 284.

15. Lezay-Marnésia, *Souvenirs,* 92.

16. *AD* Orne, J 17, letter of Tanneguy Leveneur, 28 September 1827.

17. M. R. H. de Salviac, comte de Viel-Castel, *Memoires du comte Horace du Viel-Castel sur le règne de Napoléon III, 1851–1864,* vol. 1 (Paris, 1979), 122–23.

18. Louis J. M. de Carné-Marcein, *Souvenirs de ma jeunesse au temps de la Restauration* (Paris, 1873), 8–9.

19. Viel-Castel, *Mémoires,* 122–23.

20. L. Baunard, *Etudes biographiques Mme la comtesse de Choiseul d'Aillecourt* (Paris, 1865), 2.

21. Alfred Marquiset, *Ballanche et Mme d'Hautefeuille,* (Paris, 1912), 2–4.

22. Rességuier, *Récits,* 154–55.

23. J. Boissel, *Gobineau* (Paris, 1981), 33.

24. As cited in Michel Denis, *Les Royalistes de la Mayenne,* 2 vols. (Thesis, Lille III, 1976), 1:71.

25. Charles J. M. de Tourtoulon, *L'Héredité et la noblesse* (Paris, 1862), 22. He was a *félibrige* and published poetry in provençal as well as works on noble topics: *De la noblesse dans ses rapports avec nos moeurs et nos institutions* (Paris, 1857); idem [Charles Rochenat, pseud.], *Un Gentilhomme par force majeure, comédie vaudeville* (Montpellier, 1858); etc.

26. Wesley D. Camp, *Marriage and the Family in France since the Revolution* (New York, 1959).

27. Gérard Duplessis-Le Guélinel, *Les Mariages en France,* Cahiers de la Fondation Nationale des Sciences Politiques, no. 53 (Paris 1954), 179–90.

28. Jacques Houdaille, "Analyse démographique . . . sur les descendants de Mme de Sévigné, Bussy-Rabutin et Jean Racine," *Population* 26, no. 5 (September–October 1971): 953–55; idem, "Les Descendants des grands dignitaires du premier Empire

au XIXe siécle," *Population* 29, no. 1 (January–February, 1974): 263–74; Catherine Rollet, "Généalogie et démographie: Quelques exemples récents," *Hommage à Marcel Reinhard sur la population française au XVIIIe et au XIXe siècles* (Paris, 1973), 347–557.

29. Révérend, vols. 3–5. For majorat holders see David Higgs, "Social Mobility and Hereditary Titles in France, 1814–1830: The Majorats-sur-Denande," *Histoire Sociale/Social History* 14, no. 27 (May 1981): 35.

30. Armaillé, *Quand on savait vivre heureux*, 194.

31. Houdaille, "Grands dignitaires," says "C'est probablement à elles [those families of six children and more] qu'il convient d'attribuer le relèvement de la fècondité" (p. 269).

32. T. Zeldin, *France, 1848–1945*, 2 vols. (Oxford, 1973–77), 2:967.

33. E. de Leclerc de Juigné de Lassigny, *Histoire de la maison de Villeneuve en Provence*, 3 vols. (Paris, 1900–1902), 1:147–63.

34. Abbé Berthet, "Un Réactif social: Le Parrainage du XVIe siècle à la Révolution. Nobles, bourgeois et paysans dans un bourg perché du Jura," *Annales, économies, sociétés, civilisations* 1, no. 1 (January–March 1946): 43–50. See Bradi, *Du savoir-vivre*, 19–23, on the desirability of accepting the invitation to be a godparent of "des gens d'une classe inférieure et celles des pauvres."

35. Louis Henry, *Anciennes familles génévoises: Etudes démographiques, XVIe–XXe siècles* (Paris, 1956), 26–27.

36. Louis de Bazelaire de Saulcy, *Généalogie de la famille de Bazelaire en Lorraine* (Toulouse, 1882).

37. Claude Levy and Louis Henry, "Ducs et pairs sous l'Ancien Régime: Caractéristiques démographiques d'une caste," *Population* 15, no. 5 (October–December 1960): 812, 820.

38. Houdaille, "Grands dignitaires," 263–74.

39. André-Jean Tudesq, *Les Grands Notables en France*, vol. 1 (Paris, 1964), 107.

40. Joseph du Bourg to Bruno du Bourg, 28 March 1805, cited in A. Du Bourg, *La Vie religieuse en France sous la Révolution, l'Empire et la Restauration: Monseigneur Du Bourg, évêque de Limoges, 1751–1822* (Paris, 1907), 396.

41. Révérend, 5:304.

42. Borel d'Hauterive, "Notice historique sur la maison d'Aligre," *Mémorial historique de la noblesse* 2 (1840): 113–23. The son of Etienne-François d'Aligre, first president of the Parlement of Paris, had by his second wife a son, Etienne, who in 1815 presided over the electoral college of the Eure-et-Loire. Etienne's only daughter, Etiennette, married Etienne-Marie-Charles de Pomereu (1813–89), who added the surname Aligre to his own and also inherited the vast Aligre wealth.

43. G. F. de Blay de Gaix, *Etudes historiques sur les seigneurs et barons de Gaix, près Castres (Tarn)* (Montauban, 1880), 199–203.

44. Comte de Neufbourg, in Marc Bloch et al., "Enquête: Les Noblesses. Sur le passé de la noblesse française: Quelques Jalons de recherches," *Annales d'histoire économique et sociale* 8, no. 39 (1936): 246.

45. See A. Lottin et al., *La Désunion du couple sous l'Ancien Régime: L'Exemple du Nord* (Lille-Paris, 1975).

46. W. Fortescue, *Alphonse de Lamartine: A Political Biography* (London, 1983), 15, 18.

47. Cissie Fairchilds, *Domestic Enemies: Servants and Masters in Old Regime France* (Baltimore, 1983).

48. *MC* LVIII 845.

49. *MC* LVIII 756.

50. *AD* Vienne, J 11.

51. The regional and social incidence of illegitimacy raises a cluster of complicated questions (see E. van de Walle, "Illegitimacy in France during the Nineteenth Century," in *Bastardy and Its Comparative History,* ed. R. Laslett, K. Oosterveen, and R. M. Smith [Cambridge, Mass., 1980], 264–77). There was a positive correlation of the higher illegitimacy rates and cities with populations above 40,000. Nobles were mainly urban in their residence for part of each year.

52. J. V. A. de Broglie, *Mémoires* (Paris, 1938), 115.

53. G. I. Favard de Langlade, *Manuel pour l'ouverture et le partage des successions, avec l'analyse des principes pour les donations entre vifs, les testaments et les contrats de mariage* (Paris 1811), 437.

54. Armaillé, *Quand on savait vivre heureux.*

55. *MC* LVIII 646.

56. *AD* Sarthe, M 79.

57. *AD* Vaucluse, 1M 717k, 7 February 1811. I have not been able to locate any centralized collation of this material. See also Pierre Lefranc, "Conscription dorée: Conscription des filles dans le départment de la Vienne (1809–1811)," *Revue de l'Institut Napoléon,* no. 133 (1977): 43–55.

58. A study of noblesse weddings in the Manche department (N = 173) during the nineteenth century found a rate of 85 percent endogamy, 4 percent with *titrés,* and the remaining 11 percent with bourgeois (Alain Guillemin, "Aristocrates, propriétaires et diplômés: La Lutte pour le pouvoir local dans le département de la Manche, 1830–1875," *Actes de la recherche en sciences sociales* [Paris] 42 [1982]: 40–41).

59. *MC* LVIII 720.

60. *Histoire économique et sociale de la France,* vol. 3, pt. 2 (Paris, 1976), 834.

61. R. Moulinas, "Le Pays légal dans le Vaucluse: Sa composition et son rôle dans la vie politique de 1830 à 1848" (Thesis, Advanced Studies in History, Université d'Aix-en-Provence, 1965), 33.

62. T. Zeldin, *The Political System of Napoleon III* (London, 1958), 59, 147–48; Révérend, vol. 6.

63. Duplessis-Le Guélinel, *Les Marriages en France.*

64. Charles de Ribbe, *La Vie domestique,* vol. 1 (Paris, 1877), 161.

65. R. Apponyi, *Vingt-cinq ans à Paris (1826–1850): Journal du comte Rudolphe Apponyi, attaché de l'ambassade d'Autriche-Hongrie à Paris,* 2d ed., vol. 1 (Paris, 1913), 105.

66. E. V. E. B. de Castellane, *Journal du maréchal de Castellane: 1804–1862,* vol. 4 (Paris, 1895–99), 12–13.

67. Denis, *Les Royalistes* (Thesis), 2: 645.

68. Alphonse de Lamartine, *Le Manuscrit de ma mère* (Paris, 1873).

69. *AD* Haute-Garonne, 3E 28481.

70. *AD* Eure-et-Loire, "Tableaux alphabétique des contrats de mariage, Bureau de Chartres" (1829), A. P. H. Roissard de Mainville.

71. *MC* LVIII 647.

72. *AN* BB29784, no. 160.

73. *MC* LVIII 639, 29 April 1808.

74. *AD* Hautes-Pyrénées, C 4 M, "Tableaux alphabétique des contrats de mariage, Bureau de Tarbes."

75. *AD* Haute-Garonne, WQ 5745, 5753, 5768.

76. André Armengaud, *Les Populations de l'est aquitain au début de l'époque contemporaine: Recherches sur une région moins développée vers 1845–vers 1871* (Paris, 1961), 284.

77. *MC* LVIII 646.

78. *AD* Haute-Garonne, 3E 26671.

79. *MC* LVIII 801, 11 December 1849.

80. Sample of marriage contracts drawn from the *tableaux alphabétiques* in *AD* Cher, IQ 690–92; *AD* Haute-Garonne, WQ 5745, 5753, 5768; *AD* Hautes-Pyrénées, C 4 M; and *AD* Eure et Loire, Chartes Bureau, 1800–1860.

81. For the *majorats sur demande* see *AN* BB²⁹783–84.

82. Albert Eyquem, *Le Régime dotal: Son histoire, son évolution et ses transormations au XIXe siécle* . . . (Bordeaux, 1903), 524. See on Périgueux: "plutôt l'apanage de la grande fortune et de l'aristocratie" (528); or Bourg: "La société aristocratique et la haute classe du commerce se soumettent seules au régime dotal" (p. 561).

83. J. P. Chaline, "Les Contrats de mariage à Rouen au XIXe siècle: Etude d'après l'enregistrement des actes civils publics," *Revue d'histoire économique et Sociale* 48 (1970): 254.

84. *MC* CXI 513.

85. Michel Vovelle's work on attitudes towards death in eighteenth-century Provence (*Piété baroque et déchristianisation, Attitudes provençales devant la mort au siècle des Lumières, d'après les clauses des testaments* [Paris, 1976]), with evidence drawn from 20,000 wills, sets high standards for data collection. Comments here are based on impressions from a small sample of 90 wills drawn from nobles between 1800 and 1870, mostly from a notary's office popular with a cluster of liberal Parisian aristocrats. The wills are unrepresentative of either the provincial *noblesse* or the Legitimists of the noble faubourg. Financial and geographical constraints limited me to the small numbers consulted; however, a close reading of a few wills may provide insights overlooked in the process of totaling up fragments of data from large numbers of documents in order to generate scattergrams and frequency distributions.

86. Favard de Langlade, *Manuel,* 361–97.

87. One finds exceptions: the duc de Maillé (1770–1837) began his will, "Au nom du Père, du Fils, et du Saint Esprit: je déclare avoir toujours mis une confiance en Dieu que j'ai adoré toute ma vie en le suivant moins bien que je n'aurais dû le faire" (*MC* LVIII 750), whereas his wife (d. 1851) made no religious invocations or donations and limited her charity to the servants. However, she did wish to be embalmed as long as possible to ensure that she was quite dead before burial (*MC* LVIII 808). See their marriage contract in appendix 2.

88. *MC* LVIII 649.

89. Ibid.

90. Michel Vovelle, " 'Famille, je vous ai' ": Les Faire-Part du décès dans l'aristocratie française," *Stanford French Review* 3, no. 2 (1979): 265.

91. *MC* LVIII 639.

92. *MC* LVIII 767.

93. Vovelle, "Famille," 266.

94. *MC* LVIII 756. The marquis de Boissy's second wife praised him for his extraordinary courage in specifying the shape and quality of his coffin before his death (H. E. G. R. du Coudray de Boissy, *Mémoires* . . . *redigés d'après ses papiers,* vol. 1 [Paris, 1870], 104).

95. *MC* LVIII 639, 5 May 1808.

96. *MC* LVIII 783, 3 May 1845.

97. *MC* LVIII 782, April 1845.

98. *MC* LVIII 759, May 1839.

99. *MC* LVIII 842, February 1860, with a donation of 500F to the Saint Nicholas religious association on the condition that the members accompany her coffin to the cemetery and there sing the Dies Irae, as well as say a Mass for her soul in their chapel.

100. *MC* LVIII 649, May 1812.

101. *MC* LVIII 883, 3 September 1869.
102. *MC* LVIII 847.
103. *AD* Orne, J 17, Leveneur correspondence.
104. *MC* LVIII 861.
105. Odette Voilliard, *Nancy au XIXe siècle: Une Bourgeoisie urbaine* (Paris, 1978), 29.
106. *MC* LVIII 759.
107. *MC* XXV 67.
108. *AD* Haute-Garonne, WQ 5622.
109. *MC* LVIII 805.
110. *MC* LVIII 822.
111. *MC* LVIII 805.
112. *MC* LVIII 815.
113. *MC* A. V. typescript copy, 14 April 1846. See J. Fourcassié, Villèle (Paris, 1954), 427–30.
114. *MC* LVIII 808.
115. *AD* Indre, 36 1J1 109; and H. V. Desgranges, *Nobiliaire de Berry* (Saint-Amand-Mont-Rond, 1971), provided information on the Aiguirandes.
116. As an example, C. M. H. Fornier of the Tarn described in 1800 as "cy-devant noble, bien différent dans sa conduite de son frère, le cadet, connu sous le nom de Fenayrols—tous les deux servoient dans le cy-devant Condé cavalerie. Le prévenu quitta son corps après une absence qu'il fit dans ce pays au commencement de la Révolution pendant laquelle on le présume avoir été à Coblentz sans y avoir fait un long séjour. Il est revenu dans le pays où il s'est conduit comme un véritable ennemi des principes républicaines . . . il est bien différent de son frère Fenayrols qui a constamment resté dans le même corps à son poste d'honneur, et y est encore" (*AN* F⁷3354).
117. Bradi, *Du savoir-vivre*, 86–87.
118. H. de Aldéguier, "Eloge du baron de Malaret," *Journal des propriétaires ruraux du Midi* 41 (1846): 14.
119. Alexis de Tocqueville, *Journeys to England and Ireland*, ed. J. P. Meyer (New York, 1968), xvii.
120. Armaillé, *Quand on savait vivre heureux*, 209–10.
121. A. B. N. Peat, *Gossip from Paris during the Second Empire* (London, 1903), 95. Riding in the Bois de Boulogne was already a well-established feature of upper-class male social life under the July Monarchy. Mme d'Armaillé recalled of 1840–41 that "les cavaliers de bonne compagnie avaient adopté la partie du bois qu commence au Rond Mortemart et finit à la mare d'Auteuil" (*Quand on Savait vivre heureux*, 35).
122. Elisabeth de Clermont-Tonnerre [de Gramont], *Pomp and Circumstance*, trans. Brian W. Downs (New York, 1929), 75–78; see also idem, *Years of Plenty*, trans. Florence Llona and Victor Llona (New York, 1931). These are translations of vols. 1 and 2, respectively, of her *Mémoires*, 4 vols. (Paris, 1928–35); vols. 3 and 4 have yet to be translated. On the Clermont-Tonnerre family see idem, *La Famille des Clermont-Tonnerre depuis l'an 1070* (Paris, 1950).
123. Louis Bergeron emphasized family links within the *patronat* of industrialists and businessmen, and Yves Lequin stressed family ties in the economic and social life of shopkeepers and the working class, in a history that brings out the persistence of inegalitarian and socially exclusivist attitudes in French life (see *Histoire des français: XIX–XXe siècles,* 3 vols. [Paris, 1984]).

CONCLUSION

1. Three major interpretations published in English emphasize the vigor and cunning of the rear-guard action fought by nobles at different times from the late eighteenth

century to the twentieth against the new order based on social mobility, liberal economics, and growing egalitarianism: Robert R. Palmer, *The Age of the Democratic Revolution: A Political History of Europe and America, 1760–1800*, 2 vols. (Princeton, 1959–64); Barrington Moore, Jr., *The Social Origins of Democracy and Dictatorship* (Cambridge, Mass., 1966); and Arno J. Mayer, *The Persistence of the Old Regime: Europe to the Great War* (New York, 1981).

2. Patrice Higonnet, *Class, Ideology, and the rights of Nobles during the French Revolution* (Oxford, 1981).

3. G. Paillain, ed., *Correspondance inédite du prince de Talleyrand et du roi Louis XVIII pendant le congrès de Vienne* (Paris, 1881), 339, cited in Phillip Mansel, *Louis XVIII* (London, 1981), 171.

4. Vicomte de Bonald to Joseph de Villèle, 1829, in Joseph de Villèle, *Mémoires et correspondence du comte de Villèle*, vol. 5 (Paris, 1890), 369.

5. Pierre Birnbaum et al., *La Classe dirigeante française* (Paris, 1978), 153.

6. Duc de Bassano, *Procès-verbal des séances de la chambre de pairs,* 11 March 1834, vol. 1, nos. 1–26 (Paris, 1833–34), 668.

7. *Almanach de la noblesse du royaume de France, année 1848* (Paris, 1848), back cover.

8. A. L. P. J. G. de Belbeuf, *De la noblesse française en 1861, par un maire de village* (Paris, 1861), 12. There is a similarity here to Gobineau's mindset about whites (nobles) when he wrote: "In order to avoid disappearing in the midst of inferior varieties, the white family needed to add to the power of its genius and courage a certain guarantee of numbers, even if doubtless to a lesser extent than was required by its adversaries" (quoted in Michael D. Biddiss, *Father of Racist Ideology: The Social and Political Thought of Count Gobineau* [London, 1970], 120).

9. The literary projections of the dandy as aristocrat are studied with a wealth of allusions by Domna C. Stanton in *The Aristocrat as Art: A Study of the Honnête Homme and the Dandy in Seventeenth- and Nineteenth-Century French Literature* (New York, 1980).

10. For examples see Jean Forest, *L'Aristocratie balzacienne* (Paris, 1973); Michael G. Lerner, *Maupassant* (London, 1975); and George Painter, *Proust* (London, 1966).

11. Christophe Charle, *Les Hauts Fonctionnaires en France au XIXe siècle* (Paris, 1980), 55.

12. Ibid.; see chap. 2, "Nepotisme et concours."

13. Jonathan Powis, *Aristocracy* (Oxford, 1984), 96.

14. A. B. C. Cobban, "The 'Middle Class' in France, 1815–1848," in *France since the Revolution* (New York, 1970), 19–20.

15. Louis Girard et al., *La Chambre des députés en 1837–1839*, Travaux du centre de recherches sur l'histoire du XIXe siècle, fasc. 3 (Paris, 1976), 61–75, 135–65.

16. Robert R. Locke, *French Legitimists and the Politics of Moral Order in the Early Third Republic* (Princeton, 1974).

17. Robert T. d'Hauteville, *De la mission des hautes classes dans la société moderne* (Paris, 1863), 12.

18. Michel Denis, *Les Royalistes de la Mayenne* (Thesis), 1:311. See also Pierre Simoni, "'Réproduction sociale' and Elite Values: Obituaries and the Elite of Apt (Vaucluse), 1840–1910," *Histoire Sociale/Social History* 16, no. 32 (November 1983): 331–58.

19. Jean d'Ormesson, *At God's Pleasure* (London, 1978).

20. Pierre Bourdieu, *La Distinction: Critique sociale du jugement* (Paris, 1979).

21. A. J. P. Taylor, "God Save Our Old Nobility" (review of Mayer, *The Persistence of the Old Regime* in *New York Review of Books*, 2 April 1981, 19).

Glossary

Dotation. Under Napoleon I, recompenses from public funds conferred on officials for military or civil services. Under Napoleon III, public funds placed at the disposal of the emperor and the imperial family. Also denoted the appropriation of public funds, as in the case of Marshal Pelissier, made duc de Malakoff, with a *dotation* of 100,000F which was transmissible to his male descendants who carried his title. *See also Majorat.*

Droit d'aînesse. Designation of the preeminent rights of the eldest surviving son under Old Regime testamentary law. Article 896 of the Civil Code forbade its use in post-Revolutionary France. Articles 1048 and 1049 permitted a man to bequeath to his grandchild property under the safeguard of one or several of his own children.

Faisances. All that a farmer binds himself to provide to the lessor over and above the monetary price of the lease.

Hoirie. A legal term for inheritance.

Majorat. Property the revenue of which is entailed to support the holder of a title of nobility. There are two types of *majorats:* those based on the personal property of the holder, which remain inalienable as long as the masculine descendants of the founder use the title; and those established on property derived from the *domaine extraordinaire* awarded to the holders for service to the state. This property is liable to reclamation by the *domaine extraordinaire* when the male descendance is extinguished. The owner of land for *majorats* previously sold as *biens nationaux* must submit the receipts of purchase (*AN* BB[1115]). A law of 13 May 1835 forbade the establishment of new *majorats* upon private property; it was reiterated by law on 11 May 1849.

Partage. An apportionment, sharing out of a succession.

Partage successoral. See Partage.

Pension pairiale. A royal decision of 13 December 1823 described these pensions as substitutes for *majorats. See also Majorat.*

Préciput d'aînesse. Right to a preference share for the eldest male among coheirs of an estate.

273

Préciput légal. See Préciput d'aînesse.

Référendaire. Officer of the Chancellery who reported to the imperial Senate and the Chamber of Peers under the Restoration.

Substitution. A legal disposition designating to whom a heritage passed if the legatee did not receive it. Together with the *droit d'aînesse,* it was a standard feature of pre-Revolutionary legal practice. On 25 February 1790 the Constituent Assembly abolished its use in inheritance of noble properties, and on 17 June 1790, all *substitutions,* perpetual or temporary. The law of 14 November 1792 prohibited its use.

Index

NOBLES IN NINETEENTH-CENTURY FRANCE

Designed by Martha Farlow.

Composed by The Composing Room of Michigan, Inc., in Primer.

Printed by BookCrafters, Inc., on 50-lb. S. D. Warren's Sebago
Eggshell Cream Offset and bound in Holliston Roxite A.

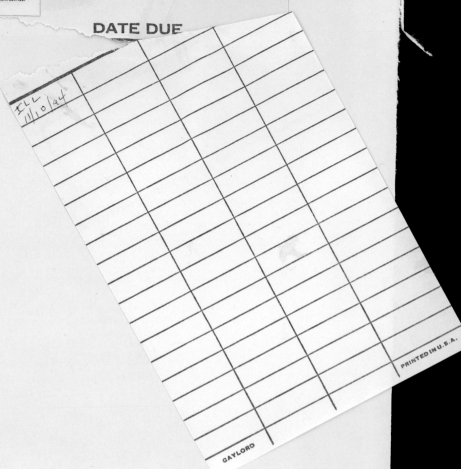